UNDERCLASS

Underclass

A History of the Excluded
1880–2000

John Welshman

hambledon
continuum

Hambledon Continuum, a Continuum imprint
The Tower Building, 11 York Road, London SE1 7NX, UK
80 Maiden Lane, Suite 704, New York, NY 10038, USA

First Published 2006

ISBN 1 85285 322 0

A description of this book is available from the
British Library and from the Library of Congress.

Typeset by Egan-Reid Ltd, Auckland, New Zealand.
Printed in Great Britain by MPG Books Ltd, Cornwall.

Distributed in the United States and Canada
exclusively by Palgrave Macmillan,
A division of St Martin's Press.

Contents

Acknowledgements   vii

Introduction   ix

1 Regulating the Residuum   1

2 A Trojan Horse   21

3 In Search of the Social Problem Group   45

4 The Invention of the Problem Family   67

5 Chasing the Culture of Poverty   87

6 Sir Keith Joseph and the Cycle of Deprivation   107

7 Uncovering the Underclass – America   127

8 Uncovering the Underclass – Britain   157

9 Social Exclusion and Cycles of Disadvantage   183

10 Conclusion   205

Notes   211

Bibliography   245

Index   257

Acknowledgements

The help of many people, over a long period of time, has made the writing of this book possible. Perhaps foremost among them has been John Macnicol, whose work I first came across as a postgraduate student. His article 'In Pursuit of the Underclass', published as long ago as 1987 in the *Journal of Social Policy*, is in many ways the starting point for this volume, and my debt to his ideas and arguments will be obvious. I would also like to thank a number of other researchers, archivists, and postgraduate students who have suggested references and helped in many different ways: Adrian Allan, Alan Bacon, Virginia Berridge, Alan Cohen, Andrew Denham, Nicola Caldwell, Anthony Feiler, Pat Garside, Hilary Graham, Chris Grover, Lesley Hall, Bernard Harris, Jane Lewis, Audrey Mullender, Paolo Paladino, Margaret Pelling, David Reeder, Adrian Sinfield, Pat Starkey, John Stewart, Mathew Thomson, Charles Webster, and Paul Weindling. Alan Deacon, in particular, has been a source of encouragement throughout. The staff at the Universities of Leicester and Lancaster have responded to many requests for interlibrary loans, and obscure references from their respective stacks.

The Economic and Social Research Council and the Wellcome Trust both financed periods of study which made some of the research possible, and in 2002 Lancaster University, the University of Leeds, and the Social Policy Association funded a workshop on the 'cycle of deprivation'. Articles exploring aspects of this story have been published in *Benefits*, the *Historical Journal*, the *Journal of Social Policy*, *Social History of Medicine*, *Twentieth Century British History*, and *Urban History*. Papers that have been relevant to this book have been given at the Universities of Aberdeen, Exeter, Lancaster, and Southampton; at conferences in Evora and Coimbra, Portugal and Oslo, Norway; at the London School of Hygiene and Tropical Medicine and University College, London; and at the Wellcome Unit for the History of Medicine, Oxford. I am grateful for the suggestions and comments that those attending have made.

The Institute for Health Research at Lancaster University provides a perfect place in which to do research. Though not themselves historians, my colleagues have always been interested in the insights that history offers, and I owe a particular debt of gratitude to the Institute's previous Director, Tony Gatrell. I would also like to thank my editors at Hambledon and London, Tony Morris and Martin Sheppard. This book first took shape at a meeting with Tony Morris, longer ago than I care to remember, and I am grateful to them both for their many suggestions, and above all for their patience. But most of all, I would like to thank my wife and children, Rose, Thomas, and Juliet, who have lived with the 'underclass' for many years. My first book was dedicated to my parents. But this one is for them, with all my love.

Introduction

In June 1997, in a speech given by Tony Blair at the Aylesbury housing estate, in the London borough of Southwark, the Prime Minister stated that the Government would deal with poverty – the 'forgotten people'. But he argued that it was not just a question of poverty, but one of fatalism, and about 'how to recreate the bonds of civic society and community in a way compatible with the far more individualistic nature of modern, economic, social and cultural life'. And he continued, 'there is a case not just in moral terms but in enlightened self interest to act, to tackle what we all know exists – an underclass of people cut off from society's mainstream, without any sense of shared purpose'.[1] Blair's point was that, though problems were caused by changes in the nature of work, and long-term unemployment, there was a danger that people were becoming detached from society, and from citizenship in its widest sense. It was suggested that solutions would have to be long-term; would require greater co-ordination across government departments than previously; and would need to be based on policies that had been shown to work.

These ideas were amplified in December of that year, at Stockwell Park School in the London borough of Lambeth, where Tony Blair gave a speech at the launch of the Government's Social Exclusion Unit. What was needed, he claimed, was a spirit of national renewal, to tackle problems now defined as 'social exclusion'. Blair defined social exclusion in the following way:

> Social exclusion is about income but it is about more. It is about prospects and networks and life-chances. It's a very modern problem, and one that is more harmful to the individual, more damaging to self-esteem, more corrosive for society as a whole, more likely to be passed down from generation to generation, than material poverty.[2]

According to the Prime Minister, part of the answer lay in improved co-ordination of government policy – 'joined up problems demand joined up solutions' – but he also warned that the approach was as much about self-interest as compassion. Since then, of course, there have been several reports from the Social Exclusion Unit – for example, on teenage pregnancy, on truancy and school exclusion, on 'rough sleepers', and on neighbourhood renewal. The thrust of this interpretation has been reflected in a plethora of government initiatives – Sure Start,

Education and Health Action Zones, the New Deal for Communities, the Single Regeneration Budget, and many more. More generally, government policy in such areas as employment and health has been characterised by an emphasis on personal responsibility, and influenced by research on ways of changing behaviour.[3]

Social exclusion derives in part from earlier continental thinking, particularly in France, and is also influenced by the more general theme of the 'third way'. We will look in greater detail at social exclusion in chapter 9. Much of the recent writing on social exclusion has sought to distance itself from an earlier under-class discourse, both in empirical terms and symbolically. Thus John Hills has concluded that data from income dynamics has indicated 'there is little evidence in the UK for a permanently excluded "underclass", doomed from childhood … what there is, however, is evidence of groups whose life chances are much less favourable than others'.[4] Nevertheless, other writing on social exclusion has tended to underline the continuities between the concept of social exclusion and an earlier 'underclass' discourse. Ruth Levitas, for example, identifies three themes in social exclusion, including a moral underclass discourse which presents the socially excluded as culturally distinct from the mainstream; focuses on the behaviour of the poor; implies that benefits are bad; and ignores inequalities among the rest of society.[5] Some academics have looked more closely at the language of New Labour. Norman Fairclough, for example, agrees with Levitas that the behavioural and moral delinquency suggested by the term 'underclass' has been carried over into the construction of social exclusion.[6]

The actual language and policies adopted by New Labour tend to support this point. It is noticeable, for example, that several phrases have been used inter-changeably. We can see this in Tony Blair's Southwark and Lambeth speeches, where he used both 'social exclusion' and the 'underclass'. Moreover in the specific case of child poverty, there are marked continuities between New Labour's focus on 'cycles of disadvantage' and the 1970s research programme on the 'cycle of deprivation'. In April 2000, for example, the *Guardian* newspaper reported that research indicated that higher state benefits were 'not sufficient to break the cycle of deprivation'.[7] The writer seemed unaware of the historical resonance of this phrase, and oblivious of the research programme into the 'cycle' carried out in the 1970s. We will examine these continuities in greater depth in chapters 6 and 9. What is sufficient to note here is that the example of social exclusion indicates that what is missing from this debate is a sense of its historical dimension. Very little is known about the extent to which 'social exclusion' marks a radical departure from previous efforts by government in this field, or whether it is simply the latest in a series of similar labels.

This book is concerned with the history of the concept of the 'underclass', and aims to fill that gap. It is arguable, of course, that the idea of the 'deserving' and 'undeserving poor' is a much older idea, and it can certainly be identified in the early modern era. However, while we briefly review the earlier history of these ideas in the next chapter, this book really covers the period from the 1880s to the present day. Its main focus is Britain, though two chapters, on the 'concept of poverty' and on the 'underclass', also look in detail at the experience of the United States. What is perhaps most important to get across is that the book is not a history of poverty *per se*, but of a particular interpretation of the causation of poverty that has reappeared periodically under slightly different labels. It seeks to understand why these ideas have been so persistent, but also how they have been moulded by the particular political, economic, and demographic concerns of specific historical periods. One issue is that of who has been inventing these labels, and of which professional groups have been defined as 'experts'. It has been pointed out, for instance, that whereas the main writers on poverty in the 1960s were sociologists, this area of research is now dominated by economists, and by the manipulation of large data sets. A further theme is that of the influence of American models on British social policy, notably in the 1960s, and of what the sociologist A. H. Halsey has described as 'ideas drifting casually across the Atlantic, soggy on arrival, and of dubious utility'.[8] The book also looks in detail at those periods when ideas underwent a process of transition, to emerge in slightly different form, and at the periods when no 'underclass' notion appeared to be in existence. It is thus concerned both with continuities and discontinuities. However its main concern is to explore the idea that an 'underclass' has been successively re-invented over the past 120 years in Britain and the USA.

This introduction seeks to set the scene for the later chapters: these are arranged chronologically and examine successive re-inventions of the 'underclass' idea over the past 120 years. But it is important to pause for a moment to look at the background to this issue. First, the introduction examines some of the difficulties that defining the 'underclass' has posed for researchers. Second, it briefly reviews earlier writing on the history of the concept of the underclass, in both the United States and Britain. Third, it makes a case for the book, arguing that earlier writing, while important, has failed to provide a systematic analysis of the history of the concept in either the United States or Britain. Fourth, it sets the book in the context of recent writing on agency and structure, outlines how the book is organised, and identifies two main questions. The first underlying question is whether the similarities between these ideas are greater than the differences. The second is whether there is sufficient linearity between these ideas to support the argument that the underclass has been periodically re-invented over the past 120 years.

Fairclough's work on the language of New Labour has been paralleled by greater interest in the vocabulary of poverty. A recent international glossary, for example, includes the phrases 'Charity Organisation Society'; 'culture of poverty'; 'cycle of deprivation'; 'deserving poor'; 'exclusion'; 'genetic explanations'; 'intergenerational continuity'; 'problem families'; and 'underclass'.[9] It notes that the term 'underclass' has been used both to describe the long-term marginalised or unemployable, and as a labelling phenomenon. Certainly the difficulties of defining the underclass, and the ambiguities of the term, have been both an obstacle for researchers, and part of its attraction for users. The *Oxford English Dictionary* notes the Swedish term *underklass*, and defines the underclass as 'a subordinate social class, the lowest social stratum in a country or community, consisting of the poor and unemployed'.[10] The earliest usage given in the *OED* is that by the Scottish poet Hugh Macdiarmid, in a biography of the Red Clydesider, John Maclean. At his trial in 1918, Maclean stated that 'the whole history of society, has proved that society moves forward as a consequence of an under-class overcoming the resistance of a class on top of them'.[11] The next reference given by the *OED*, however, is by the Swedish economist Gunnar Myrdal in 1963, when he stated 'less often observed ... is the tendency of the changes under way to trap an "underclass" of unemployed and, gradually, unemployable persons and families at the bottom of a society'.[12] The usages given in this edition, for the period 1964–85, show how Myrdal's structural expanation has become one based increasingly on behaviour.

However, it is also important to note that defining the 'underclass' has posed problems for researchers. Although it does not appear in Raymond Williams's famous book *Keywords*, the term 'underclass' can be considered in that way, as a phrase that has its own particular history, but which plays a significant role in putting across different meanings.[13] One of the interesting questions about the 'underclass' is whether it is technically a class in the Marxist sense. As John Macnicol has written, many proponents of the underclass have seen it as 'distinct from the working class – in effect, a rootless mass divorced from the means of production – definable only in terms of social inefficiency, and hence not strictly a class in a neo-Marxist sense'.[14] For Marx and Engels the 'dangerous class' was the *lumpenproletariat*. The other important Marxist concept was that of the 'reserve army of labour'. In *Das Capital*, Marx had written that a surplus working class population tended to form an 'available industrial reserve army', and it was on its formation and re-formation that the cycles of modern industry depended. General movements of wages, argued Marx, were similarly regulated by the expansion and contraction of the 'reserve army of labour'.[15] Other writers have of course suggested that the social security system reproduces a 'reserve army of labour', and functions only secondarily to mitigate poverty or provide income maintainence. The 'reserve army of labour' increases competition among workers, and acts as a downward force on wages. Norman Ginsburg has written, for example, that 'in the inter-war years the permanent existence of an inflated labour reserve army, now closely supervised by the state, performed the classic function of holding down wages and dividing the working class'.[16] What Marx meant by the 'reserve army of labour' was of course the unemployed. However, it is less clear that the 'reserve army of labour' and the underclass are synonymous. That is one question that this book seeks to answer.

These debates about how to define the underclass became particularly heated in the 1980s, as we shall see in chapters 7 and 8. The main contrast was then between those who used alternative structural and behavioural definitions. Thus William Julius Wilson has defined the underclass as:

> Individuals who lack training and skills and either experience long-term unemployment or are not a part of the labour force, individuals who engage in street criminal activity and other aberrant behaviour, and families who experience long-term spells of poverty and/or welfare dependency.[17]

Erol R. Ricketts and Isabel V. Sawhill defined the underclass as a 'subgroup of the American population that engages in behaviours at variance with those of mainstream populations'. Specifically, they argued that an underclass area was one with a high proportion of high school dropouts; adult males not regularly attached to the labour force; welfare recipients; and female heads of households. They estimated that 2.5m people, or 1% of the American population, lived in these areas, mainly in the older industrial cities.[18] But Robert Aponte countered in 1990, writing of the USA, that the term 'underclass' had never been properly defined, despite three decades of sporadic use.[19]

British underclass researchers have faced similar problems, with definitions that have stressed either structural or behavioural elements. David Smith defined the underclass as 'those who fall outside this [Marxist] class schema, because they belong to family units having no stable relationship at all with the "mode of production" – with legitimate gainful employment'.[20] Thus for Smith, the underclass lay outside the conventional class hierarchy, and below the bottom class. David Willetts viewed the underclass as the same as 'long-term or frequent claimants of income support'.[21] But British commentators have been critical of attempts to define the underclass. Writing in 1987, John Macnicol outlined three problems of defining the underclass. First, that a popular version of the concept had been internalised by ordinary working-class people as the converse of 'respectable'. Second, there was the difficulty of separating the underclass concept from wider assumptions about the inheritance of intelligence and ability that were common before IQ testing was discredited. Third, a further complication was the fact that the idea of an 'underclass' had also been used by those on the Left to describe the casualties of capitalism, and those suffering acute economic deprivation.[22] Hartley Dean and Peter Taylor-Gooby have argued that it is a concept which 'empirically speaking, is hopelessly imprecise and, as a theoretical device, has repeatedly conflated structural and cultural definitions of not only poverty, but of crime as well'. They concluded that 'underclass' was 'a symbolic term with no single meaning, but a great many applications ... it represents, not a useful concept, but a potent symbol'.[23]

These debates about how to define and measure the underclass were perhaps most marked in the 1980s. In this book we will not attempt to define the underclass since our concern is with the history of a discourse rather than an empirical reality. Equally, however, we do not regard the underclass as simply a synonym for the poor. Its use over time has generally been more precise than that – generally to define a much smaller group whose poverty is attributed in part to wider structural factors, but also with respect to the behavioural inadequacies of individual members. We are concerned with how the underclass has been defined at different times, and what these definitions illustrate about the individuals and organisations doing the defining. There are continuities in these debates, notably in the relative weighting given to behavioural factors on the one hand, and structural causes on the other. Nevertheless there are also differences in the way in which the underclass has been defined at different times, reflecting the distinctive economic, political, and social contexts of particular periods. Moreover, two of the ideas that we will look at – the culture of poverty and the cycle of deprivation – were more about outlining a process by which people became or remained poor, than about setting out parameters with which a particular social group could be circumscribed. One of the aims of the book, then, is to map these continuities and changes in debates about defining and measuring the underclass.

It is important to recognise that although the history of the concept of the underclass has never been systematically explored, there has nevertheless been important earlier work that provides a set of hypotheses and arguments that can be tested against the evidence. The theme of the deserving and undeserving poor in the early modern period is one example of this timeless discourse. But there has also been writing on the underclass in both the USA and Britain.

In the modern period, academics have explored how ideas about stigma and deviance have become incorporated in labelling. David Matza, for example, argued as early as 1966 that the 'disreputable poor' were being continually rediscovered, and that words were being constantly substituted, mainly in an attempt to reduce stigma. Matza, a sociologist based at the University of California at Berkeley, noted that terms that referred to essentially the same thing shifted rapidly, and that perhaps because of this, both researchers and practitioners remained unaware of historical continuities.[24] The latest example, at that time, was the expression 'hard to reach'. Other examples identified by Matza included the *lumpenproletariat*; Thorstein Veblen's idea of a leisure class; and the term 'pauper'. He argued that those deemed the 'disreputable poor' were 'the people who remain unemployed, or casually and irregularly employed, even during periods approaching full employment and prosperity; for that reason, and others, they live in disrepute'.[25] Matza claimed that the 'disreputable poor' was comprised of several smaller groups – the 'dregs' who tended to be migrants; 'newcomers' who were recently arrived; 'skidders', or those who had fallen from higher social standing; and the 'infirm'. In terms of the process of 'pauperisation', Matza identified a process of 'massive generation', by which this population was continually replenished, and one of 'fractional selection', by which newcomers passed into its ranks. Matza concluded the 'disreputable poor' were 'an immobilised segment of society located at a point in the social structure where poverty intersects with illicit pursuits'.[26]

Matza published a slightly different version of this chapter, that was subsequently revised and elaborated in light of the 'culture of poverty' debates of the 1960s. He argued that poverty might most usefully be seen as a series of concentric circles – the poor; the welfare poor; and the 'disreputable poor' who were 'poor, sporadically or permanently on welfare, and, additionally, suffer the especially demoralising effects of the stigma of immorality'.[27] Matza provided more statistical detail on the poor and the welfare poor, included the Aid for Families with Dependent Children (AFDC) programme. He added a further group to those that comprised the 'disreputable poor' – the 'functionaries' who oversaw the conduct of those who required assistance. What was interesting about Matza's work was that it was an early recognition that the 'poor' were socially constructed. In addition, his work was notable for the way it recognised similarities with the British experience. In particular, he noted that the 'problem family' concept was defined in terms of the alleged disorder of family life. The concept of the 'problem family' will be addressed in chapter 4.

Matza recognised that, in part, the labelling process was motivated by attempts to reduce stigma, and for this reason was likely to fail. Conversely, some terms were deliberately offensive, originating outside social work circles. Writings on the role of stigma amplified some of these ideas. Chaim Waxman, for example, has observed that social work has been dominated by a social casework approach that is based on a cultural perspective. These commentators saw the poor as manifesting patterns of behaviour and values – to escape from their poverty they had to change their behaviour and values – but as these had been internalised, it was a slow and difficult process. Waxman suggested that Matza's example of the 'disreputable poor' showed how, for some people in society, receipt of certain types of assistance was sufficient evidence of moral defectiveness, and could lead to labelling and stigma. He suggested rather that the patterns and attitudes of the poor were adjustments to the stigma of poverty; these were transmitted intergenerationally, through socialisation. To break the stigma of poverty, the poor should be 'integrated, rather than isolated'.[28]

Some of those critical of early underclass concepts located them in a longer-term historical process. In his important critique of the culture of poverty, published in 1968, Charles Valentine noted that this idea had much deeper roots in the history of American social investigation – there had long been a belief that the lower classes had a different social outlook to the middle class.[29] There was then a lull in this writing, extending from the late 1960s to the late 1980s. It was only with the emergence of the underclass in the 1980s that some commentators returned to the question of how one term replaced another. The psychologist Michael Morris, for instance, asked why the concept of the 'underclass' had replaced the 'culture of poverty'. He concluded they were similar but not identical – the traits identified by Oscar Lewis as being part of the culture of poverty were almost identical to those allegedly observed in the underclass. However, there were also important differences. The conservative argument that welfare programmes helped develop and maintain the 'underclass' had not been evident in the 'culture of poverty'; the 'culture of poverty' was less single-minded in its treatment of race; and the 'underclass' was seen as a growing problem, whereas the 'culture of poverty' was more static. Morris suggested that the term 'underclass' gained popularity because it appeared to be more neutral; it helped to define a subgroup; it could be fitted more easily into sociological frameworks; it was supported by black scholars such as William Julius Wilson; and it was more in line with the prevailing conservative ideology. Morris suggested that the evidence indicated that 'another chapter in the history of word substitution concerning the disreputable poor is currently being written'.[30]

Observers have thus commented both on the idea of the 'disreputable poor' as a labelling phenomenon, and on the processes by which one term has tended to replace another. Others have directed attention to the functions of these terms, and viewed them through a historical lens. Writing of the history of the 'underclass' in the United States, historian Michael Katz has suggested that despite the anxiety it created, the emergence of the 'underclass' in the late 1970s was a comforting discovery. It was small and concentrated enough to be helped or contained, and its prominence refocused attention on culture and behaviour, and away from income inequality and the class structure. The concept served to focus attention on a subset of the poor, and it encouraged targeted approaches through reviving discredited notions of the 'culture of poverty'. Katz concluded that:

> by diffusing an image of poor people as split into two sharply divided groups, underclass helps perpetuate their political powerlessness by strengthening the barriers that for so long have divided them against each other.[31]

More relevant for our purposes is that Katz has also suggested that the underclass is a 'metaphor for social transformation' and evokes perceptions of novelty, complexity, and danger. [32] Like Matza, Katz points out that there have always been attempts to distinguish between the able-bodied and impotent poor. In the 1920s, 'scientific racism' culminated in eugenics and immigration restrictions. Similarly in the 1960s, the work of Oscar Lewis, in propagating the notion of a 'culture of poverty', along with developments in social psychology, emphasised the helplessness and passivity of dependent peoples. At the same time, Katz is critical of the phrase 'underclass'. For Katz, the term 'muddies debate and inhibits the formulation of constructive policy' – it lacks a consistent theoretical basis, and has 'little intellectual substance'. [33]

Nevertheless some of the work of Katz and his colleagues, certainly in the edited collection The "Underclass" Debate, is arguably more about urban poverty than about the history of the concept of the underclass itself. More relevant to the concerns of this book has been the work of the American sociologist Herbert Gans. Writing in the journal of the American Planning Association in 1990, for example, Gans, at that time Robert S. Lynd Professor of Sociology at Columbia University, observed that whereas the term 'underclass' as used by Gunnar Myrdal in the 1960s had been concerned with unemployment, by the late 1970s social scientists were identifying the underclass with persistent poverty, rather than joblessness. In the same period, the term became more mixed up with 'race', and with behavioural factors. Gans argued the term should be dropped, as it had become 'hopelessly polluted in meaning, ideological overtone and implications'. [34] Gans argued the term had numerous dangers for planners. These included its power as a buzzword; its use as a racial codeword; its flexibility; and its synthesising function. It covered a number of different groups of people, and had become a stereotype. Furthermore, the term interfered with anti-poverty planning; was extremely persuasive; was associated with particular neighbourhoods; and was linked to the 'concentration and isolation' hypothesis put forward by William Julius Wilson. Finally, Gans argued that the term side-stepped issues of poverty, and was unpredictable in how it might be used. Gans suggested the phrase might signal that society was preparing for an unemployed 'caste', whose members were blamed for their joblessness, and regarded as undeserving. [35]

Gans has noted that the term can be analysed in terms of its functions, as well as its causes. He has written of the functions of the concept of the 'undeserving poor', both positive and negative, adaptive and destructive. Among these functions Gans lists risk reduction; scapegoating and displacement; norm reinforcement; spatial purification; the reproduction of stigma and the stigmatised; and the extermination of the surplus. The idea of the 'undeserving poor' and the stigmas with which people are labelled persist, he argues, because they are useful to the people who are not poor. [36] In arguably his most substantial contribution to this field, Gans has outlined what he calls the 'label formation' process. He argues that this includes a number of interested parties. First are the 'label-makers' who invent and reinvent the labels. They need to be 'alarmists', able to persuade an audience that the new word identifies a population that is responsible for alarming problems. The 'alarmists' also need to have access to the 'counters', who are able to supply the numbers on the labelled population. Labels need to refer to failings rather to processes or concepts, and also should be credible. At the same time, there may be times when no label for the undeserving poor is needed. Gans refers to a 'sorting' or 'replacement' process when a new label becomes popular after an old one has lost favour. But even the most popular labels undergo 'broadening', when they develop subsidiary meanings, or are attached to other populations. A crucial role is played by the 'label users', in being willing to listen to a new word, and also by the 'legitimators', whether academics or journalists, whose arguments justify the use of the new label. Also involved in this process are the 'labelled', the poor who are the subject of these changing terms. Gans argues that it is 'contextual conditions', embracing forces, agencies, and individuals, that ultimately account for the success of a label. Last are the 'romanticisers', who revive 'dead' labels decades after they have passed out of use. [37]

The hypothesis suggested by Gans provides a useful frame of reference against which to map the processes of change and empirical evidence explored in this book. Given that the underclass debate has been more influential in the United States than in Britain in the recent period, it is not surprising that there has been more serious historical work on the USA. But in Britain too, there has been work on the history of the undeserving poor; on images of the poor; and on the cyclical nature of particular terms. Bill Jordan, for example, was inspired by the 'cycle of deprivation' thesis advanced by Sir Keith Joseph in the early 1970s to trace the earlier history of the recurring idea of the undeserving poor, from the seventeenth century onwards.[38] Peter Golding and Sue Middleton have looked at images of the poor in the period 1890–1939, noting the role of the 'primary definers' and the popular media, and concluding that blaming the victim remains a cornerstone for conceptions of poverty.[39] The cyclical nature of ideas underlies Geoffrey Pearson's book on the history of 'hooliganism'. Pearson criticised the view that street crime and 'hooliganism' are evidence of a permissive revolution, and further evidence of a rapid moral decline from the stable traditions of the past. In fact, successive generations have voiced identical fears of social breakdown and moral degeneration, whether the 'Hooligan' gangs of the late Victorian period, or the 'muggers' of the contemporary urban streets. Pearson argued that his history of 'respectable fears' showed that street violence and disorder were a solidly entrenched aspect of the social landscape.[40] There was thus a strong cyclical element in these anxieties.

But in Britain it has been John Macnicol who has done most to point out continuities in the history of the underclass concept. Influenced by the emergence of the idea of the underclass in the United States, Macnicol argued in 1987 that those involved in the debate were only half aware of the conceptual flaws of the concept, and were ignorant of its 'long and undistinguished pedigree'. He outlined problems in defining the underclass. These problems of definition notwithstanding, also significant were the continuities that could be observed over the previous hundred years. Macnicol claimed that there had been at least six reconstructions:

- The social residuum notion of the 1880s
- The social problem group idea of the 1930s
- The concept of the problem family in the 1950s
- The culture of poverty thesis of the 1960s
- The cycle of deprivation theory of the 1970s
- The underclass debates of the 1980s

This schematic framework really provides the backbone for this book, although we look in more detail at the idea of the unemployable in the early 1900s, and at the move to social exclusion in the 1990s. Macnicol's main aim was to chart, in some detail, debates about the social problem group in the 1930s, and to demonstrate links between them and both the cycle of deprivation in the 1970s, and the underclass in the 1980s. In the interwar period, there were investigations of an hereditary social problem group, as part of a wider conservative social reformist strategy. Macnicol concluded that:

> The concept of an inter-generational underclass displaying a high concentration of social problems – remaining outwith the boundaries of citizenship, alienated from cultural norms and stubbornly impervious to the normal incentives of the market, social work intervention or state welfare – has been reconstructed periodically over at least the past one hundred years, and while there have been important shifts of emphasis between each of these reconstructions, there have also been striking continuities. Underclass stereotypes have always been a part of the discourse on poverty in advanced industrial societies.[41]

While acknowledging that the ambiguity of the underclass concept had been one of the main reasons for its on-going popularity, Macnicol also identified five important underlying strands. First, he claimed it was an artificial 'administrative' definition relating to contacts with organisations and individuals of the state, such as social workers. In this respect, it was a statistical artefact in that its size would be affected by such factors as eligibility, take-up of benefits, and changing levels of unemployment. Second, it tended to get muddled with the separate issue of inter-generational transmission, typically of social inefficiency. Third, certain behavioural traits were identified as antisocial while others were ignored – a wide variety of human conditions were lumped together and attributed to a single cause. Fourth, for him the 'underclass' issue was mainly a resource allocation problem. Fifth, Macnicol claimed that it was supported by people who wished to constrain state welfare, and was thus part of a conservative analysis of the causes of social problems and their solutions.[42]

The key question of linearity has also been addressed by Macnicol, in relation to continuities between the problem family concept of the 1950s, and the underclass notion of the 1980s. Macnicol suggests that the debate over the problem family provided a kind of rehearsal for the underclass debates of the 1980s, particularly in respect of the methodological difficulties faced by researchers. Three groups were interested – the Eugenics Society, Family Service Units, and local Medical Officers of Health – but all experienced problems in proving the existence of problem families. Most of the definitions of problem families were really descriptions of household squalor. Macnicol concludes that the emergence of the culture of poverty in the 1960s and the cycle of deprivation in the 1970s suggests a linear development between 1945 and 1995. Moreover there are similarities in the process of social distancing; the involvement of pressure groups; and a combination of administrative definitions with behavioural ones. However, he also notes that by the 1990s much had changed, most obviously in relation to the labour market, demography, and family formation.[43]

By the 1990s, Macnicol was inclined to treat the underclass less as a discursive phenomenon, and more as an empirical possibility – though he remained sceptical. The question of how and when these ideas emerge is a key theme for this book. Macnicol has suggested that underclass stereotypes will emerge most strongly at times of economic restructuring, when there are high levels of poverty, unemployment, and general social dislocation. At these times, a large 'reserve army of labour' will exist, and its 'dysfunctional' behaviour will cause concern. But he concedes that during the 1950s the concept of the problem family emerged at a time of full employment, economic optimism, a strong belief in the nuclear family, and low illegitimacy ratios. Macnicol makes the point that the term 'underclass' has become a metaphor for real problems that post-industrial societies face, such as widening social polarisation and income inequality, residential segregation, and segmented labour markets. Nonetheless he observes that as soon as one enters the debate, one enters a world of enormous empirical and conceptual complexity. The former includes such issues as unemployment, family formation and demographic trends, shifts in the social ecology of cities, and welfare spells, while debates about the meaning of social exclusion provide a good example of the latter. In the 1980s, a conservative model of underclass-formation, that stressed over-generous welfare payments and a decline in moral responsibility, was countered by a structural model that emphasised changes in the labour market, the social ecology of cities, and family formation. Overall, Macnicol has concluded that the term is most useful as a metaphor for widening social polarisation and economic inequality – it might be applied to an underclass of retired people.[44]

Given the impetus provided by Macnicol, it has often been acknowledged that the underclass concept has been periodically re-invented over the past hundred years. Hartley Dean and Peter Taylor-Gooby, for example, have argued the concept has been most interesting for what it has revealed about preoccupations with delinquency and dependency. The underclass has always been negatively defined, by the criteria of productive work and family life from which the underclass is excluded. They have written that the effect of the concept was 'not to define the marginalised, but to marginalise those it defines', and was more a potent symbol than a useful concept. It would be helpful, they suggested, to see 'residuum' and 'underclass' as discursive phenomena that provided a commentary on broader social relations.[45] Pete Alcock, writing of poverty, has argued that a pathological approach has been a recurring feature of debates about the problem of poverty in an industrial society.[46] Tony Novak has underlined the importance of the word 'underclass', despite its lack of precision, in evoking threats that the poor pose to the family, law and order, and to the labour market.[47] And researchers have begun to explore contending philosophical perspectives on the causation and resolution of the underclass.[48]

However despite this recognition of the successive invention and reinvention of different labels, academic research has not gone beyond this to provide a systematic analysis of how this process has occurred and what lessons it offers to contemporary policy-makers. In part this reflects the distaste that many academics on the Left have felt for terms such as 'underclass'. It has been argued that one of the distinctive features of social policy in the postwar period was an almost total focus on structural rather than behavioural factors in the causation of poverty and deprivation. This derived in part from the approach of its dominant figure – Richard Titmuss – and can be seen in the work of one of its most distinguished practitioners – Peter Townsend. But their disapproval for what is perceived as a focus on the behavioural inadequacies of the poor has also led to a failure to explore the meaning of 'underclass' and associated labels as discursive phenomena.

While there has been important writing on the history of the underclass in the United States, much of the writing by British-based academics has been superficial and unsatisfactory – with the important exception of Macnicol. Several of the books that have been produced have been by sociologists and social policy analysts who are interested in the history of the underclass only as a preliminary to recent policy developments. The book by Kirk Mann, for example,

The Making of an English 'Underclass', is really a history of the social divisions of welfare and labour, and is not, despite its title, a history of the concept of the underclass. He asks why the poorest members of society are so often segregated from the rest of the working class. Mann touches on the disappearance of the social residuum and the unemployables during the First and Second World Wars, and he is concerned to tackle the ideas of Charles Murray.[49] However, because of unease over the term 'underclass', the book focuses on intra-class divisions. Lydia Morris's book *Dangerous Class* does examine the historical background to the development of an underclass. She notes that a welfare system that had appeared to offer a guarantee of social citizenship in the 1940s had become transformed into a system that was associated with the underclass and social disenfranchisement. Discussions of the underclass tend to be cast in terms of a nuclear family, argues Morris, where the father is the breadwinner and the mother socialises the children. Morris sees social citizenship and the underclass as linked concepts, one representing inclusion, the other exclusion and moral failure. The term 'underclass' is useful in capturing this sense of status exclusion, though it is less convincing in explanatory terms. Morris suggests the debate should be changed from a focus on the underclass to a reconsideration of how sociologists think about social structures.[50] Nonetheless, while she relates the term 'underclass' to the history of ideas about citizenship, and to the creation of the welfare state, her book is not an exploration of the different forms that the underclass concept has taken across time.

There is therefore, despite this earlier work, no full-length study of the history of the concept of the underclass in either Britain or the United States over the past 120 years. Several of the reconstructions are known only in terms of their broad outlines, such as the cycle of deprivation debates of the 1970s, in part because of an emphasis on easily-available published sources. In contrast, archival materials remain under-exploited. There has been perhaps an inevitable focus on the underclass debates of the 1980s. Much less is known about other underclass reconstructions, such as the debates about the unemployable in the 1900s, which arguably form an additional conceptual stepping-stone. The links by which concepts in Britain and the United States served to cross-fertilise each other, and the extent to which this occurred, remains unknown, although there is increasing interest in processes of policy transfer.[51] Arguably the most glaring gap in research is that of the process by which one term replaces another. The preliminary hypotheses provided by Gans and Macnicol form a useful starting-point. But otherwise very little is known about the process by which a term comes into existence, gains popularity, falls out of favour, and then is replaced by a different, but similar, alternative. In fact as this brief survey of the secondary literature shows, there is no comprehensive history of this story, either in Britain or the United States.

The need for a study of this kind has been underlined by new thinking in social policy that has sought to look more closely at the relationship between agency, structure, and poverty. In the 1970s, commentators such as Peter Townsend stressed the importance of wider structural factors, and were unwilling to admit that either cultural factors or individual agency might have a role to play in determining the response of people faced by unemployment and poverty. However, increasingly social policy analysts are coming to concede that the structural focus of social policy in the postwar years – typified by arguably its most influential figure, Richard Titmuss – was in fact a source of serious weakness that subsequently left it ill-equipped to dealt with assaults by the Right in the 1980s. It is argued that research in the social administration tradition has been limited to distributional issues, and neglected the study of social relations. The effect of this writing has been to refocus attention on the relative importance of behavioural and structural factors in causing poverty and deprivation.

It has long been recognised that the discipline of social administration was dominated by an empiricist tradition. As Peter Taylor-Gooby has pointed out, it was concerned with charting the shortcomings of state welfare, and it ignored the place of welfare within a larger capitalist system.[52] Ramesh Mishra alleges the dominant influence in social administration was Fabian socialism – its tradition was one of pragmatism; was Britain-centred; concentrated on the factual study of social problems; focused on statutory social services; and had no theoretical approach to its subject matter. In part this was due to the influence of Titmuss – Mishra argues that he furthered the study of social policy in many ways, but was not interested in theory.[53] Mike Miller has noted that Titmuss's support for universal welfare was based in part on his belief that more selective benefits would lead to people being stigmatised.[54]

Michael Titterton, for example, has argued that the dominant paradigms in the study of social welfare have ignored the role of agency. In the early 1990s, Titterton was a consultant to the Economic and Social Research Council's (ESRC) Human Behaviour and Development Group. He claimed these paradigms were characterised by a preoccupation with pathological views of health and welfare, and by inadequate conceptualisations of the 'mediating structures' between the individual and wider social forces. The concept of 'coping', for example, showed there were variations in vulnerability and coping styles, and these were differentiated by gender, age, and social class. Titterton argued a new paradigm should try to understand people's 'differential vulnerability'; it should examine the different coping strategies that they used; and it should include the people who survived – the 'invulnerables'. Titterton drew on some of the studies that had been included in the cycle of deprivation research programme of the 1970s, and we will look further at the 'cycle' in chapter 6. He called for a new paradigm of welfare, where the focus was on the differential nature of vulnerability and risk among individuals, and their different reactions to threats to welfare. The work should:

> generate respect for informal modes of coping and helpseeking, and should create a new sensitivity towards the creative and diverse ways in which people respond to their own problems and the ways in which they help other people to respond.[55]

Titterton's plea has been taken forward by other writers. Eithne McLaughlin, for example, has suggested that the relationship between social welfare and behaviour is central to understanding the outcomes of welfare provision, and essential for modelling future demand. (Interestingly, she also noted that historians like Michael Katz were trying to place more emphasis on agency than previously). The main problem, claimed McLaughlin, was that in social science people tended to regard structure and agency as alternatives, and as having as a hierarchical relationship to each other – one must be 'on top'. McLaughlin argued rather that social welfare research should investigate the relationships between structures, values, and behaviour in the decision-making processes of individuals. It seemed likely that research into 'decision environments' would require new types of methodology and theory, and combine qualitative and quantitative techniques.[56]

McLaughlin's demand for a shift in the conceptual focus of research on poverty has been echoed by Fiona Williams and Jane Pillinger. They have argued there should be a move from researching social groups as categories to:

> integrating an acknowledgement of people's, or groups' own agency, experience and understanding of their position, and seeing them as creative, reflexive agents both constrained by and enabled by, as well as creating, the social conditions in which they exist.[57]

Williams and Pillinger noted research into poverty had become increasingly preoccupied with a pathological approach, whose concern with questions of motivation and behaviour was typified in the notion of the underclass. In response, research on poverty, unemployment, and lone motherhood had focused on meanings and discourses, including the social construction of the 'poor'. But other changes in poverty research, including the concept of social exclusion, had also paved the way for a greater recognition of the heterogeneity of the poor. Overall, Williams and Pillinger argued that a new research paradigm could bridge the conceptual and methodological gaps that dichotomies in social science research had generated, and would create 'a more multidimensional view of what poverty means in relation to the quality of life'.[58]

In a book that summarised research in an ESRC/Rowntree Foundation research programme, Fiona Williams, Jennie Popay and Ann Oakley explored a new paradigm of welfare. In particular they have been concerned to see how a new framework for research could incorporate new approaches that emphasised individual agency, without losing sight of the approach that stressed structural constraints. They were sympathetic to the efforts of Titterton in identifying a new paradigm for welfare and research, but argued he had overestimated the extent to which one could be constructed from the literature on stress, life events, coping, and social support. They suggested this literature failed to explain or illuminate the relationship between identity, agency, and structure. Williams, Popay and Oakley also questioned the usefulness of old and new paradigms, although they agreed that, with the exception of Titmuss's work on altruism, research in the 1960s and 1970s focused on structural determinants, and inequalities were seen in terms of social class.[59]

Williams and Popay concluded from this work that earlier research had neglected individual experience and agency, so that the recipients of welfare were 'at best, shadowy, largely forgotten inhabitants of the research terrain'. The dichotomy had been represented as analyses of poverty in terms of an individualist (blame the victim) versus a structuralist (blame the system) approach. Williams and Popay concluded there should be four levels of analysis – the welfare subject; the social topography of enablement and constraint; the policy context; and the dynamics of social and economic change. They concluded that while much was changing in the lives of individuals, many old inequalities were intensifying. What was needed was that:

> we begin to investigate new ways of researching these issues, new ways of breaking down the separation of the individual from the social, new ways of understanding the relationship between human behaviour and social policy, and between social policy, social inequality and social change.[60]

A slightly different perspective on the same question has been provided by Julian Le Grand, and his typology of people as being public spirited altruists (knights); passive recipients of welfare (pawns), or as self-interested (knaves). Le Grand has argued that the development of quasi-markets in welfare provision, and the supplementation of 'fiscal' welfare by 'legal' welfare, were the result of changes in the way policy-makers viewed human motivation and behaviour. Le Grand characterised the classic welfare state as 'one designed to be financed and operated by knights, for the benefit of pawns'.[61] In contrast, more recent policies have been based on a range of assumptions – that people are knaves; that knaves can be converted into knights; and that we know little about human motivation. However, Le Grand argued neither set of policies has been based on evidence, and each is as likely to fail as the other. What was needed was a more complex view of human behaviour. There was some evidence, claimed Le Grand, that recent policies had begun to incorporate this. Le Grand's work is interesting for its acknowledgement that there have always been tensions between the assumptions that people were either passive or self-interested, as seen in attempts to control the behaviour of people seen as work-shy, loafers, and scroungers.[62]

Debates about 'stakeholder welfare' have evoked related debates about character, behaviour, and human nature.[63] Frank Field argued subsequently that agency had been neglected, writing that 'the welfare state has developed no room for such a discussion of behaviour, even though such a public debate is crucial for change to be successful and supported'.[64] He maintained that the state had to allow individuals the freedom to make their own choices, while retaining the responsibility for the framework within which those choices were made. Field was critical of Titmuss, and a resurgence in neo-liberal and individualistic ideas in the 1970s and 1980s also prompted Alan Deacon to go back to Titmuss's earlier writings. Deacon was struck by Titmuss's total opposition to 'judgementalism' – Titmuss seemed to reject personal responsibility in almost all circumstances, and was extremely optimistic about human behaviour. For Titmuss, social policies had to be universal, and non-judgemental. But Deacon argued that this neglect of behaviour rendered Titmuss's analysis vulnerable to Thatcherism, including the concept of 'behavioural dependency', and to the arguments of Charles Murray and Lawrence Mead.[65]

The revival of interest in human agency in sociological and social policy debates, as they saw it, has also been considered by Alan Deacon and Kirk Mann. They have noted contradictions in the apparent similarity of developments in so-cial policy and sociology. Deacon and Mann argued that agency was neglected by participants in debates about social policy, empiricism, Fabianism, and Marxism – the poor were rarely active agents of change. Moreover, questions about agency were not just neglected in the postwar period, but were consciously dismissed, as a reaction to the individualism of the Charity Organisation Society, and the weaknesses of social casework. In particular, the denial of agency was due to the influence of Titmuss, so that 'arguments about problem families or cycles of deprivation were an irrelevance or worse'.[66] Nevertheless more recent debates about welfare have been more about behaviour than structure, more to do with dependency than poverty. Deacon and Mann characterise these new perspectives as welfare as a channel for the pursuit of self-interest; welfare as the exercise of authority; and welfare as a mechanism for moral regeneration. Overall, they conclude that the revival of agency creates opportunities for a social science that is more sensitive to the activities of poor people, and more representative of the diversity of British society.

Research on the 'Americanisation' of welfare debates has also related policy changes to moralism. Alan Deacon illustrates how American dependency theorists – Charles Murray and Lawrence Mead – pushed issues on to the policy agenda that had been neglected and suppressed in Britain. The void that developed in America around discussions on race following the publication of the Moynihan

Report (1965) seems similar to that which emerged in Britain on questions of the importance of behaviour in explanations of poverty. One example is the hostility evident in the 1970s towards the cycle of deprivation – to the idea that there might be a cultural dimension to poverty, or that deprivation might be transmitted from one generation to another. Deacon argues the direction of the research programme was altered, by the researchers themselves, and this void was filled by conservative writers. Deacon notes that many British academics remain hostile to the idea of an underclass, and to compulsion in welfare to work programmes. He concludes the 'Americanisation' of welfare has enhanced and sustained a morality that is shared by Blair and Thatcher, but distrusted by Old Labour and One Nation conservatism.[67]

Deacon has shifted his position, to an extent, in distinguishing between the 'Titmuss paradigm' and the 'quasi-Titmuss paradigm', arguing that Titmuss's rejection of individualistic or behavioural accounts later hardened into a more deterministic approach that refused to discuss such factors.[68] Other work has drawn attention to continuities between New Labour's emphasis on cycles of disadvantage and the cycle of deprivation research of the 1970s.[69] Deacon claims that the emphasis of New Labour on child poverty, and continuities in deprivation over generations, has forced it to integrate competing explanations. He outlines these as a cultural explanation; a rational explanation; a permissive explanation; an adaptive explanation; and a structural explanation. Moreover he has underlined the continuities with the cycle of deprivation research programme of the 1970s. Deacon claims that the rhetoric of New Labour is closest to the adaptive explanation. More importantly, it now has an understanding of the causes of social exclusion that is both structural and behavioural.

The interplay between agency and structure is now at the heart of contemporary theorisations of the dynamics of poverty, and agency is at the core of debates about the future of welfare. These debates have served to point out how the study of behaviour has been neglected by earlier commentators. Ruth Lister also notes the denial of agency in postwar British social policy, arguing that agency should be understood in the context of structural, cultural, and policy constraints faced by ordinary people. Interestingly, Lister argues that poverty cannot be understood in simply material terms, but needs to be comprehended in terms of social relations between the poor and non-poor. She notes how the nineteenth century is key to understanding modern American and British discourses of poverty, including the case of the underclass.[70]

But with some notable exceptions (including those of Deacon and Lister) the approach of social policy commentators has been weak in historical terms – evidence is used selectively, and there is little sense of the debate before 1950. It is assumed, without much evidence, that in the postwar period, debates about poverty were framed almost exclusively in terms of structural factors, whereas research has indicated that even Richard Titmuss was interested in personal behaviour.[71] It is arguable that a focus on the history of the concept of the underclass may endorse a pathological emphasis, and we do not regard agency and behaviour as synonymous. But in seeking to trace how underclass concepts have been successively reconstructed, as discursive phenomena, this book is a contribution to that larger enterprise, in indicating the extent to which debates about behaviour have been marked as much by continuity as by change. Fiona Williams and Jane Pillinger have argued that 'the discourses of poverty, then, are as significant for study as the numbers in poverty', and Ruth Lister that 'contemporary discourses of poverty are rooted in history'.[72]

The aim of this book, then, is to explore the history of the concept of the underclass in Britain between 1880 and 2000. The first chapter examines the longer-term history of such ideas as the 'undeserving poor', the 'dangerous class', and the *lumpenproletariat*. It then turns to the theory of the social residuum in the 1880s, the way it was used by social investigators such as Charles Booth and Helen Bosanquet, exploring its rise and fall in the period up to the First World War. Chapter 2 charts the history of the related concept of the unemployable, starting with the role of Sidney and Beatrice Webb and William Beveridge in promoting it in parallel to the social residuum, but also tracing its influence in the interwar period. It also examines how the notion of the social residuum came to be absent from the social surveys of the early 1900s – such as those by Seebohm Rowntree and Arthur Bowley. The notion of the social problem group, espoused by the Eugenics Society in the 1920s and 1930s, is taken up in chapter 3. This was succeeded by the theory of the problem family, which surfaced during the evacuation of schoolchildren at the outbreak of the Second World War, and which remained an influential concept in public health up to the early 1970s. As we have noted, one of the most important aspects of this story is not only to understand why and how these concepts came into existence, but also to examine periods of transition, such as wartime. The problem family, then, is the subject of chapter 4.

The focus of this part of the book is essentially on Britain. In the case of the culture of poverty, however, explored in chapter 5, it is the experience of the United States that is most relevant. The phrase was popularised by the social anthropologist Oscar Lewis, and had an important influence on debates about America's 'War on Poverty' in the 1960s. In Britain, the concept of the problem family re-emerged in a slightly different form, as espoused by Sir Keith Joseph. His thinking, and the research programme on the cycle of deprivation in the 1970s, is the subject of chapter 6. The underclass debates of the 1980s were much more wide-ranging, generating a huge literature, particularly in America. Here we look at the experience of the United States in chapter 7, before turning to related debates about the underclass in Britain in chapter 8. In chapter 9 we bring the story up to date with social exclusion, exploring the origins of the term, but also examining how the cycle of deprivation has been revived by New Labour in the context of initiatives designed to tackle child poverty. In the conclusion, we examine how this is a story of both continuity and change; empirical detail and conceptual complexity; the expert and the non-expert; structural constraints and alleged behavioural inadequacies. We argue, nonetheless, that despite the many differences between these concepts, there is also much evidence of a linear process at work.

Regulating the Residuum

The period 1880–1914 was an age of classic social investigation, with such well-known figures as Charles Booth and Benjamin Seebohm Rowntree. Less commented on, perhaps, is the existence of a parallel concern with an underclass or social residuum. This is partly because early historians tended to concentrate on those elements of policy, such as old age pensions, free school meals, and unemployment insurance, that appeared to prefigure the welfare state of the 1940s.[1] They assumed that the approach to social policy before 1914 was overwhelmingly empirical, and neglected its wider ideological context. With some important exceptions, it is only more recently that historians have begun to look closely at the moral assumptions that often lay behind policy. The focus has shifted towards those other, more illiberal, elements. They include such issues as proposals for labour colonies, policy in the field of mental deficiency, eugenics, and plans for the sterilisation and segregation of 'defectives'. In part, this reflects the decline of the classic welfare state, and wider changes in attitudes towards the relative roles of the statutory, private, and voluntary sectors.

David Ward's work indicates that, in the United States in this period, there was a preoccupation with the size and situation of the lowest stratum of urban society. Many housing reformers believed that there was a stratum of the poor, a 'submerged residuum', that would not respond to improved housing. For this reason, they recommended municipal lodging houses. This debate was refined following the publication of Booth's work on London. Ward claims that by 1900, reformers had modified their view of the slum to incorporate the social isolation and environmental deprivation of the poor. Thus there was then a more sustained attempt to improve the social environment, and to ensure social justice.[2] Interestingly, in the United States, Booth's structural interpretation was more influential than his behavioural analysis. The American case was different to the British context, in that the situation of the immigrant poor was more prominent. Nevertheless the experience of the United States would in turn have an important influence on British debates – especially with regard to the culture of poverty in the 1960s, and the underclass of the 1980s.

Here, we look again at the phenomenon of the social residuum in the period 1880–1914 in the light of various arguments that have been put forward by historians. The impact of his social surveys meant that Booth was arguably the most influential writer on class and poverty in the 1880s. But it was a theme that also appeared in other contemporary writing, including by H. M. Hyndman, secretary of the Social Democratic Federation; Samuel A. Barnett, warden of the East London settlement of Toynbee Hall; the founder of the Salvation Army, William Booth; and by Helen Bosanquet. More generally, the term 'residuum' can be found in a wide range of Parliamentary papers. These include the reports and evidence of the Royal Commission on Housing (1885); the Select Committees on Distress from Want of Employment (1894–96); the Interdepartmental Committee on Physical Deterioration (1904); the Royal Commission on the Care and Control of the Feeble Minded (1904–08); and the Royal Commission on the Poor Laws (1905–09).

In this chapter we look first at the way that historians have interpreted the sudden interest in the residuum in the 1880s. Second we explore the longer term history of the theme of the undeserving poor, as expressed by writers as diverse as Thomas More and Thomas Malthus, and also at related ideas such as the Marxist concept of the *lumpenproletariat*, and the contemporary concern with the 'dangerous classes'. We then turn to look in more detail at how the concept of the social residuum was used in the 1880s, by Charles Booth, Helen Bosanquet, and a wide range of other writers. In subsequent chapters we will seek to examine how the social residuum remained an important influence on later concepts, most obviously in the case of the unemployable in the early 1900s, and the social problem group in the 1930s. Overall, we are concerned with how the notion of the social residuum has influenced successive re-inventions of the underclass since the 1880s.

Although the theme of an undeserving poor has a long history, it appears nevertheless that in the 1880s the idea re-emerged with particular force, through the concept of the social residuum. Gareth Stedman Jones represents an important exception to the general rule that historians have tended to focus on liberal rather than illiberal social policies. In *Outcast London* (1971), Stedman Jones provided a powerful analysis of perceptions of the residuum in the 1880s and 1890s. Whereas contemporary observers drew comforting pictures of London in the 1870s, by the following decade it was thought that the residuum formed a significant proportion of the working class. Stedman Jones has argued that the concept of the residuum was central to the crisis of the 1880s, and was present in the thinking of every group, from the Charity Organisation Society to the Social Democratic Federation. It was dangerous, not only 'because of its degenerate nature, but also because its very existence served to contaminate the classes immediately above it'.[3] The fear was that if this situation continued, the residuum would in time contaminate and subsume the respectable working class. Although the New Liberals wooed the respectable working class, they also advocated a more coercive and interventionist policy towards the residuum, which was too great a threat to be left to natural forces and to the Poor Law. Thus both Samuel Barnett and Alfred Marshall advocated labour colonies – Marshall in response to the housing crisis, and Barnett as a solution to unemployment.[4] Stedman Jones argues that the subjective psychological defects of individuals featured larger than before. The problem was not structural, but moral, and the evil to be combated was not poverty but pauperism.[5] Stedman Jones has argued that new theories of 'degeneration' influenced the debate and served to switch the focus from the moral inadequacies of the individual, to the effects of the urban environment. This let middle-class people see poverty as the endemic condition of large masses of the population, rather than the product of exceptional improvidence or misfortune on the part of individuals. Even so, the distinction between the 'deserving' and 'undeserving' poor remained, and was simply recast in new language borrowed from Charles Darwin.

Stedman Jones suggests that the dock strike of 1889 marked a crucial turning point, since its effect was to establish, in the eyes of the middle class, a clear distinction between the respectable working class and the residuum. After the strike, the 'residuum' was regarded as a much less serious problem – a 'nuisance to administrators rather than a threat to civilisation'.[6] Stedman Jones suggests that this new distinction was amplified by the writings of Charles Booth, since Booth divided the residuum into two classes. He claims that there was a consensus among experts that it was desirable to segregate and eliminate the residuum, but also concedes that none of these proposals passed into legislation. Moreover, Stedman Jones argues that the advent of full employment during the First World War showed that the residuum had been a social rather than a biological creation. Their lifestyle had not been the effect of some hereditary taint, but the results of poor housing, inadequate wages, and irregular work. Once employment opportunities became more widely available, those previously deemed unemployable could not be found.[7] In fact, concludes Stedman Jones, 'they had never existed, except as a phantom army called up by late Victorian and Edwardian social science to legitimise its practice'.[8]

In an analysis of Booth's contribution to social theory, Peter Hennock has argued that the Stedman Jones interpretation needs to be modified. In particular, he has claimed that there are important elements of continuity with the 1860s that make it difficult to regard the 1880s as a period of significant theoretical innovation. Whereas Stedman Jones has stressed that writers in the 1880s took a new line in separating the residuum and the respectable working class, Hennock points out that these issues had been debated before, in the Reform Bills of 1866–67. He has suggested that the connections between the ideas of the 1860s and 1880s are too close to be ignored.[9]

José Harris notes that the residuum has been identified as a key concept in

Victorian social science, and a component in the shift from the rationalistic
hedonism of the New Poor Law to the 'Social Darwinism' of the age of imperial-
ism. Its emergence has been located in the 1880s. However, Harris argues that the
term was used in many different ways, and a demarcation between the respectable
and degenerate poor long pre-dated the 1880s. The debates of the 1880s showed
continuity with this earlier era in that they were partly fuelled by fears that the residuum would be given the vote. She has characterised the 1880s as an era both of
economic crisis and of popular democracy.[10] Moreover, theories of the residuum
had other sources in political and social thought, apart from the application of
Darwinism. They were fuelled as much by issues to do with extending the suffrage
to the working class, as with biological degeneracy. Finally Harris argues that in
Britain at least, there is little evidence that those who used the term 'residuum'
necessarily had any wider commitment to a framework of 'natural selection' or
'hereditary degeneration'.[11] Harris concludes therefore that the residuum issue of
the 1880s and 1890s was as much a political as a sociological phenomenon, and 'at
least as much an expression of certain ancient moral and constitutional ideas as
of new-fangled notions of science and social evolution'.[12] The debate about social
reform in the 1880s and 1890s was influenced by evolutionary language, but
this should be seen as 'emblematic verbiage rather than precise social science'.[13]
It was invoked by many different commentators, and did not preclude support
for draconian social policies. In fact, the only area of policy where a 'Darwinian'
model took hold was in the treatment of mental deficiency.

This secondary literature has been illuminating on the debate about the
residuum in the 1880s. However it has weaknesses in two respects. First, it tends
to concentrate on Booth and neglect the many other commentators who wrote
on the residuum in this period. Second, while good on the 1880s, it is much
weaker on the period after 1900, and on continuities between the concerns
about the residuum and related debates about the unemployable. Marc Brodie's
study of the political and social attitudes of the poor of Victorian and Edwardian
London has underlined the importance of assessment of individual, personal,
and moral character in working-class political judgements.[14] Nevertheless while
questioning the extent of poverty in the East End, Brodie does not deal directly
with the concept of the residuum.

It is important to recognise that underclass stereotypes have always been part of
discussions of poverty, and certainly pre-dated the upsurge of interest in the social
residuum of the 1880s. In Britain, the broad idea of an underclass dates back at
least as far as the seventeenth-century Poor Law, with its concerns about vagrancy,
and desire to distinguish between 'deserving' and 'undeserving' claimants. The
1598 Poor Law Act stated that parents and children should maintain poor people,
that children should be set to work, and also reflected concerns about public

order. Similar anxieties were expressed by contemporary writers. Thomas More's *Utopia*, for example, published in 1516, reveals a contemporary concern with the 'lusty beggar' that echoes much more recent debates about lone parents.[15]

Similar concerns were evident in the late eighteenth century, when moral judgements were based on the labour-market relevance of different claimants. The period 1790–1834 saw important changes in poor relief, and it was argued that these had led to the 'demoralisation' of the poor. One such writer was Thomas Malthus (1766–1834). In his 'Essay on the Principle of Population', published in 1798, Malthus argued that the Poor Laws had not helped deal with distress even with an expenditure of £3m. In his view, it had increased the population without increasing the amount of food available for its support. Moreover the provisions consumed in the workhouse reduced the amount for the 'more industrious and more worthy members'. Parish laws had increased the price of provisions and lowered the real price of labour. Malthus wrote:

> It is also difficult to suppose that they have not powerfully contributed to generate that carelessness and want of frugality observable among the poor, so contrary to the disposition frequently to be remarked among petty tradesmen and small farmers. The labouring poor, to use a vulgar expression, seem always to live from hand to mouth. Their present wants employ their whole attention, and they seldom think of the future. Even when they have an opportunity of saving they seldom exercise it, but all that is beyond their present necessities, goes, generally speaking, to the ale-house.[16]

Malthus argued therefore, that the Poor Laws diminished the will to save, and weakened incentives to sobriety, industry, and happiness. As we shall see, many aspects of his interpretation – the effects of welfare on behaviour; the alleged focus of the poor on the present; their failure to make adequate preparation for the future; and their tendency to spend money on enjoyment rather than saving – were to be echoed by much more recent commentators.

It was a theme that was picked up by other writers. In 1798, for example, Jeremy Bentham, in his *Outline of a Work Entitled Pauper Management Improvement*, emphasised the defective 'moral sanity' of the dependent poor, their economic unproductiveness, and the gulf between them and the ordinary working class.[17] Similar anxieties underlay the 1834 Poor Law Amendment Act, which removed subsidies on low wages and created workhouses. The principle of 'less eligibility' was adopted, and it was believed that the bulk of social evils were to be found among the poor. As Bill Jordan has written:

> The real enemy was still seen as the *moral* depravity of the poorest class, and the real solution as a system of relief which dealt with this depravity and confined it as narrowly as possible to this near-incorrigible group, thus saving the much larger poor but industrious class from contamination.[18]

Although the Poor Law Amendment Act of 1834 appeared to make no distinction between different grades of the able-bodied poor, this lack of discrimination was never completely acceptable to popular opinion.

There were signs of similar anxieties in the 1860s. Henry Mayhew had drawn on related ideas, although he did not actually use the phrase 'residuum'.[19] Jennifer Davis has suggested that the garrotting panic of 1862 in London led to a moral panic – one of those periods when public anxieties, especially as expressed by newspapers and the government, served to 'amplify deviance' and promote new measures for its control. Following the Habitual Criminals Act of 1869, a particular group of law-breakers were defined as distinct from the rest of the population – a 'criminal class' – which was useful in justifying the creation of a police force and its extension into working-class areas.[20] A further influence came across the Channel, from France. Here the writings of Balzac and Victor Hugo, along with bourgeois opinion, had helped to create the notion of the 'dangerous class'. Bourgeois opinion was concerned about where the 'dangerous class' was recruited from, whether it had similar characteristics to the labouring classes, and whether both groups were governed by similar imperatives.[21] Ideas about a 'dangerous class' drew support from contemporary beliefs about the physionomy of criminals and the poor. It was seen as a residuum of paupers and criminals recruited from the unskilled urban poor left behind by the march of progress. Jennifer Davis has explored how image and reality interacted, illuminating the process by which the residuum was identified and given concrete existence, by studying the relationship between a Kensington slum and the wider community. She has argued that Jennings' Buildings became a focus for local anxieties about the dangerous classes. Yet Davis has noted it was also part of the wider economy of Kensington, and many individuals profited from its existence. It was only in 1873 that it was finally demolished.[22]

Some writers have argued that the underclass is not a class in the Marxist sense. In the Communist Manifesto, published in German in London in February 1848, Marx and Engels argued that the proletariat was the really revolutionary class. But of the 'dangerous class' they wrote:

> the social scum, that passively rotting mass thrown off by the lowest layers of old society, may here and there, be swept into the movement by a proletarian revolution, its conditions of life, however, prepare it far more for the part of a bribed tool of reactionary intrigue.[23]

Writing of France in 1851, Marx noted:

> the lumpen proletariat ... in all towns forms a mass quite distinct from the industrial proletariat. It is a recruiting ground for thieves and criminals of all sorts, living off the garbage of society ... vagabonds, *gens sans feu et sans aveu*, varying according to the cultural level of their particular nation.[24]

Engels expressed similar ideas in his preface to the second edition of his *Peasant War in Germany*, published in October 1870. Engels wrote 'the *lumpenproletariat*, this scum of depraved elements from all social classes, with headquarters in the big cities, is the worst of all the possible allies'.[25] Every leader of the workers who relied on them as guards or allies, wrote Engels, had proved he was a traitor to the movement.

This was amplified in later Marxist writing on historical materialism. Nikolai Bukharin, for example, was to write in 1925 of a social system that included a fifth class made up of déclassé groups – categories of people outside the labour market, such as the *lumpenproletariat*, beggars, and vagrants. For Bukharin, the psychology and ideology of classes was determined by the conditions of material existence. In the case of the *lumpenproletariat* this led to 'shiftlessness, lack of discipline, hatred of the old, but impotence to construct or organise anything new, an individualistic declassed "personality", whose actions are based only on foolish caprices'.[26] He argued that in each of the classes, an ideology corresponded to its psychology – revolutionary communism in the proletariat; a property ideology in the peasantry; and in the *lumpenproletariat* 'a vacillating and hysterical anarchism'. For Bukharin, certain traits needed to be present in a class in order for it to be able to transform society. It should be a class that was economically exploited and politically oppressed; poor; one that was involved in production; was not bound by private property; and was welded together by the conditions of its existence and common labour. In the case of the *lumpenproletariat*, economic exploitation, political oppression, and a sense of a common interest were all absent. Bukharin concluded that it was 'barred chiefly by the circumstances that it performs no productive work; it can tear down, but has no habit of building up'.[27]

The modern concept of the underclass, therefore, has to be set within the context of these earlier ideas in both Britain and continental Europe. Moreover as José Harris has pointed out, in the particular case of the residuum, many recent writers have ignored the fact that debates long pre-dated the better-known anxieties of the 1880s, and had been originally associated with the campaign to widen Parliamentary and local suffrage. The term 'social residuum' seems to have been first used in a British context by John Bright, radical MP for Birmingham, in the debate on the Second Reform Act of 1867. Bright used it to define those who (in his opinion) should in no circumstances be given the vote. He argued there was a small class which should not be enfranchised, 'because they have no independence whatsoever ... I call this class the residuum, which there is in almost every constituency, of almost helpless poverty and dependence'.[28]

Bright's case against the residuum was not in terms of poverty, but in the language of property. Compared to the independent working class, the residuum were:

all of them in a condition of dependence, such as to give no reasonable expectation that they would be able to resist the many temptations which rich and unscrupulous men would offer them at periods of election to give their vote in a manner not only not consistent with their own opinions and consciences, if they have any, but not consistent with the representation of the town or city in which they live.[29]

Thus it was feared that, unlike the respectable working class, the members of the residuum would sell their votes to the highest bidder. The household suffrage provisions of the 1867 Act were deliberately designed to create a direct ratepayers' franchise in which respectable working men who paid their own rates were admitted to the constitution. Contemporaries were confused about who should be let in, but were agreed the residuum should be left out – by definition, the residuum did not include household ratepayers.

Another early example of the use of the term 'residuum' is provided by the social reformer Alsager Hay Hill (1839–1906). Trained as a barrister, Hay Hill had become interested in Poor Law and labour questions, and worked as an almoner for the Society for the Relief of Distress in East London. He later was prominent in the work of the Charity Organisation Society in the 1870s and 1880s. His paper on unemployment had originally been an entry to a competition organised by the National Association for the Promotion of Social Science, for the best essay on a 'Feasible Plan for the Temporary Employment of Operatives and Workmen in Casual Distress'. Published in 1868 as *Our Unemployed*, Hay Hill's pamphlet argued that the unemployed fell into three groups – casual labourers; representatives of the 'decaying and underpaid' trades; and an 'incompetent class'. At the same time, there was also a separate residuum of 'honest, thrifty, and industrious men' who became unemployed and destitute through the normal workings of the trade cycle. Hay Hill's solutions were a national system of registration of labour, more rigorous classification by the Poor Law authorities, and the creation of public works by Local Improvement Committees.[30]

The ambiguity of the term 'residuum', and indeed much of its appeal, is immediately apparent. For John Bright, it was a small dependent class which could not be trusted to use the vote responsibly. For Alsager Hay Hill, on the other hand, the residuum were the 'industrious unemployed', men who found themselves out of work through no fault of their own, though his 'incompetent class' may be closer to an underclass stereotype. The concept of the residuum can be seen to have had political, economic, social, and moral implications. Increasingly common was the line taken by the Charity Organisation Society, which was founded in 1869 specifically to distinguish between the 'deserving' and 'undeserving' poor.

Peter Hennock has shown that the 1880s were a period of particular upheaval. So much attention was focused on the existence of poverty that beliefs in social progress came to be questioned. These distinctive features included the publication of the pamphlet *The Bitter Cry of Outcast London* (1883–84), leading to the appointment of the Royal Commission on the Housing of the Working Classes; demonstrations and riots during the winter of distress and unemployment in 1885–86; an influx of Jewish migrants from Eastern Europe; strikes by the London matchgirls and dockers in 1888 and 1889; and the launching of the Salvation Army with William Booth's *In Darkest England and the Way Out* (1890).[31] One recurring theme was anxiety about the residuum on the part of various individuals and organisations.

Peter Keating has written of the history of social investigation in England, noting the constant references to 'wandering tribes', 'pygmies', and 'rain forests' in the period 1866–1913, and arguing that the use of the word 'abyss' in the 1890s marked an intensification of the class fear that had always been present in this writing. He argues that by the time of Rowntree's survey of York, 'rain forests' had been replaced by 'poverty cycles'; vignettes by statistical tables; the individual by the mass; and the study of the poor by the investigation of poverty. Even so, the tradition of social investigation continued in the twentieth century with increasing power.[32] The famous book *In Darkest England* (1890), by William Booth (1829–1912) provides a good example of this literature. Best known today for founding the Salvation Army, Booth's book was largely written by the journalist W. T. Stead, but it nevertheless caused a sensation. Booth argued that perhaps the most striking aspect of Stanley's African explorations had been his account of the equatorial forest – 'where the rays of the sun never penetrate, where in the dark, dank air, filled with the steam of the heated morass, human beings dwarfed into pygmies and brutalised into cannibals lurk and live and die'. The obvious parallel was between a 'darkest Africa' and a 'darkest England' – for England too had its ivory raiders (publicans), its tribes of savages, and its explorers (social reformers).[33]

An examination of some of this literature suggests that the story is more complex than earlier writers have implied. In an article in the journal *Contemporary Review* (1884), for example, the economist Alfred Marshall argued that in order to solve the pressing problem of housing, the 'London poor' should be forcibly moved to rural areas. Marshall (1842–1924) served on the Royal Commission on Labour (1891–94), and spent much time on the preparation of evidence for the Royal Commission on the Aged Poor (1893). Many people went to London in the first place, Marshall alleged, because they were 'impatient and reckless, or miserable and purposeless; and because they hope to prey on the charities, the follies, and the vices that are nowhere so richly gilded as there'.[34] The effect of living in London was to reduce their physical constitution, and in any case 'the descendents of the dissolute are naturally weak, and especially those of the dissolute in large towns'.[35] The solution was a network of labour colonies, for, as he concluded, 'till this is done our treatment of the poor cannot cease to be tender where tenderness is the parent of crime, and hard where hardness involves needless and bitter degradation and woe'.[36] Marshall used the phrase 'submerged social stratum', he was concerned about physical deterioration, and he did advocate the setting up of labour colonies. Yet his concern was with the poor and the unemployed, and he did not use the phrase 'the residuum'.

Arnold White, writing in the same journal a year later, was concerned with the condition of the class he deemed the 'nomad poor'. A popular journalist who was involved in the 'national efficiency' movement, and who is perhaps best known for *Efficiency and Empire* (1901), White estimated that 20% of this group were able to work, 40% were capable of part-time work, and the remaining 40% were 'men from whom the grace of humanity has almost disappeared'. Although White had found more 'temperate and would-be industrious folk' among London va-grants, he conceded they were a minority, arguing of the group as a whole that:

> physically, mentally, and morally unfit, there is nothing that the nation can do for these men, except to let them die out by leaving them alone. To enable them by unwise compassion to propagate their kind, is to hand on to posterity a legacy of pure and unmixed evil.[37]

White estimated from the 1881 census that some 200,000 men, women, and children formed a 'submerged social stratum' in London, and he claimed that 'physical unfitness' was increasing. He proposed to reorganise charities so that the provision of poor relief was more efficient, and to 'sterilise the vicious' by refusing charity to those whose poverty and unemployment was due to their own shortcomings. But again White did not use the term 'residuum', and his concerns were more with the 'nomad poor', claiming there had been an improvement in the 'moral texture' of the population.

Examining the case of the working class in 1887, the socialist leader H. M. Hyndman (1842–1921) argued that overcrowding had led to physical degeneration; age discrimination was a further problem; and technological change meant that men were increasingly being 'worn out' by work. A further problem was the existence of a 'certain percentage who are almost beyond hope of being reached at all'. He wrote that this group was 'crushed down into the gutter, physically and mentally, by their social surroundings, they can but die out, leav-ing, it is to be hoped, no progeny as a burden on a better state of things'.[38] While Hyndman was concerned with physical degeneration, and he noted the existence of some who were beyond hope, his main interest lay in how improvements to housing might be reflected in better health, and again he did not use the phrase 'residuum'. In fact evolutionary language was strikingly absent from his article.

In the journal *Nineteenth Century* in 1888, Samuel A. Barnett, later warden of Toynbee Hall, noted the existence of large numbers of unemployed, writing that 'the existence of such a class numbering in London its tens of thousands is a national disgrace and a national danger'. If one part of society was content with a poor standard of living, and the rest of society was indifferent to its situation, class conflict was not far away. For:

> there are tens of thousands, with the thoughts and feelings of men, living the life of beasts, greedy for what they can get, careless of the means of getting, rejoicing in low pleasures, moved by a blind sense of injustice ready to take shape in foolish demands and wild acts.[39]

Like Booth, Barnett thought one solution might be a system of labour colonies which would deter 'loafers' and reduce pauperism. Nevertheless Barnett conceded that the unemployed were not all loafers and idlers – many were steady and honest, and did want to work. Moreover, while Barnett considered labour colonies as a solution, he also emphasised the importance of character, concluding that it was for the London Poor Law Guardians to seek 'the means of settling the problem of the unemployed, of hushing that cry which is so much more bitter because it rises from men who, for want of knowledge, are in poverty, in misery, and in sin'.[40]

   The evidence of reports from public bodies was as similarly complex as the writings of individuals. In the case of the Royal Commission on the Housing of the Working Classes (1884–85), it is unclear whether the concept of the social residuum really was very influential. On the one hand, the report noted that if a 'certain class' of the poor was put into decent houses, it would wreck them. Struggling industrial workers and the 'semi-criminal class' lived side by side, and it was this latter group that was the really destructive class.[41] On the other hand, the report acknowledged that although it was said homes were dirty because of the habits of people, there was a reason why individuals appeared to be indifferent to their surroundings. Many were ignorant about sanitation, blocked up sources of ventilation, and kept corpses for many days before burial. Given this analysis, what was needed above all was education.[42] But the question really was whether the habits of the very poor who lived in overcrowded conditions, such as drinking, were the cause or consequence of their condition. As a contemporary pamphlet put it, 'is it the pig that makes the stye or the stye that makes the pig?' The Royal Commission concluded that drink and poverty acted and reacted upon one another, and the main cause was low wages:

> discomfort of the most abject kind is caused by drink, but indulgence in drink is caused by overcrowding and its cognate evils, and the poor who live under the conditions described here have the greatest difficulty in leading decent lives and of maintaining decent habitations.[43]

Despite the writing of others, arguably the key figure in advancing the study of poverty, class and employment was the social investigator Charles Booth (1840–1916). Born in Liverpool in 1840, and after some training in the Lamport and Holt steamship company, Booth began a long and successful career as a shipowner. He was a partner in the firm of Alfred Booth & Co from the age of 22, and later the Booth steamship company was formed, with Charles Booth as chairman until 1912. However, from the 1880s Booth's main energies were directed principally towards social investigation rather than business affairs. As is well known, his major achievement was the *Life and Labour of the People of London* (1889–1903), extending to 17 volumes in three series. Many of his other publications were concerned with old age pensions, including *Pauperism and the Endowment of Old Age* (1892), and Booth was appointed a member of the Royal Commission on the Poor Law in 1905.

The work of Booth has been of key importance in debates about the social residuum in the 1880s. Stedman Jones suggests that the new distinction between the residuum and the respectable working class was amplified by the writings of Booth, since he divided the residuum into two classes. Once separated from the respectable working class, the residuum was no longer a political threat – more of a social problem.[44] However, other writing on Booth has been more cautious. John Brown has explored how Booth considered the potential of the labour colonies that he called 'industrial communities'. But Brown points out that Booth always put forward the labour colony solution very tentatively, not least because it would have involved evacuating around 345,000 people out of London. As a policy option, it was both impractical and authoritarian, and was generally ignored by contemporaries. But it is true that Booth's ideas remained influential. Beveridge, for example, refined Booth's analysis through the concept of underemployment, even though the solution that he proposed was a national system of labour exchanges rather than labour colonies. Brown argues there is little reason to suppose that Booth regarded his proposals for labour colonies as a serious solution to the problem of the residuum.[45]

Similarly José Harris argues that while Booth's survey is imbued with residual-ist and evolutionary language and conceptions, he used Darwinist language loosely and metaphorically rather than in an exact and scientific way. He did not suggest that progress and degeneracy were the products of irreversible biological mutation. Instead, men and women were the products of experience and circumstance. Booth thought the 'residuum mentality' was found at all levels of society, and he did not believe degeneracy was hereditary in a physiological sense. Harris argues therefore that Booth's residuum was a cultural phenomenon susceptible to pressure and manipulation, rather than the product of a natural law. Booth certainly exploited fashionable rhetoric, but more important in his analysis was the role of personal character and rational choice. His solution to poverty was not forcible segregation, but greater efforts to develop moral character and citizenship.[46] Jane Lewis argues that Booth shared the conviction of Octavia Hill and Helen Bosanquet that individual habits and character had to be modified for change to be lasting.[47] Therefore she tends to support Harris's point that it was the role of character and personal choice that was most important to Booth. Peter Hennock too has argued that the emphasis of Booth's work was in separating out the classes, particularly between the respectable working class, and the residuum of demoralised labour. Booth's genius was not in analytical or conceptual originality, but in his perseverance and inquisitiveness. Thus Hennock concludes that 'there is therefore a strong case to be made for regarding Charles Booth as a systematiser, working within a familiar set of assumptions about the composition of society and the nature of social progress'.[48]

Booth is recognised as an extremely important figure in the development of social investigation.[49] However, with some notable exceptions his interest in the social residuum has been neglected in favour of his empirical research into poverty. This is surprising, since this thread in his thinking was evident from his first publications. The results of the early research that were later to form part of the *Life and Labour of the People of London* were given in papers to the Royal Statistical Society, in May 1887 and May 1888. In the first of these papers, Booth described the 'condition of the inhabitants' of Tower Hamlets, an area that comprised the five registration districts of Whitechapel, St George's in the East, Stepney, Mile End Old Town, and Poplar.[50] Booth divided the people who lived in Tower Hamlets into eight classes, ranging from 'A', the 'lowest class', to 'H', the 'upper middle class'. Class 'A' was thought to comprise some 6,882 people, or 1.5% of the total population. Included in it were 'so-called labourers, loafers, semi-criminals, a proportion of the street sellers, street performers, and others', along with the homeless and criminals who were also working.[51] Class 'B', that dependent on casual earnings, comprised some 51,860 people, or over 11% of the total. Of the members of class 'B', Booth wrote that 'these people, *as a class*, are shiftless, hand-to-mouth, pleasure loving, and always poor; to work when they like and play when they like is their ideal'.[52] While there was much unemployment, there was also an element of a 'leisure class'. Booth argued that 'they cannot stand the regularity and dulness [sic] of civilised existence, and find the excitement they need in the life of the streets, or at home as spectators of, or participants in, some highly coloured domestic scene'.[53]

Nevertheless, when Booth attempted to classify the population in the five districts of Tower Hamlets by employment, or 'sections', he was forced to concede that the divisions between these classes were not fixed, but constantly fluctuating. The sections 'not only melt into each other by insensible degrees, but the only divisions which can be made are rather divisions of sentiment than of positive fact'.[54] In all, there were some 39 employment groups, or 'sections'. The first section did correspond to class 'A'. These were 'casual labourers of low character, together with those who pick up a living without labour, and include the criminal or semi-criminal classes'.[55] Their food was poor, and alcohol their only luxury. Booth wrote:

> these are the battered figures who slouch through the streets, and play the beggar or the bully, or help to foul the record of the unemployed; these are the worst class of corner men who hang round the doors of public houses, the young men who spring forward on any chance to earn a copper, the ready materials for disorder when occasion serves.[56]

Booth had no doubt that the situation of these people was in part hereditary – the children of this class were the 'street arabs', and were separated from their parents in pauper or industrial schools. More numerous were the 'young persons' who belonged to this group – 'young men who take naturally to loafing; girls who take almost as naturally to the streets; some drift back from the pauper and industrial schools, and others drift down from the classes of casual and irregular labour'.[57] At the same time, the group was not homogeneous and there were some respectable individuals. Employing the metaphor of the prospector, Booth claimed that 'those who are able to wash the mud may find some gems in it'.[58]

What is most interesting for our purposes are Booth's overall conclusions. For while Booth admitted that the state of affairs revealed in his investigations was serious, it was 'not visibly fraught with imminent social danger, or leading straight to revolution'.[59] Overall, he calculated that 65% of the population were above the poverty line, 22% on the line, and 13% in distress and falling below it. His findings were therefore reassuring, in that although profound poverty was apparent, social revolution was not an immediate danger. Booth concluded:

> that there should be so much savagery as there is, and so much abject poverty, and so many who can never raise their heads much above the level of actual want is grave enough; but we can afford to be calm, and give to attempts at improvement the time and patience which are absolutely needed if we are to do any good at all.[60]

In his second paper to the Royal Statistical Society, given in May 1888, Booth reported on his attempts to extend his investigations into the Hackney School Board Division. This comprised the registration districts of Shoreditch, Bethnal Green, and Hackney, or a further 440,000 inhabitants, making a total of some 908,958 people when combined with the earlier work on Tower Hamlets.[61] Again much of the information was collected by School Board visitors. Booth retained his 8 classes, ranging from 'A' to 'H'. He estimated that in the Hackney School Board Division, class 'A' comprised some 11,000 people, or 1.25% of the total, while class 'B' numbered some 100,000 people, or 11.25% of the entire population. However Booth now argued that classes 'B', 'C', and 'D' constituted the real problem of poverty, disregarding 'A', which he regarded more as an issue of 'disorder'.

In an attempt to uncover the causes of poverty, Booth analysed 4,000 cases known to the School Board visitors as the 'poor' and 'very poor' in each district. With regard to the 1,610 heads of families in classes 'A' and 'B', 4% were classified by him as 'loafers', while 55% were in casual or irregular employment or had low pay. A further 14% were thought to be in poverty because of 'drink or obvious want of thrift', while the predicament of a further 27% was owing to 'questions of circumstance', ranging through large families, illness, and irregular work. In contrast, a similar analysis of 2,466 heads of families in classes 'C' and 'D' suggested that 68% were in poverty due to conditions of 'employment', and that fewer cases were due to questions of 'habit' or 'circumstance'.

For Booth, the main problem was posed by class 'B'; if it could be 'swept out of existence' the work it did could be taken on by classes 'C' and 'D', which would then be much better off. He wrote:

> to the rich the very poor are a sentimental interest: to the poor they are a crushing load. The poverty of the poor is mainly the result of the competition of the very poor. The entire removal of this class out of the daily struggle for existence I believe to be the only solution of the problem of poverty.[62]

Class 'A', on the other hand, represented a very small group – both in relation to the rest of the population and with regard to class 'B'. Echoing his paper of the previous year, Booth maintained that the situation was not out of control. His purpose was to reassure on the basis of his extensive social investigation, and to play down the more dramatic pronouncements of some of his contemporaries. Booth concluded, 'the hordes of barbarians of whom we have heard, who, coming forth from their slums, will one day overwhelm modern civilisation, do not exist. The barbarians are a handful, a very small and decreasing percentage'.[63]

The ways in which Booth viewed the residuum are further illustrated in the collected volumes of the *Life and Labour of the People of London*, published from 1889. These included examples of what might be termed evolutionary language. Booth wrote that 'the unemployed are, as a class, a selection of the unfit, and, on the whole, those most in want are the most unfit'.[64] Similarly he argued that periods of economic slump sorted out those men who were better managers or who had other advantages, writing that 'there result a constant seeking after improvement, a weeding-out of the incapable, and a survival of the fittest'.[65] Nevertheless, while he advocated that class 'A' should be dispersed, and that labour colonies might be used for class 'B', there was no sense that the latter was in any sense fixed, and it is not clear how seriously he viewed this as a solution. Though he termed it a 'sort of quagmire underlying the social structure', class 'B' were not paupers but 'the material from which paupers are made'.[66] Moreover, while he argued that class 'A' was hereditary, he hoped that it might become less so, partly through improved provision for children.[67] Finally, his overall message was again hopeful, since he amended his earlier warning slightly to read 'there are barbarians, but they are a handful, a small and decreasing percentage: a disgrace but not a danger'.[68] As Peter Hennock has suggested, 'the percentages that he presented, far from being grounds for pessimism, were in his opinion ones for optimism'.[69]

But what is most striking on looking again at the Booth survey is that – like Alfred Marshall, Arnold White, H. M. Hyndman, and Samuel Barnett writing before him – he made little serious attempt to define the residuum accurately, and in fact the term itself was almost entirely absent from his writings. As José Harris has suggested, Booth used evolutionary language opportunistically and rather loosely. He did not suggest that progress or degeneracy were caused by irreversible biological mutation – rather men and women were mainly the products of experience and circumstance – and if there was deterioration it was caused by the effects of the London environment. He aimed to make the transmission of bad characteristics less hereditary. And the solutions that he advocated most seriously were not dispersal and labour colonies, but the exercise of character and rational choice.[70]

What was the impact of the Booth survey? Gareth Stedman Jones has suggested that Booth's conclusions were not immediately accepted, but with the dock strike and the publication of the first two volumes of *Life and Labour*, his analysis merged with that of middle-class opinion. Once social investigation and the actions of the strikers themselves had established a clear distinction between the 'residuum' and the working class, fears of revolution subsided.[71] In his book *In Darkest England* (1890), General William Booth attempted to use Charles Booth's figures to estimate the numbers of the destitute. Adding together the poorest class, prison inmates, 'indoor paupers and lunatics', and those dependent on them, Booth estimated that this group constituted some three million of the total population of thirty one million in Great Britain. Thus from these 'ghastly figures', Booth argued the problem was one of the 'submerged tenth'.[72]

Appointed to the chair of political economy at Cambridge in 1885, Alfred Marshall published his *Principles of Economics* in 1890. It rapidly came to be seen as the greatest economic treatise of his generation. In it, Marshall made a more direct reference to the residuum. He wrote that:

> those who have been called the Residuum of our large towns have little opportunity for friendship; they know nothing of the decencies and the quiet, and very little even of the unity of family life; and religion often fails to reach them. No doubt their physical, mental, and moral ill-health is partly due to other causes than poverty: but this is the chief cause.[73]

Thus Marshall provided an explanation that located the residuum in a structural rather than behavioural context. The residuum was less to be feared than to be pitied. Ninety years later, his points would be repeated almost exactly in debates about the underclass.

Nevertheless, the Report of the Select Committee on Distress from Want of Employment (1896) suggests that the older distinction between the 'deserving' and 'undeserving' survived despite the Booth survey. Based partly on evidence from Charles Booth, the Report of the Select Committee argued that the respectable unemployed did not deserve Poor Law relief, and the Report objected to the stigma associated with it. Significantly, the Report also embodied the fear that if the 'better class of unemployed' was brought into contact with poor relief, its independence would be gradually undermined and it would rely permanently on receiving assistance. Basically, a distinction was made between the ordinary applicants for parish relief and the deserving unemployed. The needs of the former could be met in the usual way, while there were other ways to help the deserving poor. With regard to the stone-breaking test, for example, the Committee argued that this should be ended since 'the casual and deserving poor suffer by being brought into contact with the loafing class in the stoneyard'.[74] Similarly it objected to state grants on the basis that they would lead to the 'demoralisation' of the recipients, and to farm colonies which became 'the resort of the idle and vicious, to the exclusion of the efficient and deserving'.[75]

The writers and commentators featured so far had one thing in common – they were all men. Ross McKibbin, on the other hand, has claimed that the work of early female social investigators was marked by an interest in the behaviour of the poor that anticipated Oscar Lewis's culture of poverty in the 1960s. He has written of Helen Bosanquet, Margaret Loane, and Florence, Lady Bell, that 'they were all three probably the most accomplished Edwardian practitioners of a cultural sociology; but they were also all three hostile to structural explanations of poverty and collective solutions to it'.[76] These writers were concerned with familiar aspects of the life of the poor. Why, for example, were the poor so improvident in their management of money? Why was working-class behaviour marked by a sense of time that seemed confined? And why, compared to the middle class, did the urge for excitement seem so strong, and lapses of concentration sudden and frequent? McKibbin points out the striking similarities between the approaches taken by Bosanquet, Loane, and Bell, and by cultural sociology in the United States in the 1950s and 1960s. He claims that the techniques adopted by Oscar Lewis were almost identical to those of these early female investigators.

Helen Bosanquet (1860–1925) was born into the well-known Manchester Utilitarian family of the Dendys – her sister Mary, for example, was active in social work with the 'mentally defective'. After graduating from Cambridge,

Helen worked as a paid secretary for the Shoreditch District Committee of the Charity Organisation Society, from 1890 until her marriage to the philosopher Bernard Bosanquet in 1894. Helen remained committed to the world of social work within the COS, and she also edited the *Charity Organisation Review* until 1912. Helen Bosanquet was one of the most powerful intellectual and political influences on the COS before the First World War, if an increasingly isolated one. Angus McBriar has suggested that the attitude of the Bosanquets towards the residuum showed that they believed that the condition of the poor was due to their lack of will-power or strong character, and absence of self-help and independence. McBriar claims that in the 1890s the Bosanquets led the COS away from the dichotomy between deserving and undeserving, towards a more refined distinction between the 'helpable' and the 'unhelpable'.[77]

In a paper read at the Economic Club in January 1893, and subsequently published in a collection edited by her husband, Helen Bosanquet analysed the social residuum within the framework provided by neo-classical economics. She made a clear distinction between the residuum and the class of 'genuinely self-supporting wage-earners', though she also argued that members of the residuum could be found in all classes of society.[78] The difference between the two groups, according to Bosanquet, was one of 'character and disposition'. What distinguished members of the residuum was their attitude to pleasure, pain, labour, and reward. But the residuum itself consisted of two groups – those who were in 'superfluous' jobs, and unskilled labourers who supported regular wage earners in the main industries. Together, the residuum also possessed a number of other notable characteristics. Its members lacked foresight and self control, they lived entirely in the present, and had little sense of the past. According to Bosanquet, they were unable to remember street names and house numbers, they had a poor sense of direction, and they had trouble in distinguishing left and right. Family ties were loose, so that neither different generations nor siblings had much sense of mutual responsibility. As a result, the life of a member of the residuum was:

> one incoherent jumble from beginning to end; it would be impossible to make even a connected story out of it, for every day merely repeats the mistakes, the follies and mishaps of yesterday; there is no development in it; all is aimless and drifting.[79]

Most important for Bosanquet was that these variations of 'character' had economic results, in that members of the residuum had a different attitude towards labour and reward from that of 'normal' people. In the opinion of Bosanquet, it was the 'inferior' man who was most vulnerable to the ups and downs of the trade cycle – it was these workers who were 'the first to be turned off as work slackens, and the last to be taken on as it improves'. The 'residuum' cost as much to produce as the self-supporting wage earner, but generated little of real value – they had the economic worth of cracked bells. Bosanquet thought that it was almost impossible to eradicate these 'defects of character' – the best that could be hoped for was that the 'residuum' would fade away through 'natural processes'. It might 'gradually wear itself away, or in the coming generation be reabsorbed into the industrial life on which it is at present a mere parasite'.[80]

Some of the same ideas were repeated in *The Strength of the People* (1902). It is interesting that here Bosanquet tended to use the phrase 'very poor' in place of 'residuum'. In suggesting the term 'residuum' was no longer fashionable, this may provide a comment on wider changes in intellectual thought. Nonetheless Bosanquet maintained that the first step towards solving contemporary social problems was in the area of the 'individual mind and character'. Indeed any alternative approach was likely to make the situation worse rather than better. In a section that provides clear resonances with much more recent writing on social capital, Bosanquet argued that the less obvious, but ultimately more successful, strategy would be to 'approach the problem by striking at its roots in the minds of the people themselves; to stimulate their energies, to insist upon their responsibilities, to train their faculties. In short, to make them efficient'.[81]

Jane Lewis suggests that Helen and Bernard Bosanquet believed in ideas as much as social action. Only through a thorough understanding of human behaviour could social problems be solved, and it was social work that was the key to achieving social change. And it was because they placed so much emphasis on developing and reforming individual character that they favoured social work as the means of achieving change. Thus state intervention posed a danger to the exercise of individual will and effort. Lewis argues that Helen Bosanquet provided perceptive and sympathetic descriptions of working-class life. At best, the emphasis on 'character' could lead to a desire to work with and empower individuals. She was, for instance, more sympathetic to the residuum than her contemporary Beatrice Webb, and her ideas were better worked out than those of Charles Booth. At the same time, the interpretation was heavily influenced by the prevailing moral and social philosophical framework.[82] To change character would achieve more fundamental improvement than changing economic conditions. José Harris points out that for Helen Bosanquet the residuum could be reclaimed, by a mixture of tough social policies, visiting, and training in citizenship and good housekeeping.[83] As with Booth, therefore, Bosanquet saw the residuum as amenable to change rather than the product of an inexorable natural law; its members could be found in all social classes; and it was character that held the key.

There was therefore much discussion about the existence of a social residuum among social investigators in England in the 1880s, and this has to be placed in the context of older ideas about the deserving and undeserving poor, the Marxist insistence on the existence of the *lumpenproletariat*, and wider fears of 'criminal classes' and 'dangerous classes'. Influenced in part by fears of physical degeneracy, there was much concern about the poor and the unemployed in London in the 1880s, and draconian social policies were advocated that sought to segregate these social groups, including through the establishment of labour colonies. Much of Booth's analysis was concerned to separate out his 'social quagmire' from the respectable working class, and some of this was couched loosely in evolutionary language. Moreover, as the writing of Helen Bosanquet indicates, this analysis, and the use of the term 'residuum' itself, persisted into the 1890s.

However, it is also clear that a concern with a residuum existed long before the 1880s, in the debates about enfranchising the working class through the Second Reform Act, in 1867. Moreover much of the writing of the 1880s, by Alfred Marshall, Arnold White, H. M. Hyndman, and Samuel Barnett, among others, was concerned more generally with poverty and unemployment; their anxiety about a 'submerged social stratum' or the 'nomad poor' was only one of the issues that they explored; and while they may have subscribed to the idea, they did not in fact use the term 'residuum'. While these writers were concerned with the effects of physical degeneracy allegedly caused by the urban environment, they were also concerned with improvements to housing, and in fact the language of Social Darwinism was strikingly absent from their analysis. In the arguments of both Booth and Bosanquet, the main thrust of their writing was to emphasise the importance of character, and there was evidence from the Report of the Select Committee on Distress from Want of Employment (1896) that the older distinction between the deserving and undeserving survived despite the evidence of the Booth survey. As others have noted, arguments for sterilising the 'unfit' or for establishing labour colonies did not pass into legislation.

While earlier writers on the residuum have tended to see the First World War as a further turning point, and have made some connections between the social residuum and the ideas that came after, they have failed to do this systematically. Social investigators had begun to write about the unemployable in the 1890s. It is to that notion that we now turn.

2

A Trojan Horse

In order to look more closely at the transition from the notion of the 'social residuum' to the concept of the 'social problem group', we examine in this chapter the related idea of the 'unemployable'. This phrase was used by a range of writers in the 1890s and early 1900s, including Sidney and Beatrice Webb, and William Beveridge. There were both similarities and differences between the notions of the social residuum and the unemployable. On the one hand, social surveys conducted by, among others, Benjamin Seebohm Rowntree and Arthur Bowley, and published after 1900, suggest these terms fell out of favour in the years before the First World War. Nevertheless debates in the 1920s and 1930s about unemployment, which generated a 'search for the scrounger', and when contemporaries claimed to have detected a 'social psychology' of unemployment, entailed re-visiting those debates on the unemployable that had been such a feature of the 1890s and early 1900s. We argue that concern with the residuum did not ebb away, as Stedman Jones has suggested. Rather it remained a latent, but still potent, stream in intellectual thought, embodied in the Trojan Horse concept of the unemployable. In this way it served to sustain a particular interpretation of poverty that provided a fertile soil for the concept of the social problem group in the 1920s.

It was Charles Booth's eight-class taxonomy of the population of London, and particularly the case of class 'B' within it, that provided the focal point for much of the discussion of the concept of unemployables in the late-Victorian and Edwardian periods. Beatrice Potter (1858–1943) joined the COS in 1883 as an unpaid Visitor, and also worked as a rent collector in one of Octavia Hill's housing schemes. Later, she became disillusioned with social work, and moved more towards social investigation, initially by working on Booth's survey of London. After she married Sidney Webb (1859–1947) in 1892, the Webbs worked more on histories of institutions than social surveys. Working in tandem as 'the firm', their publications included histories of trade unionism, Fabian tracts on education, a history of local government, and of course the drafting of the Minority Report of the Royal Commission on the Poor Law.

Jane Lewis has made the point that whereas women's roles in nineteenth-century philanthropy have been acknowledged, the part women played as social investigators has often been overlooked. Even so, this secondary work on Beatrice Webb has not gone as far as it might to explore the ways in which she used the related concept of the unemployable. The new absence of the term 'residuum' and frequency of the phrase 'unemployable' is made clear in some of the earliest writings of Sidney and Beatrice Webb. In their book *Industrial Democracy* (1897), for example, the Webbs made the – to them – important distinction between the 'unemployable' and the 'temporarily unemployed'. While unemployment was 'an inevitable incident in the life of even the most competent and the best conducted workman', they argued that, like the poor, the unemployable 'we have always with us'.[1] The Webbs divided the unemployable into three groups. In the first category were children, older people, and women of child-bearing age. The second group was composed of the sick and crippled, 'idiots and lunatics', the epileptic, the blind, deaf, and dumb, criminals and the 'incorrigibly idle', and all who were 'morally deficient'. In the third group were men and women who:

> without suffering from apparent disease of body or mind, are incapable of steady or continuous application, or who are so deficient in strength, speed, or skill that they are incapable, in the industrial order in which they find themselves, of producing their maintenance at any occupation whatsoever.[2]

It is immediately clear that the boundaries between these groupings were blurred – older people might fit into the first and third. Nevertheless, the solution put forward by the Webbs was a dual one, influenced by current public health policy, of prevention on the one hand and treatment on the other. Like Booth, the Webbs realised that one solution was offered by labour colonies which would remove the unemployable from the labour market, and avoid the danger of 'parasitic competition with those who are whole'.[3] However, the Webbs also argued that if a policy of a national minimum of education, sanitation, leisure, and wages was adopted, it would reduce the costs of the unemployable to the state, and also begin to reduce its size. This fiscal accounting argument was typical of much thought at the time. Taxpayers, it was alleged, were concerned at having to maintain in public institutions 'an enlarged residuum of the unemployable', and a national minimum would instead 'increase the efficiency of the community as a whole'.[4] Thus the Webbs managed to combine a belief in the unemployable with solutions that emphasised the role of state action. In this, their remedies were almost the direct opposite of those of Helen Bosanquet outlined in the previous chapter.

As we have noted, the Webbs played a key role in the drafting of the Minority Report of the Royal Commission on the Poor Law (1909). The Report argued that in the end, 'character' was irrelevant in discussions of unemployment. It concluded that 'whether the men are good or bad, drunken or sober, immoral or virtuous, it is a terrible misfortune to the community, as well as to themselves, that they should be unemployed'.[5] Even so, the Minority Report did support the concept of the unemployable. The Minority Report again argued that the unemployable were not all the same – some members of the group did not actively look for work, while others did look but were unsuccessful. Another simile was to compare the unemployable to wreckage from an ocean liner, since it was composed of 'material of the most heterogeneous and sharply differentiated kinds, bright and clean and in active use, but now so battered and sodden as to appear, in bulk, almost homogeneous in its worthlessness'.[6] The Report argued that some members of the unemployable could be rehabilitated. Again employing the metaphor of the prospector, the Webbs wrote that, if properly sorted, there was much that could be useful, and some 'gems' of real value. Jane Lewis has compared Beatrice Webb and Helen Bosanquet, noting that they differed in the way they viewed the relationship between social facts and social theory. She has argued that Bosanquet was more sympathetic towards the residuum than either Booth or Webb, noting that the Minority Report, in its attitude to 'recalcitrant labour', and in recommending draconian proposals for dealing with it, and forcing it into a useful life, showed the old distrust of, and contempt for, the residuum.[7]

Industrial Democracy and the Minority Report support the argument of Lewis that Beatrice Webb was less sympathetic towards the residuum than Helen Bosanquet. But it was the expression 'unemployable' that Beatrice Webb used, more than the term 'residuum'. Certainly the work of the Webbs demonstrated how the concept of the unemployable persisted in social thought well after the First World War. In their history of the Poor Law (1929), for example, the Webbs argued that the unemployed could be classified into six groups, with the residuum constituting a final group, who might be called the unemployable. This group included:

> those who, by reason of physical, mental or moral deficiencies, have great difficulty in discovering any employer willing to engage them at any price; and also those who, finding other ways of picking up a meagre subsistence, are not, with any reality, seeking employment at all.[8]

For the Webbs, the terms 'residuum' and 'unemployable' seemed interchangeable. But they also claimed the First World War had demonstrated two things. First, there was no 'surplus' population for which occupation or wages could not be found. Second, the category of the unemployable had no definite boundary since a large proportion of those thought to be physically, mentally, or morally incapable of employment did find work in wartime.[9] Thus they continued to believe the unemployable existed, while conceding there was no definite distinction between the unemployable and the unemployed. It is debatable which strand in their thinking was the most significant. It is interesting that the point made by

Stedman Jones in *Outcast London* about the residuum and the First World War was made originally by the Webbs in relation to wartime and the unemployable. But as we shall see when we come to the problem family, it is also the case that underclass concepts can be invented in wartime, raising important questions about how and when the transition between these concepts occurs.

The Webbs' interest in the unemployable was echoed by other contemporary writing on unemployment. Geoffrey Drage, Secretary to the Labour Commission, and writing in 1894, had argued that casual labourers could fall into the lower class of the unemployable, which consisted of those 'who are permanently un-employed because through some physical or moral defect they are economically worthless'.[10] At the same time, Drage conceded that there were many temporarily without work because of economic conditions rather than their 'comparative fitness', and it was the 'least capable' or the 'least steady' who were the first to be 'turned off'. When it came to the causes of unemployment, temporary unemployment was usually due to conditions independent of the men involved, and over which they had no control. Drage did argue that unemployment could be due to 'low physical and moral condition', old age, or a physical disability. But more often it was 'faults of character – habits of intemperance, idleness or dishonesty – which constitute their inferiority'.[11] Drage was heavily influenced by the earlier work of Booth, and he attached great importance to classifying the unemployed. He also accepted that labour colonies offered the prospect of a temporary solution.

Percy Alden's study of unemployment, published in 1905, was also heavily im-bued with the concept of the unemployable. Alden had previously been warden of the Mansfield House settlement in East London, a member of the Mansion House Unemployed Committee, and secretary to a conference on unemployment held at London's Guildhall in 1903. For Alden, the unemployable was composed of two groups. First, there were the 'criminals, semi-criminals, vicious vagabonds and the incorrigibly lazy' – the able-bodied who refused to work, or were refused work because of some 'defect' in their character. Second, there were the physically and mentally deficient. The second group could be subdivided into a further four groups – the aged; the physically weak and maimed; epileptics; and 'weak-willed inebriates and the mentally deficient'.[12] Given this, the solutions were different for each group, though there was some overlap. For the former, the remedies were the abolition of casual wards; the introduction of identification papers; the provision of relief stations; and the setting up of labour colonies. For the latter, they included residential homes for old people, the provision of old age pensions, and the creation of farm colonies.[13]

Like the Webbs, Alden regarded the unemployable as a heterogeneous group, comprising both those unwilling and those unable to work. And, like them, his solutions were a mix of the 'progressive' and the reactionary. Alden had just returned from a visit to labour colonies in Holland, Belgium, and Germany, and the key theme of his book was segregation. He emphasised the separation 'of the criminal and vicious vagabond from all who may be called in any real sense irresponsible'.[14] It was also important to distinguish between 'the genuine unemployed man who is in search of work, and the vicious vagrant who is in search of opportunities for plunder and who has not the slightest intention of working'.[15] From his observations on the Continent, Alden knew that Denmark, Belgium, Germany, and Holland had set up labour colonies and workshops. His preference was for farm colonies rather than casual wards, because men were detained in the former, and the work was 'useful and humanising'. Nevertheless many of these were not hopeless cases, they were 'men of weak character, easily swayed and led by the baser kind' – they need not be permanently unemployable, but could be rehabilitated.[16] Overall the aim, as he saw it, was 'to check the wholesale demoralisation of large sections of the working classes, and restore to the people the assurance so long denied that honest work will carry with it a just and certain reward'.[17]

The concept of the unemployable can also be seen to have permeated the Departmental Committee on Vagrancy appointed in July 1904. Its 1906 Report argued that 'it [the army of vagrants] is mainly composed of those who deliberately avoid any work and depend for their existence on almsgiving and the casual wards; and also for their benefit the industrious portions of the community is heavily taxed'.[18] Numbers for 1905, for example for the casual ward population for London, had decreased slightly, but remained unacceptably high. Overall, the Departmental Committee argued that the current system made no attempt to reform the vagrant. It stressed the potential role of labour colonies and police control, and proposed that the real cause of vagrancy was 'indiscriminate charity'.[19]

Interestingly, the Report was shot through by a distinction between the 'habitual vagrant' and the 'bona fide wayfarer'. The 'habitual vagrant' was regarded as one of four identified types of the homeless, and while numbers fluctuated, it was thought there was an 'irreducible minimum' of some 20–30,000 people. The Committee claimed, for example, that 'the habitual vagrant much prefers bad accommodation with laxity of control to a well-appointed cell and strict discipline'.[20] One suggestion was that vagrants should be the responsibility of the police, rather than the Poor Law authorities. Nevertheless attempts should also be made to improve provision for the man 'genuinely' in search of work. One idea was to give him bread and cheese on leaving the workhouse, while forcing the 'other class' of vagrant to report to the police. Furthermore, the Committee recommended compulsory labour colonies for 'habitual vagrants', to clear them from the streets, force them to lead a more useful life during detention, and to act as a deterrent. These labour colonies were to be organised by local authorities or charities, with deterrent features such as unpleasant food, distinctive dress, and high walls to prevent escape. They should be self-financing through the work of the inmates – free food and cheap shelters were a 'serious evil'.[21]

Writing in the preface to Edmond Kelly's *The Unemployables* (1907), Sir William Chance echoed the recommendations of the Departmental Committee, noting the importance of abolishing the casual wards, and establishing labour colonies for the unemployed and habitual vagrants. Previously a Lecturer in Municipal Government at Columbia University, in New York, Kelly's book provided a more sustained analysis of the concept of the unemployable, or what John Burns had called the 'loafers, thieves and ne'er-do-wells'. Kelly attempted to classify the unemployed according to physical strength, blamelessness, and the causes of unemployment. For him, it was important to distinguish between the able-bodied and the non-able-bodied; between the blameless and the not blameless; and between the temporary and the permanent. Much of Kelly's book was taken up with the issue of to what extent the continental system of labour colonies could be applied in England. He argued that ultimately this might solve the problem of vagrancy and 'greatly diminish the expense of the criminal class and restore to the community all such persons of the vagrant and criminal classes as are capable of reformation'.[22] Kelly noted, for example, that colonies could ultimately become self-supporting, but could also prevent the current generation of vagrants from reproducing. Overall Kelly's work demonstrated how, in this period, discussions of vagrancy were inseparable from those around unemployability.

Changing views on the causes of unemployment were reflected in, and informed by, work by William Beveridge (1879–1963). Educated at Charterhouse and Balliol College, Oxford, Beveridge is best-known for his *Report on Social Insurance and Allied Services*. Published in December 1942 at the height of the Second World War, it was an immediate if unlikely best-seller. It remains a key document in the history of the welfare state. José Harris's biography argues that Beveridge concluded that unemployment should be seen not as a problem of social distress or personal character, but as a problem of industrial organisation. He thought there were three types – redundancy; occasional unemployment; and chronic underemployment – and these were more important than traditional explanations based on lack of skill or thrift, and moral character. Thus Beveridge cut across debates about 'character' and 'environment' by arguing that it was industrial conditions that created the character of the unemployed, and that industrial reorganisation, not just moral improvement, was essential.[23] Yet Harris's biography also makes clear that, as with many of his contemporaries, Beveridge took an interest in debates about the relative influences of heredity and environment, and there were signs that he was attracted to eugenics. His views were complex, and while at times he subscribed to an 'environmental' interpretation, at others he was swayed by eugenics, especially with regard to mental subnormality. Harris has written:

> The development of Beveridge's views on unemployment between 1903 and 1906 was therefore in many respects ambivalent. On the one hand he was intellectually committed to a purely inductive approach to social problems; yet many of his conclusions about unemployment were clearly derived not merely from facts but from contemporary social theory.[24]

In 1904 Beveridge reflected in the *Contemporary Review* on the lessons of the Mansion House Fund for tackling unemployment. The main feature of the proposals of the Mansion House Committee, supported by the Lord Mayor's Fund, had been the offer of continuous work, in colonies outside London, to male heads of families. Between December 1903 and March 1904, 467 families received relief. Labour tests and the local knowledge of the selectors had been relied upon to eliminate those deemed 'undesirable'. Beveridge argued the colony test had been effective, and 'the mass of idlers and dependents who usually expect to reap an easy harvest from the opening of relief funds ceased to apply as soon as they found that work was demanded'.[25] He suggested the main lessons from the work of the Committee had been the importance of classification, but also the persistence of the distress. Beveridge argued that the 'material' comprised three groups – the unemployable; casual labourers; and men normally in regular work. The unemployable had to be isolated, and periods of regular work and discipline in compulsory labour colonies were essential.

The inconsistencies in Beveridge's thought that Harris points to are also evident in the summary of the earlier writing in the *Morning Post* that appeared as the book *Unemployment: A Problem of Industry* (1909). Beveridge on the one hand maintained an interest in the 'personal factor' in unemployment. He asked to what extent strengths of personality could prevent unemployment, and how far weaknesses of personality should be regarded as its causes. For Beveridge, there were some men who clearly did not want to work. He wrote that:

> they are the social parasites most prominently represented by the habitual criminal and the habitual vagrant. Each of these is in truth as definitely diseased as are the inmates of hospitals, asylums and infirmaries, and should be classed with them.[26]

Beveridge believed that there were various 'defects of character' that increased the likelihood of a person being unemployed. First, there were the 'purely parasitic types' who constituted a permanent vagrant class. Second, there were men willing to work now and again, but not continuously. Third, among all men, there were 'common faults and occasional self-indulgences' whose net effect was to increase economic waste and unemployment.[27]

However although some were unemployable, Beveridge acknowledged that this term had no real meaning – the best carpenter in the world was 'unemployable' as a printer – and that the dividing line between 'this class' and the rest of the community was hard to define. Beveridge argued that the 'problem' of unemployment could only to a limited extent be solved by improvements in human character. First, the class of the unemployable was small in number. Second, human character could best be improved by eliminating the social or industrial conditions that tended to perpetuate 'idleness and irresponsibility'. Third, no likely improvement in character would eliminate the main economic factors in unemployment. Beveridge observed that one of the main problems was that many people were living on a 'quicksand' of casual and irregular work. Therefore he concluded that:

> while this quicksand and its movements are part of industry, society cannot escape some responsibility for those who live there; cannot treat as criminals those whose industrial services are there required; cannot end the evil by rescuing individuals.[28]

Thus José Harris claims that Beveridge's views on unemployment were in many ways based on traditional economic and evolutionary assumptions, especially in relation to the issue of casual labour. She points out the contradictions in the position that he, and others, adopted. The distress that resulted from unemployment was viewed as the product of a disorganised labour market, but it was also thought that casual and irregular workmen were inferior social specimens. It was important to maintain the principle of deterrence, but at the same time it was thought the labour market should be regulated and unemployment reduced. The lowest class was not seen just as inefficient or improvident, but as a degenerate class. This distinction was increasingly called into question by the leaders of the working class. However, personal criticism of the unemployed was not incompatible with a structural explanation. The solutions that Beveridge put forward embraced labour exchanges; unemployment insurance; short-time agreements and adjustments in standard wage-rates at times of depression; and the reform of the Poor Law. He believed, therefore, that social and economic activities were capable of rational administrative control.[29]

Overall, there are some respects in which it would clearly be wrong to regard the terms 'residuum' and 'unemployable' as synonymous. Unlike the residuum, which was regarded as a separate class, the unemployable was seen as a subset of the unemployed. And unlike the former, the latter was regarded as a heterogeneous group, comprising both those unable, and those unwilling, to work. Nevertheless the comment of the Webbs that there was a 'residuum of the unemployable' also hinted at continuities between the two ideas that were more than semantic. As in the case of the residuum, there were commentators whose preferred solution was a system of labour colonies. As with the social residuum, it is suggested that the concept of the unemployable evaporated with the advent of full employment during wartime. Again, like the social residuum, the concept of the unemployable was not seen as inconsistent with a structural analysis of the causes of poverty. In terms of timing, it seems that the concept of the unemployable was most obvious in the period 1880–1914 – Beveridge's classic *Unemployment: A Problem of Industry*, was published in 1909. With the Webbs, however, there was evidence that they discussed the unemployable as early as 1897, and as late as 1929. It seems likely that the term 'residuum' was succeeded by that of the 'unemployable' as less pejorative, less redolent of evolutionary language and Social Darwinism. But it also appears that terms such as 'social residuum', 'unemployable', and 'social problem group' could all be in use in the same period.

Further evidence on the appearance and disappearance of these terms after 1900 is provided by social surveys on both poverty and unemployment. The pioneering research by Charles Booth on poverty in East London was quickly followed by similar studies by other social investigators. Among the best known are those by Benjamin Seebohm Rowntree in York, published in 1901, and a social survey of working-class households in four English towns that was published by Arthur Bowley in 1915. Both are deservedly seen as landmarks in the history of social investigation – Rowntree for the distinction he drew between primary and secondary poverty; and Bowley for his innovative use of sampling methods. But the surveys have less frequently been examined for what they reveal about the ideas and assumptions of the researchers that planned and conducted them. Here we examine the work of Rowntree and Bowley to see the extent to which their surveys reflected a continuing interest in the concepts of the residuum and the unemployable, or whether they arguably marked a transition in the social theories that lay behind social investigation.

The third child of Joseph Rowntree, Benjamin Seebohm Rowntree (1871–1954) was born in York in 1871. He joined the family firm in 1889, becoming a member of the Board of Directors in 1897, and Chairman in 1923–41. He was closely associated with the charitable, social service, and village trusts that his father created, and subsequently the Rowntree firm became a leader in the field of scientific management and industrial welfare. Impressed by the work of Booth, Rowntree was determined to find out if the state of the poor in York was as serious as Booth had found in London, and *Poverty, A Study of Town Life* was published in 1901. Jonathan Bradshaw suggests that three important claims can be made for this survey – it had an important impact on public understanding of poverty; it had an immediate impact on policy; and it established the British tradition of empirical social science research.[30]

Recent writing on Rowntree has clarified the circumstances in which his first

survey came to be written, showing, for example, how his background as an indus-
trialist led him to have an interest in the 'physical efficiency' of his workers.[31]
It has also been claimed that, rather than the Booth survey, the inspiration for
Poverty was a work by Rowntree's father and Arthur Sherwell, *The Temperance
Problem and Social Reform* (1899).[32] At the outset, Rowntree outlined his aim
as being to 'throw some light upon the conditions which govern the life of the
wage-earning classes in provincial towns, and especially upon the problem of
poverty'.[33] The method chosen was a house-to-house survey of York carried out
in 1899, of 11,560 families living in 388 streets. The families comprised a total
of 46,754 people, or two-thirds of the overall population of the city. Rowntree
included an enquiry into food, rent, and other expenditure, along with a study
of social conditions, budgets, and diet. Arguably the most important conclusion
drawn was the distinction between primary and secondary poverty. Primary
poverty was defined as 'families whose total earnings are insufficient to obtain
the minimum necessaries for the maintenance of merely physical efficiency'.
Secondary poverty, on the other hand, was defined as 'families whose total earnings would be sufficient for the maintenance of merely physical efficiency were
it not that some portion of it is absorbed by other expenditure, either useful or
wasteful'.[34]

There was no doubt that serious poverty existed in York. Rowntree wrote of
the Hungate area of the city, for example, that:

> though not large in extent, it is still large enough to exhibit the chief characteristics of
> slum life – the reckless expenditure of money as soon as obtained, with the aggravated
> want at other times; the rowdy Saturday night, the Monday morning pilgrimage to the
> pawn-shop, and especially that love for the district, and disinclination to move to better
> surroundings, which, combined with an indifference to the higher aims of life, are the
> despair of so many social workers.[35]

His conclusion was that 7,230 people were in primary poverty in York (9.91%
of the total population) and that 13,072 people were in secondary poverty
(17.93%). Therefore overall, 20,302 people (27.84%) were in poverty. This was
comparable to the findings of Booth, who as we have seen estimated that 30.7%
of the population of London were in poverty. Rowntree concluded that more
attention should be given to living standards, 'for no civilisation can be sound
or stable which has at its base this mass of stunted human life'.[36]

With regard to the residuum, there are two important methodological differences between the surveys of Booth and Rowntree. First, Rowntree employed
special investigators to undertake house-to-house visits, and surveyed the entire
working-class population. Second, Rowntree classified his households by income
and household composition rather than by 'conditions of poverty'.[37] It had not
been possible to find out about income through direct questioning of households,

but income on occupation and workplace was available, and Rowntree used this to estimate earnings. Thus Rowntree adopted a four-fold classification of the working-class family (A–D), accordingly to the weekly income for a moderate family of two adults and from two to four children. The ranges were less than 18 shillings; 18–21 shillings; 21–30 shillings; and more than 30 shillings. The distribution of the population of York within Rowntree's four classes is given in table 1.

TABLE 1: Rowntree's Four-Fold Classification of Working-Class Incomes

Class	Weekly Income	Number of Households	Numbers of Persons
A	less than 18 shillings	656	1957
B	18–21 shillings	983	4492
C	21–30 shillings	3822	15710
D	more than 30 shillings	6099	24595

Sources: Rowntree, *Poverty: A Study of Town Life*, p. 31; Hennock, 'Concepts of Poverty', p. 193, table 7.1.

Rowntree divided his class 'A' (the lowest) into those earning money and those earning no money. He estimated that in the case of 1,295 people (66% of the total), the immediate cause of poverty was the fact that the main wage-earner had died or deserted the family, or was unable to work because of ill-health or old age. Economic causes, through lack of work or low wages, accounted for the poverty of 418 people (21%). He concluded that 'after full allowance has been made for public and private charity, the people in class A are chronically ill-housed, ill-clothed, and underfed'.[38]

Rowntree's moralism is well-known – his later surveys of York contained maps indicating the location of all the pubs in the city. There were occasional examples in the text when the language of national efficiency, and concepts of 'fitness', were apparent. Rowntree noted, for instance, of 'unfit' workmen that 'unfitness' meant low wages, low wages meant insufficient food, and insufficient food led to 'unfitness' for labour. The result was a vicious circle which was perpetuated in the next generation. Rowntree wrote that 'the children of such parents have to share their privations, and even if healthy when born, the lack of sufficient food soon tells upon them. Thus they often grow up weak and diseased, and so tend to perpetuate the race of the "unfit"'.[39] At other points, Rowntree employed eugenic language. He argued, for example, that the high rate of infant mortality in certain wards in York had its advantages, in that sickly children were 'weeded out'. Even so, many of those who survived did so with 'seriously enfeebled constitutions'.[40]

Like many other contemporary commentators, Rowntree referred to the ways that medical examinations of recruits had provided a commentary on the health of the population, and he compared the position of Britain to that of Germany, Belgium, Russia, and the USA, thereby equating health with concepts of national fitness.

Nonetheless, while Rowntree at times drew on the language of national fitness and eugenics, he also was aware of what today would be called poverty dynamics. He argued that people moved in and out of poverty, and also stressed that structural factors were the key causes. Rowntree argued, for example, that few people were likely to remain in class 'A'. At any time the poor might sink into it, through lack of work or the death or illness of the main wage-earner, but equally they would rise out of it when work was found, or when children began to earn money. Only older people would remain in class 'A', until they died or went into the workhouse.[41] In general, claimed Rowntree, the main causes of primary poverty were the death of the main wage-earner; incapacity of the main wage-earner through accident, illness, or old age; the fact that the chief wage-earner was out of work; chronic irregularity of work; large families; and low wages. Thus Rowntree recognised that most people moved in and out of poverty. The main determinants of these movements were structural factors such as death, illness, unemployment, and low incomes.

The closest that Rowntree came to a behavioural explanation was in his discussion of what he termed secondary poverty. Rowntree estimated secondary poverty by calculating the amount of poverty in York, and then subtracting primary poverty from the total. He conceded that 'the point at which "primary" passes into "secondary" poverty is largely a matter of opinion, depending upon the standard of well-being which is considered necessary'.[42] Rowntree argued that the causes of secondary poverty were in part in the control of individuals. They included 'drink, betting, and gambling. Ignorant or careless housekeeping, and other improvident expenditure, the latter often induced by irregularity of income'.[43] Nevertheless, Rowntree argued that the causes of 'secondary poverty' were again primarily structural, in that they reflected the wider environmental circumstances within which much of the working class lived. He wrote:

> housed for the most part in sordid streets, frequently under overcrowded and unhealthy conditions, compelled very often to earn their bread by monotonous and laborious work, and unable, partly through limited education and partly through overtime and other causes of physical exhaustion, to enjoy intellectual recreation, what wonder that many of these people fall a ready prey to the publican and the bookmaker?[44]

Subsequent writing was revealing about Rowntree's viewpoint. Helen Bosanquet was critical of Rowntree's survey in her review of *Poverty* in the *Charity Organisation Review* in May 1902. She was doubtful about the way the proportion of the population in York and London seemed virtually the same. Bosanquet argued that debates about the percentage of people in poverty would serve to distract attention from the need for improvements in housing and sanitation. She also argued that like Booth, Rowntree had relied on 'appearances' to identify the poor. Moreover in *The Times* in September 1902 Bosanquet wrote that:

> it can do no good, and may do much harm, to be constantly reiterating to people whose lives are difficult that their difficulties are insuperable. Hundreds of thousands of families throughout the country are daily proving that they are not insuperable, and proving also to those who care to look that the 'poverty line' is comparatively seldom a question of money income primarily.[45]

She argued that Rowntree had in fact 'emphasised the wonderful capacity of even the poorest to make a good life for themselves'.[46] In reply, Rowntree defended the relatively high nutritional standard he had adopted, and the reliability of his estimates of family incomes. However he suggested the main difference between Bosanquet and himself was a different view of human nature, and her attachment to:

> the extreme wing of the Individualist school [which] unduly magnifies what may be done for the amelioration of social conditions through the personal effort and self-reliance of the individual, and correspondingly minimises the sphere of State intervention.[47]

Most secondary writing has centred on Rowntree's distinction between primary and secondary poverty. John Veit-Wilson has argued that Rowntree's work was of fundamental importance in the history of social investigation, in facilitating a shift from an absolutist to a relativistic model of poverty. Rowntree's model was therefore quite comparable to the concept of relative deprivation later adopted by Peter Townsend. Unlike Booth, he acknowledged that class 'A' was not a static residuum – people might fall into it through unemployment or the ill-health of the main wage-earner, but equally could rise out of it when their circumstances improved, as when their children began to work. Although secondary poverty was caused in part by drinking, betting, and 'improvident' expenditure, Rowntree viewed these as an inevitable response to a social environment dominated by low wages. Veit-Wilson suggested that it appears Rowntree used the distinction between primary and secondary poverty as a heuristic device to convince those who favoured a behavioural interpretation that the lifestyle of the poor was in part caused by low income.[48] Nevertheless Bernard Harris argues that although Rowntree used an impressionistic method to identify poverty in 1899, he defined poverty in terms of physical and economic inefficiency. Although Rowntree moved further towards a definition of relative poverty than his contemporaries, there was still an important gap between this and the idea of relative poverty that

Townsend pioneered in the 1960s. Rowntree took cultural factors into account when estimating minimum diets, included an allowance for personal and recreational expenditure, and he did not argue that the poverty line should move upwards with the general standard of living.[49]

Jonathan Bradshaw argues that Rowntree's distinction between secondary and primary poverty was a critical element in convincing the public that poverty was a structural rather than merely a behavioural problem. Rowntree 'established for the first time that poverty was the result of structural not behavioural factors', and his facts finally 'put the nail in the coffin' of the distinction between the 'deserving' and 'undeserving' poor put forward by the COS. Bradshaw writes that if poverty in Britain has been understood, in the main, as a structural problem rather than a behavioural one, this is in part due to the legacy of Rowntree.[50] It is certainly true that while the language of national fitness and eugenics made occasional appearances, the concept of the residuum was absent from Rowntree's survey. Nevertheless Bradshaw underestimates the extent to which concepts of the underclass have been successively re-invented in twentieth-century Britain. If the concepts and vocabulary of the residuum and the unemployable were absent from Rowntree's survey, it was to prove a temporary respite.

The fact that the terms 'residuum' and 'unemployable' were now noticeable by their absence was also true of social surveys of poverty published during the First World War. Rowntree's contribution to the development of the social survey was taken further by Arthur Bowley. Whereas Rowntree was a businessman and philanthropist, Arthur Bowley (1869–1957) was a career academic. Educated at Trinity College, Cambridge, Bowley's earliest academic appointments were at the London School of Economics and University College, Reading. It was only in 1919 that Bowley became Professor of Statistics at the London School of Economics. Much of his work was in the measurement and definition of national income, and during the Second World War Bowley was director of the Oxford University Institute of Statistics. As Peter Hennock has noted, Bowley's most important contribution to the social survey was in the use of random sampling methods.[51]

Together with A. R. Burnett-Hurst, a former Research Assistant at the London School of Economics, Bowley published in 1915 a social survey of working-class households in four English towns. Their survey was based on enquires made in 1913 into economic conditions in Northampton and Warrington, and in Stanley, County Durham. A similar enquiry had been made in Reading in 1912. The most important innovation in this survey was the adoption of a random sample. This comprised one house in 23 in Northampton; one in 17 in Stanley; one in 19 in Warrington; and one in 21 in Reading. Bowley and Burnett-Hurst calculated the weekly wage rates for adult males, ranging from under 8 shillings to over 40 shillings, and compared these to Rowntree's figures for York in 1899. A further innovation was the use of a new poverty line. Bowley and Burnett-Hurst estimated the number of families above and below: firstly, the minimum standard adopted by Rowntree, and secondly, a new standard. For example, they found that in Reading, 128 of 622 families were below Rowntree's poverty line, and 127 families were below the new standard. This meant that 20.6% of working-class households, or 15.3% of all households, were below the Rowntree poverty line. With regard to the new poverty standard, the equivalent figures were 20.4% and 15.1%.[52]

Livelihood and Poverty was far ahead of its time in explaining the methods used, and in the precision of the results. Unlike Rowntree, Bowley showed no interest in mere impressions of poverty. It is not particularly surprising, therefore, that – as was the case with the Rowntree survey – the phrases 'residuum' and 'unemployable' were entirely absent. Bowley and Burnett-Hurst argued that what their survey illustrated was that much poverty 'is not intermittent but permanent, not accidental or due to exceptional misfortune, but a regular feature of the industries of the towns concerned'.[53] Overall, as shown in table 2, it was estimated that the main reasons why a household was in poverty were: because the income was inadequate for a large family; the main wage-earner had died; the main wage earner was ill or old; because of unemployment; and due to irregular work. Low wages were the most important of the causes of primary poverty.

TABLE 2: Households in Poverty by Cause (per cent)

14	death of chief wage earner
11	illness or age of chief wage earner
2	unemployment
2	irregularity of work
26	income insufficient for family of 3 children or less
45	income insufficient for family of 4 children or more
100	total

Source: Bowley and Burnett-Hurst, *Livelihood and Poverty*, p. 47.

Thus Bowley and Burnett-Hurst, through the adoption of sampling procedures and refinement of a poverty line, further advanced the move towards the modern social survey. The approach taken was precise and statistical, and one in which the moral condemnation of the unemployable had no place. The authors of the survey summarised their conclusions in the following way:

It is often implied that the causes which bring men into poverty are within their own control, that they are the masters of their own fate and the creators of their misfortunes. In many cases this may be so; yet the extent to which it is true is exaggerated.[54]

Livelihood and Poverty was published during the First World War, and attracted little interest. In fact, it was the sequel to the study, published in 1925 with the title *Has Poverty Diminished?*, that made Arthur Bowley more widely known as a social investigator.[55] In this book, Bowley compared the very different worlds of before and after the First World War, by investigating the same towns with as nearly as possible the same methods. The main developments were seen as being the fall in the birth-rate; the loss of life during the First World War; the rise in prices; the rise in wages for unskilled labour; and unemployment. But again the causes of poverty were seen as falling into two groups – first, the broken families in which the father or husband was dead or not able to earn; and second, those in which he was normally at work but at insufficient wages.[56] The relative numbers of these families had changed little. Thus this second study again confirmed the objective, statistical tone of the earlier one, a tone in which the language of 'social residuum' and 'unemployable' would have seemed an anachronism.

It appears from the evidence of the Rowntree and Bowley surveys that the language of 'social residuum', so apparent in the earlier investigations of Booth, was absent from later reports on poverty. The term 'unemployable' was also noticeable by its absence. The Bowley and Burnett-Hurst survey was published by the Ratan Tata Foundation, an organisation that had been funded by an Indian philanthropist and set up at the London School of Economics 'in order to promote the study and further the knowledge of methods of preventing and relieving poverty and destitution'.[57] Further insights into changing views on the residuum were provided by the inaugural lecture of its Director, R. H. Tawney, given at the School in October 1913. Entitled 'Poverty as an Industrial Problem', Tawney argued that economic history had led to a change:

> to approach problems of poverty, as, in the first place at any rate, problems of industry, to emphasise the fundamental economic contrasts common to numbers of men, rather than the individual peculiarities of earning and spending, to take the trade, the town, the school as the unit of enquiry rather than the isolated individual or family.[58]

Tawney argued that modern poverty was associated, not with 'personal misfortunes peculiar to individuals, but with the economic status of particular classes and occupations', and poverty should be studied, therefore, 'first at its sources, and only secondly in its manifestations'.[59] He proposed that low wages, casual employment, and juvenile labour were the most pressing areas to be studied.

Nevertheless, while the work of Rowntree and Bowley marked an important shift in the analysis of social problems, it is important not to underestimate the continuities with earlier analyses. Tawney did not regard the personal factor as unimportant. He argued that what was also needed was to increase the 'economic resisting power' of individuals and their families.[60] Furthermore in Rowntree's examination of unemployment in York (1913), he devoted a chapter to the 'work-shy'. This investigation was based on 7 June 1910, when 60 investigators called on every working-class house in York, and asked whether anyone living there was out of work, keen to find work, male or female, and in which occupation they were interested. These cases were examined by a small number of investigators – reasons given for leaving work were checked with employers.[61] In the survey, 105 men were found to be 'work-shy', defined as 'men whose inefficiency, or unwillingness to work, is not due to age, illness, or any other physical disqualification, but primarily to infirmity of character'.[62] One example was a publican who had left his job in 1906 owing to illness. He was suffering from indigestion, and was classified as 'drinker and lazy'.[63]

However, the line separating these men from the casual worker was acknowledged to be a fine one, and the state of mind of the work-shy was 'often the result of external conditions beyond their control'. Rowntree wrote that 'it is of much greater importance that we should cease to manufacture shirkers than that we should learn how best to deal with them after they have been manufactured'.[64] Of the 105, for example, 50 had been previously engaged in regular work, and were 'inferior workmen' who, once unemployed, found it difficult to compete for work against 'better men'. Among those who had lost their jobs for 'unsatisfactory reasons' were drinkers. Even here Rowntree wrote:

> Born often of a poor stock, and growing up amid a degrading environment, with a slum street for an unguarded playground, receiving the legal minimum of education with no encouragement from their parents, sent into the world at 13 or 14 to drift into whatever occupation comes their way, then, whether single or married, living in a poor house and dingy street, and returning to it night by night after nine or ten hours of unskilled work, which rouses neither interest nor ambition, with minds untrained to serious thought, and a horizon on which the marvels of art and science and literature have never dawned – what wonder if, in their effort to introduce some colour into the drab monotony of their lives, they fall victims to the allurements of the bookmaker or publican, or lose heart and join the ranks of those who have ceased to strive?[65]

Overall, Rowntree concluded that about 30% of the 105 once worked regularly and left their jobs for 'satisfactory' reasons; 30% also worked regularly but left for 'unsatisfactory' reasons; and 40% had never done any regular work.[66] Various solutions were put forward, including Care Committees and industrial training, although it was acknowledged that even if the number of unemployables was reduced, 'a residuum of unemployed men' would still exist. For them, some form of labour colony was necessary. Nevertheless the main thing was to 'cease to manufacture an unemployable class'.[67]

In 1914, Victor Branford, Honorary Secretary of the Sociological Society, wrote of the Booth survey that:

> while the Booth type of survey is admirable in giving a picture of the economic and mate-rial condition of the family, it remains deficient ... in the more difficult task of describing and estimating the family's life of leisure, its spiritual condition – what might be called its cultural status ... Here the difficult problem is to discover some method for observing and recording what the French call the *etat-d'ame*, i.e., the thoughts and emotions, the habit of mind and life, of persons in their interior and intimate relations with one another and with surroundings. The sort of question this more intensive survey has to put before itself, is – How can we decipher and record peoples' ideals, their characteristic ideas and culture, and the images and symbols which habitually occupy their minds?[68]

It was this concern with the culture of poverty that was to become so pervasive fifty years later, in the 1960s.[69]

Both in the 1930s and more recently, there have been heated debates about the alleged impact of unemployment on health. In many respects it has been hard to prove that the experience of being out of work has affected health, not least because of the difficulty of separating the effects of unemployment from those of poverty and poor housing. It is equally difficult to make a valid distinction between the experiences of health and illness of the unemployed, and those who are in work, but employed on low pay. In fact, it is arguable that ill-health has not so much been caused by unemployment, as revealed by it.[70] As unemployment worsened in the late 1920s and early 1930s, there was a concern with benefit fraud, and with those 'genuinely seeking work', that again has parallels in the early twenty-first century. In the words of one writer, those who administered unemployment insurance in the interwar years were 'in search of the scrounger'.[71] Moreover, with regard to health it is also possible to trace at this time a discourse that was more concerned with the mental than the physical effects of becoming unemployed. It was pointed out, for instance, that the campaigns of the National Unemployed Workers Movement were surprisingly peaceful, and it has been argued that this was because of the pervading sense of fatalism and powerlessness.

More specifically, some observers began to talk about the 'social psychology' of unemployment. The best known of these studies was based on the Austrian town of Marienthal. This small industrial community, on the Fischa-Dagnitz river in the Steinfeld district, suffered almost total economic breakdown in the summer of 1929. By February 1930, when the looms and turbines stopped and only a few men had been kept on to dismantle the plant, 367 of the 478 families (77%) were thought to be unemployed. These families were studied intensively, through family files, life histories, time sheets, a school essay project, and other statistical data.[72] The study was conducted by Marie Jahoda, Paul Lazarsfeld, and Hans Zeisel of the Psychological Institute at the University of Vienna, and was published in German in 1933. The responses of 100 families to the experience of unemployment were classified. It was claimed that 16 remained 'unbroken'; 48 were 'resigned'; 11 were 'in despair'; and 25 were 'apathetic'. The authors concluded of the latter two 'deteriorated forms' that:

> it now appears that they are probably but two different stages of a process of psychological deterioration that runs parallel to the narrowing of economic resources and the wear and tear on personal belongings. At the end of this process lies ruin and despair.[73]

By the late 1930s, Paul Lazarsfeld, one of the authors of the study, had moved to the United States, to the University of Newark. With Philip Eisenberg, of the University of Columbia, Lazarsfeld refined the earlier analysis into what became the classic account of the psychological effects of unemployment. In their article, published in 1938, Lazarsfeld and Eisenberg argued that unemployment made people emotionally unstable, since it disrupted time patterns. There was a loss of the sense of the passage of time, and some people indulged in irrational spending. More importantly, Lazarsfeld and Eisenberg claimed that individuals went through a process of stages of psychological adjustment to the experience of becoming unemployed. First came shock, followed by an active search for a job during which the individual remained optimistic; second, when efforts failed, the individual became more pessimistic; and third, the individual was broken and became fatalistic. Thus it was claimed that the unemployed progressed from optimism through pessimism to fatalism, reflected in an increasing sense of inferiority, the destruction of family relationships, and a weakening of interest in politics and organisations.[74]

The Marienthal study was published in German, with an English translation only becoming available in 1972. Nevertheless the theory of the 'social psychology' of unemployment was paralleled in some studies conducted in Britain in the 1930s. A report on 1,000 medical examinations for sickness benefit in Glasgow was conducted by the Department of Health for Scotland. This claimed that in 335 cases (33.5%) the cause of incapacity was 'psychoneurotic'. The Regional Medical Officer concluded that in the event of unemployment, male workers were more likely to 'break down' than female.[75] Psychoneurotic disability was lowest (compared to the employed) in those unemployed for less than three months, highest in those who had been unemployed for six months to two years, and it declined thereafter to a level similar to the employed. The author concluded that:

after falling out of work there is a short period of a sense of release (a holiday freedom); gradually anxiety and depression set in with loss of mental equilibrium; finally, after several years, adaptation takes place to a new and debased level of life, lacking hope as well as fear of the future ... we may conclude that unemployment primarily influences the mind rather than the body.[76]

Other interwar surveys that focused more directly on the experience of the unemployed provided evidence that cast doubt on the 'social psychology' theory. A study by E. Wight Bakke, an American academic from Yale, for example, was based mainly on interviews, diaries, and participant observation. Bakke found that the unemployed were not a group of social misfits, but workers subject to the normal fluctuations of industry. Unemployment had affected their nutrition and family budgets, enforcing economies, for instance, in the purchase of new clothes. Nevertheless Bakke maintained that their morale was high, and only a small proportion (7.6%) could be described as 'loafers'.[77] If they were tired, it was because of the exhausting business of looking for a job – diaries indicated that on average they spent twenty three hours a week searching for work. They were keen on the cinema and gambling, but spent little time in pubs. Overall, Bakke concluded that unemployment insurance had alleviated the worst effects of unemployment – the extra income kept peoples' diets from deteriorating, it was not necessary to sell furniture, and they were able to remain involved in organisations and associations.[78]

Apart from the material provided by E. Wight Bakke, there is evidence that the authors of the Marienthal study themselves had serious reservations about their work. Although well-known through the original, the book was only available in German until 1972. One of the authors, Paul Lazarsfeld, admitted that he refused an English translation of the Marienthal study for a long time because he was aware of its weaknesses. Lazarsfeld conceded that the sampling procedures had never been stated, the typologies were developed intuitively, attitude scales were not used, and the approach was naïve. He admitted that 'I can excuse all this only by remembering the adventurous pioneering spirit that propelled us; but it made me uncomfortable enough that for a while I refused any offer to publish a translation'.[79]

As Ross McKibbin has argued, it is very likely that unemployment had an important effect on the psychological health of unemployed workers. However it seems clear that the 'social psychology' theory of unemployment is less convincing. Lazarsfeld and his colleagues had argued that 'demoralisation' showed itself in four ways – in the disintegration of daily routines; in an inability to devise alternative work; through the collapse of intellectual interests; and in the abandoning of political activity. But there is little evidence, from contemporary surveys, that any of these things happened. In the 1930s the unemployed did not disintegrate, they did not lose interest in work, and they did not become apolitical. What is more surprising is how little these things happened. The extent to which people who were unemployed remained interested in reading, went to the cinema, were politically active or joined clubs seemed to depend to a large degree on how much they had done these things when they were employed. McKibbin concludes that many unemployed people remained tied to aspects of working-class life. Indeed, the reason why the unemployed were so resilient may very well be because they were not wrenched from their communities, and because family life remained intact.[80]

But in interwar social surveys, an individual analysis of unemployment went further than being simply the 'social psychology' of unemployment. In his social survey of Merseyside (1934), David Caradog Jones conceded that the unemployed were a heterogeneous group of workers; it was not a permanent group; and the main causes were economic conditions rather than personal defects or industrial capacity. Those deemed unemployable by the Ministry of Labour were people 'whose industrial value is so low that an employer would never select him for a job unless no other applicant was available and the job had to be done at once, i.e. that an employer would only engage him in the last resort if at all'.[81] Nevertheless Caradog Jones also argued unemployment was due to 'personal shortcomings, in body, mind or character' which might be inborn defects or 'the evil effect produced by the perpetual action of a bad environment upon a poor hereditary endowment'.[82] He classified the chronically unemployed as one of his 'subnormal types', writing that 'persons who are so handicapped are at least sub-normal in the sense that they fall definitely and chronically below the average in the amount of employment they succeed in getting'.[83] The survey regarded any able-bodied man, aged 22–50, and continuously in receipt of public assistance on grounds of poverty due to unemployment for two years or longer, as subnormal in employability. A survey of the 'subnormal unemployed' explored their age and occupational grade; the number married and single; family size; and classified the cleanliness and tidiness of their homes.[84] His definition of 'abnormality' was actually extremely weak – it included three main groups – those with some form of disability; others with 'moral' failings; and a third group defined through its dependence on welfare.[85]

The authors of the Pilgrim Trust survey (1938) noted in their chapter on 'Psychological Problems' that one of the most frequently discussed of all the problems of unemployment was the willingness of the unemployed to work. The close relationship between Unemployment Assistance and wages was the main factor determining the attitudes of those men who remained out of work. But there clearly were also men who were 'work shy', especially among the younger men. The group was not large, and could be distinguished from those who had looked for work and given up. The authors of the survey noted that 'the chances are that he is mixed up with some betting concern, or that he keeps greyhounds, or picks up something here and there in addition to his Unemployment Assistance by hawking or street singing'.[86] Often his wife would not know if he was working or not. Besides those who were 'work shy' were those who could not work on account of some physical or mental defect. Again numbers were small. Overall the problem was perceived as being one of maintaining the work incentive for those men regarded as on the labour market, and to reconcile those retired from industry to unemployment.

The theory of the 'social psychology' of unemployment has had an important influence on research in this field. One of the original authors of the Marienthal study, Marie Jahoda, continued to argue in favour of this analysis as high unemployment returned in the 1970s and 1980s. Jahoda maintained that the onset of unemployment was marked by shock and a period of constructive adaptation, and was then followed by successive feelings of deterioration, boredom, and lack of self-respect, ending in fatalistic apathy. She argued that physical deprivation undermined psychological resistance, while the absence of the sense of organisation that accompanied work led to a sense of uselessness. In other writing, Jahoda returned to the four-fold classification of the earlier Marienthal study – that which had sorted the unemployed into the categories of the 'unbroken', the 'resigned', those 'in despair' and the 'apathetic'.[87] Writing in 1981, on the return of mass unemployment, Adrian Sinfield argued the 'social psychology' theory was receiving increasing support. At the same time, he noted that the hypothesis had been illustrated and supported rather than tested. Writers had tended to look for 'social psychology' patterns in the unemployed workers that they interviewed, and ignored evidence to the contrary.[88]

There were important differences between the 'social psychology' of unemployment, and the concept of the unemployable in the early 1900s. Whereas the 'social psychology' theory was mainly about the effects of the experience of unemployment on the mental well-being of workers, debates about the unemployable were more about the character of individual workers, which, it was claimed, meant they had a predisposition to becoming unemployed. Moreover, those deemed unemployable were perceived as being a heterogeneous group, comprising both those who were unwilling to work, and those unable to take paid employment. Even so, there were also marked continuities.

There were important changes in social thought in this period, which permeated debates about the causes of unemployment. Even though the concept of the unemployable remained popular among commentators that included the Webbs and William Beveridge, there were signs that unemployment was recognised much more as having structural causes, so that the solutions included a national system of labour exchanges, and attempts to mediate the effects of the casualisation of labour. With regard to unemployment, both Beveridge and the Webbs believed that the move from moral and personal to industrial and environmental explanations of unemployment was one of the main characteristics of a new analysis of the subject at the end of the nineteenth century. Perhaps most importantly, being unemployable was not, in general, seen as a hereditary condition that was inter-generational in effect. Rather it was a reflection of economic forces allied to personal inadequacies. The effect of these changes can be seen after 1900, when the language of the 'residuum' was almost entirely absent from the social surveys of Rowntree and Bowley. As the Webbs pointed out, the advent of full employment during the First World War seemed to destroy the concept of the unemployable.

Ater 1900, many of the ideas that had sustained the concept of the residuum in the 1880s were absent. The language of Social Darwinism had waned in its influence, and the emphasis on 'character' seemed less apparent in discussions of unemployment. The draconian proposals for setting up labour colonies were less in evidence. If, as has been argued, fears of the residuum were more about constitutional issues than a belief in degeneracy, the nation was adjusting to an enlarged working-class franchise. Perhaps most importantly, full employment during the First World War meant there was less of a focus on the idea of being unemployable. Finally, in the hands of social investigators such as Rowntree and Bowley, a more scientific style of research was evident, stressing structural rather than moral factors. The work of Bowley marked a decisive shift towards apparently neutral techniques, and in the 1930s it was the search for the scrounger that was more apparent than the focus on the unemployable.

Nevertheless, what is perhaps more striking is the resilience of these ideas. It is arguable that the concept of the unemployable was simply the social residuum reborn, shorn of its evolutionary language and connotations, and reshaped so that it could co-exist with a more structural interpretation of unemployment. The Webbs believed in the existence of the unemployable; it shaped the Minority Report of the Royal Commission on the Poor Law; and as late as 1929 the Webbs were still including the unemployable in their discussions of unemployment. Beveridge too, argued that there were people who did not want to work, and that 'defects of character' meant that unemployment was more likely for some – his points about unemployment as a problem of industry, and recommended solution of a system of labour exchanges notwithstanding. The alternative solution of labour colonies continued to lurk in the background. Rowntree continued to explore the condition of the work-shy; even Tawney believed that the 'personal factor' in unemployment was not unimportant; and the quotation by Branford indicated that some observers, at least, thought that the culture of the poor deserved greater emphasis in the work of social investigators. The 1920s and 1930s were marked by the search for the scrounger, and by the 'social psychology' theory of unemployment. Perhaps the era of Bowley, and the absence of residuum and unemployable is best seen as a hiatus in the history of the underclass. If so, it was short-lived. For it was in the 1920s that, inspired chiefly by the Eugenics Society, the search began again for an underclass, now called not the social residuum, but the social problem group. It is to that later period, and to the social problem group that we now turn.

3

In Search of the Social Problem Group

As we have seen, there was considerable interest in the concept of the social residuum in the late nineteenth century on the part of a large number of individuals and organisations. Among these Charles Booth was arguably the best known. Slightly different, but related, ideas were embodied in the idea of the unemployable, by the Webbs and William Beveridge among others. It is clear that this behavioural emphasis was less clear cut after 1900, and that a more structural interpretation was reflected in the work of Rowntree in York and the Bowley social survey. At the time of the First World War, full employment suggested that there did not exist a group termed the 'unemployable'. However, various factors including the economic depression of the 1920s, along with the assumption that mental deficiency was increasing, meant that the earlier concerns about the social residuum and the unemployable reappeared in the interwar years, albeit in slightly different form.

One obvious source of support for the concept of a social residuum lay in the work of the Eugenics Education Society, founded in 1907. Following on from the work of Sir Francis Galton, its interest lay in improving 'national efficiency' through selective breeding, with the information for this being assembled by eugenists. Established initially in London, it gradually set up a network of provincial branches. While the group was a heterogeneous one, most members would have agreed that human characteristics were determined by inheritance according to laws that were knowable; that they could identify desirable and undesirable human characteristics; and that policies should be devised to increase the fertility of those with desirable characteristics (positive eugenics) and to limit that of those with undesirable characteristics (negative eugenics).[1] Historians have pointed out that eugenics appealed particularly to the professional middle class, especially those who were involved in social policy, though there were some notable exceptions, such as Medical Officers of Health (MOsH), the nature of whose work inclined them more to an environmental or structural interpretation.[2] There has also been debate over the extent to which eugenics appealed to 'progressive thinkers'.[3] Historians have shown how, reflecting anxiety about the future of the race, a eugenic influence can be detected in contemporary debates about education, birth control, slum clearance, and mental deficiency.[4] However, John Macnicol has pointed to various interpretative problems – many prominent political figures used eugenic ideas tactically and opportunistically; it is difficult to rank in significance and influence the range of eugenic ideas; and measuring the impact of any elitist group is always difficult. Moreover the explicit policy outcomes of eugenics were few. Macnicol has concluded therefore that 'the eugenics movement is undoubtedly interesting – indeed, perhaps more interesting at the periphery of its influence than at the centre – but one must be cautious of overstressing its importance'.[5]

The new underclass concept of the 1920s and 1930s was that of the social problem group, and the relative merits of a policy of sterilisation was one of the key areas of debate. Historians interested in eugenics have explored how the Society used the concept of the social problem group in the 1920s and 1930s. Pauline Mazumdar, for example, has argued that the eugenics movement was part of a larger trend – an attempt by the upper middle class to understand and control the urban poor. The COS (1869); the Moral Education League (1898); the National Association for the Care and Protection of the Feeble-Minded (1896); and the Fabian Society each had its own solutions, but the Eugenics Society believed its explanation undercut all of them.[6] Greta Jones has argued that the social problem group notion illustrated the marriage of two concepts – that there was a stratum of society of low intellectual endowment deemed the 'feeble-minded', and that most social problems were a product of this stratum. Thus the social problem group represented a medicalisation of the residuum.[7] R. A. Soloway locates the interest in the social problem group in the context of evidence that differences in the birthrates of social classes were moderating – eugenists therefore turned to smaller sectors of society, such as unskilled manual workers and casual workers, and chronic paupers. New reform-minded eugenists were not sure what constituted hereditary fitness and where it was found in society. But most eugenists were still able to recognise racial fitness even if it was not precisely defined – in the skilled working class, and the middle and upper ranks of society. Similarly there was more of a consensus about unfitness, and that defects were heavily clustered in the new social problem group.[8] Desmond King has agreed that it was in attempting to define the target of sterilisation that commentators turned to the social problem group.[9]

John Macnicol has argued that, at a time of recession and unemployment, when mass democracy and the newly established Labour Party appeared to threaten the existing order, and when the emerging medical, psychiatric, and social work professions were on the rise, the social problem group provided a theory of social reform for newly-professionalised groups. This coincided with concern over the increase in mental deficiency as highlighted in the Wood Report on Mental Deficiency (1929). Macnicol argues that the concept was sustained by a small group of eugenists, but their concerns reflected wider insecurities within conservative professional middle-class opinion, and was constructed in relation to the solution of sterilisation. However, proving the existence of the social problem group led to serious methodological difficulties. By the late 1930s, the credibility of both eugenics and sterilisation was being weakened. Nevertheless, Macnicol argues that in the 1940s, the idea of the social problem group was to re-emerge as the notion of the problem family.[10]

The social problem group has thus been the subject of some work by historians interested in the history of eugenics, mental deficiency, and birth control. Despite the research by Macnicol, this work has not yet been integrated into the longer-term history of the underclass in either Britain or the United States. This chapter looks at how the Eugenics Society embraced the concept of the social problem group, particularly in relation to debates about sterilisation. It begins by exploring how eugenics was drawn into debates about vagrancy in both Britain and the USA. It traces studies on individual families published in the United States in the 1890s, and explores the work of individual researchers, such as E. J. Lidbetter in London, and David Caradog Jones in Liverpool. A final section of the chapter looks at the problems that the Eugenics Society faced in trying to prove the existence of a social problem group in the 1930s, but also, conversely, at how this concept was transformed into that of the problem family in the early 1940s. The chapter argues that the theory of the social problem group served as a conceptual stepping stone, effectively linking the ideas of the social residuum and the unemployable, current in the 1880s and 1900s, to the theme of the problem family that was to emerge in the 1940s.

One way in which eugenics pervaded discussions of social issues in the interwar period was in relation to the perceived 'problem' of homelessness. Tim Cresswell has argued that in the United States, the family histories of vagrants were examined for characteristics such as headaches, drinking, and crooked feet, that might make it possible to diagnose or predict those who would subsequently become tramps. Through these diagnoses, and other observations that linked tramps to the spread of syphilis, Cresswell claims it is possible to map the ways in which normality was being defined in relation to the pathological mobility of the tramp. He argues that 'observers sought to encode the bodies of tramps as pathological, as diseased and genetically unsound … tramps were metaphorically a pathology in the wider social body'.[11] In the minds of investigators, the causes of mobility were not linked to wider structural factors, but were located in the tramps' own minds and bodies – the solution was to prevent tramps from reproducing. Methods of dealing with tramps were justified through the alleged threat of disease, and the need to restore health and normality. Thus Cresswell concludes that:

In the process of pathologisation, social reform, medicine and eugenics were all impli-
cated in the construction of American society as a body threatened by the pathology of
tramphood, just as the body of the tramp – one with suspect heredity and racked with
disease – was made up as an embodied sign of danger and deviance.[12]

Discourses similar to those identified by Cresswell were evident in Britain. The
Departmental Committee on the Relief of the Casual Poor, which was appointed
in September 1929 and reported in 1930, provides evidence both on the way
that the homeless were treated, and on attitudes towards them.[13] The Report
on the Relief of the Casual Poor was similar to the 1906 Report on Vagrancy in
that it continued to distinguish between those seeking work and those who were
'habitual vagrants'. It was calculated, for example, from a census conducted on
one night in February 1928, that casual wards in London had a population of
some 2,582 people. But more interesting was the way in which this group was
subdivided. The Report estimated that 12.5% of this group were seeking work;
31.5% were probably seeking work; 33% were 'habitual vagrants'; and 23% were
probably 'habitual vagrants'.[14] The Departmental Committee argued that there
was a marked overlap between the 'casual poor' and mental deficiency. One of
the Board of Control's inspectors, Dr E. O. Lewis, had examined 592 'casuals'. It
was claimed that of these, 93 (15.7%) were 'feeble-minded'; 32 (5.4 per cent) were
'insane'; and 34 (5.7%) were in a 'psychoneurotic' condition.[15]

While the Report of the Departmental Committee continued to distinguish
between types of vagrants, it also tempered this with a more liberal policy. For one
thing, it admitted that casual wards fell short of the ideal standards – conditions
in many were 'infamous and intolerable'. Tasks were trivial, while the attitude
of the officers was harsh – they had lost hope and all interest in the men that
they were responsible for. The Committee argued that the effect of improving
standards of treatment and accommodation would not be to attract men to a life
of vagrancy, but would improve the self-respect of the casual population, and
make it easier for them to be reintegrated into society. Recommendations were
made for proper arrangements for bathing, sleeping, cleaning, feeding, and work;
properly qualified staff; regular medical inspection; and better co-ordination
and administration.[16] The Report noted further that the population of the
casual wards was a heterogeneous one. The men who passed through the ward
of a large provincial workhouse, for example, included labourers, bootmakers,
carpenters, cooks, clerks, grooms, porters, firemen, painters, sailors, and tailors.
Echoing Beveridge's report on unemployment (1909), the Report argued that the
habit of 'tramping' in search of work served no useful purpose that could not be
provided through labour exchanges.[17]

This conclusion was supported by the third volume of the New London
Survey, published in 1932, which showed that many of the inmates of common

lodging houses were in more or less regular work. By then, there were 155 licensed common lodging houses in London, with about 16,900 beds. Common lodging houses provided a bed, washing accommodation, and the use of a common kitchen, with a charge that varied from five pence to one shilling.[18] The New London Survey found that the occupation of the homeless depended very much on location – in the riverside boroughs of Stepney, Poplar, Deptford, Greenwich, Woolwich, and Southwark one might find dock-labourers, seamen, and ships' firemen; in the boroughs of St Pancras, Paddington, and Islington coal porters near the railway terminals; and in the boroughs near the markets porters for fish and other goods. It was the same for women. In Paddington and Kensington they tended to be laundry hands; and in inner boroughs such as Holborn waitresses, washers-up, servants, office cleaners, and charwomen. The survey claimed that hawkers and older women in receipt of old age pensions could be found in all common lodging houses, flower and match sellers more occasionally, and prostitutes in those that were privately managed.[19]

Despite the evidence that the inhabitants of common lodging houses were in regular work, when it came to vagrancy the New London Survey continued to use a behavioural interpretation of homelessness, with eugenic overtones. Its editor, Hubert Llewellyn-Smith, wrote that only a few vagrants could be rehabilitated, with the remainder continuing to live 'aimless, hopeless and useless lives'.[20] In fact there were very few vagrants in the common lodging houses, and the 'habitual tramps' were found more in the casual wards. He wrote of the homeless that:

> They include a large element of the vagrant, criminal, mentally deficient and physically subnormal, and their ranks are continuously recruited by the deposit of the moral, physical and economic dregs which filter down from all the grades above them. Most of them have little will power and no hope.[21]

Llewellyn-Smith rejected Booth's classification of vagrants as degraded and semi-criminal – rather they were economically 'subnormal' and living below the poverty line. At the same time, there was evidence that vagrancy and mental deficiency continued to be seen as linked together. Because of the 'low-grade character of the human material dealt with', solutions would only affect one in ten of the homeless.[22]

In the USA, one early example of writing on vagrancy is the study of 'the hobo' by Nels Anderson (1921) under the auspices of the Chicago School. Anderson reported that many tramps were physically or mentally defective, and he concluded that 'disease, physical disability, and insanitary living conditions seem to be, as things are, the natural and inevitable consequences of the migratory risk-taking and irregular life of the homeless man'.[23] Similar ideas, though less punitive, pervaded Frank Gray's popular book *The Tramp* (1931). This was more in the tradition of picaresque writing that viewed the tramp as a 'gentleman of the road'. Here the tramp was viewed as a kind of Pinteresque noble savage, superior in knowledge and conversation to the average person. His life was one of freedom, he was an expert on geography and also on famous criminal trials, he was a fund of knowledge on the countryside, on 'the habits of the police and of the birds and hares'.[24] The needs of the tramp were few, and his outlook meant he was 'at war with the community from whom he receives and takes'.[25] Nevertheless Gray also claimed that a high proportion of tramps were criminals, mentally deficient, feeble-minded, or mentally 'peculiar'. While he argued that poverty was not one of the key causes of vagrancy, the physique of tramps was so poor they were 'physical degenerates'.[26]

Overall then, there is evidence in Britain, in the early decades of the twentieth century, of similar concerns to those that Cresswell has identified for the United States. Several reports made recommendations to improve the state of casual wards, the principle of deterrence notwithstanding. Those who used the casual wards were casual labourers, and it was recognised that labour exchanges might be a more effective system than 'tramping' in search of work. In London, it was known that many of those who inhabited common lodging houses were in regular work. Nevertheless the desire to distinguish between the 'habitual tramp' and the wayfarer 'genuinely in search of work' was also remarkably persistent. The tramp was pathologised, and labour colonies were again put forward as a solution. As we shall see in the following section, similar views pervaded debates about the social problem group.

The way that the issue of vagrancy was pathologised provides the background to the narrower search for the social problem group in the interwar years. It was this group that allegedly produced the phenomenon of tramps, among other social undesirables. It has been suggested that there was renewed interest in the residuum or social problem group in the 1920s because the postwar recession and unemployment convinced many eugenists that the effects of differential fertility were manifesting themselves in poor economic performance and an expanding army of unemployables. Second, the rise of the Labour Party created a situation in which existing class privileges appeared to be threatened. Third, the rise of the medical, psychiatric, and social work professions highlighted the possibility of therapeutic intervention; a conservative aspect of this was the application of Mendelian laws of inheritance and remedies such as sterilisation. Eugenics offered newly-professionalised groups a strategy of conservative reform. Fourth, there was the concern in the 1920s over an apparent increase in the incidence of mental deficiency.[27]

The background to this later interest in the social problem group was earlier interest in the effects of heredity and the environment in individual families, particularly in the United States. Charles Rosenberg locates an increase in hereditarian explanations of individual disease and anti-social behaviour from the 1840s, especially in explaining the origin and intractability of the incarcerated and stigmatised. He claims American populisers of hereditarian ideas in the 1870s reflected various influences – that of French degeneration theorists; a need to elaborate mechanisms in scientific terms; an emphasis on environmental reform; and a diffuse evangelicalism.[28] In 1877, the social reformer Robert Dugdale published an exhaustive examination of the notorious Jukes family – a family whose members were allegedly marked by a high incidence of 'antisocial' habits. Dugdale had studied the family while working as Secretary of the New York Prison Association. He argued that 'fornication' was the key feature of the behaviour of the Jukes family, while secondary features included prostitution, 'exhaustion', and disease.[29] On the Jukes themselves, Dugdale estimated that successive generations of the family – 709 members in all – had over 75 years 'cost' the state some $1.3m, in expenditure associated with pauperism, outdoor relief, prison, prostitution, illegitimacy, begging, and charity.

But Dugdale argued not for sterilisation, but for environmental reform and control. In the introduction, Franklin H. Giddings argued that:

> the factor of 'heredity' whatever it may be, and whether great or small, always has the coefficient, 'environment', and if bad personal antecedents are reinforced by neglect, indecent domestic arrangements, isolation from the disturbing and stimulating influences of a vigorous civilisation, and, above all, if evil example is forced upon the child from his earliest infancy, the product will inevitably be an extraordinary high percentage of pauperism, vice, and crime.[30]

Dugdale referred to two earlier enquiries, one conducted into county jails in 1874, and one on state prisons in 1875. Elisha Harris, of the Prison Association of New York, had observed from these that although in theory any young person could become trapped in a downward spiral, in practice the number of 'well-born' and 'well-trained' children who descended from virtue to vice was very small. He wrote that 'habitual criminals spring almost exclusively from degenerating stocks; their youth is spent amid the degrading surroundings of physical and social defilement, with only a flickering of the redeeming influence of virtuous aspiration'.[31] Criminals, vagrants and paupers – the 'ignorant, vicious and incapable' – arose out of the 'same social soil'.[32] Thus it was the corrupting environment that was emphasised.

It is interesting to contrast Dugdale's study of the Jukes with those of later social investigators, who were concerned more with heredity and with mental deficiency. The best-known is that of the Kallikak family (1912) conducted by Henry Herbert Goddard, of the Training School at Vineland, New Jersey, for Feeble-Minded Boys and Girls. Among the pupils at the School was Deborah, a girl aged 22 who had been classified as 'feeble-minded'. Goddard began to research her family history, and claimed to have found evidence of 'feeble-mindedness' in earlier generations. He argued that this provided a natural experiment in heredity. A young man of a good family had become through two different women the ancestor of two lines of descendants – one good and the other allegedly characterised by mental defect in every generation. One side of the family comprised 496 people, prominent in nearly every walk of life. In this family and its branches there was nothing but 'good representative citizenship' – there were doctors, lawyers, judges, teachers, traders, landholders, and men and women prominent in every area of social life. On the other side of the family (480 descendants including Deborah) were found 'paupers, criminals, prostitutes, drunkards, and examples of all forms of social pest with which modern society is burdened'.[33] It was estimated that 143 of the 480 were 'feeble-minded', 46 'normal', and the rest 'unknown' or 'doubtful'. A further 36 were illegitimate, 33 sexually immoral (mainly prostitutes), 24 confirmed alcoholics, 3 epileptics, 82 died in infancy, 3 were criminals, and 8 kept houses of 'ill fame'. An additional total of 1,146 – that included those who had married into other families, allegedly included 262 who were 'feeble-minded', 197 'normal', and 581 'undetermined'.[34] Goddard wrote that:

> the conclusion is inevitable that all this degeneracy has come as the result of the defective mentality and bad blood having been brought into the normal family of good blood, first from the nameless feeble-minded girl and later by additional contaminations from other sources.[35]

The solution advocated by Goddard, as by many other writers on the 'feeble-minded', was that of segregation. However, he acknowledged that there were two problems. One was how to identify the 'feeble-minded'. The other was how best to deal with them even when they had been found. Colonies offered one solution, sterilisation another. In the case of the latter, there were a further two problems. First, there was public opposition to the operation. Second, there was the difficulty of knowing who were the right people to operate on, owing to persisting uncertainty about the exact laws of inheritance. Nevertheless Goddard concluded 'for practical purposes it is, of course, pretty clear that it is safe to assume that two feeble-minded parents will never have anything but feeble-minded children'.[36]

Thus earlier discussions that had emphasised the influence of the environment were increasingly replaced by studies that had a biological reductionism and emphasis on authoritarian solutions, such as segregation and sterilisation. The earlier study of the Jukes had attempted to balance the effects of heredity and environment, but in 1911 Dugdale's original notes were found, and a eugenics field worker, Arthur H. Estabrook, began to trace the contemporary descendants of the family. Estabrook traced a further 2,111 Jukes, arguing that half of the Jukes were feeble-minded, and all the criminals were feeble-minded. After 1910, the Jukes and the Kallikaks were joined by numerous other families – the Pineys, the family of Sam Sixty, the Happy Hickory family in Ohio, the Nam family, the Hill Folk, and the Dack family – all accepted as proof of the idea that from heredity flowed feeble-mindedness and social failure.[37] From 1907, the Eugenics Society in Britain began to produce reports on the family histories of paupers. This echoed the studies in the United States of the Jukes and the Kallikaks. Family record forms were produced for Society members, and these included the category 'presence of any special tastes, defect, gift or peculiarity of mind or body'.[38] Advice on preparing family pedigrees was also circulated by the Eugenics Society at this time.

Aside from its research on family histories, the most focused research of this kind was the support that the Eugenics Society gave to the work of E. J. Lidbetter, a Poor Law official in the East End of London. Lidbetter (1877–1962) is now largely a forgotten figure in the history of social investigation. Nevertheless his early work, and the support that the Eugenics Society gave to it, is an important example of early research into the existence of an inter-generational underclass. Working as a Relieving Officer in Bethnal Green, Lidbetter had in his spare time begun to look more closely at the family histories of the people that he was dealing with. At the National Conference on the Prevention of Destitution in 1911, for example, Lidbetter summarised the eugenist point of view rather neatly, arguing, 'it is the view of the Society that destitution, so far as it is represented by pauperism (and where there is no other standard) is to a large extent confined to a special and degenerate class'.[39] The solution to the 'problem', as Lidbetter saw it, was detention and segregation. The Society had formed a committee on pauperism in 1910. In 1911 and 1917, he published articles in the Society's journal, the *Eugenics Review*, the first of which was about what he termed the 'defective community'. From 1913, Lidbetter had begun an investigation into pauperism and heredity, but this was abandoned during the First World War.

In 1920, at the Second International Eugenics Congress, Lidbetter argued that pauperism was not hereditary, but that it was 'a consequence of inherent and transmissable defects of character' and dependant on mental, moral, and physical defects. What had been neglected, in his view, was the 'essentially personal element'. From some 400–500 pedigrees of paupers that he had compiled, Lidbetter suggested that there were three groups – those characterised by the inheritance of mental defect; a low grade type of 'mildly incompetent persons'; and a group that was 'distinctly non-moral'. The two main questions were whether the existence of a certain type of pauper family could be proven, and whether the cause of pauperism was of 'definitely transmissable character'. Lidbetter argued that there existed 'a definite race of chronic pauper stocks, intermingled with the general community, not recruited to any large extent from the normal population, and not sensibly decreased by the agencies for the promotion of human efficiency'. In his view the laws of heredity meant that this class could be reduced.[40]

Lidbetter remains an elusive figure, especially in this early period when the archival sources make only occasional references to him. But by the early 1920s he was in fairly close contact with the Eugenics Society, as well as writing articles for newspapers like the *Daily News* on such topics as the 'marriage of the unfit'.[41] Lidbetter became more closely involved with the Eugenics Society from May 1923 when a small research committee was formed. This included some of the key figures in the Society – Dr Cyril Burt, Professor A. M. Carr-Saunders, Professor Julian Huxley, and Sir Frederick Mott. The exact status of this new committee remains something of a mystery. It noted that the earlier investigations of 1913–15 had not been completed, and one of the committee's aims was to assist Lidbetter in his on-going work into the family histories of paupers. More specifically, it agreed to pay for a research assistant, so that his survey could become more sophisticated – for instance by including a random sample and control group. Correspondence indicates that Lidbetter was highly thought-of at this time. In January 1928, for example, an MP asked the Society for a speaker who could address the Conservative Health and Housing Committee on the theme of 'Eugenics and the Cost of the Unfit'. Its Secretary recommended Lidbetter, writing 'I have in mind someone who has studied this problem at firsthand very thoroughly and he has really data of greater practical value than any man in England or America'.[42]

The Eugenics Society contributed to the costs of a book that Lidbetter was writing. Nevertheless there were signs that the Society's new Secretary, Carlos Blacker, was concerned about Lidbetter's methodology. In June 1931, for instance, Blacker reported on a recent meeting he had had with Professor Lancelot Hogben, then Head of the Department of Social Biology at the London School of Economics. One of the things they had discussed was the possibility of securing additional funding through the Rockefeller Foundation. Blacker was anxious to increase the academic credibility of the Society's research by improving links with the School. However, Blacker warned Lidbetter that Hogben's willingness to approach Rockefeller 'depends to a great extent, upon your ability to discriminate between different kinds of pauperism, in particular between that which implies social inadequacy and that which implies misfortune without social inadequacy'.[43]

Lidbetter himself provided further insights into his work in an article published in the *Eugenics Review* in 1932. He argued that concern about a social problem group, expressed in the Wood Report on Mental Deficiency of 1929, was nothing new. Similar concerns had been expressed in articles in the *Eugenics Review* in 1910, and publicised in newspapers including *The Times*. His aim was to examine the personal, family, and wider relationships of paupers in the

East End, and to collect 'pedigrees' in selected cases. Lidbetter argued that these revealed 'that there is in existence a definite race of sub-normal people, closely related by marriage or parenthood, not to any extent recruited from the normal population, nor sensibly diminished by the agencies for social or individual improvement'.[44] The pedigrees provided insights as to how this group had been created: the main reason was inbreeding, and the recurring intermarriage of 'defective' people. The greatest danger, in fact, was the case of the 'high-grade defective and the mildly incompetent, but apparently normal, person'.[45] Lidbetter conceded that the more he studied this problem, the less certain he was about what should be done about it. What was needed most was intensive research, carried out by responsible academics, and properly funded. Despite this proviso, the first volume of Lidbetter's research was published in 1933. The book could only summarise a fraction of the research that Lidbetter had carried out in the East End of London between 1910 and 1928. In fact, this first volume contained only 26 pedigrees. Nonetheless, as in his article of the previous year, Lidbetter argued that the pedigrees provided evidence for the existence of a social problem group. He wrote that 'there is some evidence that the persons included in the pedigrees have a sufficiency of common characteristics such as to constitute a class by themselves'.[46]

Some observers were quite impressed with the results of Lidbetter's labours. The Secretary of the COS, J. C. Pringle, for instance, congratulated Blacker that the book had finally been published. He wrote that he and his colleagues had long been convinced it was going to be 'one of the most important contributions to the elucidation of difficult problems of our life-time'.[47] Others were less happy. When Carr-Saunders reviewed the book for the Society, he admitted to Blacker that 'all that I say in praise of it is really meant. What I do not say is that his introduction rather alarms me. He finds difficulty in telling a plain story. One can hardly make out from it what he has been doing. Also bias is evident'.[48] Blacker replied to Carr-Saunders that 'I quite agree with you about the dangers of Lidbetter making questionable deductions from his material, and I much hope that the contents of the later volumes will be adequately supervised'.[49]

Only the first volume of the proposed survey was published, and John Macnicol has suggested that what is most apparent from the book is how vague Lidbetter's evidence actually was. On the one hand Lidbetter argued that many 'degenerate tendencies' could take a variety of forms, and were due to biological weakness transmitted through heredity. On the other, he argued that the group were sufficiently similar to constitute a separate class. The social problem group had to be presented as being sufficiently large to represent a serious problem, but also needed to be shown to be an identifiable unit with a single cause. While Lidbetter made no reference to social conditions in the East End of London, he did concede that military call-up and improved employment opportunities during the First World War had reduced the pauper population. Furthermore, the Boards of Guardians had relaxed the administration of outdoor relief to the able-bodied, so that the numbers of 'persons chargeable' rose rapidly. This illustrated how the social problem group was ultimately a statistical artefact. A final weakness was that little information was given on individual family members. As Macnicol has noted, a recurring feature of the history of the underclass has been the repeated insistence that more research is necessary.[50]

As this discussion of Lidbetter's role has indicated, the wider context to his work was provided by the way the Eugenics Society propagated the concept of the social problem group in the 1920s and 1930s. Lidbetter had noted that the key event in spreading the concept of the social problem group was the Report of the Committee on Mental Deficiency (1929). This had been appointed in June 1924 by Sir George Newman, Chief Medical Officer of the Board of Education, to consider problems posed by the mentally defective child. In 1925 its remit was widened to include adult defectives. It became a Joint Committee of the Board of Education and the Board of Control. Chaired by Arthur Wood, a civil servant in the Board of Education, the members included the prominent eugenists Sir Cyril Burt and Dr Alfred Tredgold, respectively Professor of Education and Lecturer in Mental Deficiency at London University, and Evelyn Fox of the Central Association for Mental Welfare.[51] The Wood Committee met 42 times, and its report was completed in January 1929. Overall, the Committee estimated that there were around 105,000 mentally defective children, or about three times the number then known to Local Education Committees. There were about 30,000 lower grade defectives under 16. And it was thought there were around 150,000 adult defectives, or twice as many as had been certified by the Board of Control. Thus the Wood Committee claimed that some 300,000 children and adults in England and Wales were mentally defective.[52] Eugenics clearly was an important influence on the work of the Committee. The report commented that 'the science of eugenics is doing invaluable service in focusing scientific thought and public opinion upon the racial, social and economic problems that the subnormal group presents to every civilised nation'.[53]

The most important aspect of the report was the alleged increase in the incidence of mental deficiency. Dr E. O. Lewis, the Committee's Medical Investigator, attempted to assess the number of mental defectives by investigating six areas with a population of 100,000. The Wood Committee argued, for example, that feeble-mindedness was more likely to occur among populations of a low mental or physical level, in slum districts or poor rural areas, and was more likely to be prevalent in a 'sub-normal' group. It was suggested that 'primary amentia' was both a family and a group problem. Mental defectives could be found in all social classes. However, the report argued that if families containing mental defectives were segregated, this group would contain a higher proportion of paupers, criminals, the unemployed, 'habitual slum dwellers', and prostitutes than an equivalent group.[54] Most of these families would belong to a 'social problem' or 'subnormal' group, comprising the bottom ten per cent of the population. In terms of prevention, the options were segregation and sterilisation. The key problem was that the families of the 'subnormal' group remained large, while families of the 'better' social groups were becoming smaller.

Following the publication of the Wood Report, some members of the Eugenics Society were cautious about the concept of the social problem group, suggesting it would offer a target to the Society's enemies. Others argued that it should be brought to the attention of the general public, and linked to the Society's policy on voluntary sterilisation. Bernard Mallet, the Society's then Secretary, wrote:

> surely few more challenging statements than this have ever been uttered by a Departmental Committee. Four million persons in England and Wales who are the great purveyors of social inefficiency, prostitution, feeble-mindedness and petty crime, the chief architects of slumdom, the most fertile strain in the community! Four million persons in a socially well-defined group forming the dregs of the community and thriving upon it as a parasite thrives upon a healthy and vigorous host. It is difficult to conceive of a more sweeping or socially significant generalisation.[55]

Mallet proposed to form a Social Problem Investigation Committee to look in detail at such areas of study as epileptics, slum dwellers, unemployment, and prostitution. He suggested that inquiries might be carried out at the local level, and a short book published by the Society. It is clear that the impact of the Wood Report permeated provincial intellectual life. Some Medical Officers of Health were interested in the alleged links between feeble-mindedness and the 'social problem group', and it was featured in radio broadcasts by some of the Eugenics Society's members.[56]

Successive Secretaries of the Eugenics Society promoted this issue. Bernard Mallet called for an investigation of the social problem group in his article in the *Eugenics Review*, and in May 1932, Carlos Blacker asked for collaborators, hoping that there might be ten separate studies, each investigating 50 families. The aim was to select families that exhibited 'multiple social problem' characteristics and to see if the incidence of mental defectiveness was higher in these families than in the population as a whole. This reversed the procedure of the investigation carried out by Lewis for the Wood Committee.[57] By November 1932, Blacker was claiming that local studies were being carried out in London, Hull, Southampton, Liverpool, Newcastle, and Reading.[58] As a result, the Social Problem Group Investigation Committee that had been set up in 1923 and supported the early Lidbetter work, was effectively reconstituted in June 1933. Chaired by Sir Allan Powell, it included David Caradog Jones and E. J. Lidbetter.

With segregation, sterilisation had long been recommended as a solution to the problems posed by the underclass in its different forms. The social problem group became the focus because it provided the means of defining the target for sterilisation policies.[59] Following the publication of the Wood Report, the Eugenics Society intensified its efforts in support of a policy of sterilisation, and it sought to build a coalition of support among the social work, mental health, and public health professions. A Committee for Legalising Eugenic Sterilisation was organised by Carlos Blacker of the Eugenics Society, and a Private Member's Bill was introduced by the Labour MP Major A. G. Church in July 1931. However, this was unsuccessful, and the Eugenics Society turned instead to lobbying civil servants and bodies such as the Central Association for Mental Welfare. Public meetings in support of sterilisation were held up to the outbreak of the Second World War.[60]

The Departmental Committee on Voluntary Sterilisation, set up by the Ministry of Health in June 1932, was largely in response to the fears triggered off by the Wood Report. But it also represented a coup for the Eugenics Society in influencing the policy-making elite, and the Departmental Committee would also in turn further support the concept of a social problem group. Its terms of reference were to:

> examine and report on the information already available regarding the hereditary transmission and other causes of mental disorder and deficiency; to consider the value of sterilisation as a preventive measure having regard to its physical, psychological, and social effects and to the experience of legislation in other countries permitting it; and to suggest what further inquiries might usefully be undertaken in this connection.[61]

Chaired by Sir Laurence Brock, a senior civil servant in the Ministry of Health and Board of Control, its members included a mixture of civil servants, experts in mental deficiency, and others sympathetic to the Eugenics Society. The Report produced by the Departmental Committee argued that mental defectiveness was more common in the 'lowest social stratum' than in the rest of the population. Here one could find 'an unduly high incidence of mental defect, insanity, intellectual dullness, epilepsy, as well as tuberculosis and other physical defects'.[62] The Committee attached particular importance to the social problem group, and argued that the solution of voluntary sterilisation was especially relevant. Mental defectives were unable to support themselves, drifted to the slums, and married others like them. Thus the social problem group increased the number of mental defectives, and children of low intelligence. The Committee rejected compulsory sterilisation, but overall, recommended that voluntary sterilisation should be legalised for mental defectives and other 'transmissible' mental disorders and physical disabilities.

Despite the recommendations of the Departmental Committee, the campaign for the voluntary sterilisation of mental defectives was not successful. This illustrates the dangers of exaggerating the impact of eugenics on policy. There was confusion between the voluntary and compulsory options of sterilisation. Historians John Macnicol and Desmond King have together suggested there were four main reasons that account for the failure of the campaign. First, the Minister for Health, Sir Hilton Young, had reservations about sterilisation and was not co-operative; second, the labour movement was joined in its opposition by the Catholic Church; third, there was never a strong scientific case for sterilisation, and the British Medical Association refused to endorse it; and fourth, the proposed sterilisation programme was damaged from January 1934 by revelations of the Nazi campaign of compulsory sterilisation and euthanasia. Overall, the campaign for the voluntary sterilisation of mental defectives revealed both the wide appeal of eugenics, but also the obstacles that the Society faced.[63]

Although the campaign for voluntary sterilisation was ultimately unsuccessful, the report of the Departmental Committee had also provided support for the concept of the social problem group. By the early 1930s, the Eugenics Society was beginning to realise that eugenics was becoming discredited through attacks on it by legitimate scientists. Evidence was emerging from Nazi Germany about the compulsory sterilisation of the feeble-minded, following the 1933 Eugenic Sterilisation Law. The Society was starting to turn to positive eugenics and to wider population questions. Nevertheless Blacker remained determined to find clear proof of the existence of the social problem group.[64] Embarrassed by the obvious weaknesses in Lidbetter's methods, the Eugenics Society placed more hope in the work of other investigators. David Caradog Jones (1883–1975) was educated at King's School, Chester, and later won an open mathematics scholarship to Pembroke College, Cambridge. After the First World War, Caradog Jones was first Lecturer in Mathematics at Manchester, and later Lecturer in Sociology at Liverpool.[65] In this latter post he planned and directed the Merseyside Social Survey.

It has been suggested that Caradog Jones was a typical member of the Eugenics Society at this time. In his autobiography, he recorded that his parents were born 'of good Welsh farming stock'. During the First World War he was a conscientious objector, spending time in the detention room at Newcastle Barracks, sewing mailbags. The interest of Caradog Jones into aspects of personality was apparent at an early stage. In 1913, for example, he published in the *Journal of the Royal Statistical Society* a study of the extent of 'economic moral failure' among regular workers. This listed such traits as drink, dishonesty, misconduct, negligence or irregularity, and incompetence.[66] As John Macnicol comments:

by background and temperament, therefore, Caradog Jones was in many respects the archetypal inter-war eugenist; newly professionalised, he had worked his way up by considerable effort; to a strong religious faith was added an interest in social policy and a non-socialist reformism.[67]

Caradog Jones was able to find an outlet for these interests in the Merseyside Social Survey. Funded through the Rockefeller Foundation, the Merseyside Survey was intended to complement the New Survey of London Life and Labour. Chapter 14 of the third volume dealt with 'sub-normal types', defined as being the mentally deficient and epileptic. Here Caradog Jones wrote that one of the most important questions was 'how to identify those persons who outwardly are normal but who inwardly carry defective "genes", seeds which if transmitted produce defective stock some time in the future'.[68] Using data based on children attending Special Schools, and adults supervised by the West Lancashire Association for Mental Welfare, Caradog Jones explored the relationship between defectiveness, sex, and age; families; social class; and home conditions. He suggested that where families had two or more mentally defective children, it was likely that the defect was hereditary – marriages of defectives should be closely monitored. He referred to the work of Lewis on the Wood Report, claiming that Lewis had shown how feeble-mindedness was more common in the social problem group. Overall, Caradog Jones concluded that in any large urban area there was a social problem group which was 'the source from which the majority of criminals and paupers, unemployables and defectives of all kinds are recruited'.[69] In general, Caradog Jones maintained that structural measures were not sufficient for social reform, writing that it was not enough to improve the 'framework of society'. Instead, attention should also be directed to 'the quality of the people from whom that society is increasingly recruited'.[70]

The fact that these concerns were evident in the Merseyside Social Survey is generally well known. Caradog Jones provided the Brock Committee on Voluntary Sterilisation with a summary of the material he had collected. What is much less appreciated is the extent to which it was this aspect of the Survey that was noted by reviewers, in newspapers and other periodicals. The social problem group was mentioned, for example, in a review in the *Liverpool Post* in June 1934, while the *Daily Dispatch* commented 'amazing revelations of the intimate lives of thousands of sub-normal people and mental defectives in Merseyside are made in the University's three-volume social survey'.[71] Other newspapers echoed the concern that the birth rate was higher among these 'undesirable groups', and questioned whether the 'unfit' should marry. There were some doubts expressed about the methodology employed in the survey. In the *Political Quarterly*, for instance, its reviewer argued that the main criticisms of the chapters on subnormal types were that they 'were not always presented with the scientific integrity and detachment that one would expect in a publication of this kind'. There was evidence, he suggested, of a preconception in favour of a hereditary social problem group.[72] On the other hand, the *New Statesman* thought the detailed survey of subnormal types one of the most original aspects of the survey. Its reviewer noted: 'it goes beyond an analysis of their economic condition and attempts to trace the incidence and hereditary nature of both physical and mental defects'.[73]

Nevertheless Caradog Jones's work on the social problem group was bedevilled by many of the same problems with which Lidbetter had struggled. In September 1929, Caradog Jones had told the Secretary of the Eugenics Society that:

> among other investigations I have initiated one concerning certain types of abnormal people: those who are born blind, the very deaf, the epileptic, the mentally deficient, those who are persistently addicted to drink, crime or vice, and those who are constantly coming upon the Guardians or some charitable institution for assistance.[74]

This illustrated how weak his definition of 'abnormality' actually was. It included three main groups: those with some form of disability; others with 'moral' failings; and a third group that was defined through its dependence on welfare. The cards that were prepared for the survey included for those born blind or partially blind; for the very deaf; the epileptic; those mentally retarded and deficient; those persistently addicted to immorality, crime and alcohol; the chronically destitute; and those 'in any other way abnormal', such as being tuberculous or deformed.[75] Caradog Jones wrote that in all these cases there was 'some lack of physical, mental, or moral balance, or some failure of social and economic adjustment which makes them a burden upon the community'.

Caradog Jones hoped that in the survey, Lewis's concept of the social problem group might be broken down into its different components.[76] These methods were borne out in the published Survey, where different chapters dealt with the blind, the deaf, physical defectives, alcoholics, criminals, the 'immoral', and the unemployed. He defined the group as being a section of the population that is 'largely dependent upon others for support'.[77] In addition to its being a heterogeneous group, Caradog Jones faced difficulties in proving mental defectiveness was hereditary. Even in the chapter on mental deficiency, he was forced to admit that out of 912 children attending schools for mental defectives, only 11 had a parent recorded as ex-Special School or suffering from a more serious grade of defect. He argued, unconvincingly, that the figures were misleading, since there had been no special school in Liverpool before 1900, and the West Lancashire Association for Mental Welfare had been in existence only since 1915. He was forced to fall back on the work of the eugenist A. F. Tredgold to argue that the 'neuropathic diathesis' could be transmitted, but that it might be several generations before it resulted in mental defect.[78]

By the late 1930s, various factors were combining to weaken the legitimacy of eugenics and sterilisation. The mood of crisis that had characterised the early 1930s had evaporated by the latter half of the decade, as the economy began to recover, and the social and political fabric had shown itself to be strong enough to withstand the strains to which it had been subjected. Demographic investigations were destroying the foundations of many eugenic theories, such as the phenomenon of the differential birth rate. Eugenics was increasingly under attack from scientists such as Hogben, and research, such as that of John Boyd Orr on nutrition, directed attention more to environmental than hereditarian factors. In particular, an emerging Keynesian middle-way consensus was holding out an optimistic and convincing strategy for non-socialist reformism. In this context, many began to argue that environmental reform was a complementary component of eugenics.[79]

Research on the social problem group therefore took place within a changed intellectual climate, where the emphasis was on what has been called 'reform eugenics'. E. J. Lidbetter, for example, was aware that by the late 1930s the intellectual climate had changed dramatically. Writing in January 1936, he warned that an attempt to link housing to eugenics or to the social problem group would lead to a torrent of (arguably justifiable) criticism being directed at the Society.[80] Moreover the Eugenics Society still faced the problem of proving that the social problem group actually existed. In 1937, a book was published from the work sponsored by the Social Problem Group Investigation Committee. C. P. Blacker argued that, from the point of view of 'negative eugenics', no question was more important than that of whether a 'social problem group composed of persons of inferior hereditary condition' actually existed. If it did exist, and had recognisable biological characteristics, it was important that the fertility of the members should be restricted.[81] However the composition of the group remained extremely heterogeneous. Different chapters dealt with the mentally retarded child; mental disorder; epilepsy; drunkenness; prostitution; recidivism; paupers; neurasthenia, and unemployment. Moreover the tentative title, *A Social Problem Group?*, showed that the findings remained inconclusive. Despite his belief that research was essential, Blacker was forced to concede that 'the social problem group constitutes a very difficult subject for accurate and impartial investigation'.[82]

Some investigators continued to believe in the group. Raymond Cattell, for example, wrote in 1937 that 'such sub-average types are often only fitfully employed, cannot co-operate in hygienic measures and in enlightened methods of bringing up children, and cannot comprehend political issues'.[83] Similarly David Caradog Jones maintained in the foreword to *A Social Problem Group?* that:

> our acquaintance with the detail of human inheritance of various defects and disabilities and of the effect of the environment upon them is still astonishingly meagre, but enough

is known in a broad sense to provide us with guiding principles in our attitude towards social conditions.[84]

Others drew on the concept for opportunistic or tactical reasons. In his study of regional variations in infant mortality, for example, the young Richard Titmuss repeated the mantra that the social problem group was 'the source from which all too many of our criminals, paupers, degenerates, unemployables and defectives are recruited'.[85]

Despite the doubts expressed in *A Social Problem Group?*, Blacker remained persistent into the 1940s, encouraged by the formation of the Royal Commission on Population. In April 1944, he wrote to Lidbetter of the social problem group that 'the line that I have in mind is that such a group exists and that it may well seek to abuse the measures of social security which are designed to secure freedom from anxiety, want and fear'.[86] In June 1944, he told Lidbetter that copies of *Heredity and the Social Problem Group* should be given to members of the Royal Commission, writing that 'the fact that social security schemes will break down if unemployment and other forms of dependency exceed a certain minimum should make people conscious of the parasitic character of the social problem group'.[87] However, many of the leading members of the Eugenics Society remained embarrassed about Lidbetter and his work. In June 1944, Carr-Saunders recommended that copies of Lidbetter's volume should not be presented to the Royal Commission, warning that its members would argue most of the 'defects and ill-behaviour' had social and environmental causes.[88] Blacker admitted to Carr-Saunders that on re-reading the book he was disappointed by the introduction. He continued 'indeed, I felt that I had rarely come across such a clear instance of the reader's mind being muddled or even prejudiced against a piece of careful work by a bad general presentation'.[89]

By the Second World War, even Caradog Jones appeared to be more cautious. While he argued that Lidbetter's pedigrees confirmed that the social problem group existed, he conceded that the Brock Committee were probably right in saying there was less agreement about its size. He maintained that people of subnormal intelligence who were not certified defectives could be the carriers of certain genes that were defective in one way or another. What was crucial was where to draw the line defining 'subnormal' intelligence – a bit like the poverty line.[90]

The reactions of Leon Radzinowicz and Lord Horder to this piece were revealing. Radzinowicz observed that although the work of Booth, Rowntree, and Bowley had revealed much about the economic and social facts of the social problem group, less was known about its 'physical and mental peculiarities'. Little was known about the relationship between poverty and mental defect, and it was not established that the social problem group was the source of criminality.

Radzinowicz suggested, perceptively, that these ideas were more of a discursive phenomenon. Whereas the concept of the '*classes dangereuses*' belonged to the period of the Industrial Revolution, that of the social problem group was linked to plans for a system of universal social security. Lord Horder observed that Caradog Jones said little about the relationship between economic and mental poverty, and he too, remained undecided about whether the social problem group really existed.[91]

In a textbook on social surveys, published in 1949, Caradog Jones asked:

> is the so-called 'social problem group' a class radically different from the rest of the population, or is the term one which conveniently, but perhaps rather confusingly, covers a heterogeneous mass of persons suffering from defects and disabilities which have no more than a superficial relationship to one another?[92]

At the same time, he was enthusiastic about the new theme of the problem family. He wrote that 'in my experience the majority of such families seem, in fact, to be incapable of economic thought, or at least of forethought'. The fundamental cause was subnormal intelligence, and the only useful approach was that of the Family Service Units – which persisted with 'utterly useless human material'.[93] Thus, as the following chapter will illustrate, many of those attracted to the concept of the social problem group in the 1930s were able to transfer their interests to the new theme of the problem family in the 1940s.

There was thus much evidence that the earlier concepts of the social residuum and unemployable persisted into the interwar period. One illustration of this is provided by the attempts to pathologise the tramp. But the main sense in which these ideas were propagated was in the new concept of the social problem group. This was a key element in the work of the Eugenics Society. Early attempts to study mental defectiveness and heredity in families and paupers were given further support in the way that the social problem group was identified in the Wood Report, supported by the Brock Committee. Compared to the social residuum, ideas about mental deficiency were crucial in sustaining the concept of the social problem group – there was more concern about methodology, and a desire for academic respectability. Nevertheless, other key aspects of earlier concepts were evident – a sense that the group constituted around 10% of the population; an emphasis on inter-generational continuities; a stress on the potential importance of sterilisation and segregation; and a continuing belief in the role of the expert. Against the background of the depression, and in the context of anxieties about the rise of the Labour Party, the social problem group provided middle-class professional groups with a single-cause explanation of social problems. Moreover in the 1930s, the social problem group was constructed in relation to the advocated solution of sterilisation. The social problem group thus entered the lexicon of fashionable eugenic language, to be exploited by opportunists who were on the margins of the Eugenics Society.

Despite this symbolic importance, the efforts of the Eugenics Society were weakened by the fact that the existence of the social problem group could not be proven. E. J. Lidbetter argued that it was characterised by biological weakness and was also a separate class, and while the group had to be large enough to create concern, it was also an identifiable unit with a single cause. Lidbetter made little reference to social conditions, and his admission that pauperism declined during the First World War and rose in the recession showed that it was a statistical artefact. In his work on the Merseyside Social Survey, David Caradog Jones argued that the group was made up of three factions – those who had some form of disability; those marked by moral failings; and a third group that was dependent on welfare. But like Lidbetter, Caradog Jones struggled to demonstrate convincingly that mental defectiveness was hereditary, arguing that while it could be transmitted, it might be several decades before mental defect showed itself. Both therefore linked vague ideas of social inefficiency to pseudo-scientific ideas about heredity. Both were forced to fall back on the argument that, while the existence of the group was self-evident, more research was necessary.

The Wood Report and Lidbetter research would surface periodically in the later researches of both supporters and opponents of related ideas, such as the cycle of deprivation in the 1970s. But while the concept of the social problem group remained popular in the late 1930s, wider factors such as the emerging Keynesian 'middle-way' consensus had also begun to weaken both the credibility of eugenics and the attractions of a policy of sterilisation. The position of the Society was further weakened following the publication of the Beveridge Report of 1942. By the mid-1940s, the concept of the social problem group had already begun its transformation into the notion of the problem family. This was first apparent in accounts of the schoolchildren evacuated from the cities to the countryside in September 1939. One account in particular, the survey *Our Towns*, by the Women's Group on Public Welfare (1943), was particularly important in this respect. Perceiving that the mounting evidence of Nazi experiments and the wider climate of social reconstruction made its ideas appear out of date, the Eugenics Society sought to take on board this shift and use it for its own ends. It was not surprising, therefore, that in the late 1940s the Society was in the forefront of proposals to investigate the new phenomenon. It is the new concept of the problem family that the next chapter seeks to explore.

4

The Invention of the Problem Family

In an article published in September 1944, Dr R. C. Wofinden, the Deputy Medical Officer of Health (MOH) for Rotherham, described the typical 'problem family' in the following way:

> Almost invariably it is a large family, some of the children being dull or feeble-minded. From their appearance they are strangers to soap and water, toothbrush and comb; the clothing is dirty and torn and the footwear absent or totally inadequate. Often they are verminous and have scabies and impetigo. Their nutrition is surprisingly average – doubtless partly due to extra-familial feeding in schools. The mother is frequently sub-standard mentally. The home, if indeed it can be described as such, has usually the most striking characteristics. Nauseating odours assail one's nostrils on entry, and the source is usually located in some urine-sodden faecal-stained mattress in an upstairs room. There are no floor coverings, no decorations on the walls except perhaps the scribblings of the children and bizarre patterns formed by absent plaster. Furniture is of the most primitive, cooking utensils absent, facilities for sleeping hopeless – iron bedsteads furnished with fouled mattresses and no coverings. Upstairs there is flock everywhere, which the mother assures us has come out of a mattress which she has unpacked for cleansing. But the flock seems to stay there for weeks and the cleansed and repacked mattress never appears. The bathroom is obviously the least frequented room of the building. There are sometimes faecal accumulations on the floors upstairs, and tin baths containing several days' accumulation of faeces and urine are not unknown.[1]

It was a description that was to remain powerful, if misleading, for much of the early postwar period.

Although there was much interest in the concept of the social problem group during the interwar period, at the end of the 1930s social investigators remained unable to prove that it actually existed. By the early 1940s, the theme of the social problem group had been superseded by that of the problem family. It was this concept that represented a further step in the evolution of the concept of the underclass. The problem family concept is arguably the least-studied link in the chain, and has attracted limited interest from historians. Some studies have sought to explore the problem family in terms of the concept's usefulness to professional groups including public health doctors and social workers, relating this to wider processes and organisational changes culminating in the Seebohm Report (1968).[2] Pat Starkey, on the other hand, has argued that it was the

Children and Young Persons Act (1963) that transferred responsibility for these families to Children's Departments. Drawing in part on a case-study of Bristol, Starkey also maintains that the continuing use of the term masked changes in the type of family it was used to describe.[3] Elsewhere, Starkey has related the issue of the problem family to the wider stigmatisation of the feckless mother, pointing out that 'problem family' really meant 'problem mother', and that the physical conditions of the home and children were given more importance than any other aspect of their welfare. Starkey writes that the problem mother was 'at the intersection of eugenic, class and social anxieties, all concerned with the quality of post-war British life and represented by groups of professionals who had an interest in reforming her'.[4] Finally Alan Cohen and Pat Starkey have traced the history of problem families in the context of the early history of the voluntary Family Service Units, showing how the metaphor changed from a biologically deterministic one to a medical one, from corrective to therapeutic work.[5]

Perhaps most interestingly, John Macnicol has explored the shift from the problem family debates of the 1950s to the underclass anxieties of the 1980s. Macnicol argues that discussions about problem families provided a rehearsal for underclass debates, indicating continuities in the discourse, but also showing how much had changed in British society over the past fifty years. Macnicol notes how the Eugenics Society, the Family Service Units, and public health doctors had become interested in the problem family in the 1940s, and also explores in some detail methodological problems that bedevilled this early research. Most definitions of problem families, for example, were essentially definitions of household squalor, and the Eugenics Society faced big problems in attempting to carry out a survey. Macnicol also charts the growing criticisms of the problem family concept in the 1950s. Acknowledging the related ideas of the culture of poverty and the cycle of deprivation, Macnicol asks to what extent there is a linear development from problem family to underclass in the period 1945–95. On the one hand there are continuities in the process of social distancing based on class, gender, and age; in the way the idea was pushed by a small but active pressure group; in the combination of administrative and behavioural definitions; and in the agreement that a problem existed but disagreement over its causes. But on the other hand, there have been significant changes in the labour market; and in demographic and family formation behaviour. Given very real concerns about widening social polarisation in the 1990s, Macnicol concluded that in contrast 'the 1950s do appear to be years of optimism and hope'.[6]

This chapter examines these earlier interpretations against the empirical evidence. It explores the concept of the problem family through the eyes of four different interest groups, whose members and ideas overlapped, but which can nonetheless be considered as having separate identities. These comprise the Eugenics Society and other individuals interested in eugenics; the voluntary

Family Service Units; medical personnel including public health doctors; and a broad coalition of academics and practitioners in the emerging social work profession. The chapter argues that the problem family can be seen as further conceptual stepping stone between the social problem group idea of the 1930s, and the cycle of deprivation notion of the 1970s. The problem family provides important evidence on how these ideas emerge, and also how they acquire a pejorative connotation and fade away. However, the links between the problem family idea and the American culture of poverty theory are much less easy to trace, with important differences, most notably in the treatment of race.

It is well known that the evacuation of schoolchildren from the cities to the countryside in September 1939 led to an important debate about the effectiveness of health and welfare services, and contributed to the content of the Beveridge Report.[7] It was in the course of these discussions that the transition from the notion of the social problem group to the concept of the problem family occurred. One of the most influential reports on the evacuation experience was the survey *Our Towns*, published by the Women's Group on Public Welfare in 1943. This was a group of middle-class women, who had previously been active in a range of voluntary organisations. In many respects, the report made incisive criticisms of the performance of organisations such as the School Medical Service in the 1930s. On the other hand, the report also reflected a pathological or behavioural interpretation of poverty. Most obviously, the introduction to the report argued that one effect of the evacuation had been to 'flood the dark places with light' and show that the 'submerged tenth' described by Charles Booth still existed in cities. In language that was later echoed by Oscar Lewis, the authors of the survey argued that the members of the submerged tenth seldom joined trade unions, friendly societies, classes, or clubs, and rarely attended church. And *Our Towns* claimed that within this group were the problem families who were:

> on the edge of pauperism and crime, riddled with mental and physical defects, in and out of the Courts for child neglect, a menace to the community, of which the gravity is out of all proportion to their numbers.[8]

Next to the problem families were others who were 'grey rather than black', who were dirty, but were nevertheless capable of improvement through better education and higher living standards. The authors of the *Our Towns* report suggested that a social survey of 'this class of the population' was seriously needed.

The *Our Towns* report was a beguiling mixture of reactionary and 'progressive' views, emphasising the role of education on the one hand, and the importance of improved living conditions on the other. While it advocated nursery classes and 'clubs for mothers', it also recommended family allowances and minimum wages. Part of the reason why it became an unlikely best-seller was because it caught the mood for social reconstruction. But it was the comment on problem families that caught the eye of other social commentators. David Caradog Jones, for example, who had been prominent in the search for the social problem group in the 1930s, used a piece on the *Our Towns* report in the *Eugenics Review* to press for a new survey.[9] The *Our Towns* survey inspired several public health doctors to write articles about problem families, and also generated other social surveys. In Luton, for example, a study on post-war reconstruction included a report on problem families that was funded by a small grant awarded by the Eugenics Society and written by an administrator in the local public health department. He claimed that problem families were those which:

> For their own well-being or the well-being of others, for reasons primarily unconnected with old age, accident, misfortune, illness or pregnancy, require a substantially greater degree of supervision and help over longer periods than is usually provided by existing social services'.[10]

Health visitors, district nurses, and sanitary inspectors were asked to submit details of families that fitted this definition, and the 167 families reported were investigated further by a health visitor. The report suggested that the causes of the problem family phenomenon were numerous – 'subnormal' mental capacity, broken families, frequent pregnancies, ill-health, absent husbands, and alcoholism. What was really needed was education and rehabilitation, intervention by central government, and a national survey. Luton's MOH agreed that 'an aspect of the rekindled interest in the social problems of our times has been an increased attention to the problem family'.[11]

Prominent among these observers was the Eugenics Society, which had been the prime mover in the search for the social problem group in the 1930s. By the end of the Second World War, the association between Nazism and eugenics, the election of a Labour government, and declining anxieties about the birth rate all seemed unfavourable for the objectives that the Eugenics Society had espoused in the 1930s. David Caradog Jones observed of the Luton report that it was unclear what was cause and what was effect, and that the author might have been 'too drastic in his pruning'.[12] More significant was an attempt by the General Secretary of the Society, C. P. Blacker, to summarise the findings of the growing number of reports on problem families, and to outline methods for a national survey. Blacker argued that what seemed important was 'temperamental instability' in the mother or father, along with large families. He accepted that defining the problem family still posed problems, especially for borderline cases, but he claimed the families were well-known at the local level and thought that, through several small-scale surveys, it would be possible to estimate the size of the social problem group.[13] Thus Blacker aimed to shore up support for the Eugenics

Society by updating the concept of the social problem group, and by cashing in on the vogue for the problem family.

Following meetings between Blacker and the MOH for Luton, and the awarding of a small grant, the Eugenics Society now formed a Problem Families Committee. Its first meeting in July 1947 was attended by prominent members of the Society such as David Caradog Jones, Lord Horder, and Richard Titmuss, and a number of interested MOsH.[14] It was recommended that a survey needed to be undertaken of the size of the social problem group, and the MOsH present agreed to undertake pilot enquiries in their areas, in Bristol, Warwickshire, Luton, Rotherham, the West Riding of Yorkshire, and the London borough of Kensington. Problem families would be defined in terms of the multiple problems they presented to statutory and voluntary organisations. Further changes to the definition were necessary. Problem families were not just families with children, and older people were excluded. It was thought that the four main features were 'intractable ineducability'; 'instability or infirmity of character'; 'the presentation by the family of multiple social problems'; and a 'squalid home'.[15]

The idea was to use local authorities to collects lists of families that presented various problems. In fact, organisations were asked to submit details of any family which over at least six months 'has confronted you with a *chronic and relatively intractable problem for which our present social services provide no lasting remedy*'.[16] These were to be returned to the MOH who would prepare a complete list. Following a conference, a list of 'possible problem families' would be agreed. It was suggested that in a large area, such as the West Riding of Yorkshire, a sample of 100 should be selected for more intensive study and visiting. Those deemed 'biological or social casualties' in the Luton survey should be removed, and so the list of 'possible problem families' would be 'pruned' and reduced to a smaller list of 'authentic problem families'. Details of these families were to be sent to Blacker, at the Eugenics Society.[17] Nevertheless it was recognised that however carefully the final list was prepared, there were likely to be different standards of assessment by the MOsH in the different areas. It was suggested, therefore, that there should be close co-operation between all concerned with the fieldwork, and between the study sites and the centre, with C. G. Tomlinson, author of the Luton survey, co-ordinating the pilot studies.

These doubts about the methodology were reflected in the cautious claims made in support of the project. In January 1948, it was said that the purpose of the pilot enquiries was simply to devise a workable method of counting problem families, and to standardise a method of investigation that might be adopted on a larger scale.[18] It was hoped that each area would produce reports on 50–100 'authentic problem families'. But it was also admitted that the six areas were not representative, and were simply those where the local MOsH were sympathetic to the 'problem', and linked to the Eugenics Society.[19] In March 1948, an observer from the Ministry of Health reported that the Committee was focusing on two characteristics, 'intractable ineducability' and 'instability or infirmity of character', declaring that:

> these together express themselves in the persistent neglect of children (if there are any), in fecklessness, irresponsibility, improvidence in the conduct of life, and indiscipline in the home wherein dirt, poverty and squalor are often conspicuous.[20]

Despite the attempts at ensuring some consistency in the fieldwork, doubts about the methodology persisted. In April 1949, for example, it was suggested that each investigator should send to Blacker a detailed account of three problem families regarded as typical in their area.[21] These concerns were highlighted by evidence of dissension within the team. In Bristol, it became clear on reading case histories that notorious problem families had not been included on the lists. The procedure was changed, so that a list of names and addresses was circulated to the organisations, who were asked to give more information about them. Dr R. C. Wofinden, then the MOH for Bristol, revealed that his list of problem families had been whittled down from 212 to 155, and he admitted of the attempt to establish a procedure for a national survey that 'the method tried out has not been a complete success'.[22] The MOH for Rotherham argued that the term 'problem family' was unfortunate, suggesting that 'there is, of course, no clear-cut division between respectable citizens and those whose habits make them a nuisance and a burden to the rest of the community'.[23] And criticisms were voiced by Dr E. O. Lewis, who had worked on the survey of the social problem group for the Wood Report. In February 1952, Lewis wrote that the results were disappointing since variations in the number of notifications indicated they were far from thorough, and suggested that the MOsH knew little about social problems in their areas.[24]

The role of Richard Titmuss in the problem family debate was particularly interesting. As we have seen, Titmuss was one of the original members of the Committee, but he thought that rehabilitation deserved more emphasis, and quietly stopped attending the meetings. Titmuss used this as an excuse to distance himself from the final report when it was published in 1952, and he asked that his name be removed from the list of contributors.[25] The reasons for Titmuss's embarrassment were not difficult to see. C. P. Blacker admitted that 'none of us is unaware of the defects in these inquiries or of the pitfalls involved in comparing them', and the pilot surveys were best thought of as 'experiments in method'.[26] Nevertheless the final report claimed that the five pilot surveys (Warwickshire had been dropped) had found 379 problem families. In terms of incidence, there were 2.6 problem families per 1,000 families in North Kensington; 1.4 in Bristol; 1.2 in the West Riding of Yorkshire; 3.5 in Rotherham; and 6.2 in Luton.[27] Blacker acknowledged that some tables, such as those on the physical appearance of housewives, where impressions had simply been recorded by health visitors, were rather subjective. He attributed the 'ineducability' of parents to mental subnormality and to their 'weak and vacillating characters', and he argued that the families were characterised by their inability to benefit from education, by the dirt and chaos of their homes, and the high number of children. Heartened by a recent Government circular on child neglect, Blacker suggested that MOsH should co-ordinate future surveys of the problem family.[28]

The Eugenics Society now turned its attention from problem families to the theme of 'promising families'. More generally, other aspects of post-war Britain, including the creation of the welfare state, changing attitudes towards mental health, and the baby boom, contributed to a decisive turning point in intellectual life, after which eugenics had less influence on public policy.[29] The 'mentally handicapped', for example, had proved that they could work, and it was no longer possible to argue that labour market failure was caused by genetics.[30] Even so, there remained a eugenic interest in problem families into the 1960s, particularly in connection with birth control. In 1965, for example, it was reported that a domiciliary birth control service had been started for problem families in Southampton, funded in part through the Marie Stopes Foundation. The author wrote that 'eleven families have left the area – the nomadic instinct is noticeable in these families; they move about, believing that the distant fields are greener, and to keep track of them is often impossible'.[31] C. P. Blacker remained involved in a sterilisation project for the Simon Population Trust. As late as 1966, he wrote that 'for problem families sterilisation is especially appropriate. Here socio-economic indications commonly overlap therapeutic ones, especially when the mental health of the mother is in question'.[32] This then provides the link between the problem family debate and the notion of the cycle of deprivation. As we will see subsequently, it was the problem family concept rather than the American culture of poverty notion that was the main influence on Sir Keith Joseph and his cycle of deprivation theory.

Although it is a commonplace that the Second World War witnessed the evolution of universal health services and the creation of the welfare state, less is known about the fortunes of voluntary organisations in this period. These included existing charities like the Red Cross, and semi-official bodies such as the Women's Voluntary Service. To these we can add the Pacifist Service Units that were formed by small groups of conscientious objectors in a few large cities. The most prominent Pacifist Service Unit was the Liverpool branch formed in October 1940. It began work in the air raid shelter in the crypt of Holy Trinity Church, in St Anne Street. Here the workers tried to find billets for homeless people, and, by 1941, were helping individuals and families through emergency hostels. Many of the Unit's volunteers were members of the Society of Friends, and the approach was essentially pacifist and religious, with the workers identifying closely with their clients. As the chairman of the Liverpool Unit later wrote of his colleagues, 'they were cut off from, and, in some measure, ostracised by society, and they found in the men, women and children in the hostels a like group of people'.[33]

Although the Pacifist Service Units prided themselves on their independence from professional organisations, their growing interest in casework was an important step in the evolution of social work. The Liverpool Unit, for example, took on casework at the end of 1941, by providing more personal help to families and individuals in need. By May 1942, it had begun to classify the stages that 'rehabilitation families' passed through. Its approach to social work was one that was innovative and relied on the personal relationship between workers and clients, but which nonetheless stressed the value of practical help of a physical nature and was essentially amateur. The Unit noted that what it termed 'rehabilitation families' posed particularly difficult challenges; by 1944 it was diagnosis, and the problems of those families deemed 'baffling cases', that were receiving more attention. The Units were generally small, consisting of a fieldwork leader, a secretary, and a team of caseworkers. Caseworkers usually handled about 15 cases, and casework meetings were held weekly. Training was provided, and some workers were graduates in social science. The emphasis on casework was taken up by the Manchester and London Units, and a new National Casework Committee was formed.[34] Thus, the Pacifist Service Units had their own distinctive agenda, but also adopted an approach that was to become an important stepping stone for the emerging social work profession.

The 'rehabilitation families' were the forerunners of the problem families, and by the end of the Second World War, the Pacifist Service Units had become closely identified with the latter concept. In 1944, Tom Stephens of the London Unit wrote that problem families were characterised by a combination of irregular income, but also by mismanagement. He argued that aspects of their condition, such as their 'disordered' lives, the fact that the children were often late for school, and the 'inefficiency' of the mothers and fathers showed that the main cause was one of 'character'. However 'outside' factors, such as poverty, illness, and large families were also important. The problem, then, was both a failure of character and the pressure of circumstances. Stephens wrote that the solution was the restoration of normal family life. He wrote that:

> the problem family are left untouched by much of the help they need: they stay behind when their neighbours are rehoused, their children are not taken to the clinics, and the most undernourished child never gets his free milk and vitamins.[35]

Despite close links with the Eugenics Society, both in terms of personnel and with regard to how they conceptualised the families, the approach of the Family

Service Units was one in which ideas of biological determinism were mitigated by humane values, which saw worth in every person.[36]

Further insights into the way that the Pacifist Service Units viewed problem families were provided in a book edited by Stephens and published in November 1945. It followed on from a conference on casework held in Liverpool in 1944. The book set out the nature of the 'problem', provided a series of descriptions of families considered typical, reviewed the work of the Pacifist Service Units, and appealed for additional funds. Stephens echoed the Eugenics Society in arguing that, while the problem family could not be defined, it was easy to recognise. Thus the problem family lived in a filthy home and possessed little furniture, the mother could not manage the home or the children, and the father was in irregular employment such as casual labouring. At the same time, his prognosis was more hopeful, with the solution consisting of 'personal treatment for the individual families'.[37] In the estimation of Stephens, problem families were essentially 'the misfits who fail to benefit from the provisions which suffice for average people'.[38] Stephens argued that the strength of the Pacifist Service Unit approach derived from its combination of professional competence and warmth and sincerity, but he admitted that it was founded on practical help, so that 'cleaning, decorating, removing, repairing and disinfesting were the first forms of service, and on this basis the rest was built'. Thus the hope was that, through practical example and training, the problem families could be educated into 'the highest possible standards of social and domestic life'.[39]

The book sold well and both publicised the work of the Pacifist Service Units and propagated the concept of the problem family more widely. Some reviewers interpreted its findings as being further evidence of the existence of a residuum or 'a kind of social sediment of persons and families'.[40] Others were less interested in the number of families and thought that practical work was the correct approach, arguing that to treat the family members and ignore the home would be 'to treat the symptoms and leave the focus of disease untouched'.[41] The Pacifist Service Units had always intended to continue their work in peacetime and, in January 1947, a new national organisation named Family Service Units was formed. Discussions held at this time also indicated that the *Our Towns* report had provided important support for this work. New Units were formed in 1948 in several London boroughs and gradually spread to provincial cities so that, by 1954, there were ten, with two in London and others in Liverpool, Manchester, Sheffield, Leicester, Birmingham, York, Bristol, and Bradford. From 1954, the Ministry of Health allowed local authorities to provide grants towards the work of the Family Service Units. Even so, while a skeleton national organisation had been created, the influence of the Liverpool Unit remained significant.

Some of the Family Service Units made attempts to adopt a more innovative approach, by experimenting with groups for adolescent girls and camps, extending their work to cover new housing estates, and by appointing full-time workers who possessed academic qualifications in social work. Yet, in many ways, the approach seemed little different to that of the Pacifist Service Units in the early 1940s. While the new National Secretary argued that phrases such as 'derelict families' and 'unsatisfactory households' were not interchangeable, and the terms 'social problem group' and 'problem families' not synonymous, his language remained eugenic in tone. Moreover, his emphasis on the defining characteristics of the families echoed that of Stephens, so that eating habits, for example, continued to be used as a benchmark for social norms.[42] This approach was replicated at the local level. Workers in the Liverpool Unit rejected a more professional approach, arguing they were successful only in 'a warm sympathetic relationship of friendship and involvement', while their Chairman admitted in 1963 that the work was continuing as it had begun, 'with an offer of practical help made in a spirit of friendship'.[43] The Family Service Units appointed a research worker in the late 1950s, but his findings lacked originality and essentially drew on the ideas of others. One article, for example, concluded that workers should act as parents, claiming that 'extreme immaturity' was a common characteristic among problem families.[44]

The approach of the Family Service Units remained embedded in the experiences of the early 1940s, and belated attempts to assess the effectiveness of casework were unconvincing.[45] Yet this is to miss much of the importance of the Units, which lay more in their contact with more influential organisations and individuals. Many of those who sought to professionalise social work looked to the Units for a viable alternative to the approach of local health departments. One survey of social work in London, for example, wrote that the local Unit was 'both unique and extremely effective in its methods'.[46] Similarly, the Younghusband report on the role of social workers claimed the Units had shown that problem families were not a homogeneous group, and had influenced the work of local authorities.[47] Particularly significant were the close links forged with academics in university departments, illustrated in the involvement of Unit members in the 'rediscovery of poverty' and in the formation of the Child Poverty Action Group.[48] In these ways, the Units played a key role in the development of the emerging social work profession. However, most significant in this context was their role in the concept of the problem family, with which the Family Service Units remained most closely identified.

Some members of the medical establishment were sceptical of the value of the Family Service Units. One review concluded that 'the cure of this social disease is often impossible, and until the causes of family failure are better understood prevention cannot begin to operate'.[49] In part, this attitude reflected a desire to prevent the Units from encroaching on the empire of local MOsH. These doctors had originally been appointed by local authorities in the late nineteenth century, to monitor public health and to tackle the rise in infectious disease that had accompanied the growth of large cities. In the interwar period, MOsH had begun to treat tuberculosis and venereal disease, to manage personal health services for mothers and infants, and supervise municipal hospitals. Under the National Health Service Act, the MOsH lost their hospitals and clinics, and the role of public health was to become increasingly problematic in the post-war period. In many ways, the involvement of the MOsH with problem families, and the subsequent policy of the Ministry of Health on family welfare, represented an attempt to come to terms with the impact of these wider changes.

The *Our Towns* report on the evacuation of schoolchildren, published in 1943, was the key source for the concept of the problem family. Towards the end of the Second World War, half a dozen or so MOsH also began to publish articles in their professional journals on problem families in their respective areas. It was these MOsH who subsequently were linked with the Eugenics Society's Problem Families Committee. One was Dr R. C. Wofinden, whom we met at the start of this chapter, subsequently MOH for Bristol. He argued that 'derelict families' were those with 'social defectiveness of such a degree that they require care, supervision and control for their own well-being or for the well-being of others'.[50] Wofinden thought that the 'ascertainment and disposal' of mental defectives might be improved through sterilisation and segregation, but also advocated training centres and further research.[51] Though the doctors may have had similar motives for becoming interested in problem families, they came up with radically different solutions, illustrating that, while some had a lingering affection for eugenics, others were more in tune with the Pacifist Service Units.

Another was Dr C. O. Stallybrass, deputy MOH for Liverpool. She wrote that *Our Towns* had revealed that 'the norm of many areas is horribly low', and defined problem families as those 'presenting an abnormal amount of subnormal behaviour over prolonged periods with a marked tendency to backsliding'.[52] Stallybrass recommended both prevention and treatment, including marriage guidance, bodies similar to the Pacifist Service Units, and hostels and training homes for mothers and children.[53] Like Wofinden, Stallybrass placed a heavy emphasis on characteristics. She wrote that:

> If one makes a list of their unpleasant aspects of social life, one will invariably find that these families offend in several of them, e.g., squalor; vermin and dirt; truantism – the whole family may be discovered in bed at an hour when the children should be in school; delinquency; indecent overcrowding; failure to pay the rent; irregular and uncertain mealtimes; an almost complete absence of furniture especially inadequacy of cooking utensils, and of beds and bedding; for these latter they are frequent applicants to charitable agencies, largely on account of the insanitary habits of the children, or even of the adults; these insanitary habits, in turn, give a characteristic odour to the house.[54]

The language employed by Stallybrass was remarkable. She wrote that problem families were 'like animals in a cave, or a cage – often a cage of their own making', and were 'like rudderless barques with flapping sails drifting on the social tide, driven hither and thither by any momentary gust of emotion'.[55]

Another of the MOsH involved with the Eugenics Society was Dr S. W. Savage, MOH for Hertfordshire. He stated that 'problem mothers' did not give their children a minimum level of care, refused to co-operate with health visitors, and did not use the advice given to them.[56] Dr J. L. Burn, MOH for Salford, suggested that the problem family was one where 'the conditions of the home are dirty and disordered, and where the care of the children is bad'.[57] Burn organised the making of a short film strip on the issue of the problem family. Dr Fraser Brockington, MOH for the West Riding of Yorkshire, was also closely associated with the Eugenics Society. He advocated registers, changes in the law, and a new approach to delinquency, but also thought local authorities should appoint social workers, arguing that 'what is required is someone who will take off his coat and get down to restitution of civilised conditions'.[58] In many respects, the authors of these articles, and their emphasis on characteristics, had an important influence on the approach subsequently adopted by the Eugenics Society. More generally, these doctors seized on the issue of the problem family to illustrate that they were at the cutting edge of social welfare, and to prevent further erosion of their medical specialism.

In the 1950s, further articles appeared in public health journals on problem families in a range of rural and urban areas, including Herefordshire, Sheffield, Worcestershire, London, and Southampton.[59] The concept continued to be propagated in textbooks for MOsH and other health professionals. Uncertain attempts were made to incorporate the notion of the problem family into the new discipline of social medicine. One Professor of Social Medicine argued that the families were characterised by dirty homes, primitive cooking arrangements, verminous children, and erratic time-keeping. Indeed, he wrote that the characteristics of the problem family were so distinctive 'that they may fairly be deemed pathological, in the sense that the family as a group is diseased'.[60] Some of these textbooks were written by former MOsH who, by the mid-1950s, had become academics in the new discipline of social medicine. At Manchester, Professor Fraser Brockington acknowledged that there was no precise definition and that each family was unique, but still argued, nonetheless, that 'the problem family is one of the great social diseases of modern times'.[61] The concept was also promoted within particular groups of health professionals. A textbook for health visitors, for example, included the problem family in a chapter on the 'abnormal family'. The suggested characteristics were a lack of order; the weekly income was 'wrongly' spent; 'bad' feeding; the furniture and other equipment were poor; the sleeping arrangements were unsuitable; and the clothing was inadequate.[62]

This writing was matched by some limited activity at the local level. Some local authorities had taken action in the early 1940s. Norwich, for instance, had appointed a 'home advisor' who scrubbed floors, cleaned children, and taught mothers the basics of mending, cooking, and household management.[63] However, while the Ministry of Health monitored the wave of interest in problem families, it did not take action, perhaps because it was preoccupied with other changes in the structure of health services. It was only in the early 1950s, and following the publication of the survey sponsored by the Eugenics Society, that the term 'problem family' cropped up in new Ministry of Health circulars on child neglect and family break-ups. First, in July 1950, a joint circular by the Home Office, Ministry of Health, and Ministry of Education sought to tackle child neglect, and avoid the need to remove children from homes. This was to be achieved mainly through improved co-operation by statutory and voluntary agencies.[64] Second, in a further circular issued in 1954 it was suggested that local authorities should use health visitors and home helps to tackle problem families.[65] Henceforth, this area of social welfare began to be included in the work of many local health departments.

Official reports suddenly began to mention problem families. In 1951, for example, the Chief Medical Officer wrote that, with improvements in child health, more time could be devoted to the problem families that comprised 2–3% of families in most areas.[66] In particular, the Ministry of Health encouraged local authorities to draw on the recently-created home help service, arguing that these women could often make families more resourceful and independent.[67] In the same period, these families began to appear in reports on the School Health Service. One report commented that children with head lice tended to be the offspring of problem families, and that treatment was particularly difficult owing to the ignorance, neglect and indifference of the parents.[68] Other surveys used the phrase in passing. The report of a government working party on the future of health visiting commented that problem families were 'merely the most obvious sign of the social ill-health that many think is endemic in a modern industrial society'.[69] While the issue was a minor feature of health provision as a whole, the Ministry of Health clearly regarded the families in clinical terms, as having a disease with recognisable causes and symptoms and which could be cured through practical help.

Certainly these ideas were translated into practical reality since many local health departments, in both urban and rural areas, began to make provision for the problem family. Herefordshire, for example, appointed a welfare worker for this purpose in 1949, arguing that with the 'rough dirty woman of independent spirit' it was best to concentrate on the children.[70] In Bristol, where the MOH remained uneasy about the problem of definitions, the local authority made sure health visitors had small caseloads, drew on the resources of the Family Service

Unit, and also sent families to recuperation centres.[71] Other local authorities, including Leicester and Kent, preferred to rely on their large pool of home helps.[72] The approach taken usually depended on the age of the MOH, the relative strengths of the health visitor and home help services, and the degree to which voluntary organisations could be relied upon. Whatever method was employed, it can be seen with hindsight to have been characterised by a degree of self-confidence and complacency. Indeed one medical journal claimed in 1957 that 'most medical officers of health know personally or through their health visitors, the great majority of problem families in their areas'.[73]

In the 1960s, the concept remained alive at the local level in many local authorities. Although formal responsibility for this issue had been transferred to Children's Departments through the 1963 Children and Young Persons Act, the health dimension continued to be important.[74] In Sheffield, for example, the Health Department carried out follow-up surveys on the problem families they had supposedly identified in the 1950s. This study concluded that, overall, housing and living standards had improved, as part of the general rise in living standards, but employment and child care continued to pose problems.[75] There was much evidence that a judgemental approach continued to prevail. It was reported, for instance, that families were irresponsible in their attitude to money, with the authors writing that:

> articles commonly found in households where the family income does not cover bare necessities because of heavy debts, include tape recorders, radiograms, cocktail cabinets, and quite often one or more large pedigree dogs.[76]

The Sheffield studies underlined the need for contraception for large families, and it was in this respect that the concept of the problem family, and eugenic language in general, was most prominent at the national level. Many local health departments targeted family planning services at their problem families, and this was a policy advocated by central government departments.[77] In 1968, for example, the Chief Medical Officer wrote that family planning was particularly important for families characterised by 'squalor, ill-health, an inability to cope and limited intelligence'.[78] Public health was usually the outlet for these ideas, but the term 'problem family' remained attractive to other medical specialisms, like psychiatry, into the 1970s.[79] What was particularly striking was that the concept displayed remarkable resilience and longevity, at least in medical circles, long after it had been discredited among the emerging social work profession.

Noel Timms has argued that social workers have shown little interest in the history of their profession, and that the story of social work remains 'largely untold'.[80] Although the *Our Towns* survey of evacuation did much to promote the concept of the problem family, other reports published in the 1940s were more critical, suggesting for example that the answer lay with trained social workers.[81] Moreover, as we have seen, the Pacifist Service Units, with their emphasis on rehabilitation through social casework, had also provided an important counter to the claims of the Eugenics Society. Although the British Federation of Social Workers had been established in 1936, social work remained in its infancy and the first generic course was only established at the London School of Economics in 1954. The numbers of social workers on the ground remained small into the late 1960s. As social workers grew in confidence, however, many became increasingly critical of the concept of the problem family, and of the work of local health departments. In this sense, the issue became bound up in the 1960s with the wider struggle between the public health and social work professions for control of the personal social services.[82]

When the Eugenics Society published its report on problem families in 1952, many of the medical journals carried favourable reviews, claiming that these families displayed consistent symptoms.[83] However, many of the social work journals were more critical, questioning whether the label 'problem family' was useful and proposing that rehabilitation deserved more emphasis.[84] Other practitioners in new specialisms such as psychiatric social work were also sceptical. Elizabeth Irvine, for example, thought that casework by psychiatric social workers was the most useful approach and was critical of the Eugenics Society's survey, noting that 'problem families are easy to recognise and describe, but surprisingly hard to define'.[85] Workers employed by organisations such as the Family Welfare Association agreed on the symptoms and definitions, but concurred that more study was required. Furthermore, other surveys on related subjects suggested that local authorities should increase the scale of casework. In his study of health visiting in Manchester and Salford, for example, David Donnison argued of problem families that 'some of the complaints made against such people by those in the social services sound like the grumbles of respectable citizens against neighbours with a more Bohemian way of life'.[86]

These reservations and doubts were strengthened by academic research which, from the mid-1950s, began to examine the term 'problem family' with a greater degree of intellectual rigour. Some of these theorists had previously worked in Family Service Units, and many were keen to establish the distinctiveness of social work as an emerging professional group. Noel Timms, for example, noted in 1954 that casework was being taken up by social workers, arguing that 'the so-called "problem family" is becoming respectable'.[87] In a similar vein, he argued the following year that the term covered an extremely heterogeneous group, and suggested earlier studies were essentially descriptive and lacked theoretical sophistication. He doubted whether the social problem group and problem family were synonymous, and thought sociological factors had been ignored. Drawing on theories about deviance, he examined the attitudes of problem families towards goals and standards, concluding that some displayed the 'retreatism' previously described by Robert Merton.[88] It is interesting that Merton himself acknowledged this work, writing that examples of 'retreatism' had recently been identified among problem families in England.[89] Indeed, these links between Britain and the USA are worthy of further examination.

Supported by the Family Service Units and encouraged by academics such as Richard Titmuss, by then Professor of Social Administration at the London School of Economics, Timms elaborated these ideas in other publications. In 1956, for example, he argued that 'previous research into the problem family suffers from deficiencies in theory and in research method; it has proceeded largely on unexamined biological assumptions and has relied on the techniques of the social survey'.[90] This work culminated in the book *The Problem of the 'Problem Family'*, which was co-written by Timms and Fred Philp and published in 1957. In the foreword, Titmuss argued that the debate about the problem family had been conducted 'in a singularly uncritical manner' so that 'what knowledge has been gained from all these inquiries has not accumulated on any theoretical foundations'.[91] Philp and Timms noted that no satisfactory definition had emerged and that previous writers had usually avoided the issue by stating that the problem family was 'hard to define, but easy to recognise'.[92] Of the emphasis on cleanliness and dirt, they commented that social workers often used middle-class, rather than working-class standards. They noted that the deployment of health visitors by local authorities rested on an assumption that the problem was largely one of faulty domestic and child-care standards, and were sceptical about the value of co-ordinating committees. Overall, they concluded that previous studies had failed to show how behavioural and structural factors related to each other, and suggested that ideas about heredity had obscured the value of sociological and psychological theory.[93]

The book was a significant turning point, both in the history of the problem family and in the context of the wider struggle to establish the professional identity of social work. Not surprisingly, the social work journals reviewed it favourably. David Donnison, for example, now suggested that the term 'problem family' should be abandoned, arguing that earlier work on the subject was 'a shocking indictment of the intellectual level of much that is written about social work and social policy'.[94] Similarly, others were increasingly critical of the co-ordinating committees that many local authorities had established in 1950. One study doubted whether the MOH was 'sufficiently cognisant of social work needs to be able to use the committee effectively'; argued that trained caseworkers were needed; and began to consider the idea of a family department.[95] Others summed up the approach of this group when they wrote of the problem family that 'it is the complexity and depth of its individual problems which need to be understood and dealt with, not the presenting symptoms which are offensive to society'.[96]

These articles reflected the growing professionalism of social work, and a more general trend away from ideas of biological determinism towards social science. As we have seen, the Younghusband report looked more favourably on the work of Family Service Units than on what the Eugenics Society had done, and suggested that problem families were only an entity in that 'they represent a problem to society'.[97] The Younghusband report had argued that psychology, psychiatry, and sociology were more influential than ideas about genetics, but it was an attack on social casework that was the central concern of Barbara Wootton's *Social Pathology and Social Science*, also published in 1959. Wootton noted that the earlier surveys had been motivated by ideas about social pathology and were marked by techniques and findings of poor quality. In particular, Wootton argued that previous work on the social problem group had failed to distinguish between personal inadequacy and economic misfortune, and suggested that it had not 'advanced beyond the descriptive stage, establishing the recurrences of recognisable syndromes of problem behaviour'.[98]

Although Wootton's work hinted at an important sea change in thinking, it is important to appreciate that the approach of this lobby was not one of simple consensus. There were differences of interpretation between the various interest groups that were subsumed, for convenience, under the social work umbrella. Psychiatric social workers, for example, had their own agenda, with the concept of 'immaturity' being one area of disagreement.[99] Moreover, some studies were able to combine a more sophisticated attitude to other aspects of social welfare with a continuing belief in the problem family. A study of unmarried mothers, for example, adopted a sympathetic approach that diverged sharply from the earlier pathological emphasis, but also claimed that the 10% of children in problem families were 'more trouble to the authorities than all the rest put together'.[100] Nevertheless, there was evidence of an uneasy coalition that was broadly critical of the Eugenics Society and of the approach subsequently adopted by local health departments. In 1962, Noel Timms wrote that 'we are still faced with a variety of "symptoms" but no one is quite sure what they are symptoms of'.[101] Similarly, a local case-study of delinquency suggested that failure was not on the part of problem families, but in the inadequacies of social services.[102] Other studies specifically excluded the 'problem families' known to the local authority, and argued that co-ordinating committees simply provided a forum for the outlet of underlying medical and social work tensions.[103]

The changing climate of opinion was particularly evident in successive editions of Penelope Hall's guide to social services. Although she had devoted a whole chapter to problem families in the first edition published in 1952, by 1965 she emphasised integration into the community rather than separate 'treatment' and hoped that the term would disappear.[104] These changes both reflected the earlier Ingleby report on juvenile delinquency, and anticipated many of the recommendations of the Seebohm Committee on social services departments.[105] In this sense, the issue of the problem family became bound up with the wider struggle between the public health and social work professions for control of the personal social services. The Ingleby Committee distinguished between the problem family and the 'family with a problem', and it was more critical of co-ordinating committees than of Family Service Units.[106] Following the 1963 Children and Young Persons Act, in many areas it was the Children's rather than the Health Departments that had the responsibility for problem families. In many ways, the Seebohm Committee represented the culmination of this particular debate on the respective roles of the public health and social work professions. On the specific issue of the problem family, the report hinted that work of this kind should not be undertaken by local health departments, argued that co-ordinating committees had not been effective, and thought that health visitors could not operate as social workers.[107] The creation of social services departments in 1970 represented a crushing defeat to the health departments, which subsequently disappeared in the 1974 health service reorganisation. It was an intriguing irony that Richard Titmuss, an original member of the Eugenics Society's Problem Families Committee, was also one of the main forces behind the Seebohm Report. In this respect the Seebohm Committee accelerated the process already begun through the 1963 Children and Young Persons Act, in taking these areas of social work away from local MOsH.

The case of the problem family therefore represents a further step in the evolution of the concept of the underclass, effectively linking the notion of the social problem group of the 1930s with the theory of the cycle of deprivation that was to become prevalent in the 1970s. In this chapter, we have tried to explore the history of the problem family in terms of its usefulness to a range of interest groups. It is easy to exaggerate the differences between these interest groups, and arguable that the overlaps in ideas and membership are equally important. Nevertheless four broad approaches can be distinguished. The Eugenics Society, which had taken up the social problem group in the 1930s, sought to use the concept of the problem family at a time when wider political and demographic trends were unfavourable to its objectives. The Pacifist Service Units, on the other hand, began as a group of conscientious objectors who invented an essentially amateur and self-styled branch of social work, and whose identity remained bound up with the concept of the problem family. The medical establishment, and MOsH especially, became interested in the problem family at a time when the decline of infectious disease raised questions about the need for public health. In the 1950s, efforts to tackle problem families became part of the work of local public health departments, often working in tandem with Family Service Units. However the concept of the problem family itself was also coming under increasing criticism from a broad coalition of practitioners and theorists in the emerging field of social work, who were opposed to the approach favoured by the Eugenics Society and others, and who used this aspect of social welfare as a means of establishing the identity of their own profession.

In many respects, the problem family was a more hopeful concept than that of the social problem group since, apart from the Eugenics Society, the emphasis was on rehabilitation rather than sterilisation and segregation. Several strands of the notion reflected the wider economic, political, and social climate of the 1950s. In the first place, the focus was very much on women, reflecting the strength of contemporary views on the traditional nuclear family and attitudes towards the place of the wife and mother in the home. By contrast, the father was a shadowy figure. Second, what was most striking was the stress on behavioural rather than structural factors, with child care rather than poverty being emphasised. In this, the concept of the problem family illustrated the perception that most people were enjoying a period of full employment, along with new universal health and welfare services. Third, the concept relied to an extent on the failure to develop effective and robust methodologies for social science research, and it was only belatedly that the Eugenics Society survey came in for sustained criticism. In the 1960s, with the rediscovery of poverty, the emphasis on social casework implicit in the term 'problem family' was to become increasingly unacceptable to social workers who favoured structural explanations.

What is perhaps most interesting is whether there is a linear trend in the history of the concept of the underclass. How exactly did the social problem group mutate into the problem family, and then change again into the cycle of deprivation formulation? There are some important differences. While the history of the problem family was very interesting in the 1950s it was nonetheless a debate that was contained within professional circles, and did not have the popular or media dimensions associated with similar debates in the 1980s. Interestingly too, it was a concept that evolved in wartime, while we have previously argued that in the case of the social residuum the idea evaporated with the advent of full employment during the First World War. These are important questions, to which we will return in the conclusion. For the moment we turn to the 1960s, and to events on the other side of the Atlantic, where the notion of the culture of poverty was to play a significant role in similar debates in the United States.

5

Chasing the Culture of Poverty

In Britain, as we have seen, developments in public health and social policy were influenced by the theme of the problem family into the 1960s. On the other side of the Atlantic, in the United States, the 1960s saw the emergence of the 'War on Poverty'. Given the belief in the 'American Dream', the discovery of poverty was arguably more disturbing to Americans than to their British counterparts. Introduced by the Kennedy administration, but continued in the Johnson administration, a wide-ranging new programme that came to be called the 'War on Poverty' sought to eradicate poverty once and for all. Amendments to the Social Security Act, in 1962 and 1967, aimed to provide training schemes, day nurseries, and family planning advice to make mothers self-supporting. Another strand was provided by community action, embracing techniques that had originally been employed in developing countries. New structures and initiatives that were set up at this time included the Office of Economic Opportunity, and within it, the Community Action Programme. By 1969, there were 972 Community Action Areas in the United States.[1]

Those involved in these programmes later admitted that it remained unclear whether the target was really the individual or the community.[2] It was argued by some, for example, that community action was emphasised too heavily, and that greater attention should have been paid to creating jobs and raising income levels. These critics suggested that little thought was given to the difference between poverty (a lack of money) and a culture of poverty (essentially a lifestyle).[3] In part this was because the 'War on Poverty' was influenced so heavily by concepts like lower-class culture and the culture of poverty. In 1964, for example, when presenting the Economic Opportunity Act to Congress, Sargent Shriver, Director of the Peace Corps and a special assistant to the President for the poverty programme, said:

> being poor … is a rigid way of life. It is handed down from generation to generation in a cycle of inadequate education, inadequate homes, inadequate jobs and stunted ambitions. It is a peculiar axiom of poverty that the poor are poor because they earn little and they also earn little because they are poor.[4]

As this quotation indicates, for some the fundamental question remained unresolved – are people poor because they behave differently, or do they behave differently because they are poor?

This chapter examines the way that the theory of the culture of poverty influenced these debates in the United States, and to a lesser extent in Britain. It explores the emergence of the culture of poverty as put forward by Oscar Lewis, and an earlier history of writing about lower-class culture, and the influence of both on the Moynihan Report (1965). We also look at the critical reception the concept received in the late 1960s; the extent to which it was imported into Britain; and how it influenced initiatives such as the Educational Priority Areas. The culture of poverty provides a further step in the history of the underclass, successfully linking the theme of the problem family in the 1950s, to the concept of the cycle of deprivation in the 1970s. One final point on language is that we retain the use of the term 'negro' as it was commonplace at the time, even though now rightly regarded as a stigmatising device.

Alice O'Connor locates the emergence and influence of the culture of poverty in terms of wider postwar changes that affected social scientific thinking about the poor. First, the political economy of affluence, that created the idea that America was becoming a classless society. Second, the postwar institutionalisation of the behavioural sciences, which encouraged a psychological emphasis on class and race. Third, the resurgence of middle-class domesticity in Cold War ideology and culture, which reinforced the patriarchical family as a psychological and social norm. Fourth, the rise of poverty as a global political issue. She argues that all of these converged in the idea of the culture of poverty, and more broadly in the paradox of poverty in the affluent USA. O'Connor writes that although the culture of poverty was rooted in an earlier era, it can be understood 'as an expression of the broader trends in postwar political economy, politics, and culture that reshaped liberalism as an ideology as well as its approach to social knowledge and to the poor'.[5]

The culture of poverty hypothesis can be located in the context of earlier writing on blacks and migrant groups. However in other respects its source was outside the United States, since it was generated by anthropological fieldwork. What is clear is that it was the creation of one individual – Oscar Lewis, Professor of Anthropology at the University of Illinois from 1948. Lewis had previously carried out fieldwork in Tepoztlan in Mexico, but from the mid-1950s his work took a new course and he worked increasingly with tape recorders. He was never again to do as much historical work, or as thorough an ethnography, as he had carried out in Tepoztlan. Susan Rigdon, Lewis's biographer, argues that he now committed himself to areas of investigation in which he was ill-equipped to carry out research. One of these was his involvement with the culture of poverty thesis.[6]

From 1956, Lewis began to look at lower-class culture patterns in Mexico City, reported in his book *Five Families: Mexican Case Studies in the Culture of Poverty* (1959). In this work, Lewis sought to present a picture of daily life in five Mexican families, four of which were in a lower income group. Yet at this point he had not provided a description of the culture of poverty. He wrote that his purpose had been to 'contribute to our understanding of the culture of poverty in contemporary Mexico and, insofar as the poor throughout the world have something in common, to lower-class life in general'.[7] But at this stage it was just a means of linking two things he was interested in – culture and poverty. Lewis went on to investigate this further in *The Children of Sanchez* (1961). He warned readers that it was important to distinguish between poverty and a culture of poverty, and pointed out that not all people who live in poverty share a common subculture. But he used the phrase inconsistently, and failed to make it clear that most of his informants did not live in a culture of poverty.[8] Lewis was further influenced in his interest in the culture of poverty by clinical psychology, through his friendship with Carolina Lujan. It was this that provided the basis for his list of the characteristic traits in the culture of poverty. Lewis was later to find that he had gone too far in explaining the culture of poverty by reference to psychological damage.[9]

Fieldwork in Puerto Rico gave Lewis the chance to test out his theory, and the classic account of the culture of poverty appeared in the introduction to *La Vida* (1966), although this was simply an expanded version of the introduction to *The Children of Sanchez*. In this work, Lewis compared 100 low-income Puerto Rican families from four slums in Greater San Juan with their equivalents in New York. He wrote that as an anthropologist he had tried to understand poverty as 'a culture or, more accurately, as a subculture with its own structure and rationale, as a way of life which is passed down from generation to generation along family lines'.[10] Thus the culture of poverty was not just a matter of economic deprivation, but had a positive connotation. It had advantages for the poor, and indeed it was arguable that without it, they would be unable to carry on. According to Lewis, the culture of poverty flourished in particular types of societies. But certain features had to be in place. These included a cash economy; high unemployment; low wages; a lack of social, political, or economic organisation for the low-income population; the existence of a bilateral kinship system; and the existence, in the dominant class, of a set of values that stressed the accumulation of wealth and property, upward mobility, and thrift. Thus the culture of poverty showed how the poor both reflected the environment in which they found themselves, and adapted their culture accordingly. It was 'both an adaptation and a reaction of the poor to their marginal position in a class-stratified, highly individuated, capitalistic society'.[11]

Lewis argued that the culture of poverty could be studied from a number of viewpoints, of which the first was the relationship between the subculture and the larger society. One characteristic of adults as opposed to children was the way that the poor did not participate in, or were not integrated by, the major institutions of the larger society. People with the culture of poverty, it was alleged, did not belong to trade unions, were not members of political parties, were not participants in the welfare system, and did not make use of banks. It was this 'low level of organisation' that gave the culture of poverty its marginal quality in a highly complex and organised society. Even so, Lewis was quick to point out that the culture of poverty was not just an adaptation. Once established, it tended to perpetuate itself through the generations, because of its effect on children. By the age of six or seven, argued Lewis, children 'have usually absorbed the basic values and attitudes of their subculture and are not psychologically geared to take full advantage of changing conditions or increased opportunities which may occur in their lifetime'.[12]

Lewis claimed that the families who displayed the features of the culture of poverty had various other characteristics. At the family level, these included the absence of childhood as a 'prolonged and protected stage in the life cycle', early initiation into sex, abandoned wives and children, authoritarianism, and lack of privacy. At the individual level, individuals were said to suffer from feelings of marginality, helplessness, dependence, and inferiority. Other significant 'traits' included a high incidence of maternal deprivation, a 'strong present-time orientation with relatively little ability to defer gratification and to plan for the future', and a sense of resignation and fatalism.[13] However, Lewis was also keen to distinguish between a culture of poverty and poverty *per se*, and he pointed to countries where the poor did not have a way of life that could be described as a culture of poverty. These included many primitive or preliterate peoples studied by anthropologists; the lower castes in India; the Jews of eastern Europe; and socialist countries like Cuba. Lewis argued that the culture of poverty existed in countries like Mexico that were at an early free-enterprise stage of capitalism, whereas the United States had much poverty but little culture of poverty. Overall, Lewis argued that improved economic opportunities were not the whole answer. It was easier to eliminate poverty than the culture of poverty.[14]

Susan Rigdon points out that by this stage, Lewis was heavily dependent on collaborators and assistants, and his project had become unmanageably large. The culture of poverty was a dramatic yet conveniently vague phrase that helped to call attention to the problem of the poor.[15] Of all Oscar Lewis's voluminous writings, it was the relatively brief section that proposed the existence of a culture of poverty that proved to be the most influential. It was reprinted in numerous different collections, and had a profound influence on the 'War on Poverty'. Historian Michael Katz has noted that the culture of poverty had complex origins. It originated among liberals, and was used to justify more active, generous, and interventionist policies. This in turn, reflected a larger assumption in the liberalism of the time – that dependent people were mainly helpless and passive, and, without the leadership of liberal intellectuals, were unable to break the cycles of deprivation that characterised their lives.[16] By the early 1960s, American commentators who were reporting on the rediscovery of poverty began to discuss this phenomenon in terms of a culture of poverty or underclass. Michael Harrington's book, *The Other America* (1962), for example, was widely read, including by President Kennedy himself. Harrington presented an eye-witness account of poverty in contemporary America. He argued that a culture of poverty did exist. The poor had their own language, psychology, and view of the world. To be impoverished, wrote Harrington, was 'to be an internal alien, to grow up in a culture that is radically different from the one that dominates the society'.[17]

Despite his intentions, Lewis's theories were easily appropriated by conservatives in search of a modern label for the undeserving poor. The problem of poverty could be solved without major political or economic restructuring. Alice O'Connor writes that this deprived population was perceived as needing the galvanising force of outside intervention to break the vicious circle of deprivation in order to benefit from the opportunities the affluent society could provide.[18] Furthermore, in the hands of a writer like Edward C. Banfield, the culture of poverty became a conservative concept. In *The Unheavenly City Revisited* (1974), for example, Banfield argued there was a single problem – 'the existence of an outlook and style of life which is radically present-oriented and which therefore attaches no value to work, sacrifice, self-improvement, or, service to family, friends, or community'.[19] Noting that within the poverty areas were huge enclaves that were almost entirely Negro, Puerto Rican, or Mexican-American, Banfield argued that 'the existence of a large enclave of persons who perceive themselves, and are perceived by others, as having a separate identity', constituted a danger to law and order and to the well-being of society in the long run.[20] Banfield claimed that, along with an allegedly high incidence of mental illness, this warranted the implication that lower-class culture was pathological.

In part, this disjunction between Lewis's intentions, and the way in which his ideas were used by others, reflected Lewis's premature death in 1970. Rigdon argues that Lewis had little interest in the analysis of data. She sees it as a paradox that a man who was so innovative in his fieldwork was so derivative in his conclusions. She writes that 'in reading Lewis on the culture of poverty one sees not the results of a reasonably systematic analysis of his data but a mosaic of shards culled from the literature of anthropology, psychology, psychiatry, sociology, and economic history, as well as from novels about the poor'.[21] Lewis was always imprecise in his use of language, as in his use of the term 'slum culture', and the selective use of his data. Summing up his life and work, Rigdon argues that 'his research was not the revolutionary act he idealized it to be, nor was it even a catalyst for serious reform. It was, however, at the very least, a good work passionately pursued'.[22]

Thus the inventor of the term 'culture of poverty' was the anthropologist Oscar Lewis in the 1950s and 1960s. But with hindsight, it is clear that Lewis's notion was simply the latest in a line of similar ideas that had been around in the United States since well before the Second World War. As James Leiby has noted, Amos Warner had written in 1894, for example, of a 'vicious circle' or cycle of poverty – what was new seventy years later was the academic respectability implied in the term 'culture'.[23] Between these two periods there was much writing that adopted a pathological view of urban life, and also explored in some detail lower-class culture. In 1925, for instance, the Chicago sociologist Robert Park had written that the city had a moral as well as a physical organisation, and cities and their inhabitants moulded and modified each other. Under the influence of the urban environment, he suggested, local attachments broke down, and restraints and inhibitions were weakened . The result was an increase in vice and crime. Park argued further that 'in the great city the poor, the vicious, and the delinquent, crushed together in an unhealthful and contagious intimacy, breed in and in, soul and body'.[24] In fact 'moral regions' and the people that inhabited them were part of the normal life of the city. There were areas where a 'divergent moral code' applied, and good and evil were to be found side by side. In general, suggested Park, the city revealed all the human characteristics and traits that were hidden in smaller communities. It was this that made urban areas so suitable for research, and would 'make of the city a laboratory or clinic in which human nature and social processes may be conveniently and profitably studied'.[25]

Park's argument was about the way that urban life allegedly undermined working-class culture, and was not specially about race. Ideas that provide antecedents for the culture of poverty can also be found in the work of Franklin Frazier, then Professor of Sociology at Howard University. In his influential book, *The Negro Family in the United States*, for example, first published in 1939, Frazier argued that although the ending of slavery had emancipated black Americans, increasing urbanisation since 1900 had 'torn the Negro loose from his cultural moorings'.[26] Welfare agencies, he suggested, were unable to cope with the new tide of family disorganisation – 'family traditions and social distinctions that had meaning and significance in the relatively simple and stable southern com-munities have lost their meaning in the new world of the city'.[27] Social problems that had been unimportant in rural areas gained much greater significance in the city. Illegitimacy, for instance, had become a much more serious economic and social issue. Overall, Frazier concluded that immorality, delinquency, and broken homes were the inevitable result 'of the attempt of a preliterate people, stripped of their cultural heritage, to adjust themselves to civilisation'.[28]

Although Frazier's subject was the black family, his arguments were echoed in studies of other migrant groups. During the Second World War, the anthropologist-ethnographer William Foote Whyte published a study of a slum district in a city on the East Coast that he called 'Cornerville'. Seeking to 'build a sociology based upon observed interpersonal events', Whyte had lived there for three and a half years, including eighteen months with an Italian family – he admitted he had been heavily influenced by the work of the Chicago School of sociologists. His argument was that in 'Cornerville', the only opportunities for people to get on were through racketeering and local politics. Whyte argued that the problem was not that the society was 'disorganised', but that the people of the district had insufficient opportunities to participate in the wider society. Whyte's recommended solutions followed from this analysis. Thus he argued that if people had access to greater economic opportunities, they would be in a position to take more responsibility to shape their own destinies.[29]

Other work associated with the Chicago School in the 1940s explored opportunities and motivations, and began to argue that culture was an adaptive response to the wider environment. One of these writers was Allison Davis. Davis had trained in social anthropology, was the co-author of *Children of Bondage*, an examination of the black adolescent personality, and had also written *Deep South*, a study of the social organisation of a southern city. In a collection edited by Foote Whyte, he argued that the habits of 'underprivileged workers', such as 'shiftlessness', 'irresponsibility', lack of ambition, absenteeism, and 'quitting' were normal responses to the environment in which they lived. They constituted 'a system of behaviour and attitudes which are realistic and rational in that environment in which the individual of the slums has lived and in which he has been trained'.[30] Davis subsequently argued further that each social class had developed its own differentiated and adaptive form of the basic American culture. Behaviour regarded as delinquent, shiftless, or unmotivated was in fact a realistic and respectable response to the wider physical, economic, and cultural environment. Davis claimed that studies of child-rearing practices had found numerous differences between white, Negro, middle-class, and lower-class families. For example, lower-class children stayed up longer, were in the streets later, and went to the cinema more often. Davis concluded that lower-class children had 'fuller gratification of their organically based drives' – in the case of a habit like eating, these drives were trained and eliminated much more gradually in the lower class, and relapses were treated more leniently. Davis concluded that 'lower-class people look upon life as a recurrent series of depressions and peaks, with regard to the gratification of their basic needs'.[31]

These arguments about the alleged characteristics of lower-class culture were further elaborated in the 1950s. One of the most influential articles of the early postwar period, on 'lower-class culture' in the context of adolescent street gangs, was published in 1958 by Walter B. Miller. Miller argued that the 'lower-class' way of life was characterised by a set of focal concerns which together constituted 'a distinctive patterning of concerns which differs significantly, both in rank order and weighting from that of American middle-class culture'.[32] These focal concerns included trouble, toughness, smartness, excitement, fate, and autonomy. For Miller, the adolescent street gang represented an adolescent variation of this lower-class structural form, and had two additional concerns – with belonging, and with status. In general, Miller suggested that lower-class culture should not be seen simply as the opposite of middle-class culture. Instead it was 'a distinctive tradition many centuries old with an integrity of its own'.[33]

However, while influential, these ideas coexisted with alternative explanations. One example of the latter was the 'lower-class value stretch' elaborated by Hyman Rodman. In 1959, Rodman wrote that many of the alleged characteristics of lower-class life – illegitimacy, promiscuity, and desertion – should be seen not simply as 'problems', but as solutions to the problems that people faced. Rodman had carried out fieldwork in Trinidad, in the Caribbean, and he claimed that on issues such as illegitimacy, observers tended to judge lower-class behaviour with middle-class values. In fact, argued Rodman, the lower class both subscribed to the general values of society, and had its own values. With regard to illegitimacy, it tolerated both legal marriages and non-legal unions.[34] Rodman elaborated his theory of the 'lower-class value stretch' in 1963. By the 'value stretch', Rodman meant that the lower-class person, without abandoning the general values of the society, developed an alternative set of values. With regard to questions such as the value placed upon success, or on marriage and legitimate childbirth, the lower-class person had a wider range of values. This might be called a 'stretched value system with a low degree of commitment to all the values within the range, including the dominant, middle-class values'.[35] Rodman argued that the lower-class value stretch provided the best explanation for juvenile delinquency and illegitimacy. He concluded that 'the lower-class value stretch is the predominant response of lower-class individuals to their deprived situation'.[36] It was through this mechanism that some of the apparent contradictions about a common or class-differentiated value system could be explained.

A more sensitive approach to culture than that displayed by Franklin E. Frazier was evident in the work of the sociologist Herbert Gans. In *The Urban Villagers* (1962), Gans had presented a study of an inner-city Boston neighbourhood where many native-born Americans of Italian parentage lived. Gans argued that in the West End the working-class subculture differed considerably from lower- and middle-class subcultures. These subcultures were '*responses* that people make to the *opportunities* and the *deprivations* that they encounter' (Gans's own italics).[37] In the long run, the form they took was closely related to the availability of employment – the lower-class female-based family was a response to, or means of coping with, the lack of stable male employment. Downward mobility was possible. But conversely, when opportunities were available, individuals and families responded by attempting to put into practice their hopes for a better life, and improved their standard of living accordingly. Gans suggested, therefore, that what was distinctive about lower-class life may simply have been a situational adaptation.

One of the most sophisticated of these researchers was Elliot Liebow, whose work on 24 black men who shared a street corner in a district of Washington was summarised in the book *Tally's Corner* (1967). Most were unskilled manual workers or were unemployed, and were aged between 20 and 50. Liebow tried to explain their behaviour as a direct response to the conditions of lower-class life, rather than a compliance with historical or cultural imperatives. Taking the case of unemployment, Liebow argued that 'this inside world does not appear as a self-contained, self-generating, self-sustaining system or even subsystem with clear boundaries marking it off from the larger world around it'.[38] Unemployed men turned to the street corner where a shadow system of values accommodated their perceived failure. The street corner acted as a kind of sanctuary, where failures could become successes, and weaknesses strengths. In general, Liebow wrote that the 'streetcorner man' did not have his own subculture, but his outlook was 'his way of trying to achieve many of the goals and values of the larger society, of failing to do this, and of concealing his failure from others and from himself as best he can'.[39]

Overall, then, there was a tradition of writing about the poor that embraced blacks and migrant groups such as Italians. Charles Valentine was later to locate the culture of poverty in the context of this earlier writing. With regard to Franklin E. Frazier, for instance, Valentine argued that Frazier's picture of the family life of blacks was of a world without culture. Frazier appeared unaware of the biased nature of evidence from social work, the police, or the courts, and he made a leap from social statistics, deviance in terms of middle-class norms, to a model of disorder and instability. Valentine wrote that 'one comes to suspect that "social disorganisation" is little more than an academic-sounding label for behaviour which Franklin Frazier feels is contrary to his own value system'.[40] Valentine was similarly critical of the work of Walter B. Miller. He claimed that Miller's interpretation illustrated how the middle class tended to view the poor as a threat to public order, and to project their unresolved problems onto it. In this, Miller reflected middle-class ambivalences about legality, masculinity, shrewdness, boredom, luck, and autonomy.[41] But while some of these commentators had advanced theories about a distinctive lower-class culture, others were more concerned with the way that behaviour might be adapted because of the influence of the environment.

This early writing continued to exert an important influence on debates in American social policy in the 1960s. Frazier's *The Negro Family in the United States*, in particular, went through numerous editions and became known to successive generations of social scientists. His approach was later reflected in the work of Nathan Glazer in the 1960s, who argued that the book had not been supplanted – 'its major framework remains solid and structures all our thinking on the Negro family'.[42] But its most direct link with policy came with the Moynihan Report on *The Negro Family*, published in 1965. Its author, Daniel Patrick Moynihan, was Assistant Secretary of Labor, and Director of the Office of Policy Planning and Research. Moynihan wrote that 'Negro social structure, in particular the Negro family, battered and harassed by discrimination, injustice, and uprooting, is in the deepest trouble'.[43] A quarter of urban black marriages were dissolved, one in four black births were illegitimate, and a quarter of black families were headed by females. Overall, Moynihan claimed that the breakdown in the black family had led to a startling increase in welfare dependency. Noting that 14% of black children, but 2% of white children, were in receipt of Aid for Families with Dependent Children (AFDC), Moynihan argued that the steady expansion of this welfare programme charted the steady disintegration of Negro family structure in the previous generation. At the centre of the 'tangle of pathology' was the weakness of family structure. This was 'the principal source of most of the aberrant, inadequate, or anti-social behaviour that did not establish, but now serves to perpetuate the cycle of poverty and deprivation'.[44]

The response to the Moynihan Report has been well-documented.[45] It has been suggested that it deterred liberal scholars from acknowledging the role of agency or behaviour in debates about race and urban poverty for decades. Certainly the theory of the culture of poverty came in for sustained criticism. Among the earliest critics were Jack Roach and Orville Gursslin. In 1967, they argued that there were several problems with the theory that Oscar Lewis put forward. The first, they claimed, was that Lewis moved from the theme of subcultures to generalise about an assumed culture of poverty. Second, they suggested that Lewis failed to show what purpose the concept really served. Third, Roach and Gursslin argued that the description of the subcultural characteristics that Lewis claimed to have detected was inadequate. Fourth, they maintained that independent and dependent variables were not specified. Perhaps most importantly, Roach and Gursslin argued that it was important to distinguish between description and causation, and they emphasised what was, to their mind, the key role played by structural factors in poverty and deprivation.[46]

The article by Roach and Gursslin was an important early contribution to an emerging debate. However, the most thorough and perceptive exploration of the 'culture of poverty' was by the anthropologist Charles Valentine, in a book-length critique published in 1968. One of the most valuable parts of Valentine's book was the way that he placed the culture of poverty in the longer-term history of social investigation. Valentine's training as an anthropologist meant he was able to examine the culture of poverty more thoroughly than had been done previously. For one thing, he looked much more closely at the way that 'culture' and 'poverty' were defined.[47] Valentine argued that this was a misapplication of the original concept of culture. Valentine's point was that, like the approach taken by Franklin E. Frazier and other earlier writers, the culture of poverty concept served to distract attention from the structural characteristics of the social system. In his writing, Lewis moved between the individual, the family, and culture, but transitions between the different levels of analysis were not entirely clear. For Valentine, this problem was highlighted by the way that Lewis's books were organised. In general, argued Valentine, the autobiographies remained a mass of material that needed more analysis and evaluation. It was difficult to determine their validity, reliability, and relevance. As well as looking at how the books were written, Valentine argued that families and local communities had wider interests and concerns than Lewis gave them credit for. What the reader ended up with instead was 'a series of overlapping family portraits or self-portraits presented in isolation from their natural or actual context'.[48] The argument was that all those writers who wrote about a cultural way of life peculiar to the poor failed to outline the relationship between individuals or families and the society as a whole. They ignored important aspects of the concept of a subculture.[49]

Charles Valentine's book was a powerful statement of the case against the concept of the culture of poverty.[50] At the time, his criticisms were echoed by other writers, such as Eleanor Burke Leacock, Professor of Anthropology at the Polytechnic Institute of Brooklyn, and William Ryan. But the culture of poverty remained an influential interpretation, its identified weaknesses notwithstanding. More important was the way Valentine's suggestions for ethnographic fieldwork were taken up by other researchers – and the way their findings strengthened his criticisms of Lewis. These included the work of the sociologist Herbert Gans, following on from *The Urban Villagers*, and fieldwork carried out by Ulf Hannerz and Lee Rainwater. Rather than a debt to Franklin E. Frazier and Walter B. Miller, this work owed more to Hyman Rodman and the 'lower-class value stretch', and to Elliot Liebow's *Tally's Corner*. As William Julius Wilson was later to suggest, its emphasis on structure rather than behaviour may have been in part a reaction to the Moynihan Report and the reception it received. The general thrust of this literature was to support the argument that the admittedly different culture of the lower class was an adaptive response to the wider society and environment.

Eleanor Burke Leacock, for example, now argued it was through the culture of poverty, that the nineteenth-century idea that the poor were poor through their own lack of ability and initiative had 're-entered the scene in a new form, well decked out with scientific jargon'.[51] Like Valentine, she argued that the culture of poverty theory focused on a negative, distorted, and truncated view of the cultural whole, and implied an untenable view of the process whereby cultural traits were evolved and transmitted. In a collection published in 1971, she concluded that 'sociocentric methods of data collection and analysis, plus a nonhistorical theory of culture and its relation to personality, have contributed to stereotypical and distorted views of these class-linked cultural variations'.[52] William Ryan's famous book *Blaming the Victim* was published the same year. Ryan argued that in the vast sociological literature on differences between the poor and the middle class, the middle class came out top every time. For Ryan, the most important aspect in understanding poverty was that it was caused by lack of money. The ideology of the culture of poverty was therefore a means of avoiding the obvious solution – that the poor needed money and power – which would require substantial changes and the redistribution of income. For Ryan, the theme of lower-class culture was similarly a means of maintaining inequality between social classes in America.[53]

Valentine had argued that empirical studies and rigorous fieldwork were necessary to test the hypothesis of the culture of poverty. He suggested that Elliot Liebow's ethnographic approach was thorough and that (unlike Frazier) he was aware of biases. Liebow had argued that men experienced their lives as being devoid of success and satisfaction because they shared the standards and criteria for success of the wider society. Rather than having his own subculture, the streetcorner man lived 'in continual and painful awareness of American values and sentiments'.[54] Other research studies carried out at this time produced findings that supported the argument of Gans and others that the behaviour of lower-class people was essentially adaptive. Ulf Hannerz, for instance, argued that the culture of poverty thesis tended to imply that the way of life of the poor was self-perpetuating. His fieldwork did not fit the pattern described by Lewis. On the basis of fieldwork conducted in the Winston Street neighbourhood of Washington, DC, in 1966–68, Hannerz felt there was a need for new analyses to show how the actions of these people were adaptations or understandable reactions to the situations in which they found themselves. Hannerz favoured an approach similar to Rodman's 'lower-class value stretch', and he tended to define 'culture' as something that could easily change in response to outside influences.[55]

Lee Rainwater's argument was that in their own communities, black families developed their own solutions to recurrent human issues. His study *Behind Ghetto Walls* (1970) dealt with the Pruitt-Igoe project in St Louis, an all-black housing project of more than 10,000 adults and children. The subculture of these families, Rainwater argued, was a creation of a range of institutions, notably social networks, entertainment, and the family, that represented a response to the conditions of life set by white society. Such a culture, then, was 'the repository of a set of techniques for survival in the world of the disinherited, and in time these techniques take on the character of substitute games with their own rules guiding behaviour'.[56] The critical element of any culture was its dynamic, adaptive quality. Rainwater claimed that in Pruitt-Igoe, the lower-class world was defined by deprivation and exclusion – ways of living were adaptations to the disjunction between the demands society made, on the one hand, and the inadequate resources that these people held, on the other.[57]

By 1970, Herbert Gans was arguing that the most important question in the area of culture and poverty was 'to discover how soon people will change their behaviour, given new opportunities, and what restraints or obstacles, good or bad, come from that reaction to past situations we call culture'.[58] Many if not most of the problems of poor people could be solved by providing incomes and jobs. Nevertheless Gans also conceded that new research methods were needed to answer the question of whether there was a culture of poverty and a lower-class way of life. Nearly twenty years later, William Julius Wilson was to argue that it was Hannerz's book *Soulside* that had identified the key question – whether there was a difference between the person affected by structural change, and the person influenced by the behaviour of others affected by those changes.

Hyman Rodman attempted to revive the concept of the culture of poverty through his on-going studies of Trinidad.[59] However, David Harrison pointed out in a review of this work that there were problems in the culture of poverty as used by Hyman Rodman. One was the extent that the culture of poverty was connected with material deprivation. A second was that Lewis's traits were found in cultures which were not poverty-stricken. Third, the descriptions of individual participants focused on negative aspects, and concentrated on the family. Finally, there were difficulties in the notion that the culture of poverty was an adaptation and reaction by the poor. Overall, Harrison claimed that Rodman's study, based on the concept of the culture of poverty, had inherited many of the conceptual inadequacies inherent in the model as put forward by Lewis.[60] Harrison argued that cultures and subcultures should be regarded as positive, and a meaningful framework for those who participated in them. Cultures and subcultures should be studied on their own terms. And research problems should not interfere with the basic aim to understand other cultures.[61]

It is important to examine the extent to which the concept of the culture of poverty, invented in the United States, was taken up in Britain, and the processes of policy transfer by which this transmission of ideas occurred. John Macnicol has pointed out that the apparent similarities between American and British social policy in this period were rooted in shared economic experiences. Structural changes in the economy reawakened concern about social problems, particularly the persistence of poverty and social disadvantage. Similarly, the solutions that were proposed reflected the different welfare traditions of the two countries, with each having both radical and conservative elements.[62] At the same time, there is also evidence of considerable resistance to the idea of the culture of poverty among British commentators.

Some earlier British studies had attempted to untangle the effects of structure and behaviour. A study of families and social networks, for example, by the psychiatrist Elizabeth Bott, had argued in 1957 that there was a general bias in favour of economic and socio-structural rather than cultural interpretations. She argued that the work of American academics like Walter B. Miller and Herbert Gans was meaningful only when related to economic and occupational factors. But in the second edition of her book (1971), Bott was more willing than she had been in 1957 to admit that economic and social determinism could also be naïve.[63] As we have seen in the previous chapter, the stress on the problem family in the British context provided potentially fertile ground for a favourable reception for the culture of poverty. Other policy developments, such as the stress on Educational Priority Areas (EPAs) in the Plowden Report (1967), reflected a similar preoccupation with culture, deprivation, and environment. It has been suggested that the EPAs provide an example of how social-science theory is translated into public policy. Nevertheless the proposal was remoulded to fit the contours of administrative and political life, and the resulting policy was a pale reflection of the original idea.[64]

One early example of these ideas in circulation was provided in the Plowden Report, *Children and their Primary Schools* (1967). In August 1963, the then Minister for Education, Sir Edward Boyle, had asked a group 'to consider primary education in all its aspects, and the transition to secondary education'.[65] The two-volume report produced by this group was in many ways a 'progressive' document. It initiated a move against 'rote learning' for instance, was one of the first reports that gave a place to parents, and favoured systematic nursery education. The Plowden Report also favoured granting schools in socially deprived areas extra staff and funds. But one innovation was the proposal to create EPAs, where there would be positive discrimination for the Areas and the children in them. The criteria for the selection of EPAs included such features as family size; overcrowding; poor attendance and truancy; the proportions of 'retarded', disturbed, or 'handicapped' pupils; and the number of children unable to speak English.[66] It was assumed that the number of these Areas would increase quickly, and that a maximum of 10% of the child population would be in EPAs by 1972–73.[67] The emphasis on EPAs in the Plowden Report was one of the first examples of a new-found enthusiasm for area-based initiatives, reflecting the experience of the United States in the 'War on Poverty'. Reactions to the Report indicated the strength of lay beliefs in individual pathology. The *Economist*, for example, argued that education was 'of course not designed to solve the social problems of the present generation of adult slum-dwellers among whom lie to a pretty large degree the origins of the other social disorders that our society is heir to'.[68] Nor, it claimed, could the measures advocated by the Plowden Committee tackle problems of deprivation that were behavioural rather than structural, and which might exist in the best-planned suburbs.

While there was no direct mention of the culture of poverty, the Plowden Report seemed inspired by American initiatives. This is supported by the review of EPAs that was edited by A. H. Halsey, then Director of the Department of Social and Administrative Studies at Oxford. Halsey argued that it was more accurate to speak of 'poverties', since poverty had multiple if related causes. Halsey argued that, in the United States, the culture of poverty had dominated the War on Poverty and the 1964 Economic Opportunity Act, providing the rationale for the emphasis on community action and social work, rather than employment policies and a redistribution of income. He suggested that the 'poverties' of industrial societies:

> must be understood to have their origins in both situational and cultural characteristics of those minorities which suffer disadvantage and discrimination and to have their cures in both economic and cultural reform, not only at the local or community level but also in the total structure of society.[69]

For Halsey, the choice was between emphasising opportunities and motivation, and in the British context it was the latter that the EPAs concentrated upon.

Similar debates about the relative importance of structural and behavioural factors were evident in the Community Development Projects (CDPs) that were announced by the Wilson Government in 1969 as part of the larger Urban Programme. These were a direct copy of the Community Action Areas that had been created during the 'War on Poverty' in America. The aim of these was to provide feedback to central and local government on the impact of existing policies and services, to encourage innovation, and to improve co-ordination. In Britain, the CDPs ran for ten years, and comprised twelve projects in all. Most were in large provincial cities such as Coventry, Newcastle, and Liverpool, or in deprived London boroughs including Southwark and Newham. The budget was £5m. Arguably the most interesting feature of the CDPs was the way in which control of the projects shifted from the Home Office and into the hands of local activists.

Martin Loney has argued that one of the key developments in the background to the establishment of the CDPs was the development of social work. Social work was attractive to the Labour Government, since it held out the promise of ameliorating social problems in a non-punitive fashion, it was relatively cheap, and it involved limited social change. The same climate that facilitated the Seebohm Report helped the CDPs. There was also interest in community work funded by the Gulbenkian Foundation, and a growing 'community focus' within social work itself.[70] These social workers increasingly rejected the traditional model of social work, leading to conflict. It was these developments that provided the context for the establishment of the CDPs. Loney argues that the original assumptions of the CDPs were strongly focused on personal rather than structural failings, and those societal failings that were recognised had more to do with the failure of the social services to direct appropriate attention to the deprived. A more effective social services approach was seen as a possible way of changing the characteristics and lifestyle of the deprived themselves.[71] It was likely that a programme that originated within the civil service would operate within that consensus. Martin Loney has written that social pathology approaches are attractive to governments who are reluctant to engage in significant social change. He notes that 'by analysing social problems in terms of the characteristics of individuals, families, or even communities such approaches legitimate small-scale programmes of social intervention which do not threaten powerful interests in society'.[72]

The community development objectives of the CDPs followed on logically from the same basic project assumptions. Community development could act as a catalyst to break up social pathology by revitalising the poor and involving them in constructive plans for improvement. Community malfunctioning was to be tackled 'from within'. Thus claims Loney, 'the role of community action was closely related to the underlying suppositions about the nature of deprivation and its social pathology'.[73] A further premise was that problem families were found in particular areas. This was both a cause and effect of the individual pathology of the poor. Aspects of Oscar Lewis's culture of poverty, such as blaming the victim, were accepted, but the rest was ignored. Thus a diluted version came to complement traditional casework methods. Initially the Home Office perspective was to break the cycle of deprivation, and its instructions emphasised a behavioural analysis of poverty. In the event, the local CDPs rebelled against this and produced reports that emphasised the structural causes of poverty. The result was conflict between the Home Office and the more radical CDPs. The effect was that by 1976 the programme had been abandoned.[74] The CDPs incorporated elements of the culture of poverty, but like Coates and Silburn (see below), also reflected the British preoccupation with problem families.

By the time that the CDPs petered out, the culture of poverty was also coming in for criticism from the wider social science academic community. Halsey was a member of the Social Science Research Council (SSRC) Panel on Poverty, along with other leading researchers and social policy analysts of the day – David Donnison, Michael Young, and Brian Abel-Smith. More direct evidence of the influence of the culture of poverty was provided in the Panel's review of concepts of poverty, published in 1968. The SSRC included the culture of poverty as one of six main strands it identified – the others were 'crisis poverty'; 'long-term dependencies'; 'life-cycle poverty'; 'depressed-area poverty'; and 'downtown poverty'. In the case of the culture of poverty, the Panel conceded that 'a combination of financial hardship, squalid environment, family structure and personal capacities and relationships may produce a pattern of adaptation characterised by particular time orientations and value systems'.[75] But it also argued that more research was needed on the links between income and behaviour, exclusion from the labour market, and the operation of the social services. The SSRC's Panel concluded that the term 'culture of poverty' was 'as likely to mislead as to enlighten: the word "culture" covers too many different factors which are better studied separately'.[76] Thus while it conceded that the concept of the culture of poverty had been influential, the SSRC Panel interpreted it as an adaptive phenomenon, and was generally hostile.

Other British commentators were attracted to the concept of the culture of poverty, but were unsure whether it really provided a convincing theoretical framework for their empirical work. Ken Coates and Richard Silburn were lecturers at Nottingham University. In their famous exploration of deprivation, *Poverty: The Forgotten Englishmen* (1970), Coates and Silburn thought that Lewis's theory did have parallels with what they had observed in the course of their research in Nottingham. Among the people that they studied, there seemed to be the same feeling of hopelessness and despair, and a similar lack of participation in institutions. At the same time, Coates and Silburn argued it was difficult to decide what were middle-class values, writing that:

> rather, there are clusters of subcriminal groups, colonies of problem families, which, as we have shown, are among the heaviest crosses which their respectable but equally poor neighbours feel themselves unjustly called upon to bear.[77]

Despite this emphasis on problem families, Coates and Silburn argued that the poorer and more isolated workers in their study did not comprise a homogeneous group. In fact, there seemed to be two groups. One shared the values and criticisms of the mainstream culture. The other had more modest aspirations, and a complacent and resigned approach to family and social life. It was reviled by residents and labelled by authorities as 'multi-problem' families, but it did not have any common identity. The aspirations of this second group seemed more modest than those of the rest, but Coates and Silburn argued this could not be attributed to a cultural pattern. In fact the poorer households in the second group had the same expectations and demands as the rest of the population. They wrote that:

> excepting the so-called 'problem families' the poorer households could not be said to be culturally distinct from the richer; they appeared to respond to the same values, to share the same basic assumptions, to accept similar restraints.[78]

Coates and Silburn tried to relate what they had discovered in Nottingham back to what Lewis had written on the culture of poverty. However, they concluded that 'from our knowledge of this one urban community, it would be very hard to maintain with any assurance that the poor constitute a single subcultural entity'.[79] There were some contradictions in the position that Coates and Silburn adopted. It was not clear if they viewed problem families as an invention of local authorities, or a group whose existence could be empirically proven. These issues notwithstanding, they managed to combine a belief in problem families with a resistance to the idea that there was a culture of poverty.

More clear-cut was the position of other British academics concerned with poverty who displayed a fiercer resistance to the idea that poverty might have anything other than structural causes. Peter Townsend was perhaps foremost among British academics in this field. In a collection published in 1970, when he was Professor of Sociology at the University of Essex, Townsend argued that poverty was produced by systems of international social stratification. Thus he rejected theories that placed the responsibility for poverty with the individual, or with a culture of poverty. Townsend wrote that:

> the concept of the culture of poverty concentrates attention upon the familial and local setting of behaviour and largely ignores the external and unseen social forces which condition the distribution of different types of resources to the community, family and individual.[80]

Townsend argued that the elimination of poverty required not the reform, education, or rehabilitation of the individual, or even, as in the American 'War on Poverty', the creation of additional opportunities for upward mobility. What was needed was the 'reconstruction of the national and regional systems by which resources are distributed, or, alternatively, the introduction of additional systems which are universalistic and egalitarian'.[81] This was the position that Townsend maintained through the 1970s. In his classic work *Poverty in the United Kingdom* (1979), Townsend argued that Oscar Lewis's approach was interesting but was concerned with individuals rather than societies. The methodology was uncontrolled, biased, ambiguous, it was difficult to confirm the theory, and the concept could not be applied consistently. Townsend conceded that the author of *La Vida* did provide an accurate description of the penalties and stresses of being poor. But Lewis did not distinguish clearly between working-class culture and a subculture of poverty. In the view of Townsend, Lewis could not disentangle the effect on behaviour of a lack of resources from other cultural influences.[82]

What is perhaps most surprising from the standpoint of today is the exclusive focus of these researchers on structural factors. Certainly the viewpoint of Townsend was shared by many other British social scientists. Dorothy Wedderburn, Lecturer in Industrial Sociology at Imperial College, London, argued that evidence generated in studies of older people illustrated that this was a type of poverty where there was little opportunity for a common culture to develop. Older people who were poor might come from working-class backgrounds. But these were not necessarily backgrounds of working-class poverty, and the working life of these people had, for the most part, not been spent in poverty.[83] Her point was that evidence based on the experience of older people tended to cast doubt on the culture of poverty. Bill Jordan, then in the Department of Sociology at Exeter University, made the point that Lewis's choice of phrase was misleading. The culture was not characteristic of uniformly poor communities, but of stratified social structures. And the continuities in family patterns observed by social workers were 'part of a subcultural adaptation to the conditions of life in city slums, overlaid with reactions to the policies of officials of those social services which characteristically are involved with the urban poor'.[84]

Questions about the way the culture of poverty was received in Britain, and how much influence it exerted, are therefore not easy to answer. The EPAs, and the corresponding focus on educational and cultural deprivation, did appear to mirror the War on Poverty. It is interesting that the SSRC did include the culture of poverty as one of its six key poverty concepts, and some researchers, such as Coates and Silburn in Nottingham, were initially attracted to the theory as a means of explaining the findings of their fieldwork. The CDPs, too, reflected American experiences in their social work and community emphasis. However, there was also much resistance in Britain to cultural or behavioural explanations of poverty from the mid-1970s. The SSRC's review of concepts of poverty showed that it was critical of the work of Oscar Lewis, preferring an adaptive explanation. In the CDPs too, there was a marked difference between the behavioural perspective of the Home Office and the much more structural analysis adopted by social workers at the grassroots level. Much more typical of the reaction of the British social science community was the Townsend view that poverty was caused by large-scale structural factors. The role of culture, and by implication behaviour, was at best a distraction, at worst an irrelevance. This reflected a much older tradition in social administration, which, guided by its chief theorist Richard Titmuss, had always steered clear of the view that the poor might in any way be responsible for the situation they found themselves in. In light of recent research interest, which has increasingly sought to combine structural and behavioural explanations of social exclusion, the stance taken by the British social science community in this period was strikingly united.

It is important to see the culture of poverty in the context of a much longer-term tradition of writing about blacks, lower-class culture, and migrant groups. Even within this tradition there were marked differences of emphasis. It is possible to contrast, for instance, the pathological interpretation of Franklin E. Frazier with the much more sensitive analysis of Elliot Liebow. The analysis adopted in the Moynihan Report was that of Frazier, but the adaptive interpretation taken on board by later researchers was recognisably that of Liebow. What is perhaps most interesting is how influential the culture of poverty was, its weaknesses notwithstanding. Charles Valentine, in particular, presented a sustained and devastating critique. Even so, Oscar Lewis gained an international reputation on the basis of the culture of poverty, one that would have been further perpetuated had he not died in 1970. There were several features that explain why the theory proved so enduring. First, it provided a deceptively simple explanation for complex problems to do with poverty. Second, the focus on alleged characteristics was always a proven means to popular acceptance, as we have seen with the problem family. Aspects of this, such as the alleged focus on the present, and corresponding inability to plan for the future, were recurring elements in underclass stereotypes. Third, Lewis made the important point that these patterns were passed on in successive generations, through the effects on the children. In the end, in terms of popular acceptance, these elements were much stronger than Valentine's sophisticated critique of ethnographic methodology and anthropological fieldwork.

Howard Glennerster has made the point that seminars on poverty are now dominated by economists, and by the analysis of large data sets, whereas in the 1960s they were influenced by sociologists.[85] That says something about how the study of poverty has changed over the past forty years. At the same time, the culture of poverty thesis has continued to attract attention. William Julius Wilson, for instance, has argued that it is the cultural-transmission aspect of the theory that has received most attention. At the same time, he writes, it is possible to recognise the importance of wider structural factors, but also to see the merits of a cultural analysis of a life in poverty. Ghetto-specific practices, such as public drinking, are more common in inner-city ghetto neighbourhoods, and the transmission of these modes of behaviour by precept and role-modelling is made easier.[86] At the time, the British response to the culture of poverty was more subdued. In fact it was only in the early 1970s that the next step in the history of the underclass was created. As ever, its origins were unusual, and can be dated with some precision to a speech by Sir Keith Joseph, in June 1972. In Britain, it was not the culture of poverty notion that was to gain both research funding and popular attention, but a rather different notion, called the cycle of deprivation. The rise and fall of the cycle of deprivation is the subject of the next chapter.

6

Sir Keith Joseph and the Cycle of Deprivation

One of the main aims of 'New Labour' has been to end child poverty, and it is striking that descriptions of policy initiatives, such as the Sure Start programme for under-fours, use the phrase 'cycle of deprivation'. What is interesting is that journalists and civil servants appear ignorant of the earlier history of the term, and its historical resonances. The 1970s and early 1980s were marked by battles between academics and civil servants over this very terrain. The books that were produced at that time are now largely forgotten, and instead gather dust on the shelves of the social policy sections of university libraries. This debate raised key questions. Was there evidence that a pattern of deprivation was in some way transmitted from parents to their children, so that there are marked inter-generational continuities in experiences of poverty? If true, to what extent was this because of cultural patterns of behaviour, and how far was it the result of wider structural factors? And was the phrase 'cycles of disadvantage' in fact a more appropriate term than the 'cycle of deprivation'?

This chapter examines debates over the cycle of deprivation in the 1970s and early 1980s, and the way that these fit into the longer-term concept of the underclass. The key figure in this field was the Conservative politician Sir Keith Joseph, then Secretary of State for Health and Social Services. In June 1972, he espoused the theory of a cycle of deprivation, and a large-scale Department of Health and Social Security (DHSS)/Social Science Research Council (SSRC) research programme followed directly from his speech. We trace the wider political context for both the 1972 speech, along with a better-known speech given in October 1974, and the origins of the cycle in Joseph's earlier concern with problem families. We are concerned too, with the ways in which academics drawn into the DHSS/SSRC programme sought to challenge and subvert Joseph's original thesis. By the mid-1980s, academics had displaced the theory of a cycle of deprivation, and wrote instead of patterns of cycles of disadvantage. In chapter 9, we will consider again how far New Labour remains attached to the theory of a cycle of deprivation.

Sir Keith Joseph (1918–1994) is a fascinating political figure.[1] Educated at Harrow School and Magdalen College, Oxford, his father had largely founded the successful Bovis construction company. As Conservative MP for Leeds North

East, Joseph displayed a compassionate interest in questions of health care and social policy from the 1950s onwards. He first entered Cabinet in 1962, under Harold Macmillan, as Minister of Housing and Local Government, but had been a junior minister from 1959. As Secretary of State for Health and Social Services, 1970–1974, Joseph played a central role in the background to the 1974 health service reorganisation. Joseph was a key advocate of monetarism in the mid 1970s, as well as founding the think-tank, the Centre for Policy Studies. In the 1980s, he served in the Thatcher governments as Secretary of State, first for Industry and then Education. Some have argued that increasingly Joseph can be seen as an 'intellectual godfather' to New Labour.[2]

Joseph remained an enigmatic character whose honesty, belief in intellectual rigour, courtesy, agonising scrupulousness, and 'intensely nervous disposition' were apparent to all who met him. As his obituary in *The Times* noted, though with some inaccuracy, 'tense and intense, and much moved by his religious certainties as a Jew, his personality, despite public parody, was not that of someone given to extreme views'.[3] It was all the more surprising then, that in a speech, given on 29 June 1972, Joseph raised the theme of a cycle of deprivation. The speech prompted much discussion, both at the time and since. Nicholas Timmins, for instance, has written that:

> The speech brought forth profoundly different interpretations. To some on the left it looked like an appeal for community action. To others it appeared to blame the individuals and deny the state's responsibility. To the right it appeared to be a defence of the family. To many it seemed just common sense.[4]

Yet the origins of the speech and the controversy it provoked have never been properly explained. Few attempts have been made to explore how and why Joseph suddenly expressed these ideas in the 1972 speech. Little is known about the ways in which the academics recruited into the DHSS/SSRC research programme sought to subvert the original thesis. And little work has been done to show how the cycle of deprivation fits into the longer-term history of the underclass.

Although relatively well known, the cycle speech has usually been judged through an abridged version, and the full text contains some surprises. The speech was given at a conference for local authorities organised by the Pre-School Playgroups Association, at Church House, Westminster, on 29 June 1972. In it, Joseph announced a capital grant of £9,500 towards the work of the Association, and a recurrent annual grant of £45,000. This came under the umbrella of the Urban Programme, since in May 1972 the Government had allocated over £1m for day-care provision for the under-fives. This money was to be spent on building day nurseries, as well as providing additional funding for playgroups.

But it was in the second half of the speech that Joseph developed his main theme, asking why it was 'that, in spite of long periods of full employment and relative prosperity and the improvement in community services since the Second World War, deprivation and problems of maladjustment so conspicuously' persisted.[5] By deprivation, Joseph meant 'those circumstances which prevent people developing to nearer their potential – physically, emotionally and intellectually – than many do now'.[6] He acknowledged that deprivation took many forms and had complex causes, including those that were economic, personal, and to do with patterns of child rearing. But he continued 'perhaps there is at work here a process, apparent in many situations but imperfectly understood, by which problems reproduce themselves from generation to generation'.[7] He proposed there was not a single process. But it seemed that in a proportion of cases, the problems of one generation were repeated in the next. Social workers and teachers could often be sure that because of family background, a child 'is operating under disadvantage and prone to run into the same difficulties in his turn as his parents have experienced'.[8]

Part of Joseph's speech was a call for more research, since he recognised that the cycle was poorly understood. Joseph admitted that his theory was not underpinned by scientific research. He maintained that 'the cycle is not a process that we fully understand, but a number of objective studies do tend to bear out the subjective belief of many practitioners that cyclical processes are at work'.[9] Nevertheless the evidence that he advanced in its support was decidedly shaky. It included follow-up studies in Sheffield on problem families; research at the Cambridge Institute of Criminology; evidence from the National Child Development Study (NCDS); studies that seemed to show that parents who had been ill-treated went on to ill-treat their own children; and a comparison of parenting in the USA and USSR that appeared to put England at the bottom of an international league table of parental involvement.

Interestingly, Joseph acknowledged that poverty did play a role in the causation of deprivation. For this reason, he said, the Government recognised the need to increase welfare spending, introduce new benefits, and improve access to those that already existed. Research was also needed into the dynamics of family poverty – 'about such matters as not only the mechanisms and circumstances which lead families into poverty, but also its duration and effects, and the mechanisms and circumstances which enable some to leave whilst others remain in poverty'.[10] This was relevant to, and complementary to, the 'cycle'. Sir Keith therefore recognised the value of longitudinal studies. In the meantime, his remedies were noticeably more limited. Apart from playgroups and services for the under-fives, they focused on family planning; support for parents; and attention to the needs of children. He claimed, for instance, that if effective family planning was more widely practised, the numbers caught up in the cycle would be much reduced. Similarly Joseph argued that 'inadequate people tend to be inadequate parents and that inadequate parents tend to rear inadequate children'.[11]

Joseph ended the speech with the hope that there would be more discussion about these issues, since he wished to see 'a development of fresh thinking and fresh initiative in this whole area'.[12] The speech was reported in the main broadsheet newspapers, but met with a fairly muted response. In a leader article, *The Times* noted that the most urgent requirements were more playgroups and domiciliary family planning. Nevertheless the paper also argued that improved co-operation between parents, teachers, and social workers had to go hand in hand with attention to poverty, poor housing, and the impact that living in a decaying area had on individual morale and ambition. The paper commented that 'all these causes need to be tackled as part of a combined approach to the problems of deprived areas, because deprived areas and deprived people go together'.[13] What was needed, according to *The Times*, was an enlarged version of the Urban Programme that looked at improvements to service delivery, notably the personal social services, but also explored the influence of these wider structural factors.

The cycle of deprivation speech is in fact less well known than a speech that Joseph made in Birmingham two years later, in October 1974. The wider context was that the Conservative Party had lost the election of 10 October, and there was speculation as to who (if anyone) might succeed Edward Heath as leader. Joseph had been urged to stand by Norman Fowler and Norman Lamont, and his speech to the Edgbaston Conservative Association on 19 October was clearly designed to highlight his leadership potential. Joseph began his speech by arguing that politics was about more than economics. He attacked left-wing theorists and the permissive society, and held up Mary Whitehouse as an example of one who had opposed postwar decadence.[14] Yet Joseph also went on to claim that 'a high and rising proportion of children are being born to mothers least fitted to bring children into the world'. Many of these mothers in social classes IV and V were unmarried, deserted, or divorced, and were of low intelligence and low educational attainment. According to Joseph, they were 'producing problem children, the future unmarried mothers, delinquents, denizens of our borstals, subnormal educational establishments, prisons, hostels for drifters'. Overall, 'the balance of our population, our human stock is threatened'.[15] Unless family planning was extended to these groups, the nation would move towards degeneration.

In drafting this section of the speech, Joseph was particularly influenced by an article in the journal *Poverty*, a publication of the Child Poverty Action Group. In this paper, the social researchers Arthur and Margaret Wynn had examined the question of whether family planning could do more to reduce child poverty. The Wynns pointed out that the number of children with parents on Supplementary Benefit had doubled, to a total of 936,000 in 1972. Falls in the birth rate meant that the proportions of children born into poorer families had increased, compared to the numbers born into social classes I, II, and III. Poverty seemed to be both a cause and a consequence of illegitimacy, but so far family planning had not been very effective among women in social classes IV and V. The Wynns concluded by pointing out that there were no cheap solutions to the problems of child poverty. Allowances for one-parent families, increases in family allowances, cheap milk, and free school meals were all essential.[16]

Joseph focused on the Wynns' parting shot that mothers under 20 might, in future, be the mothers of possibly 35% of all British people, and he singled out family planning as a means of alleviating poverty at minimal expense.[17] Although this section came towards the end of the speech, the effect was similar to the Powell 'rivers of blood' tirade. In the words of his biographers, Joseph had underestimated 'the extent to which careless words could be taken as validation for the prejudices of the ignorant'.[18] The Times noted the speech provoked a 'tinderbox of reaction, most of it hostile', and Frank Field, for example, argued that the speech was disturbing in that it attempted to show that the poor were undermining society.[19] Joseph's attempts to respond to press criticism only did further damage, and provided revealing insights into his interest in problem families. Joseph argued, for instance, that 'I suppose I had regarded myself as a person long associated with concern for problem families, and it seems to me grotesque for people to suggest that my motives in making this speech were improper or sinister'. He said he had been 'intensely interested and concerned with problem families' from the beginning of 1971.[20]

The difference between the 1972 and 1974 speeches was that the latter was given in the context of a leadership challenge, and as a consequence received much greater attention. Given to promote Joseph's leadership claims, the speech had the opposite effect, and effectively ended his chances of succeeding Edward Heath as leader of the Conservative Party.

It has been suggested that the hypothesis of 'transmitted deprivation' was a 'sort of burp from a debate about poverty and pathology that had been rumbling on for decades, if not centuries'.[21] The earlier chapters of this book support that argument. While the publications that were generated by the DHSS/SSRC research programme after the 1972 speech are relatively easy to trace, even if now largely forgotten, a more difficult task is to explore the background to the 1972 speech. It is unclear to what extent the speech expressed ideas that Sir Keith Joseph had previously voiced in speeches and articles. Was he influenced by the British problem family debate, or was the American culture of poverty notion a more significant aspect of his thinking? In what ways was the cycle of deprivation associated with other aspects of social policy, such as the inner city, deprivation, and family planning? And what exactly determined the timing of the delivery of the speech, in the summer of 1972?

As Conservative MP for Leeds North East, Joseph was in the 1950s clearly interested in the effectiveness of health and social care provision for vulnerable groups. Parliamentary questions by him, for example, focused on such issues as the geographical coverage of the home help service. But Joseph was also at this stage keenly interested in the future of the family. In the 1950s, in his policy work on Arts and Amenities, for example, Joseph had noted that young people lacked 'a sense of purpose and of personal responsibility'. In 1959 he suggested that work camps, or youth clubs in church halls, might provide a means of channelling the energies of adolescents.[22] It is clear, too, from policy documents published in the 1960s, that Joseph's thinking was influenced by the concept of the problem family. In his speech *Social Security: The New Priorities*, published as a pamphlet in 1966 by Conservative Political Centre, Joseph, at that time Opposition Spokesman for Labour, put forward ideas for social policy. Joseph argued that a competitive society could be a compassionate society: in fact 'unless society is efficient – and only competition can ensure that – there just will not be the resources for effective compassion'.[23]

Among categories of need, Joseph included problem families whose poverty was not caused primarily by lack of income, but by difficulties in managing it and in using social help. He wrote that:

> problem families have a number of inter-related difficulties – of temperament, of intelligence, of money and of health. The numbers involved may be small but their difficulties tend to be chronic, to recur in the next generation and to blight the lives of the children.[24]

Joseph located problem families within a larger set of groups – deprived children, deserted wives, families of alcoholics and prisoners, and those who had experienced broken marriages or broken homes. What these groups had in common, he suggested, was that their misfortunes were inflicted 'from within'. He called this group 'home-made casualties'. In language that echoed the Wood Report (1929), he argued that these groups were dominated by families of low income and low intelligence, with more than the average number of children. A cycle was created and repeated, whereby broken homes and bad parents reproduced broken homes and bad parents.[25]

Joseph acknowledged that structural and behavioural factors were mutually reinforcing. He conceded, for instance, that 'we know some of the breeding-grounds of warped lives; we know the close interaction of poverty, bad housing, over-sized classes, inadequate parents'. Nevertheless the solutions he proposed for problem families were more modest. More social workers and home helps should be recruited to provide care in the home.[26] Money was important, but an effective social service – that provided a means of identifying families at risk early, that channelled additional resources into school, and that offered opportunities for adolescents to gain self-respect – was also crucial. Joseph claimed that 'if the community can intervene effectively in what is often in itself misery and may also be an incubator of future misery and delinquency, then we would be narrowing the breeding-grounds of crime and unhappiness'.[27]

The key elements of the 1972 speech were thus already evident some six years earlier. Similar themes are evident in some of his speeches on housing. In 1967, he stated of between two and three million people living in privately-rented houses that 'here are the overcrowded: the families living in single rooms carved perfunctorily out of unconverted, insanitary, multi-occupied rabbit warrens. Here are the seed-beds of delinquency and even crime'.[28] There was also evidence that, in the context of housing policy, these ideas influenced his thinking well after the 1972 speech. In 1975, for example, Joseph questioned what had been achieved through compulsory purchase orders and slum clearance programmes. In his view, bulldozers had destroyed communities. And many council estates had inevitably become 'foci of social pathology'.[29]

It is therefore possible to trace the influence of these ideas in Joseph's speeches from the mid-1960s. In the early 1970s, as Secretary of State for Health and Social Services, Joseph was more closely involved with the translating of policy into practice. He was actively involved in debates about abortion and family planning, and played a key part, for example, in the setting up of the Lane Committee. Many people were unhappy about existing provision, seeking a comprehensive and free family planning service, with abortion on demand. It has been argued that Joseph's proposals for abortion and family planning were heavily influenced by his thinking on social deprivation. Joseph instructed officials to concentrate on a comprehensive domiciliary service for 'problem' groups, with encouragement for sterilisation in the case of 'really bad problem families'.[30] The Community Development Projects provided a means of funding family planning services, and Joseph linked family planning and deprivation in speeches in early 1971. In the event, the new arrangements for family planning passed into law in July 1973.

It is clear that, Joseph's recognition of the complexities of the issue notwithstanding, the cycle of deprivation matches a number of key strands in the underclass concept. Joseph was concerned with the transmission of deprivation between generations; his solutions were behavioural rather than structural; he acknowledged that there was little evidence to support the existence of the 'cycle', so that more research was necessary; and the main appeal of the phrase was symbolic and rhetorical. In fact, as we have seen, the 1972 cycle speech was only a more dramatic version of ideas that Joseph had been thinking about from the mid 1960s. What was new was the suggestion that the situation of problem families was in some way repeated in successive generations. In this, Joseph may well have been influenced by the research carried out in Sheffield into successive generations of problem families. What is clear is that the problem family idea played a more influential part in his thinking than the rival American culture of poverty concept.[31] There is no evidence that Joseph was influenced by Oscar Lewis or other American theorists. Instead his thinking on the cycle was moulded by a genuine concern with family poverty; by the earlier debates about problem families; and by wider debates in the early 1970s about family planning and deprivation.

Joseph's biographers note that the 1972 speech was not so much 'a call for open debate as an invitation to researchers to find empirical support for ideas which he held already'.[32] They suggest that, following his experiences at the Department of Housing, Joseph tended to be torn between a desire to reach firm conclusions and a need to think things through carefully before stating his own position. Recognising that the issues were complex and the research likely to be long-term in nature, advice was taken from the SSRC as to whether the problem of the cycle of deprivation could in fact be researched. It was international research on parenting that led to early discussions between the DHSS and SSRC on a possible research programme. This Joint DHSS/SSRC Working Party on Transmitted Deprivation was convened in June 1972, and a discussion paper on possible research strategies was presented at a seminar at All Souls College, Oxford, in April 1973. This was attended by researchers and others involved in the implementation of social policy. Joseph's way of working was that of an academic – he had won a Prize Fellowship at All Souls in June 1946, and was to remain closely linked to the College for the rest of his life. In addition, a review of the literature was commissioned, to be carried out by Professor Michael Rutter and Nicola Madge. Though this was not finally published until 1976, a large part was ready remarkably quickly, by June 1973. It had an important impact on the Working Party.

By August 1974, when its first report was published, the membership of the Joint Working Party had changed slightly. There were seven DHSS representatives on it, including two each from the Local Authorities Social Services Division, the Social Work Services Division, and the Research Management Division. Other bodies represented were the Central Statistical Office; Department of Education and Science; and the Medical Research Council. There was a similar number of SSRC representatives, but from more diverse backgrounds, including Professors Tony Atkinson, the economist then at Essex; Maurice Freedman from the Institute of Social Anthropology at Oxford; Roy Parker from the Department of Social Administration at Bristol; and Michael Rutter, of the Department of Child Psychiatry at the Institute of Psychiatry. Richard Berthoud has suggested that whereas the SSRC regarded the problem as one taking in all the social sciences, the composition of the DHSS representatives reflected its belief that it was a problem of individuals, and that the personal social services would hold the key.[33]

The real purpose of the Working Party at this time was to consider whether the cycle of transmitted deprivation would in fact be a fruitful area for research. When it met in June 1973, the Working Party decided that there was so much material in the literature review that it would be sensible to allow more time for it to be studied before outlining areas in which research might be undertaken. The first report by the Working Party, presented in October 1973, outlined why research would be worthwhile and the kinds of research that might be undertaken. The Working Party acknowledged that both 'deprivation' and 'transmitted' were ambiguous terms. 'Deprivation' was used to describe a condition, such as being poor, unemployed, badly housed, and so on, and also a hypothesis as to the causes of that condition – having been deprived of certain advantages. People might not agree on characteristics of 'deprivation', including the deprived people themselves. Moreover 'transmission' might also assume how continuities were caused. The Working Party noted that they might be not familial, but the influence of a common environment on successive generations.[34] These problems notwithstanding, the Working Party also concluded that:

> there is convincing evidence that intergenerational continuity is an important feature of deprivation, but that the causal mechanisms are not well understood, and that there is a good prospect that more research will contribute to improvements in social policy.[35]

It recommended a number of parallel studies, including additional work being grafted on to studies that were already under way, and it thought that roughly seven years would be required for the research. Statistical data relating to samples of individuals or families was a key resource, as were longitudinal studies such as the NCDS. These, though, were to be supplemented by intensive studies of samples in particular regions, and no new longitudinal studies were to be commissioned. Attention was also to be directed to the 'distinguishing personal or environmental characteristics' that enabled individuals to break out of the cycle.[36]

There was no firm theoretical framework for the whole programme. Thus there was room for anthropological studies of families in their social context that would produce hypotheses rather than test them. Other areas for research included the components of deprivation; intra-generational continuities; and concepts of deprivation. On the theme of inter-generational continuities, it was suggested that research might explore income and poverty; reliance on social services; 'colour'; and housing. It was recognised that identifying causal mechanisms would be the most difficult part of the research. These might include the influence of the family; social stratification; the educational system; areas and neighbourhoods; and stigma. Interestingly too, the Working Party did not discount the influence of the culture of poverty, where families and individuals 'form a sub-culture of their own, with mores dissonant with those of the broader culture, but adapted to their own circumstances'.[37] Intervention was also covered, such as housing policies, social security, and provision for the under-fives. Overall, the Working Party recommended that the DHSS and SSRC should begin to explore how this research might be carried out. This would include the completion of the literature review, and discussions about how the proposed research might be managed. The programme of research could take seven years, with a budget rising to £150,000 per year – an extremely large research programme at that time.

At the same time as the deliberations of the Working Party, there were also in the early 1970s consultations with professional, voluntary and other organisations. These indicated that Joseph had become more cautious. In *Preparation for Parenthood* (1974), Joseph stressed that debate about the cycle had not distracted the government from its priorities in the areas of low income and poor housing. He admitted that he had used the term 'cycle' to describe the apparent persistence of problems from one generation to another, and conceded that the term was 'a shorthand one and, as such, imprecise and open to much conceptual questioning'.[38] One aim was to prepare people better for parenthood, partly through providing knowledge, understanding and support; but Joseph was cautious, noting the need for more research. This was amplified by the experience of the All Souls seminar held in April 1973. Again, writing in the foreword to *Dimensions of Parenthood* (1974), Joseph conceded that the effect of early discussions in territory which, for the government at least, was unfamiliar, had been to 'alert us to the complex issues involved and to warn us against over-simple and under-sensitive reactions to the problems we perceive in families, struggling to cope with multiple deprivations'.[39]

Joseph's more conciliatory stance was partly in reaction to the hostility that the theory had provoked in some quarters. At a social work conference held in March 1974, Peter Townsend condemned the cycle of deprivation as being 'a mixture of popular stereotypes and ill-developed, mostly contentious, scientific notions. It is a conceptual bed into which diverse travellers have scrambled for security and comfort'.[40] Townsend made four points about the theory as expounded by Joseph. First, only certain types of deprivation had been chosen. Second, only certain causal factors had been selected. Third, certain interpretations of the term 'transmission' had been chosen. Finally, only particular solutions to the 'problem' had been selected. Townsend's paper was also important in that it showed an appreciation of the historical antecedents of these ideas, including the Wood Report and the Lidbetter research of the early 1930s. He repeated his earlier criticisms of Oscar Lewis and the culture of poverty. In general, Townsend argued that the theory diverted attention from structural factors, and tended to blame the victim.[41] A different critique was put forward by Bill Jordan, then Professor of Social Work at Exeter University. Jordan suggested that it was perfectly proper to ask why, in an era of increased prosperity and improved public services, some people were still poor. He argued, however, that this question had nothing to do with maladjustment. It was confusing to set up research into poverty and maladjustment among the poorest sector, when only the former was a distinguishing characteristic of this group. Jordan argued 'it is not a question of how these factors persist, as Sir Keith Joseph suggests, but of how they are reinforced by conditions of prosperity'. Jordan concluded of the cycle of deprivation theory that it 'encapsulates a number of myths that are very prevalent in both the academic and the political spheres of social policy at the present time'.[42]

Another critic at this time was Bob Holman, then Senior Lecturer in Social Administration at the University of Glasgow. Holman was critical of the behavioural emphasis of the concept of the cycle of deprivation.[43] Holman subsequently pointed out that there were differences between the cycle of deprivation and the culture of poverty. In the latter, the poor were seen as a sub culture separate from the rest of the population, whereas in the former they were part of mainstream culture, but their upbringing and education in conditions of deprivation meant that they were unable to take advantage of the wider opportunities that society offered. They were deprived of those aspects of culture that allowed other members to keep themselves from poverty. Nevertheless, Holman linked the two theories together as essentially behavioural interpretations of poverty. Overall, Holman rejected the cycle of deprivation thesis, claiming the research was inadequate, and that child-rearing practices were essentially adaptive.[44]

These criticisms notwithstanding, by August 1974, when the report of the Working Party was published, the DHSS and SSRC had signed a contract whereby the former would finance and the latter administer a programme of research into transmitted deprivation. A smaller Organising Group, chaired by Professor Peter Willmott, was to consider applications for funds from researchers wanting to work on transmitted deprivation, to discuss areas that needed to be investigated, and to encourage applications in those areas.[45] Richard Berthoud argues that the Working Party failed to identify the fundamental relationship between individual behaviour and the power of social institutions. He notes that 'by failing to define deprivation, the Working Party allowed researchers working on the programme to interpret it as they liked, but also permitted a strong assumption in favour of the equation of poverty with personal inadequacy'. Perhaps more importantly, the SSRC at that time operated very much in 'responsive' mode. It publicised its presence to the research community, and waited for social scientists to come up with projects. This meant that promoting a pre-planned multidisciplinary research programme was something of an uphill struggle. Berthoud alleges that, in 1972, the SSRC had 'never been asked an important question by an outsider'.[46]

The research programme that was organised through the Working Party was to span eight years. It cost around £750,000 (at 1970s values), and generated some nineteen studies, fourteen literature reviews, and four feasibility projects. Richard Berthoud wrote in 1987 that:

> Sir Keith Joseph is widely reported nowadays to scorn the social sciences in general, and sociology in particular. Such a blanket condemnation suggests little power of discrimination, but if the contribution to the debate on deprivation made by his most direct critics from the social sciences contributed to his view, one can have some sympathy for it.[47]

Thus it is important to explore the research programme to see why it played such an influential role in colouring Joseph's view of the social sciences in general. To what extent did the researchers diverge from the original cycle of deprivation theory, as propounded in the 1972 speech? What was the relationship between the civil servants at the DHSS and the academic community? And what changes occurred in the wider social and political climate, in the period between the first report of the Working Party in 1974 and the final report on the programme published in 1982?

As we have seen, one of the first tasks undertaken by the Working Party was to commission a literature review, a consultancy subsequently accepted by Michael Rutter and Nicola Madge. Both were based at the University of London – Rutter was then Professor of Child Psychiatry at the Institute of Psychiatry, while Madge was a Research Officer at the Thomas Coram Research Unit. The purpose of their review, published in 1976, was to examine what evidence existed that might support the 'cycle of transmitted deprivation', and to consider what it was that created these alleged continuities between generations. Rutter and Madge admitted, however, that it had quickly become clear, when they had begun work, that there were some serious problems with their brief, and that changes would be necessary. Most importantly, Rutter and Madge decided that they preferred the term 'disadvantage' to the original 'deprivation'; they substituted the plural 'cycles' for the singular 'cycle'; and they dropped the phrase 'transmitted'.

These changes would have an important bearing on the research programme as a whole. In trying to summarise the current state of knowledge, Rutter and Madge also made several other important provisos. They emphasised that they did not equate poverty with maladjustment; the suggested focus on the family was too narrow; and they would discuss environmental and constitutional factors bearing on deprivation and disadvantage. Rutter and Madge pointed out, for instance, that there were as many discontinuities as continuities in the experiences of these families. They argued further that intergenerational continuities in disadvantage were only part of the broader question of disadvantage, and should be examined in that context. Rutter and Madge argued that many children brought up in conditions of severe disadvantage developed normally and went on to produce perfectly happy families of their own. Although intergenerational cycles of disadvantage did exist, 'the exceptions are many and a surprisingly large proportion of people reared in conditions of privation and suffering do *not* reproduce that pattern in the next generation'.[48] They pointed out that there was little research on people trying to break out of cycles of disadvantage. Rutter and Madge remained sceptical about Oscar Lewis's culture of poverty, claiming that 'neither a wholly sub-cultural nor a wholly situational interpretation of the behaviour and attributes of poor communities is tenable'. Each had its own limitations and both failed to take account of individual differences. It was also unlikely that the concept was relevant to Britain – Lewis had said it was most likely to develop in 'rapidly changing societies', which Britain plainly was not. Overall Rutter and Madge concluded that 'the culture of poverty concept is inadequate for an analysis of British society'.[49]

The literature review included historical studies. In the case of problem families, for instance, Rutter and Madge traced the work of Charles Booth, E. J. Lidbetter, the Wood Committee and C. J. Blacker, and the shift in emphasis from social conditions to personal problems. Studies of problem families were essentially studies of particular characteristics, the analysis was tautological, and therefore the concept of a distinct problem family lifestyle was open to 'serious objection'.[50] In many ways, the findings of different studies, and the differences between investigators, were simply a function of how the groups had been defined, and merited little serious attention. It was not justifiable to discuss problem families as a homogeneous group separate from the rest of the population – in the opinion of Rutter and Madge they were not. Nonetheless, Rutter and Madge argued that it was important to consider families who suffered from a combination of severe disadvantages or problems. There was a marked overlap between different forms of social disadvantage, and for problem families an improvement in social circumstances might be as important as help with personal problems and relationships. Problem families did not constitute a group that was qualitatively different from other members of the population. Rutter and Madge concluded that 'just as stereotypes of "*the* problem family" are to be distrusted, so are package remedies based on notions of a homogeneous group'.[51] Yet families with multiple social disadvantages and/or personal problems did give cause for concern, both in terms of the present and with regard to problems that might persist into the next generation. While the concept of the problem family was too vague for it to be possible to estimate numbers, the evidence apparently showed there were a substantial number of families with multiple problems, some of which involved extended dependency on social services.

In terms of Sir Keith's original thesis, the authors of the literature review argued that there was no single problem of a cycle of transmitted deprivation. Rather there were many forms of disadvantage that arose in various ways, and which showed varying degrees and types of continuities between generations.

There certainly were continuities over time. However, only some were familial – there were marked regional continuities, for example, in disadvantage. There were many discontinuities. Many children born into disadvantaged homes did not repeat the pattern of disadvantage in the next generation. Even where continuities were strongest, many individuals broke out of the cycle. Equally, many people became disadvantaged without having had disadvantaged parents. Rutter and Madge summed this up by stating that 'familial cycles are a most important element in the perpetuation of disadvantage but they account for only a part of the overall picture'.[52] For instance, they thought the continuities were weaker over three generations than two. They noted that the extent of continuity varied according to the type and level of disadvantage.

Despite these arguments, Rutter and Madge did echo Joseph in arguing that behavioural and educational factors might be as significant as socio-economic deprivation. They claimed, for example, that it was possible to influence cycles of disadvantage without necessarily embarking on wholesale social change. In the first place, cycles of disadvantage were found at all levels of society. Secondly, Rutter and Madge argued that in other respects, correlations with inadequate living conditions provided a poor guide to levels of disadvantage. Although overcrowding, for example, was worse in Scotland than in England, evidence from schools indicated that Scottish children were better readers, on average, than their English counterparts. The reasons for this remained unclear. Thus research was needed into why children might be disadvantaged in one respect, but were often not disadvantaged in another.[53] It was in this way, argued Rutter and Madge, that patterns in cycles of disadvantage might be broken.

Many of the books that resulted from the various projects were published by Heinemann in the series that was associated with the research programme. Some studies, such as those by psychiatrists and psychologists, appeared to support Sir Keith Joseph's original behavioural emphasis. For example, the team led by the psychiatrist W. L. Tonge focused on problem families in Sheffield.[54] Similarly the team of paediatricians and psychologists led by Professor Israel Kolvin, then Professor of Child Psychiatry at the University of Newcastle-upon-Tyne, sought to follow up some of the families interviewed in Newcastle as part of the famous 'thousand families study' conducted by Sir James Spence in the 1950s.[55]

Others, published by academics whose sympathies lay more with the Townsend emphasis on structural factors than with the Joseph thesis, ended up far from their starting point, and in some cases showed barely disguised scorn for it. What is perhaps most striking, from the standpoint of today, is the rejection of the role of behaviour, and the emphasis on the essentially passive role of the family or recipients of welfare. Writing in 1979, Peter Townsend argued that the cycle of deprivation showed little awareness of its historical antecedents. On the other hand, it had a clear political ideology, and reflected the government's interest in area deprivation policies. Both the concept of area deprivation and assigning responsibility to the individual and family were in his view closely linked to the culture of poverty hypothesis. Deprivation was 'treated as a residual personal or family phenomenon rather than a large-scale structural phenomenon'.[56]

Townsend's work was an important influence on many of the researchers who worked on the Transmitted Deprivation research programme. For example, Mildred Blaxter, a sociologist then based at the Institute of Medical Sociology at the University of Aberdeen, sought to examine questions to do with continuities in health disadvantage among children. Blaxter tended to downplay the social patterning of beliefs, in favour of the effects of poverty and other environmental factors.[57] A study published by Juliet Essen and Peter Wedge in 1982, based on the NCDS at the National Children's Bureau, was a source of longitudinal data since it had monitored the progress and circumstances of all people in Great Britain born in one week in March 1958. Overall, Essen and Wedge were forced to concede that there was much discontinuity in disadvantage.[58] The same was true of the literature reviews of housing, education and managing money.[59] Research by the economist Tony Atkinson and his team examined continuities in economic status between generations. The Atkinson team focused on 'disadvantage', however, and denied the existence of a 'cycle'.[60] The authors of a literature review of the impact of social policy on 'transmitted deprivation' admitted quite openly that they had departed from their original brief. Roger Fuller and Olive Stevenson, both from the University of Keele, acknowledged that the terms of their remit were 'deeply problematic' – the phrase 'transmitted deprivation' was difficult to define, and the cycle of deprivation a 'shadowy phenomenon'. Overall, 'the tight conceptual framework misleadingly promised by the terminology of our remit was inevitably lacking'.[61]

It is not possible here to look at all the projects that were commissioned. Among the projects funded by the Working Party was one that sought to examine the cycle of deprivation through intensive case studies. The project was interdisciplinary in scope, and aimed to combine the approaches of psychology, sociology and anthropology. It was based on participant observation of a small number of 'multi-problem' families in an industrial town in the Midlands, and the team was led by Frank Coffield, then at Keele University. Four families were selected – the Barkers, representing a large family; Ada Paterson, an 'inadequate' mother; the Martins, a long-term unemployed family; and the Fieldings, a family regarded as 'coming out' of deprivation. The team entered the social world of these families for two years, and acted as participant observers by joining family celebrations such as wedding anniversaries, birthday parties, and Christenings, as well as more general family activities.

The volume that Coffield and his team produced was published in 1980, the first of the original studies to appear in book form. But as with Rutter and Madge's literature review, the findings of this study tended to challenge, rather than confirm, the theory of the cycle of deprivation. Vince Barker, head of the Barker family, in many ways fitted the culture of poverty stereotype put forward by Oscar Lewis. He certainly lived for the present and did not defer gratification, perhaps because he anticipated a time when he might be less physically robust and incapable of earning an adequate wage packet. Nonetheless there were other features that contradicted the traditional stereotype. For one thing, the Barkers possessed fire insurance following a fire at their home. Similarly Elsie Barker saved for Christmas, and managed her debts as carefully as she could. Coffield and his colleagues argued of the Barkers that it was only the dynamic interplay of both personal and structural factors 'which, in our opinion, can in any way do justice to the complexity of the lives we are struggling to understand'.[62] The case of the other families was similarly complex. In the Martin household, for example, there was evidence that possessions were not neglected but in fact were looked after carefully. The garden was cultivated, at least for a time, and ornaments were carefully arranged in the front room. Sally Martin spent a lot of her time washing and ironing, while Peter Martin was constantly repairing or improving household objects.[63] He, too, was interested in gardening, and also managed to keep his first job at a garage for over a year.

Reviewing the problem family literature, Coffield and his colleagues argued that this phrase, along with the term 'transmitted deprivation', should be abandoned. They were also critical of the follow-up studies conducted in Sheffield that influenced Joseph in the run-up to the 1972 speech.[64] An individual explanation of failure was favoured in these studies, and the authors were unable to explain how the children came to be involved with the same social work agencies. Overall, Coffield and his colleagues argued from their fieldwork that the cycle of deprivation was too simple an idea to explain the complex lives of the four families that they had spent so long studying in such minute detail. Employing a different metaphor, they concluded that 'the *web* of deprivation, rather than the *cycle* of deprivation, depicts more accurately the dense network of psychological, social, historical and economic factors which have either created or perpetuated problems for these families'.[65] The complexity lay in the interacting and cumulative nature of the deprivations – no single hypothesis could explain the complex mesh of factors. Although the cycle of deprivation had an appealing simplicity, the reality was that families moved in and out of established categories of deprivation. In general, Coffield and his colleagues argued that the term 'cycle of deprivation' tended to simplify complex issues. While there were factors that might increase the probability of a family being labelled as a problem, 'the causal processes are many, complex and interrelated, the exceptions numerous, and the critical precipitating events different in each case'.[66]

Reflecting on the project a year after publication, in his inaugural lecture as Professor of Education at Durham University, Frank Coffield came to the same conclusions. The idea of a circle created the wrong mental image, because it implied a simple linear progression, whereas the data that his team had collected showed how the different variables were complex, and both interacted with, and were contaminated by, each other. The 'transmission' of deprivation could not be attributed to any one single factor. Importantly, in light of recent debates, Coffield argued the data indicated that it was a mistake to focus exclusively on either behaviour or structure. The team rejected the idea that there was a small group that could be labelled as 'problem families'. Coffield concluded:

> our families were caught in a dense web of economic, medical, social and psychological problems which overlapped and interacted; their problems needed amelioration, no matter what their parents or grandparents were like. Moreover, our families moved in and out of the official categories of deprivation even during the two years of fieldwork.[67]

However, Richard Berthoud has argued that while the Coffield team identified the key issues, it adopted a research method which was unlikely to yield answers. The project was extremely small-scale, and was only able to illustrate the characteristics of 'deprived' individuals and families. In this it replicated the earlier problem family studies, though it was critical of them. Berthoud argues that the Coffield study was more useful in 'advancing the question, than in providing an answer'.[68]

Given the diverse nature of the books and literature reviews, it was hardly surprising that these modifications of the original concept were noted by those who had the task of reviewing the whole programme. In the words of Richard Berthoud, they had to 'make bricks with very little straw'.[69] Reviewing the Transmitted Deprivation programme ten years on, in 1982, Muriel Brown and Nicola Madge, from the London School of Economics, drew several conclusions. Much of the research had been concerned with broader issues of deprivation and disadvantage in society at large, and had in fact been concerned with the influence on poverty of structural rather than behavioural factors.[70] Perhaps not surprisingly, the research had not been guided by a consistent viewpoint, and Sir Keith himself had changed his stance. As we have seen, the original speech was dogmatic, mentioning the role of economic factors and living conditions, but highlighting personal factors and child-rearing. Whereas in 1972 Joseph had stressed parental influence, by 1979 he was convinced that the cycle was not inescapable. There was similar caution on the part of the academics, notably on the difference between 'attributes' and 'burdens', and on the meaning of transmission and the means by which it could be studied.[71]

Brown and Madge noted that researchers had diverse approaches. While general understanding of the meaning of deprivation had been enhanced by the debate, they concluded that 'it is fair to conclude that no real consensus was reached on the subject'. Brown and Madge found that there were some correlations between income level and occupational level across generations, and noted that health, criminality and emotional experiences in childhood could lead to poor parenting behaviour in adulthood. With regard to housing circumstances, educational attainment, and general parenting skills, however, it was harder to say if the continuities were any more than coincidental. One of the main findings was that there were many exceptions, even when the strongest family patterns were found. Brown and Madge argued that 'cycles of deprivation do not inevitably exist although they may emerge in relation to particular individuals and families'.[72]

Like Coffield and his colleagues, Brown and Madge concluded from the research that there was no single simple explanation of deprivation. First, deprivation was not unitary, with both consistent and idiosyncratic patterns. Secondly, most forms of deprivation were influenced by so many factors that it was impossible to single out specific variables – the patterns of association could not be assumed to be cause and effect. They concluded that 'neither the notion of causation implicit in the "cycle of deprivation" thesis, nor the diametrically opposed view that structural factors are all to blame for society's troubles, can be accepted'.[73] It was impossible to disentangle the many influences important for deprivation and its transmission.

Richard Berthoud has argued that Brown and Madge reviewed the research programme in rather a neutral way, without putting forward their own independent views. There was no hint that any of the studies were disappointing, or that the activities were less than well-conceived or successful. Brown and Madge accepted the failure of the Working Party to define 'deprivation' adequately, and did not explore what deprivations had in common. They claimed, unconvincingly, that despite their 'diverse approaches', the researchers came up with similar conclusions. Brown and Madge summarised this common ground through the hypothesis that 'much deprivation is deeply rooted in the structure of our society and affected by the network of unequal opportunities and life chances that the structure maintains'.[74] Berthoud contrasts the approach of Brown and Madge with the earlier literature review by Rutter and Madge, which in his view had asked questions, opened doors, and refused to reach conclusions. He was also critical of their use of the American term 'invulnerable' for those who had escaped deprivation, writing:

> If social forces merely alter probabilities, those 'who escape' are simply those whose number did not come up, but the term 'invulnerable' suggests they may have had some special armour which protected them from an otherwise inescapable destiny.[75]

Finally, Berthoud noted Brown and Madge were poor on policy recommendations. Given the problems in establishing the causes of deprivation and agreeing on explanations, Brown and Madge argued that no single policy change could touch on more than a fraction of the problem of deprivation and disadvantage.

What is interesting is how the inspiration for the cycle of deprivation thesis lay in the earlier problem family debate. It was typical of Joseph that in private he continued to study his alleged cycle. As Secretary for State for Education in the early 1980s, Joseph came to the department determined to help those he regarded as the victims rather than the beneficiaries of policy. Yet Joseph's social philosophy also explains why he was intellectually attracted to opposition to the voucher scheme. The idea behind vouchers was that parents could use them to choose schools for their children, thereby forcing schools to compete for the 'custom' of parents. Joseph opposed vouchers. He argued that, badly educated themselves and transmitting their lack of ambition to their children, parents in the lower classes would fail to make the effort. Instead the state should pour resources into these 'sink' schools, in an effort to try to recruit the best teachers. However, having learnt from some of the mistakes he had made earlier in his political career, Joseph was careful not to openly link his theories on deprivation to his opposition to the education voucher scheme. A further example of the continued influence of the cycle of deprivation came in Joseph's support for the Home-Start charity in the House of Lords in the early 1990s. This organisation uses volunteers to befriend families and provide assistance to those struggling to bring up children.[76]

It is clear that the research programme departed dramatically from Sir Keith Joseph's original thesis. A cycle of deprivation that was essentially a behavioural interpretation of poverty, that stressed the importance of inter-generational continuities, became instead a cycles of disadvantage concept. It was concerned more with structural factors and emphasised the discontinuities in the experiences of families. There were several factors involved here. First, part of the problem lay with the original report of the Working Party, which failed to define both 'deprivation' and 'transmitted' adequately. Second, in this period the SSRC was not accustomed to running a pre-planned multidisciplinary programme of this kind, and found it difficult to commission the type of studies that were thought to be required. Third, the composition of the DHSS and SSRC membership of the Working Party indicated important differences between the two groups on the possible causes of the 'problem'. Fourth, what is perhaps most striking in light of current debates is the lack of consensus among the academics. While they were able to reject the term 'cycle of deprivation' in favour of 'cycles of disadvantage', they were less successful in identifying the relative roles of behaviour and structure in the perpetuation of poverty.

As we noted at the outset, the idea of a cycle of deprivation continues to have currency at a policy and popular level. On the death of the then Lord Joseph in December 1994, *The Times* noted in a leader article that 'tough decisions rather than sentimental social engineering were needed to break the "cycle of deprivation" which so afflicted, and afflicts, our inner cities'. It defended the 1974 speech, arguing that it reflected not eugenics but Joseph's 'lifelong concern with poverty, the family and the growing dependency culture'.[77] Moreover there are marked similarities between the ideas espoused by Joseph and the policies adopted by New Labour. In introducing the Sure Start programme in April 2000, Health Minister Yvette Cooper echoed Joseph in arguing that increased benefits alone could not compensate for other factors affecting disadvantaged children.[78] The early Thatcher governments were unlikely to be influenced by the literature reviews and books that were generated by the Working Party on Transmitted Deprivation. Nevertheless, what is again striking from the perspective of today is the way that researchers are only beginning to respond to the challenge of unravelling the combination of behavioural and structural factors identified by Brown and Madge and their colleagues. The link between the cycle of deprivation and the contemporary emphasis on social exclusion is provided by the underclass concept of the 1980s. As with the culture of poverty, it requires us to cross the Atlantic once again, to examine the emergence of the underclass idea in the United States.

7

Uncovering the Underclass – America

The life-skills class convenes on Tuesday and Friday mornings, and among the twenty-two students registered for it are people who have been murderers, muggers, stickup men, chain snatchers, pimps, burglars, heroin addicts, drug pushers, alcoholics, welfare mothers and swindlers.[1]

By any standards this was an unusual school. The class was called Basic Typing 27, and it was run through the auspices of the Wildcat Skills Training Center in New York, a training programme in 'life skills' for ex-offenders, ex-addicts, unemployed women, and school drop-outs. It was devised by a non-profit-making organisation, the Manpower Demonstration Research Programme. The teacher of the life-skills class was Howard Smith, a former heroin addict who had spent several years in jail. The writer was Ken Auletta of the *New Yorker* magazine. It was 1981.

There are parallels between the uncovering of the underclass in the 1980s, and the discovery of the social residuum a hundred years earlier. Economic recession and high unemployment exacerbated fear and anxiety about the apparent emergence of a group detached from society as a whole. Moreover in both cases, the running was made by journalists, with academic interest lagging some way behind. Although, as we shall see, there were mentions of the underclass in the social science literature of the 1970s, its real emergence as a theme of much greater social and political significance can be attributed to its articulation in the popular press. As with the culture of poverty in the 1960s, the earliest moves came from America. In particular, the work of two writers, Ken Auletta and Nicholas Lemann, gave the concept of an underclass much greater prominence.

In previous chapters, we have examined such concepts as the social problem group of the 1930s, the problem family of the 1950s, and the cycle of deprivation in the 1970s. However, it is fair to say that although these were important themes in social thought, they were never part of mainstream public debate. Confined to a narrow though influential band of 'experts', or distinctive professional groups, they were never taken up by the popular press. It was only in the 1980s, with the emergence of the concept of the underclass, that questions about its origins, composition, and implications became issues of interest to a much wider constituency. As with the culture of poverty, the theory of the underclass initially proved popular with both Right and Left. In the case of the former, the term was used to refer to a group of apparently unemployed and unemployable people who faced lives of misery in the inner-city, characterised by violent crime and illegitimacy. With regard to the latter, the underclass was seen as a group of undereducated and unskilled workers apparently left behind by profound shifts in technology and in the economy as a whole. For the first time, academics began to look at the history of these labels, and to explore the processes through which they rose to prominence and subsequently lost favour.

In this chapter, we examine the limited use of the term 'underclass' in academic studies published in the 1960s and early 1970s. We then contrast this interpretation with the rather different analysis that was offered by journalists in magazine articles published in the early 1980s. We also explore the different positions that were adopted by contributors to the underclass debate in the 1980s and early 1990s. In many respects these present an over-simplification of the complex and often contradictory positions taken by various observers. Even so, it is possible to disentangle four – first, a position that saw the problems of the underclass as essentially those of behaviour; second, those that located its emergence more in terms of structural factors; third, a group that was attracted to the idea, but found no empirical evidence; and fourth, those who rejected the idea outright. Moreover, although there were important links between the debate about the underclass in the United States and in Britain, there were also significant differences in the way that the debate was constructed. Most obvious, of course, was the way that discussion of the underclass in the United States was dominated by the theme of 'race'. We look first of all at the debate in the United States. In the following chapter, we turn to the British experience.

Recent American writers, such as Jacqueline Jones, in her study of the history of the 'dispossessed' between the American Civil War and the present, have used the term 'underclass' as a synonym for the poor, and this creates some problems of definition.[2] In his study of the parole system in the United States between 1890 and 1990, Jonathan Simon argues that crises in the criminal justice system were caused not so much by problems of punishing offenders, but by much wider changes in society and the political system. Thus he claims that the great increase in prison populations must be seen in relation to the decline of industry as a source of employment for the labour force, and the emergence of an urban underclass. Simon's underclass is made up of ethnic minorities, and lives in zones of poverty. In his view, the aim of the criminal justice system has been to consolidate a process of social control 'both to secure the underclass and to secure others against it'.[3] Writing in 1993, Simon was well aware of the contested nature of the underclass debate, and of its key contributors. Nevertheless he argued that it was not necessary to resolve this debate, since for him the underclass was a synonym for the poor.[4] Most of the chapters in Michael Katz's potentially useful collection similarly focus more on urban poverty than on the underclass debate as a form of discourse.[5]

However, it is arguable that regarding the underclass as a synonym for urban poverty in practice limits the opportunities for exploring successive re-inventions of the label over time. The phrase 'underclass' was first used in the early 1960s by Gunnar Myrdal, who used it to describe the effects of technological change on the American workforce. Myrdal was then Professor of International Economics at the University of Stockholm. In *Challenge to Affluence* (1963), Myrdal, commenting on economic change, wrote that the causes of unemployment were comparatively well-known in America. Less often commented upon was the way technological and economic change tended to trap an underclass of unemployed and unemployable people at the bottom of society.[6] Myrdal argued that unemployment and poverty were creating 'an "underclass" of unemployed, unemployables, and underemployed, more and more hopelessly divorced from the nation at large and without a share in its life, its ambitions and its achievements'.[7] Myrdal argued further that the effects of these processes were perpetuated in successive generations. The fact that underclass children tended to share their parents' resources and life chances limited the extent to which the education system could contribute to social and economic mobility.[8]

Myrdal's book is generally accepted as the first modern use of the term 'underclass'. He suggested that most people in America thought of themselves as being middle-class, and were therefore unfamiliar with what might be seen as a neo-Marxist analysis. But there were studies published shortly after *Challenge to Affluence* that, like Myrdal, claimed to demonstrate the emergence of a separate lower-class culture. These included those by Elliot Liebow, Lee Rainwater, and Ulf Hannerz. What was interesting was that they did not use the term 'underclass' for the changes that they claimed to be observing, preferring instead 'lower-class culture'. Debate focused on whether these groups had a separate sub culture, or their behaviour was simply an adaptation to the circumstances in which they found themselves. The most likely explanation for this is that, through the work of Myrdal, the term 'underclass' was associated with technological and economic change. It was linked to a structural rather than a cultural or behavioural explanation of the causes of poverty.

Even studies that did look at the impact of structural change on the outlook of workers did not use the phrase 'underclass' for the changes that they detected. This was true, for example, of John Leggett's study of race and labour relations in American cities. In Detroit, Leggett drew a distinction between what he called the 'marginal' and the 'mainstream' working class. He claimed that the former group belonged to 'a subordinate ethnic or racial group which is unusually proletarianized and highly segregated'. Workers of this type had marginal roles in heavy industry, and faced economic insecurity, whereas the 'mainstream' working class were more educated and highly skilled, and more economically secure as a result. Sharing the same 'sub-cultural' traditions, the 'marginal' group was isolated from the rest of society and from the middle class in particular.[9] Leggett noted the distinction that Marx made between the employable workers and the *lumpenproletariat*. He agreed on the basis of his study that at the bottom of the working class was the *lumpenproletariat*, similar in many ways to the poor of early modern society.[10] Nevertheless he did not use the term 'underclass'.

So despite the example of Myrdal, very few writers used the term 'underclass' before the mid-1970s. It is possible, of course that this was simply a difference of language, and that the same ideas were expressed through different labels. However, the shift in language was more significant than this implies. Several reasons can be put forward to account for it. First, politicians, whether Democrat or Republican, continued to accept the ideological premises that underlay the 'War on Poverty' – the conservative argument that welfare programmes helped develop and maintain an underclass was not evident in this period. Second, the economy remained comparatively buoyant, and this masked the need for fundamental change in the older heavy industries. Third, poverty in the inner cities seemed to be less intense than it was later to become, and was not viewed as a growing racial problem – possibly because more affluent blacks had not yet migrated to the suburbs. Fourth, commentators were less concerned about aspects of behaviour – violent crime, illegitimacy, and welfare dependency – that were later to be viewed as hallmarks of the underclass.[11] The result was that within the academic community, discussion focused on the culture of poverty debate, with the reference point being Oscar Lewis rather than Gunnar Myrdal.

For much of the 1970s, the underclass debate was fairly quiet. However, by the late 1970s, recession and unemployment meant there was a disillusionment with the idea that social welfare could achieve a process of social engineering. Rapid decline of the older heavy industries and an obvious worsening of the condition of the poorest challenged the belief in inexorable economic progress. The recession of the early 1980s increased the proportion of the population in poverty in the USA, from 11.7% in 1979, to 15.2% in 1983.[12] In this situation, the re-emergence of the underclass as an important theme in public discourse was arguably inevitable. As in the 1960s, it provided a means of portraying, in dramatic form, the effects of technological and economic change on those at the bottom of the class system. But in the 1970s, Myrdal's term was also to be transformed in intellectual and ideological terms, so that by the end of the decade it had become a behavioural term for poor people, mainly black, who behaved in ways that were viewed as criminal, deviant, or simply different from the middle class.

The way that Oscar Lewis's work on the culture of poverty was reinterpreted by conservative commentators such as Edward Banfield was an early example of this process.[13] Then, in August 1977, for reasons that remain unclear, but were linked to a spate of looting in New York, *Time* magazine decided to feature the underclass as its cover story. Much of the content was a descriptive account of the minority poor in large-scale cities, accompanied by a series of photographs that featured blacks and Hispanics. Although the *Time* journalist did not link the characteristics of the underclass with a definition, the emphasis on behaviour was a departure from Myrdal. The definition of the underclass was vague, but several points stood out. In the mind of the writer, the underclass was a subset of the poor; it was urban; it was prone to crime and violence; its family structures were weak; and it had values that could be regarded as deviant. For instance, the *Time* article noted that:

> ... out there is a different world, a place of pock-marked streets, gutted tenements and broken hopes. Behind its crumbling walls lives a large group of people who are more intractable, more socially alien and more hostile than almost anyone had imagined. They are the unreachables: the American underclass.[14]

The writer noted that in cities like Chicago and New York, the underclass had been hit by the movement of manufacturing firms to the suburbs and the sunbelt. It was jobs, improvements to education, and training projects embracing partnerships between the federal government and private business that were needed most.

The *Time* article did not succeed in generating a public debate about the emergence of an underclass. Only in 1981, with the publication of the three-part article by Ken Auletta, did the underclass debate really take off. Initially appearing in the *New Yorker* magazine, these ideas gained a wider readership in the book that Auletta published in 1982. Based on the case-study of the Wildcat Skills Training Center in New York, Auletta concentrated on the behaviour and characteristics of the underclass, and it was this that gave his writing a greater impact. He cleverly moved between individual case studies of those who attended the 'life skills' class, and more general comments on the emergence of the underclass. Auletta claimed that there was no doubt that an underclass did exist. There had always been beggars, criminals, and damaged individuals that had operated outside the normal boundaries of society. At the same time, something new seemed to be happening. What was disputed was the causes of this phenomenon. Those on the Left claimed that the underclass was the victim of much larger economic forces, while those on the Right said the problems were caused essentially by the behaviour of individuals. In reality, claimed Auletta, there were as many causes of the underclass as 'there are combinations of notes on a piano keyboard'.[15]

How big was the underclass, and was it a growing problem? Auletta acknowledged that this depended partly on the way the term was defined. In 1979, there were 25m Americans classified as poor, of whom it was estimated 30% were 'acutely poor'. Other estimates based on studies of poverty dynamics claimed that around 45% (9.5m people) were the long-term poor. Including the unemployed, those with mental illness, or those who lacked support networks would raise the figure still higher. Earlier work by Oscar Lewis and Edward Banfield, among others, had produced estimates of between 1 and 20%.[16] Auletta argued the underclass was made up of four distinct groups. First came street criminals. Next were mothers whose dependency on welfare had become a way of life. The third group were 'hustlers' who earned a living in the black economy. Finally there were the 'traumatised', including patients released from mental asylums into the community. But the example of the street criminals and the 'hustlers' showed that members of the underclass were not necessarily poor. The underclass could be defined as much through behaviour as simple lack of income. What were not in doubt were the effects of the underclass. Auletta wrote, for instance, that 'members of the underclass are responsible for a disproportionate amount of the crime, the welfare costs, the unemployment, and the hostility which beset many American communities'.[17]

Auletta was concerned not just to describe the underclass, but also to see what might be done about it. He argued that policy-makers needed to agree on the nature of the problem. If it was an issue of racial and economic discrimination, then clearly structural changes were necessary. If it was a problem of behaviour linked to a culture of poverty, there was little that could be done. If it was assumed the causes were varied and complex, there was a midway position between 'revolution and resignation'.[18] In reality, argued Auletta, it was difficult to agree on what to do about the underclass because there was no agreement on the causes of the problem and its scale. The Left believed in fundamental economic and social change, the Right favoured intervention by business, and there was also a laissez-faire option. John Macnicol has observed that one of the enduring features of the underclass debate has been the recurring call for more research. For Auletta, this meant study of the medical and biological causes of the underclass, rather than its economic, sociological and psychological background. He concluded that 'one of the few subjects about which there is a consensus is the need for further research in the underclass'.[19]

If Auletta provided a readable but superficial account of the underclass, rather in the tradition of picaresque writing, Nicholas Lemann offered an analysis of the emergence of an underclass that was arguably more convincing. Published in the *Atlantic Monthly* in 1986, the location for Lemann's case-study was the South Side and West Side of Chicago, and the Robert Taylor Homes housing project where some 20,000 people lived. Lemann was interested in the way in which the existence of a black underclass culture might be linked to the migration of sharecroppers from the South, and subsequent changes in the composition of ghetto areas. Lemann wondered how the two versions of black life fitted together, and concluded that there was a divide in black America, a split between a middle class and an underclass that never made it. He argued that his study of a ghetto showed:

> The black underclass did not just spring into being over the past twenty years. Every aspect of the underclass culture in the ghettos is directly traceable to roots in the South – and not the South of slavery but the South of a generation ago. In fact, there seems to be a strong correlation between underclass status in the North and a family background in the nascent underclass of the sharecropper South.[20]

Lemann pointed out that the first wave of migration from the rural South to the urban North occurred in the 1940s, 1950s, and 1960s. The effect of this migration north was to transfer the black societies of small southern towns to Chicago. The second wave began in the late 1960s, when the black working and middle classes began to migrate out of the Chicago ghettos to the suburbs. Around 1970, for instance, the composition of the ghettos changed from being exclusively black to exclusively black lower class, and there was no alternative to the 'venerable, but always carefully contained, disorganised side of the ghetto culture'.[21] Several factors then turned the small underclass from the South into the large separate culture that it had become, and facilitated a descent into 'social disorganisation'. Lemann suggested that in Chicago, the area of North Lawndale showed these processes at work – first, the migration north; next the migration from the ghettos; finally the decline into disorganisation.

In the second part of his article, Lemann tackled the question of what could be done about a culture that appeared to be 'self-sustaining'.[22] He reiterated that the problems that seemed overwhelming – illegitimacy, unemployment, crime, and poor educational achievement – had existed in the ghettos for half a century. Until the late 1960s, when the middle class migrated from inner-city areas, these problems had been kept in check. Indeed, 'ghetto culture' was defended as being a rational response to economic and social circumstances. Community development, Lemann claimed, was the most appealing idea, since this could tackle both cultural and economic problems. The key theme should be integration, since the ghettos were the product of years of complete segregation from the neighbourhoods, schools, economy, and values of the rest of the country. Lemann concluded 'people don't like living in ghettos. They want to get out. Society should be pushing them in that direction'.[23]

Leaving aside the article in *Time* magazine, it was only in the early 1980s that the underclass debate really took off. As had happened in London a century earlier, articles in popular magazines served to provoke more serious academic study. Together, the articles in the *New Yorker* and the *Atlantic Monthly* provide a clear summary of the main themes of the two sides of the underclass debate. Auletta's insistence that the underclass could be defined as much by behaviour as by income was in the tradition of Oscar Lewis and others, and set off a chain of writing by commentators that could broadly be identified with the New Right. The work of Lemann, in contrast, associated underclass behaviour with changes in the social composition of American cities, and in the nature of southern black cultural patterns, and anticipated that of William Julius Wilson. Thus these two early articles contained the essence of the two strands of the underclass debate. They were to raise fundamental questions about the nature of economic change, the social composition of American cities, the effects of welfare on behaviour, and about patterns of racial segregation.

We will turn first to the position that defined the underclass in terms of the behaviour of its members. But before that it is necessary to examine briefly the work of one of its most influential writers – Charles Murray. Arguably the most influential book on social policy published in America in the 1980s was Murray's *Losing Ground* (1984). This was a brilliantly argued polemic against liberal assumptions about the American welfare programmes of the 1960s. Murray's point was that, through encouraging patterns of dependency and deterring people from working, welfare was part of the 'problem' rather than the solution. Murray argued, for example, that basic indicators of well-being took a turn for the worse in the 1960s, most noticeably in the case of the poor. The causes of this phenomenon were rather surprising. In Murray's words, the poor responded, as they always had, to the world as they found it. But what had been changed were the rules that governed their behaviour. He claimed that the poor were encouraged to behave in ways that were advantageous in the short term but destructive in the long term. Second, social policy masked these long-term losses, and subsidised mistakes that ultimately could not be corrected. Thus Murray argued that 'steps to relieve misery can create misery', and a 'moral dilemma' underlay the history of American social policy between 1950 and 1980.[24]

Losing Ground was concerned both with establishing data and providing an explanation for it. Murray examined the timing of trends in poverty, unemployment, and out-of-wedlock births in relation to the 'War on Poverty' programmes of the 1960s. He admitted that a decline in poverty had occurred in the USA, from 30% in 1950, to 13% in 1968. However, the improvement slowed in the late 1960s and stopped altogether in the 1970s, so that by 1980 it had crept up again to 13%. Surprisingly, it seemed that the number of people in poverty stopped declining just when public assistance programmes were at their height, and the rate of increase in those budgets was greatest.[25] Murray argued that 'latent poverty' (those who were below the official poverty line, plus those who were above it only because of welfare payments) had decreased in the 1950s, but began to increase again after 1972, to reach 22% by 1980. Calling this the 'most damning of statistics', Murray argued that economic independence was the key factor in determining the quality of a family's life. He attributed the alleged increase in 'latent poverty' to two factors. The first was the collapse of the family, especially the black family; the second, the withdrawal from the labour force of young men, especially young black men.[26]

Murray was also concerned with trends in unemployment. In the early 1950s, black youths had unemployment rates that were almost identical to those of whites. But in the second half of the 1950s, the rate of unemployment among black youths increased. Although it stabilised in the 1960s, this was at the comparatively high rate of one in four of the black labour force. In the late 1960s, black youth unemployment began to rise again, and continued to do so in the 1970s. What was interesting was that the same thing did not seem to be happening among older blacks. Between 1950 and 1980, unemployment among those over 25 decreased, while in those under 25 it increased – by 40% in those aged 18–19. Murray put forward the theory of the 'discouraged worker'. But he also claimed that the labour force participation rates of blacks and whites (a measure of the proportion of the total population either working or unemployed) were much closer in 1950 than in 1980. It was in the 1970s that they had diverged most markedly. Murray wrote that:

> What was happening, of course, is that the same people were getting older…We are watching a generational phenomenon. For whatever reasons, black males born in the early 1950s and thereafter had a different posture toward the labour market from their fathers and older brothers.[27]

Murray's argument relied on trends in out-of-wedlock births. He noted that overall birth rates for women aged 15–44 had declined, from 118 per 1,000 live births in 1960, to 68 per 1,000 live births in 1980. However, an increasing proportion of new births were illegitimate, and the problem was most acute for blacks. Although the number of out-of-wedlock births fell, those births represented a higher proportion of the total, since the number of legitimate births were falling even faster. What was most important here was the illegitimacy ratio, what Murray called 'illegitimate births not as a rate per 1,000 women, but as a percentage of all births'. The percentage of live births to black single women had increased from 17% in 1950 to 48% in 1980. White out-of-wedlock births increased as well, from 2% in 1950 to 11% in 1980. But the rise was sharpest among teenage black women, so that by 1980, for example, 82% of all births to black women aged 15–19 were out of wedlock. The result was a dramatic increase in the number of families headed by a single mother, and in the proportion of children being brought up in such families. In general, unmarried women were exercising a new freedom not to have children. The exceptions were single women aged 15–19 (black and white), and single white women aged 20–24. Murray suggested that 'for this narrow population of women, something overrode the broad social (and medical) trends that produced falling birth rates among everyone else'.[28]

What was most interesting about *Losing Ground*, and made the book so influential, was Murray's explanation for these trends. His argument was that things got much worse for the poor and disadvantaged from the second half of the 1960s than they should have, given the federal programmes on poverty, employment, wages and occupations, education, crime, and the family. As indicated above, the trends included increasing unemployment among the young, increased dropout from the labour force, and higher rates of out-of-wedlock births and welfare dependency. Murray argued that what was important was the changes that social policy made in the 'rewards and penalties, carrots and sticks, that govern human behaviour'.[29] It should have been possible to predict that these would lead to important changes in behaviour which were simply rational responses to the business of surviving. Murray argued that:

> all, poor and not-poor alike, use the same general calculus in arriving at decisions; only the exigencies are different. Poor people play with fewer chips and cannot wait as long for results. Therefore they tend to reach decisions that a more affluent person would not reach.[30]

Murray claimed that the effects of social policy on people's behaviour had been largely ignored. He illustrated this with an account of the different decisions that a fictional but typical couple, Harold and Phyllis, would have taken in 1950 and in 1970. Harold and Phyllis had just graduated from an average public school in an average American city. They were the children of low income parents, they were not interested in going to college, and they had no particular skills. Harold and Phyllis also found themselves in a familiar teenage predicament, since Phyllis was pregnant. Murray's argument was that in 1950, Harold would have got a poorly paid job (such as in a laundry) and the couple would have got married. In 1970, on the other hand, and finding themselves in the same situation, the couple would not have got married. Instead, Phyllis would have been able to claim Aid for Families with Dependent Children (AFDC) while cohabiting with Harold, and he would have supplemented her welfare cheques with part-time work. Murray concluded:

> There is 'no breakdown of the work ethic' in this account of rational choices among alternatives. There is no shiftless irresponsibility...There is no need to invoke the spectres of cultural pathologies or inferior upbringing. The choices may be seen much more simply, much more naturally, as the behaviour of people responding to the reality of the world around them and making the decisions – the legal, approved, and even encouraged decisions – that maximise their quality of life.[31]

As the case of Harold and Phyllis allegedly demonstrated, choices affecting work, marriage, and bringing up a family were bound up with economic considerations. In the 1960s, the environment in which young people grew up changed in ways that were mutually reinforcing. Changes in welfare were strengthened by changes in the risks attached to crime, and changes in education. Murray claimed that together they radically altered the 'incentive structure'. This went hand in hand with what he called the 'destruction of status rewards'. The poor became a homogeneous group, with all being viewed as victims. The welfare system was 'cleansed of stigma'.[32] Overall, Murray argued that the reforms of the 1960s were flawed, on both practical and moral grounds. He wrote that:

> It was wrong to take from the most industrious, most responsible poor – take safety, education, justice, status – so that we could cater to the least industrious, least responsible poor. It was wrong to impose rules that made it rational for adolescents to behave in ways that destroyed their futures.[33]

The implication was that fundamental changes to social policy were necessary. When they finally happened, it would be 'not because stingy people have won, but because generous people have stopped kidding themselves'.[34]

Murray's analysis reflected his unconventional academic background. He had studied Russian politics at Harvard University, and then worked in Thailand, initially for the Peace Corps and then for the United States Agency for International Development. In the mid-1970s, he was employed on an evaluation of Great Society programmes. The research for *Losing Ground* was funded by the conservative think-tank the Manhattan Institute. Important criticisms were made of Murray's radical interpretation. He said nothing about the costs of welfare. Welfare was defined narrowly, since almost all the evidence related to AFDC and food stamps for the non-disabled and non-elderly. The black population was equated with the poor, whereas the white population was implicitly the non-poor. Other critics argued that the definition of 'latent poverty' was misleading; Murray's data related to only one state (Pennsylvania); AFDC was not a major influence on out-of-wedlock births; and the increase in unemployment was unrelated to the expansion of welfare.[35] But Murray's arguments were influential. His argument was that the rules and regulations that governed entitlement to benefits and services must reward those activities and attributes which should be encouraged, and penalise those that need to be discouraged. Otherwise they would lead people to damage themselves and the communities in which they lived.

Murray only mentioned the underclass in passing. He wrote that 'if the behaviours of members of the underclass are founded on a rational appreciation of the rules of the game, and as long as the rules encourage dysfunctional values and behaviours, the future cannot look bright'. However, the impact of *Losing*

Ground was to focus attention on the apparently intractable nature of trends in unemployment and out-of-wedlock births. In many ways, it served to strengthen the behavioural interpretation of the underclass advanced by Ken Auletta. Clement Cottingham, for example, argued that, as some Marxists had predicted, technological change had seen the emergence of a redundant black and Hispanic underclass. It lay at the bottom of the urban class system, and seemed unable to adapt to the requirements of an advanced industrial society. The problems of the underclass included very low incomes, erratic employment patterns, low levels of skills, and limited access to education and social services. To these, Cottingham added what he called 'defective familial and individual socialisation processes', claiming that these had existed for generations.[36] The problem, then, was not just poverty, but the fact that patterns of deprivation showed continuities between generations. And there was a high degree of 'disconnectedness' from family and economic institutions. Cottingham's pathological analysis recalled some of the writing of the Chicago School in the 1920s. He wrote that, trapped in homogeneous ghettos, the underclass suffered from 'nutritional, health, neurological, or organic afflictions associated with densely populated, poverty-ridden, inner-city, urban environments'.[37]

This interpretation was supported in some of the academic research commissioned through the National Research Council's Committee on National Urban Policy. It had been established in February 1981, to carry out a four-year study. Kenneth B. Clark, author of *Dark Ghetto* (1960), and Richard P. Nathan, an academic at the Urban and Regional Research Centre at Princeton, contributed a chapter on the underclass to its first annual report. They agreed with Auletta that the underclass was not simply distinguished by lack of income, arguing 'the people in this group generally lack education, experience in the labour market, literacy skills, mobility options, and stable family relationships'.[38] What made the problem particularly serious was that underclass status appeared to be a permanent condition. Clark and Nathan identified some of the key questions and tasks. In particular, they tried to use multiple indicators from the 1980 census to answer the questions they had posed. They claimed, for example, that the underclass was concentrated in large cities, especially in the North Eastern and Northern states. Evidence on welfare dependency among black families suggested that poverty was passed to successive generations.[39] Clark and Nathan hypothesised that:

> The underclass appears to be walled off from the benefits of economic growth because of low earned incomes, low rates of labour force participation, and welfare dependency. People in the urban underclass are not geographically and occupationally mobile in a manner that enables them to respond to new opportunities, thus isolating them from the benefits of economic growth.[40]

Nonetheless they admitted that many of the questions they had posed could not be answered. Echoing Auletta, they argued that more research was needed.

In an article published five years later, Nathan, by then Professor of Public and International Affairs at the Woodrow Wilson School, Princeton University, queried whether the 'problem' of the underclass would ever be solved. He argued that underclass conditions were multifaceted – they were economic, behavioural, and geographically focused. Nonetheless Nathan maintained that the underclass was 'a distinctively urban condition involving a hardened residual group that is difficult to reach and relate to'.[41] On the question of solutions, Nathan was more optimistic, arguing that the principles of new-style workfare offered an important way forward. The principle was that welfare dependency was bad for people; it undermined their motivation to support themselves; and it isolated and stigmatised welfare recipients.[42]

The approach taken by George Cabot Lodge and William R. Glass was to ask what business could do for disintegrated urban communities. Both were associated with the Harvard Business School. They looked at the potential of neighbourhood organisations, organisations that could channel funds, co-operative efforts sponsored by the federal government, semi-governmental development organisations, and direct corporate intervention. Their analysis was that the underclass had to be re-integrated into social and economic life, but they conceded the task was not an easy one. Private businesses would have to show commitment, but also have a strong community perspective, and corporations should co-operate with other organisations, while at the same time leading the federal government. Nevertheless Cabot Lodge and Glass still used a behavioural definition. They wrote that 'disproportionately black, Hispanic, and young – although by no means exclusively so – the underclass is composed of single mothers, high school dropouts, drug addicts, and street criminals'.[43]

A writer whose analysis fitted this frame was Myron Magnet. His warning was that the problems that characterised underclass communities – 'urban knots that threaten to become enclaves of permanent poverty and vice' – could affect the larger society. The underclass comprised around 5m people, a relatively small proportion of the 33m Americans with incomes below the poverty line. What distinguished this group for Magnet was its behaviour – 'their chronic lawlessness, drug use, out-of-wedlock births, nonwork, welfare dependency, and school failure'.[44] It was both a 'state of mind' and a 'way of life', as much a 'cultural' as an 'economic' condition. One cause was that identified by Lemann and later elaborated by William Julius Wilson, the flight of the middle class and respectable working class from the ghettos, leaving behind the unsuccessful who gave themselves up to underclass behaviour. A second was that highlighted by Charles Murray – a welfare system that allegedly encouraged cohabiting, out-of-wedlock births, and unemployment. Magnet's proposed solutions included a consensus on welfare reform that embraced workfare, and specific measures targeted at children.

Gaither Loewenstein, from Lamar University, argued that it was unemployed young people who constituted the 'new underclass' in the United States. As young people became increasingly aware that they were confined to a secondary labour market, and had limited chances for upward career mobility, they took on behavioural characteristics normally associated with the underclass. These included 'low self esteem, present orientation (inability to plan for the future), high incidence of social alienation, low aspirations and a propensity towards deviant behaviour, such as alcohol and drug misuse and sexual promiscuity'.[45] In forming this argument, Loewenstein drew on labour market segmentation theory, the concept of a dual labour market, and the culture of poverty. The hypothesis was tested through a quantitative analysis of government statistics, interviews with the unemployed, and life histories. However, Loewenstein claimed there were important differences between this new phenomenon and the classic underclass. First, patterns of the new underclass were cyclical; second, the parents of the children were workers who were relatively well-off, and who had contributed to a sense of relative deprivation in their children; third, not all these young people had fallen into the ranks of the permanent underclass.[46]

Others acknowledged that defining the underclass was difficult, but continued nonetheless to develop definitions based on behavioural criteria rather than income. Erol Ricketts and Isabel Sawhill, for example, developed a definition of the underclass that was essentially based on behaviour, and used this to estimate its size and composition using the 1980 census. Ricketts was a sociology professor at the City University of New York, while Sawhill was a Senior Fellow at the Urban Institute. They defined the underclass as 'people whose behaviour departs from these norms [attending school, delaying parenthood, adult men and women in regular work, and being law-abiding] and in the process creates significant social costs'.[47] Thus it followed that an underclass area was one where the proportion of people engaged in these behaviours was significantly different from the average for the population as a whole. They focused on high school dropouts; males aged 16 and over not regularly working; welfare recipients; and female heads of households. Ricketts and Sawhill concluded that in 1980, 2.5m people, or about 1% of the population of the USA, lived in underclass areas, which were overwhelmingly urban.[48]

One of the main efforts on the part of the research community was the Social Science Research Council's Committee for Research on the Urban Underclass. Papers given at a conference held in October 1989 were subsequently published by the Brookings Institution. Many of these looked in great detail at the economic situation of the underclass and at issues such as racial segregation. Yet for Christopher Jencks, the underclass was synonymous with what was previously called the 'lower class' – both were characterised by unemployment, poor literacy, out-of-wedlock births, violence, and despair. His argument was that the underclass could be defined in various ways: according to income, where that income came from, cultural skills, and moral norms. Thus it was possible there was an impoverished underclass; a jobless male underclass; a jobless female underclass; an educational underclass; a violent underclass; and a reproductive underclass.[49]

Despite the work of Myrdal, there was not much mention of the underclass in the 1960s and early 1970s. Even books that looked at related themes, such as that by Leggett, chose not to use the term 'underclass'. In other respects, the focus was on the culture of poverty and the work of Oscar Lewis. This began to change with the *Time* article of 1977, and in particular following the publication of the Auletta articles in 1981. But the change was not just in the use of the word 'underclass', but in what was meant by that term. Here the work of Murray, and the argument advanced in *Losing Ground*, seemed to have a decisive impact. The argument now had a novel dimension: that it was the welfare system that was to blame rather than people themselves. By the 1980s, the meaning of the term 'underclass' had changed significantly. The focus was less on welfare and more on people. In the words of William Julius Wilson, the dominant image had become 'one of people with serious character flaws entrenched by a welfare subculture and who have only themselves to blame for their social position in society'.[50]

But those who favoured this interpretation did not have it all their own way. Other observers agreed an underclass was emerging in American cities, but gave precedence to structural rather than behavioural causes. They argued that if cultural factors were at work, they were evidence of an adaptive response to a wider environment, rather than evidence of a separate sub culture. It was an argument that built on Lemann's points about successive waves of migration, first north to the cities and then from the inner cities to the suburbs, but also went back to the work of Lee Rainwater and Ulf Hannerz in the late 1960s. These commentators tended to link the underclass more closely with economic change and income, and to emerging patterns of racial segregation in the inner cities. In this scenario, the underclass was the outcome of social and economic change, the result of which was that a significant minority had become economically redundant. This version of the concept was espoused by economists such as John Kasarda, radical black academics like Douglas Glasgow, and liberal scholars such as William Julius Wilson. Wilson's contribution to the debate was particularly interesting, in that he argued that scholars should move beyond the old dichotomy between structural and cultural interpretations.

The influence of this view was evident in some of the earliest official reports on the underclass. In October 1979, President Jimmy Carter had established the

President's Commission for a National Agenda for the Eighties. One panel was on Policies and Prospects for Metropolitan and Nonmetropolitan America. Its report (published in 1982), on urban America in the 1980s, was one of the most controversial. Interestingly, though the report appeared amid the controversy aroused by the Auletta articles, its chapter on the underclass viewed the issue almost entirely in economic terms. Its solutions included retraining those whose skills had become redundant or obsolete, with the report employing the appropriate industrial metaphor of 'assisted mid-life retooling'. Another key suggestion was that of internal migration, in order to improve access to economic opportunities. The report stated that public policies should seek to loosen the ties between 'distressed people and distressed places'.[51]

This analysis closely followed that of sociologists and economists. The work of John Kasarda, a sociologist based at the University of North Carolina at Chapel Hill, served to highlight the wider structural trends that allegedly provided the background to the growth of the underclass. Kasarda argued that cities were experiencing important changes in their functions, in that they were moving from being manufacturing to predominantly service industries. Change was also evident in their demographic make-up, in that the residents were now predominantly blacks and Hispanics. As the number of jobs decreased, the white middle class had moved to the suburbs, while there was a developing gap between the jobs that did exist and the skill levels of the disadvantaged residents. This process had particularly affected cities in the northern industrial belt, such as New York and Chicago. The result was that low-income communities had become spatially isolated, and these cities were characterised by urban poverty. Moreover, federal urban programmes had had little effect. Kasarda wrote that many people found themselves 'socially, economically, and spatially isolated in segregated inner-city wastelands, where they subsist on a combination of government handouts and their own informal economies'.[52]

The underclass concept was also drawn on by radical black writers, the earliest of whom actually preceded the Auletta *New Yorker* articles. Douglas Glasgow, for example, had initially gathered data in the Los Angeles suburb of Watts following the riots in 1965, and completed a follow-up study in 1975. Professor of Social Welfare and former Dean of the School of Social Work at Howard University, Glasgow wrote:

Over the past fifteen years, the nation's inner cities have witnessed the growth and consolidation of a population of poor and unused Black youth, confined in economic poverty and social decay. A significantly younger population than the poor of previous generations, these young Blacks, some as young as thirteen or fourteen, are already earmarked for failure – they are undereducated, jobless, without saleable skills or the social credentials to gain access to mainstream life.[53]

Glasgow's aims were to see what institutional rejection could do to individual aspirations; to identify the structural factors responsible for the development of an underclass; and to see why attempts to improve the life of the poor in the inner-city had failed. Thus for Glasgow the key themes in the formation of a black underclass were a declining domestic market, technological change, an increasing reliance on overseas labour leading to a decline in entry-level jobs, and institutional racism.[54]

Glasgow noted that, almost unnoticed, the term 'underclass' had become part of a national vocabulary, conveying the message that another problematic group required society's help. Although poorly defined, and thought by some as undeserving of serious attention, he maintained there was 'a permanently entrapped population of poor persons, unused and unwanted, accumulated in various parts of the country'.[55] Large numbers of blacks were persistently poor and unable to move, and the fact that these problems persisted from one generation to the next meant they were long-term in nature. A further feature identified by Glasgow was a lack of connections with social institutions, such as unions, the civil service, banks, and credit unions. He claimed the underclass was distinguished from the lower class by its lack of mobility rather than its moral unworthiness – its members were not necessarily lacking in aspirations or motivations to achieve. In fact, wrote Glasgow, many of the long-term poor, employed at a bare subsistence level, were essentially part of the underclass. For these reasons, the key issue was employment and jobs the solution, both inside and outside the inner city. He argued that 'no amount of social rehabilitation, community participation, or motivational programs will substitute for being able to earn a way with self-respect'.[56]

Glasgow thus located the underclass in relation to wider structural changes in technology and the economy, while at the same time arguing that it was a problem of cultural isolation and inter-generational transmission. It was difficult to separate the underclass from the long-term poor. Glasgow's position and arguments were reinforced by similar views expressed by other writers. Alphonso Pinkney's *The Myth of Black Progress* (1984) was an influential work in the early 1980s. For Pinkney, the most obvious characteristics of the underclass were its poverty, including youth unemployment, and the social decay in which it lived. Like Glasgow, he thought that one of the characteristics of the underclass was that it had few organisational ties. But Pinkney was more willing to link it with an urban street culture in which drugs, dropping out of high school before graduation, and standing on street corners featured prominently.[57] It was an analysis that Pinkney acknowledged was similar to that advanced by Elliot Liebow in *Tally's Corner*.

The most important contributor to the underclass debate in the USA has arguably been William Julius Wilson, Professor of Sociology at the University of Chicago. Wilson had written that in the 1970s, economic class had become more important than race in securing employment and occupational mobility. He estimated that in 1974 around 31% of the underclass had been black; and by 1978, a third of the entire black population was in the underclass.[58] But it was in the 1980s that Wilson made his most distinctive contribution to the underclass debate. One of Wilson's points was that following the debate about the Moynihan Report (1965), liberals had left discussion of these issues to the conservatives. Liberals avoided ascribing any behaviour that could be regarded as unflattering or stigmatising to the residents of the ghetto. In fact, they refused to acknowledge the term 'underclass', and emphasised selective evidence that denied its existence. While they acknowledged that there had been important changes in the inner city, they argued that racism provided the explanation. Wilson argued that the liberal perspective on the underclass became less influential and persuasive because many of its advocates failed to 'address straightforwardly the rise of social pathologies in the ghetto'.[59] The combined effect was to render liberal arguments ineffective, and to enhance the arguments of the conservatives, even though these had their own problems of interpretation and analysis. Whereas the most influential arguments in the 1960s had been by liberals, in the 1980s they were by conservatives. But Wilson claimed that these amounted to little more than the application of Lewis's culture of poverty theory to the ghetto underclass. Although Lewis had noted the effect of structure, conservatives focused on the links between cultural traditions, family history, and individual character. The change in the 1980s, illustrated by *Losing Ground*, was that conservatives also now argued that the problems were exacerbated by liberal social policy.[60]

Wilson's declared aim was to show how the liberal perspective might be refocused to challenge the dominant conservative views about the ghetto underclass, and provide a more balanced intellectual discussion. He concluded that liberals would have to propose explanations of the rise in inner-city social dislocations that emphasised the dynamic interplay between cultural characteristics and social and economic opportunities. The task for liberals was to produce an alternative or competing view of the underclass that was more rooted in empirical research and theory.[61] Wilson pointed out that poverty in the United States had become more urban, more concentrated, and more firmly entrenched in large cities, especially the older industrial cities with large and highly segregated black and Hispanic residents. This increase in ghetto poverty was mainly confined to cities in the Northeast and Midwest. Wilson's argument was that historical discrimination and a migration to large cities that kept the urban minority population relatively young created a problem of weak 'labour force attachment' among urban blacks. Especially since 1970, this had made them particularly vulnerable to the industrial and geographical changes in the economy. These problems were particularly severe in the ghetto neighbourhoods of large cities, because the poorest people lived there, and because the areas had become less diversified. Since 1970, inner-city neighbourhoods had experienced a migration of middle and working-class families to the suburbs. Combined with the increase in the number of poor caused by rising joblessness, this meant that poverty was more sharply concentrated in these areas. The number of inner-city neighbourhoods with poverty rates above 40% had increased dramatically.[62]

One of the interesting aspects of this analysis was how Wilson dealt with changes in behaviour. He conceded that by the 1980s there was a large sub-population of low-income families and individuals whose behaviour was different to that of the general population. In contrast, and in the years before 1960, inner-city communities had shown signs of social organisation. People had a sense of community, they identified with their neighbourhood, and they adopted norms and sanctions against behaviour they regarded as wrong. Wilson argued that the central problem of the underclass was unemployment that was reinforced by an increasing social isolation in impoverished neighbourhoods. What he called 'weak labour-force attachment' was caused by two factors: macro-structural changes in the wider society and economy, and the social milieu of individuals. Cultural values emerged from specific circumstances, life chances, and class structure. Like other writers in the 1960s, he argued that culture and behaviour were an adaptive response to the circumstances in which individuals found themselves. Wilson wrote, for example, that:

> if ghetto underclass minorities have limited aspirations, a hedonistic orientation toward time, or lack of plans for the future, such outlooks ultimately are the result of restricted opportunities and feelings of resignation originating from bitter personal experience and a bleak future.[63]

Wilson further clarified how his approach differed from the culture of poverty as defined by Oscar Lewis. He noted that it was the cultural-transmission aspect of the thesis that had received most attention, and Ulf Hannerz had made the point that Lewis had failed to distinguish between causes and symptoms. He had not separated objective poverty created by structural constraints, and culture as people trying to cope with objective poverty. The notion of the culture of poverty was thus used in a diluted sense as a 'whole way of life', and the emphasis was on the modes of behaviour learnt in the community.[64] Wilson preferred the term 'social isolation', arguing that reducing structural inequalities would decrease the frequency of 'ghetto practices', and also restrict the way that they were spread. The transmission of these practices was part of what Wilson called 'concentration effects' – that is, the effects of living in an impoverished neighbourhood. With regard to the social milieu of individuals, Wilson wrote that:

> a social context that includes poor schools, inadequate job information networks, and

a lack of legitimate employment opportunities not only gives rise to weak labour-force attachment, but increases the probability that individuals will be constrained to seek income derived from illegal or deviant activities.[65]

It followed, then, that the problems of the underclass could be most meaningfully addressed by a comprehensive programme that combined employment and social welfare policies, and featured universal rather than race- or group-specific measures. Macroeconomic policy should include child support, family allowances, and a child care strategy. Wilson was opposed to workfare-style solutions.[66] He wrote that the challenge for liberal policymakers was to enhance life chances for the ghetto underclass by emphasising programmes 'to which the more advantaged groups of all class and racial backgrounds can positively relate'.[67]

With regard to the concept of the underclass itself, Wilson was aware that its meaning had changed significantly, as it had come to be focused on behaviour. Some scholars argued it was not scientifically useful, and should be dropped altogether. However he argued that to ignore the term 'underclass' in favour of more neutral terms such as 'working class' was in his opinion to 'fail to address one of the most important social transformations in recent United States history'.[68] Changes had taken place in ghetto neighbourhoods, and the groups left behind were different to those that had lived there in earlier years. It was difficult to describe these trends accurately if the term 'underclass' was rejected. At times, Wilson used the alternative term 'ghetto poor'.[69] But while accepting the arguments of those who argued that the term 'underclass' should be dropped, he maintained that the underclass could be defined. He reaffirmed that 'what distinguishes members of the underclass from those of other economically disadvantaged groups is that their marginal economic position or weak attachment to the labour force is uniquely reinforced by the neighbourhood or social milieu'.[70]

The importance of Wilson's contribution has been that it has attempted to combine structural and cultural interpretations. Yet Douglas S. Massey and Nancy A. Denton, from the Universities of Chicago and New York, have pointed out that major gaps in knowledge remain. No study has tested Wilson's hypothesis that the degree of spatial separation between poor and non-poor minority families has increased, and that this helped explain the rising concentration of poverty. They argue that race and racial segregation hold the key to understanding the underclass and urban poverty. Racial segregation rather than class segregation is the crucial factor. Rejecting the notion of a culture of poverty, Massey and Denton argue that residential segregation has created a structural niche, and within this a culture of segregation has arisen and flourished. They claim this resolves several issues in the underclass debate. It explains why the underclass is composed of blacks and Puerto Ricans; it explains why it is confined to the

Northeast and the Midwest; and it is also consistent with research showing that upper-income blacks remain highly segregated from whites. Thus Massey and Denton conclude racial segregation should be the central focus of the underclass debate.[71]

The result of this increasing agnosticism regarding the term 'underclass' is that recent writers interested in poverty in the inner-city have preferred to use the term 'ghetto poor'. Paul A. Jargowsky and Mary Jo Bane, for example, suggested that there were various concepts of poverty – persistent poverty, linked to long periods of time; neighbourhood poverty, associated with geographically defined areas; and underclass poverty, seen in terms of attitudes and behaviour. But Jargowsky and Bane did not attempt to define or measure the underclass. Instead they defined ghettos and counted the ghetto poor in all metropolitan areas. A ghetto was defined as being an area in which the overall poverty rate in a census tract was greater than 40% – the ghetto poor were those who lived in these areas. Measured in this way, the number of ghetto poor in the USA increased by 29.5% between 1970 and 1980. To an extent this supported the Wilson thesis, since the dynamics of these areas suggested that the increase in ghetto poverty was caused by movements of the non-poor out of areas which in 1970 had been mixed income. But in the four cities Jargowsky and Bane studied – Cleveland, Memphis, Milwaukee, and Philadelphia – the processes by which they became, stopped being, or stayed ghettos were complex.[72]

Despite the popularity of the term 'underclass' in the United States, from the outset some commentators remained sceptical, pointing out it was more a mirage than a moral threat. Data taken from the Michigan Panel Study of Income Dynamics (PSID) survey has played a central role in these debates, and deserves to be looked at more thoroughly. The PSID is a longitudinal survey on family economic status that is co-ordinated from the Survey Research Center at the University of Michigan. It is based on repeated annual interviews with a sample (or panel) of 5,000 American families. Some have claimed that the PSID data shows the dangers of using cross-sectional data to draw conclusions about the extent and causes of change. The early results showed that there was much turnover in the low income population. While many people were forced to have recourse to welfare at some point in their lives, very few were dependent on it for extended periods of time. And evidence indicated that there was little association between people's attitudes and economic success.[73] All of this therefore served to cast doubt on the existence of an underclass.

One of the key questions for the PSID team was whether it was environmental or behavioural patterns that led to improvements in economic status. Attempts were made to measure, over five years, people's attitude to time, whether they planned ahead, if they avoided risks, the extent to which they drew on sources of information and help, if they economised, and if they increased their incomes by working at home. Yet the team found very little evidence that behavioural patterns like these had a consistent effect on people's income level. Similarly on attitudes and personality, the team tried to measure people's aspirations and ambitions, if they trusted or were hostile to others, their confidence in their own abilities, and whether they planned ahead. Again, these had little effect on changes in economic status over time. The team argued that what mattered most were people's demographic characteristics, including their age, sex, education, race, and family background. In an early report (1974), researchers conceded it was important to acknowledge that, in part, people were victims of their past, their environment, luck, and chance. But overall the report concluded that:

> It is after all difficult to believe that there are not some situations where individual effort matters – in seizing opportunities for better jobs, moving to new areas or avoiding undue risks. But for public policy purposes and for arguments about the extent to which one could reduce dependency in our society by changing the behaviour and attitudes of dependent members, the findings certainly do not encourage expectations that such changes would make much difference.[74]

Reviewing the PSID data in 1984, Greg Duncan, one of the Michigan researchers, summarised some of the main findings on the importance of people's attitudes. It seemed to be common sense that the most successful people were highly motivated, looked to the future, and were in control of their lives. However, Duncan pointed out that the association between attitudes and success at a single point in time did not prove the attitudes caused the success. In fact it might well be the other way around, the success causing the positive attitudes. In further research, the team had examined the relative importance of attitudes; behaviour patterns; skills; demographic characteristics; and life events. Tests were devised to explore people's motivation to achieve, their self-confidence, and if they looked to the future. Again, the PSID data showed that the most important cause of changes in income level were shifts in family composition, through births, deaths, children leaving home, and especially divorce and marriage. In contrast, there was little evidence that people with more positive attitudes were more likely to be successful.[75]

But the PSID data was much more wide-ranging than providing evidence solely on attitudes and behaviour. For one thing, it showed there was considerable turnover in the low-income population. Only just over half the individuals living in poverty in one year were found to be poor in the next, and less than half those who experienced poverty remained persistently poor over ten years. The PSID data also provided insights into the extent to which people relied on welfare. In the period 1969–1978, for example, a quarter of the population derived income from some form of welfare on at least one occasion. But only

2% of the population were dependent on this income for extended periods of time. For the rest, investigation showed that many of these families were in the early stages of an economic crisis caused by the death, disability, or departure of a husband. When family members found full-time employment, or the mother remarried, they were no longer forced to rely on welfare. The PSID data showed, then, that those people with persistently low incomes were not an underclass of young adults living in large cities. Instead poor people were very likely to be black, older, and living in rural areas, especially in the South.[76] The picture that emerged was one of temporary need. There certainly was a small but not insignificant number of people who lived in households where poverty was the rule rather than the exception. The characteristics of the 'persistently poor' were different from the population as a whole, in that three-fifths of this group were black. But one of the main findings of the PSID data was that apart from the 'persistently poor', the poor were not a homogeneous, stable group. One in four of the population was found to have lived in a poor family in at least one of the ten years 1969–78, but for half this group, poverty years did not occur more than twice. Unlike the 'persistently poor', these people were no different from the population as a whole.[77]

With the PSID data, it was possible to examine the argument that welfare programmes led to dependency in successive generations of families. The team examined parental families headed by a woman, that in 1968 had a family income just above the poverty line, but that did not receive income from welfare. In 1976, 7% of the white women from these families, and 25% of the black women, received welfare income. To an extent, then, it seemed dependency was transmitted between generations. However, most people who received welfare were not dependent on it, and most of the rest were dependent only for short periods. Most adult children from families that had previously been on welfare were not on it themselves. And most of the adults that were on welfare did not come from families that previously had been. Was it more likely that parents who were on welfare would produce children who were also dependent on welfare? The evidence provided no clear answer. Even when some continuities between generations could be found, the way these mechanisms operated remained unclear.[78] Greg Duncan argued that although case studies of families in poverty (such as those of the underclass) did provide a more vivid and complete picture of circumstances than statistical studies, they could not be considered to be representative of any larger group.[79]

The PSID data serves as an introduction to a third group of commentators – those who were agnostic in that they believed the underclass was a theoretical possibility, but could find no empirical evidence. Reviewing Auletta's book in 1983, for example, Douglas Muzzio argued that discussion of the underclass had always been characterised by the vague and shifting nature of the term. Based at Baruch College, at the City University of New York, Muzzio pointed out that there had always been underclasses in American society, and periodic outbursts of concern about the extent and effects of severe poverty. Above all, the failure to define the term 'underclass' meant that confusion and misunderstanding were guaranteed, with explanations spanning a spectrum from Marxism to Social Darwinism. For Muzzio the more interesting question was why the debate persisted. He suggested the answer lay in the way it served as a useful weapon in much bigger political and ideological battles. In his view, the underclass generated 'more commitment than detachment'.[80]

Other observers pointed out that the term 'underclass' covered too many disparate groups of people, and thereby inflated their numbers. William Kornblum thought the key questions were whether the diverse population of the underclass formed a homogeneous group with its own institutions and culture of poverty, and what policies should be adopted to deal with it. Kornblum provided some case studies of typical members, but suggested restricting the use of the term to people below the poor:

> in that they cannot survive unharmed for any length of time by themselves, because they lack both material resources and the ability to organise their lives. They are the people who are outside both the class system of capitalist production and any local community.[81]

To his mind, criminals and the poor should not be included in a definition of the underclass. Kornblum noted that, in the hands of conservatives, the culture of poverty thesis too easily became an excuse for ignoring the issue. His proposed solutions embraced community-based education and training opportunities, and improved employment in working-class areas.

Like Kornblum, Emmett D. Carson thought that it was community-based self-help strategies that could do most to change the attitudes of the underclass and enable its members to take advantage of the opportunities that existed. However, Carson, who had completed a Princeton PhD thesis on the underclass, agreed it was not a homogeneous group, but was composed of subgroups that were defined as 'any group of economically disadvantaged individuals who display a common deviant behaviour, and who also possess specific deviant attitudes with respect to the behaviour they display'.[82] One programme with ex-offenders had used criteria based on low incomes (economic status), deviant activity (behaviour), and asocial attitudes towards work (attitudes). However, like the PSID team, Carson argued that it was not possible to decide if attitudes caused behaviour or behaviour caused attitudes. He argued that there needed to be better understanding of the dynamics of the underclass before any government programmes aimed at helping its members could be devised. It was too early to settle on self-help strategies that tried to help the black population, but limited the role of government to reducing discrimination and promoting full employment.[83]

Others shared the concerns that these writers expressed regarding problems in defining the underclass. Robert Aponte, a colleague of William Julius Wilson at the University of Chicago, pointed out that the term had never been defined, despite thirty years of sporadic use. Aponte was particularly critical of the behavioural definition advanced by Ricketts and Sawhill, asking to what extent the underclass really represented a 'class', and what evidence there was of turnover. Aponte himself preferred a definition based on persistent poverty.[84] The academics Sheldon Danziger and Peter Gottschalk agreed with William Julius Wilson that a reduction in segregation and a rise in the living standards of some blacks had enabled the middle class to move out of inner-city neighbourhoods. Nevertheless they pointed out that although Wilson had put forward an attractive argument, much of it had not been tested. They accepted that changes had occurred in the spatial concentration of poverty, but argued that it was not possible to answer the question of whether they had contributed to the development of an underclass among the black poor.[85] Danziger and Gottschalk, now based at the Universities of Michigan and Boston College, have remained hesitant about using the term 'underclass'. They argue that the popular American ideal that anyone who works hard can get ahead tends to foster the idea that those who do not are personally responsible for their situation. In fact, they claim, people's behaviour is much less important in determining income level than major economic changes.[86]

Walter W. Stafford and Joyce Ladner fit into the agnostic position, that the underclass is a theoretical possibility, but there is little hard evidence. Like Michael Morris, they point out there have been both similarities and differences between debates about a culture of poverty and debates about an underclass. In both cases, there was a widespread assumption that low income groups can be reintegrated into society if they change their behaviour, and that cultural and behavioural traits associated with poverty are transmitted between generations. They suggest the concepts have been promoted at times of racial tension, and that both have been characterised by broad generalisations about patterns of deviant behaviour based on limited observations. Nevertheless there are also important differences. In the underclass debate, the role of structural factors has been more prominent; there have been more serious attempts to shape and use the concept; and there is more emphasis on class differences within the black community. Furthermore, with the underclass, there has been more emphasis on dependency as a political concern; more explicit assumptions have been made about the relationship between racism and poverty; and blacks themselves played a more prominent role in the promotion of the underclass concept.[87]

Importantly, Stafford and Ladner have pointed out that the debate has had a much wider political dimension. The underclass underwent a 'claims-making process', similar to that associated with medical breakthroughs, in which newspapers and magazines, policy institutes, and social scientists were all involved. The term gained popularity for three reasons: it was a broad term that easily stratified groups who appeared to be deviant; it enabled liberals to become involved again in debates about behaviour and dependency; and it encouraged wider participation in the debate about the norms and values of non-white populations. But they also suggested that despite the efforts of William Julius Wilson and others, definitions remained 'value laden, concerning behaviour, and difficult to measure'.[88] Measuring the underclass – through such variables as concentration and isolation, intergenerational welfare dependency, crime, marriage and families, and labour markets – has also been problematic. Stafford and Ladner argued that some liberal proponents of the underclass concept were in fact reinforcing conservative assumptions about the poor and their behaviour.

Other writers were more hostile to the term 'underclass'. Unlike the agnostics, who suggest there is a theoretical possibility but no evidence, the critics argue that the term has no scientific value or useful purpose. This strand of the debate is more difficult to trace, since many of these commentators simply write about problems of urban poverty without mentioning the word 'underclass'. But Adolph Reed, for example, then Professor of Political Science at Northwestern University, claimed in 1990 that the concept of the underclass was based on prejudice, focused on inner-city blacks and Hispanics, and concentrated on behavioural indicators. An important aspect was perceived deviance from behavioural norms, and it was for this reason that the term was attractive to so many different groups. Reed suggested that prejudice should be exposed, and efforts should concentrate on exploring the causes of poverty in the American political and economic system – on deindustralization; inequalities of wealth, income, and opportunity; race and gender; and public policy. Policy changes should be fought for – in employment, housing, education, and drug rehabilitation. For Reed, the main problem was the 'poverty of discourse about poverty'.[89]

Some writers have maintained an outright opposition to the term 'underclass'. Michael Sherraden, for example, argued that it was unclear who the underclass were, where its members were located, and when it emerged as a perceived social problem. More importantly, the phrase tended to set people apart and dehumanise them. Interestingly and unusually, Sherraden located the contemporary interest in the underclass in the longer-term context of the studies of the Jukes and Kallikak families in the late nineteenth century. In his view, the main shortcomings were that, like the concept of the culture of poverty, there was an exaggeration of the 'deep-seatedness' of poverty, and secondly, that effects were emphasised rather than causes. Sherraden was based in the School of Social Work at Washington University. He advised social workers to avoid the word 'underclass' since in his opinion this had served to 'separate and to oppress the disadvantaged'.[90]

In reality these different positions in the debate are more complex than this implies, since they tend to merge into one another. Often it is not possible to distinguish between analyses that have both structural and behavioural components. But a final, and distinctive, position on the underclass is occupied by those academic commentators who are hostile to the idea of an underclass, but interested in the functions the term has served. This is important in the context of this book since these writers have acknowledged the longer-term history of these concepts, and they have been interested in exploring the similarities and differences between them. Michael Morris, for example, Professor of Psychology at the University of New Haven, compared and contrasted the debates on the culture of poverty in the 1960s with those on the underclass in the 1980s. He suggested that both Left and Right had something to gain from a change in language, and suggested while the term 'underclass' remained flexible, changes in the wider political climate were unlikely to threaten its popularity.[91] In the hands of these writers, the term 'underclass' becomes an important metaphor of social transformation.

As we noted in chapter 5, Herbert Gans had been a contributor to this debate since the 1960s. He is well aware of how the meaning of underclass has changed, from unemployment in the 1960s, to persistent poverty in the 1970s, and to behaviour in the 1980s. By the 1990s, he was Robert S. Lynd Professor of Sociology at Columbia University. Writing in the journal of the American Planning Association, Gans argued that for planners, the term had numerous dangers. These included its power as a buzzword, its use as a racial codeword, its flexibility, and its synthesising function. It covered a number of different groups of people, and became a stereotype. Furthermore the term interfered with anti-poverty planning, was extremely persuasive, was associated with particular neighbourhoods, and was linked to the 'concentration and isolation' hypothesis put forward by William Julius Wilson. Finally the term sidestepped issues of poverty, and was unpredictable in how it might be used. He argued that the term 'underclass' should be dropped, as it had become 'hopelessly polluted in meaning, ideological overtone and implications'.[92]

While Gans had become critical of the term 'underclass', he nonetheless continued to search for an alternative that might provide a suitable description of the changes that were occurring in the nature of work. His argument was that workers who had become marginalised when Myrdal was writing in the 1960s had become excluded from the postindustrial economy thirty years later. Gans speculated that they had become an 'undercaste', whose members were blamed for their joblessness and regarded as undeserving. Many people now faced the prospect that they would never be included in the formal labour market, and would spend all their working lives in the informal sector. As with those at the bottom of caste systems, they would be shunned by the rest of society, and have extremely limited chances of higher social status and mobility. Gans admitted that he wrote about an 'undercaste' with some hesitation, since once the shock value had worn off, the basic problems with any form of alarmist terminology would become apparent. Both 'underclass' and 'undercaste' were umbrella terms, and the umbrella was 'open to anyone who wishes to place new meanings, or a variety of stereotypes, accusations and stigmas under it'.[93]

More recently, Herbert Gans has looked at the longer history of terms like 'undeserving poor' and 'underclass', and at the functions of these phrases as well as their causes. The 'undeserving poor', for example, had functions that were both positive and negative, adaptive and destructive. Among these Gans listed risk reduction, scapegoating and displacement, norm reinforcement, spatial purification, the reproduction of stigma and the stigmatised, and the extermination of the surplus. But the idea of the undeserving poor and the stigmas with which people are labelled persisted, he argued, because they are useful to people who are not poor. [94]

Writing of the history of the underclass in the United States, the historian Michael Katz has been critical of the phrase 'underclass'. To his mind, the word has 'little intellectual substance', it reinforces the tradition of blaming the victim, and it is a concept that 'muddies debate and inhibits the formulation of constructive policy'. The contributors to a book Katz edited did not manage to agree on a definition of the underclass, or even on how useful the term really was. They claimed that what united their work was a common concern with persistent and concentrated urban poverty.[95] But Katz is also aware that there have always been attempts to distinguish between the able-bodied and impotent poor, and that these labels have had important functions. In the 1980s, conditions within the inner cities were new, they had complex causes, and they were perceived as a danger to the rest of society. But for the middle class, at least, the underclass was a comforting discovery. The perceived problem was small and concentrated enough to be helped or contained, and its prominence refocused attention on culture and behaviour, and away from income equality and the class structure. Katz claimed the concept served to focus attention on a subset of the poor, and it encouraged targeted approaches through reviving discredited notions of the culture of poverty.[96] Elsewhere Katz has claimed that the term 'underclass' was simply a 'metaphor of social transformation'. It evoked three widely shared perceptions: of novelty, complexity, and danger. [97]

British commentators have of course been extremely interested in developments on the other side of the Atlantic. John Macnicol has concluded of the underclass debate in the United States that it is 'kaleidoscopic and multi-layered, operating on both an empirical and a symbolic level'.[98] Writing in June 1990, Macnicol argued that the empirical evidence did not support the underclass interpretation. Like the Webbs and Stedman Jones, he argued that a massive stimulus of the old industrial sector would be accompanied by the disappearance of the underclass – as had happened during the Second World War.[99] By 1994, Macnicol had altered his stance somewhat. He suggested the key questions were whether a new type of poverty was emerging, and, more controversially, over the question of causation. Macnicol made three points in relation to the USA – that it was not welfare that had caused the rise of single-parent families and new family forms, but changes in marital and reproductive behaviour; that unemployment was the most important factor destroying social life in inner-city communities; and that the economic trends were long-term ones originating well before the 1960s. He argued that if people allowed themselves to be swayed by the well-orchestrated campaign to popularise the 'welfare-created' underclass model, they were in danger of misunderstanding 'what may turn out to be the major item on the social agenda of the 21st century'.[100]

Commentators seemed to adopt one of at least four positions. For many on the Right, the underclass represented a group whose problems were essentially those of behaviour – illegitimacy, family breakdown, violent crime, and unemployment. This interpretation was strengthened by the distinctive contribution of Murray, in *Losing Ground*, which claimed that it was the social policies of the 1960s, rather than people themselves, that were to blame. The second position was typified by writers like William Julius Wilson, who tended to locate the emergence of the underclass in terms of structural factors such as shifts in employment trends and changes in the spatial concentration of poverty in the inner cities. Wilson acknowledged that culture and behaviour were important, but like Rainwater and Hannerz in the late 1960s, he argued that underclass culture was an adaptive response to the social environment. A third group was attracted to the notion of an underclass, but argued there was no real empirical evidence. In the case of the PSID data, this tended to indicate that behaviour and attitudes were relatively unimportant, and that people moved in and out of poverty. Finally a fourth group was less interested whether there was empirical evidence for the existence of an underclass, and preferred instead to look at the functions of the term, seeing it much more as a metaphor for urban transformation. As we shall see in the next chapter, these positions were replicated almost exactly in the debate on the underclass in Britain. However, there were also important differences, of which arguably the most significant was the much less prominent role of 'race'. It is to the experience of Britain that we now return.

8

Uncovering the Underclass – Britain

The underclass debate in the United States was wide-ranging and multi-faceted, raising fundamental questions about poverty, economic change, the effects of social policies adopted in the 1960s, and patterns of racial segregation in American cities. In earlier chapters we have noted that some underclass concepts did reflect an intellectual dialogue between America and Britain. This was most evident, for example, in the culture of poverty theory of the 1960s. At this time, social scientists were clearly interested in the ways that Oscar Lewis's ideas might be applied in the British context. On the other hand, American commentators often seemed impervious to ideas generated on the other side of the Atlantic. This was certainly true of the concept of the problem family in the 1950s. There was little evidence that in developing the notion of the cycle of deprivation Sir Keith Joseph had in any way been influenced by the theory of the culture of poverty. Robert Moore has suggested that there are problems in applying the arguments of William Julius Wilson in the British context. First, Britain does not have an equivalent of the black ghettos of American cities. Second, the rise of the welfare state has implied a contract between capital and labour that makes it different from the more open and competitive American society.[1]

Nevertheless, by the 1980s, in Britain the term 'underclass' had become part of popular vocabulary in discussions of poverty and social change. The direct link was through Charles Murray. Writing in 1997, Andrew Adonis and Stephen Pollard suggested that 'for all its drawbacks, the word underclass captures the essence of the class predicament for many at the bottom: a complete absence of ladders, whether basic skills, role models, education or a culture of work'.[2] As was the case in America, British commentators adopted several different stances on the underclass. Observers can be regarded as holding one of four basic positions. First, a 'moral turpitude' thesis that stressed behaviour, and saw the underclass as threatening the moral and social order. This approach tended to be dominated by ideas of culture and individualism, and was essentially a conservative analysis. Second, a position that was endorsed by some on the Left and accepted that an underclass had been created by structural factors in economic and social change. Third, a more agnostic view that acknowledged that there was a theoretical possibility of an underclass but no real empirical evidence. In arguing that more research was needed, their arguments sounded suspiciously like those of the

Eugenics Society in search of the social problem group in the 1930s. And fourth, a position that rejected the concept outright, regarding it as politically dangerous, empirically unsupported, and theoretically confused. For them, the underclass was a kind of 'ideological red herring'.[3] This typology forms a framework for the analysis attempted here. But first we look more closely at the earlier history of the term 'underclass' in the British context.

The *Oxford English Dictionary* records that the Scottish communist John Maclean was one of the first to use the term 'underclass'. In 1918, Maclean wrote that 'the whole history of Society has proved that Society moves forward as a consequence of an under-class overcoming the resistance of a class on top of them'.[4] This is rather different from the way that the term has been used since, in that the connotation was positive, and it was not clear that the underclass was necessarily at the bottom of society. Moreover, as we have seen in earlier chapters, the phrase 'underclass' was absent from subsequent discussions about the social problem group, the problem family, and the cycle of deprivation. These were seen as groups that were poor, as much through behaviour as lack of income, and there was a corresponding focus on mechanisms and processes, including an alleged inter-generational transmission of deprivation. Yet the type of neo-Marxist interpretation that was implied by the term 'underclass' was alien to these commentators – it implied a class interpretation of society that was not part of their mental outlook. There were times when observers came close to this position, as in discussions of the social residuum in the 1880s. But in general, it is not surprising that the term 'underclass' did not enter the lexicon of discussions of social change in Britain until the 1980s. It was only with the emergence of long-term unemployment that it appeared to offer an appropriate description for those apparently left behind by economic and social change.

In the mid-1960s, at least one British commentator endorsed Gunnar Myrdal's argument that economic change and technological advances were threatening to create an underclass of under-educated and potentially unemployable people. Richard Titmuss, Professor of Social Administration at the London School of Economics, argued in 1965 that technological change was responsible for 'the solidifying of a permanent underclass of deprived citizens, uneducated, unattached and alternating between apathetic resignation and frustrated violence'.[5] But when the term 'underclass' was used in discussions of British society, it was usually in relation to the position of ethnic migrant workers. In a textbook on class structure published in 1973, Anthony Giddens argued that where ethnicity served as a 'disqualifying' factor in the market, and where ethnic groups were concentrated in the poorest paid jobs, or were unemployed or semi-employed, it was possible to talk about an underclass. Drawing on the research carried out by John Leggett in Detroit, Giddens argued that these 'distributive groupings' were formed by neighbourhood clustering and by certain types of status group formation. However, their form varied according to differences in the size and density of urban areas, and in the social and political structures of capitalist societies. Giddens suggested that the existence of a large underclass cut across any clear-cut distinction between middle- and working-class neighbourhoods.[6]

Giddens accepted that the size and demographic composition of the United States made it something of a special case. Nevertheless he maintained that in Europe, too, it was possible to see an emerging underclass. In many European countries, the lack of an indigenous ethnic minority led to a transient underclass being imported from outside. Similar developments were evident, Giddens argued, in Britain and France. Composed of recent migrants in urban and industrial areas, the underclass formed the basis of a pool of highly 'disposable' labour. First, its members had few educational qualifications, and were unskilled manual workers. Second, if certain jobs were done by migrant workers, the existence of an underclass made it easier to separate jobs that would be more acceptable to the working class.[7] Like Leggett, Giddens was interested in whether this underclass was of potential political significance. He argued that the underclass could be viewed as a force for revolutionary change, or as reinforcing conservative attitudes. Giddens predicted that 'hostile outbursts' were likely, because the underclass was unable to exercise the kind of citizenship rights enjoyed by everyone else. However, despite its radical potential, he concluded it was more likely that the overall effect would be conservative.[8]

The way that Giddens identified the existence of an ethnic underclass is particularly interesting in light of his writing on the 'third way' and social exclusion. Other commentators in this period, though, were more hesitant about using the term 'underclass' to describe the position occupied by ethnic minority groups in Britain. This was true of the work of John Rex and Robert Moore in Birmingham in the late 1960s. Although they argued that migrants were excluded from the full benefits of the welfare state, for instance in areas such as housing, they did not use the term 'underclass'.[9] In 1975, the sociologists John Westergaard and Henrietta Resler argued similarly that in Britain, ethnic minorities were not concentrated uniformly at the bottom of the economic order. Although they undoubtedly faced serious obstacles in the labour market, as indeed in society in general, they did not constitute an underclass. Descriptions of migrant labour as an underclass, they suggested, were more applicable to other continental countries, such as Germany and Switzerland, that had recruited large numbers of foreign workers into poorly-paid jobs.[10]

When the term 'underclass' was used, it was deployed in a rather different way, and had a more positive connotation. In their Birmingham case-study, John Rex and Sally Tomlinson argued that there was much evidence that migrants were discriminated against, and also stigmatised in the way that the welfare state operated. They acknowledged that there was some tendency for the black community in Britain to operate as a separate class or underclass, but resisted the idea that its members were an inert mass with a ghetto mentality or a culture of poverty. Rather they argued that ethnic minorities organised and acted in their own underclass interests. But two factors pulled migrant workers away from a quasi-Marxist 'underclass for itself'. First, the affiliations that migrant workers had with the mainstream working class, and secondly, the influence of their homelands.[11] Rex and Tomlinson concluded of their Birmingham case-study that the car industry provided unstable but highly unionised conditions, with good wages for workers. Other factories and foundries had few unions, and provided work that was poorly paid but secure. They claimed that distinctions of this kind in the labour market were a 'necessary but not sufficient condition' for the emergence of an underclass.[12]

In later work, John Rex restated this position, conceding that migrant workers had been excluded from business activity and from participation in employment, housing and education. He argued, however, that they had organised themselves and demonstrated a degree of political consciousness. Thus Rex again dissociated himself from the negative definition of an unemployed and unemployable class caught in a culture of poverty, in favour of an analysis where migrants had their own forms of organisation, culture, ideology, and politics. In the phrase adopted by Rex, this was an 'underclass-for-itself'.[13] Other writers on ethnicity have followed Rex in dissociating themselves from the underclass thesis, arguing that despite the attempts of William Julius Wilson, the term has been part of a racist discourse, and a vocabulary of coded panic terms.[14] Even in the 1980s, the concept of the underclass in Britain has much less connection with race than it does in the American context.

Overall, in the period before 1980, the term 'underclass' was only used in a very limited sense in the British context. Even when it was thought it might provide an apt description of the position of workers from ethnic minority groups, researchers subsequently decided that the concept was not supported by empirical evidence. This work was concerned with migrant workers and ethnic minority groups rather than with the white working class. One of the few early attempts to apply the term 'underclass' to other social groupings was by Peter Townsend. In his classic survey of poverty, published in 1979, Townsend noted that older people, the disabled, the chronic sick, the long-term unemployed, and one-parent families were not part of the conventional workforce. He argued that the way in which they had been denied access to paid employment, had subsistence-level incomes, and low social status meant that they constituted a kind of modern underclass.[15] Thus Townsend widened the concept of the underclass away from ethnic minority groups to embrace the experience of vulnerable white groups whose low income separated them from the rest of society. This is all the more interesting given Townsend's rejection of behavioural factors in poverty and deprivation, and his hostility to the notions of the culture of poverty and cycle of deprivation. Townsend saw the underclass in structural terms, and included the long-term unemployed as one of his vulnerable groups. As unemployment worsened in the early 1980s, the term 'underclass' would come to be seen by many as an appropriate description for the kind of society that these economic and social changes were threatening to create.

Inspired in part by the Ken Auletta articles in the *New Yorker*, a new approach became evident in Britain in the early 1980s. Writing in the *New Statesman*, for instance, the sociologist Ralf Dahrendorf claimed that mass unemployment and reductions in the real value of wages had increased the size of an underclass that threatened social order and morality. For Dahrendorf, the underclass was 'a cancer which eats away at the texture of societies and metastasises in ways which can increasingly be felt in all their parts'.[16] In addition to unemployment and low wages, the underclass suffered from an accumulation of social pathologies – poor education, illiteracy, 'incomplete families', and poor housing. In the United States, it was clearly also an issue of race. Above all, according to Dahrendorf, the 'syndrome of deprivation' led to a ghettoised existence – people were 'clinging precariously to a "normal" world of jobs and expanding life chances, but settling in a life cycle of their own'.[17] Although caused partly by economic dislocation, for Dahrendorf the underclass was expressed in other changes. One was the increasing problem of football hooliganism. The traditional working-class sport had apparently become an underclass game. The culture included 'a lifestyle of laid-back sloppiness, association in changing groups of gangs, congregation around discos or the like, hostility to middle-class society, peculiar habits of dress, of hairstyle, often drugs or at least alcohol'.[18] Dahrendorf himself doubted whether the phrase 'class' was appropriate, but had no doubt that striking changes were evident.

These comments notwithstanding, Dahrendorf's approach was also a liberal one, since he argued that there were moral, social, and practical reasons why the members of the underclass should not be forgotten by the rest of society. He pointed out that the affluent middle class did not endorse social mobility, and he argued that 'the existence of an underclass casts doubt on the social contract itself'.[19] With regard to solutions, Dahrendorf claimed there was no macroeconomic answer to the 'problem' of the underclass, and in fact there was no single solution. Education was clearly critical, as a means of improving employment chances. Basic income held the key in affirming the basic principle of citizenship. For Dahrendorf, the 'existence of an underclass violates the fundamental assumption of modern, free societies which is that everyone without exception is a citizen with certain entitlements common to all'.[20] Thus the main task of government was to extend full citizenship rights to all.

While Dahrendorf's approach was a curious mixture of conservatism and liberalism, the key writer in this arena was again Charles Murray. As we saw in the previous chapter, his book *Losing Ground* (1984) had been a brilliantly argued polemic against liberal assumptions about the value of the welfare state. Encouraged by the *Sunday Times* newspaper and the Health and Welfare Unit of the Institute for Economic Affairs (IEA), Murray's ideas were widely publicised in Britain. In an article in the *Sunday Times Magazine* in November 1989, Murray described himself as 'a visitor from a plague area come to see whether the disease is spreading'.[21] He repeated some of the arguments of *Losing Ground*. Murray was quite clear that underclass did not refer to poverty, but to the type of poverty identified by Henry Mayhew in nineteenth-century London and referred to as the 'undeserving poor'. He argued that Britain had an underclass, though it was out of sight and smaller than in the United States. He wrote that Britain had 'a growing population of working-aged, healthy people who live in a different world from other Britons, who are raising their children to live in it, and whose values are now contaminating the life of entire neighbourhoods'.[22]

According to Murray, the underclass was growing rapidly, and was characterised by three features – out-of-wedlock births, violent crime, and unemployment. During the period 1945–60, Britain had a very low and even slightly declining 'illegitimacy ratio' – that is, births to single women as a percentage of all births. In 1960–78, the ratio increased, but remained low compared to other countries. Then it began to rise very rapidly, to 14.1% in 1982, 18.9% in 1985, and 25.6% by 1988. Murray claimed, from birth data on municipal districts and the census, that the increase in these out-of-wedlock births was concentrated in the lowest social class. In poor neighbourhoods, out-of-wedlock births could constitute the majority.[23] Unlike the United States, the role of ethnicity was much less significant. Out-of-wedlock births were higher in the black community, but this represented a comparatively small proportion of the British population as a whole. Murray claimed from educational research that the children of single parents did worse than those of married parents. And Murray was particularly critical of the absence of fathers in inner-city communities. He wrote that 'the key to an underclass is not the individual instance but a situation in which a very large proportion of an entire community lacks fathers, and this is far more common in poor communities than rich ones'.[24]

Murray also focused on crime, claiming that the habitual criminal was a classic member of the underclass since he 'lives off mainstream society without participating in it'.[25] But crime also fragmented communities, and changed its norms of behaviour. Figures for property crime, for example, were allegedly higher in Britain than in the United States. In 1988, England had 1,623 reported burglaries per 100,000 population, compared to 1,309 in the United States. Thefts of motor vehicles also seemed to be higher. Violent crime was lower in England and Wales than in the United States, but it was rising rapidly, especially from 1968 onwards. By 1988, England had 314 violent crimes reported per 100,000 people. And this was despite the demographic decline in the group most likely to commit these crimes (teenage males). Murray claimed that violent crime was spatially concentrated in poor communities where the 'underclass is taking over'.[26]

The third strand of Murray's argument was based on an alleged decrease in labour force participation. Murray claimed that the 1981 census indicated that municipal districts with high proportions of household heads in Class V (unskilled labourers), also tended to have the highest levels of 'economically inactive' people of working age. (Whereas the unemployment figures included those available for work, the 'economically inactive' included those who declared they were not available for work.) Murray claimed that people of working age who were neither working nor looking for work were more likely to be found in the slums than the suburbs. From largely anecdotal evidence, Murray's hypothesis was that Britain was experiencing a generation gap by class. Lower-class men in their teens and twenties had a changed attitude towards the labour force. Work was no longer regarded as a source of self-respect, and a means of escaping the benefit system. This contributed to the breakdown of communities. Young men who were not required to support families found other ways to prove that they were men, which allegedly took destructive forms.[27]

Murray attempted to explain the causes of the emergence of the underclass by applying the analysis of *Losing Ground* to the British situation. He disagreed that it was linked with the election of the Thatcher government in 1979, and a subsequent increase in inequality. Instead, as in the USA, 'the rules of the game changed fundamentally for low-income young people. Behaviour changed along with the changes in the rules'.[28] Murray claimed that the clear-up rates for crimes such as robberies had fallen, and penalties had become less severe. Figures for 1982 and 1987 showed an increase in the number of indictable offences, but a decline in the number of convictions, and in the number of prison sentences. With regard to out-of-wedlock births, too, social stigma had declined, while the benefit system made it possible to have a baby without the support of a father. Benefits for single women began to rise in the 1970s, while the 1977 Homeless Persons Act prioritised the claims of pregnant women and single mothers to local authority housing. Murray argued that these social problems were interconnected, and would not be solved by a decline in unemployment.

Murray argued that social policy in both the United States and Britain was driven by the same intellectual impulses and had had similar effects. Britain, however, could learn little from America, since politicians were unwilling to face the fact that they were powerless to deal with an underclass once it existed. Murray's solution was more self-government for poor communities, giving them greater responsibility for criminal justice, education, housing, and the benefit systems. Murray's message for Britain was bleak, in that there was evidence of an underclass, and it was growing. But there also seemed little evidence that a Conservative or Labour government would do much about it.[29] It was clear that Murray defined the underclass through behaviour. He wrote, for example, that:

> When I use the term 'underclass' I am indeed focusing on a certain type of poor person defined not by his condition, e.g. long-term unemployed, but by his deplorable behaviour in response to that condition, e.g. unwilling to take jobs that are available to him.[30]

Nevertheless Murray claimed that he did not agree with the notion of a culture of poverty, and was well aware that some families managed to break out of a 'cycle of disadvantage'. At several points, Murray indicated that his arguments were based on direct observation in deprived communities, including Birkenhead and the Easterhouse estate in Glasgow. But as the above summary makes clear, the analysis was essentially the same as in *Losing Ground*, supported by different data.

Murray's writing was extremely influential, especially in the popular press. The Director of the IEA's Health and Welfare Unit, David G. Green, for example, wrote that Murray did not apply the term 'underclass' to all the poor, but only those 'distinguished by their undesirable behaviour, including drug-taking, crime, illegitimacy, failure to hold down a job, truancy from school and casual violence'.[31] Murray made a further contribution to the underclass debate, in a two-part article published in the *Sunday Times* in May 1994. This again looked at three 'symptoms' – crime, illegitimacy, and economic inactivity among men of working age – but was based on figures for 1992. Murray's figures indicated that since 1989, property crime in England and Wales had increased a further 42%, and violent crime by a further 40%. The illegitimacy ratio had increased to 31.2% in 1992. In terms of economic inactivity, the 1981 census had indicated that 11.3% of working-aged men (aged 16–64) were unemployed, and that 9.6% of working-aged men were economically inactive altogether. The 1991 census showed that 11.0% of working-aged men were unemployed, but that the percentage of working-aged men who were economically inactive had increased by a third, to 13.3%. It was not clear what this meant, but Murray regarded it as a worrying development.[32] Furthermore he claimed that the term 'underclass' had a new legitimacy compared to four years earlier.

Murray made three main points. The first was that the family was undergoing unprecedented change. Second, the family in the upper middle class was 'in good shape', but in the lower classes was likely to deteriorate further. Third, that wholesale overhaul of the benefit system was necessary. He claimed that the evidence could be found in four areas of family life – out-of-wedlock births; divorce; cohabitation; and their relation to social class. One cause of the rise in out-of-wedlock births was the dramatic increase in divorce that followed the 1969 Divorce Reform Act. At the same time, rates of marriage began to fall, and cohabitation became much more common. Statistics for 1991 showed that 74% of births outside marriage were jointly registered, and 70% of these were to parents living at the same address, or cohabiting. Overall, the census indicated that for families with children born in 1991, 70% were born to married couples, 16% to unmarried couples living at the same address, and 14% to a woman living on her own.[33]

Murray was particularly keen to relate these trends to social class. The census revealed that the proportions of married couples in households with dependent children varied according to geographical area. Inner London had the lowest percentage (57%), while outer London had a much higher figure (75%). Figures were higher still in local authorities classified as 'remoter, largely rural' (81%), and were highest in those classified as 'mixed urban-rural' (82%). Murray claimed from the 1991 census that out-of-wedlock births bore a strong relationship to social class. In the ten local authorities with the lowest percentage of households in Class V, 18% of the children were born out-of-wedlock in 1991. In the ten local authorities with the highest percentage of households in Class V, 40% of the children were born out-of-wedlock in 1991. Murray claimed from this data that 'the England in which the family has effectively collapsed does not consist just of blacks, or even the inner-city neighbourhoods of London, Manchester, and Liverpool, but lower working-class communities everywhere'.[34]

Murray argued that this 'breakdown' in the English family varied according to social class. He tried to illustrate changes since the 1970s by choosing the ten districts with the highest proportion of Class V households in the 1981 and 1991 censuses. These included Middlesbrough, Hartlepool, and Liverpool. He then chose the ten districts with the lowest proportion of Class V households. These included Wokingham, Surrey Heath, and South Buckinghamshire. In 1974, the two-parent family was the standard in both types of area, as were other aspects of community life. They had the same 'social template'. In 1991, on the other hand, there were areas of Middlesbrough (with 45% of its births out-of-wedlock) and Wokingham (with 15%) that were dramatically different. Murray predicted that society would be split between the 'New Victorians' and the 'New Rabble'. The first would edge back towards traditional morality, while the second would come to resemble the American underclass.[35]

Murray argued further that British social policy would sustain the disintegration of the family in the lower income groups. Part of Murray's argument was that fraud and abuse were widespread in the benefit system. But he also argued that individuals were making choices to opt for benefit rather than paid work. As with Harold and Phyllis in the USA, to people in the low-skilled working class, marriage made 'no sense'. An additional element of Murray's argument was that these cultural norms would become embodied in successive generations. For young men, marriage acted as a 'civilising process', but unmarried parenthood offered no means of socialising young boys. In terms of solutions, Murray argued that full employment would have little effect on out-of-wedlock births. He advocated changes to the benefit system, so that single mothers were not favoured over married mothers, arguing that 'the welfare of society requires that women actively avoid getting pregnant if they have no husband, and that women once again demand marriage from a man who would have them bear a child'.[36]

Murray's later comments on changes in family life found some supporters. The journalist Melanie Phillips, for example, agreed with Murray, writing that 'the collapse of the family is a social disaster. It weakens the cultural and moral transmitters down through the generations. It lies at the heart of many of our social problems'.[37] There were communities in which fatherlessness had become the norm. Phillips wrote that:

> These communities are truly alarming because children are being brought up with dysfunctional and often antisocial attitudes as a direct result of the fragmentation and emotional chaos of households in which sexual libertarianism provides a stream of transient and unattached men servicing their mothers.[38]

Marriage had become devalued, and children were simply another set of 'consumer commodities'. At the same time, Phillips disagreed with Murray's scenario of the 'New Victorians' and the 'New Rabble', and also disputed that it was welfare that had created these new social norms. The greatest increases in out-of-wedlock births had occurred in Classes I and II, and arguably the danger was that society would become divided within each class. Phillips argued that intellectuals and politicians should support the family, as should the state, through the tax and benefits system.

Whereas in 1989 Murray had been interested in economic change and the emergence of an underclass, five years later he was more concerned with changes in the family. This change was significant, reflecting the criticism that his arguments had aroused. We will look more closely at those criticisms shortly. For the more thoughtful commentators on the Right, the underclass continued to pose problems of definition, making them more cautious than their American counterparts. David Willetts, for instance, was at the time associated with right-wing think-tanks, and a prospective Conservative Parliamentary candidate. Willetts suggested that three groups were likely to be on Income Support – the long-term unemployed, unskilled workers in erratic employment, and younger single mothers – and the underclass could be defined most simply as long-term or frequent claimants of benefit. He agreed with Murray's economic model, and claimed there was a group called 'the respectable poor' for whom values were important. While the idea of an underclass was controversial, it forced people to look at questions of poverty and social security. Willetts also acknowledged that there appeared to be little connection between his three underclass groups. He used the term provisionally and hypothetically, and 'enclosed within imaginary quotation marks'. Willetts noted that in *Losing Ground*, Murray was mainly concerned with AFDC, and thus 'welfare' in the USA and 'social security' in Britain were not the same thing.[39]

The point in summarising Murray's arguments here is not to endorse them, but to try to indicate why they attracted so much attention. As he had argued in the American context, Murray's analysis was essentially about the effects of social policies on human behaviour. His closest counterpart in the British context was Frank Field, who had earlier been Director of the Child Poverty Action Group and later was Director of the Low Pay Unit. In 1971 he was the co-author of an article that had invented the term 'poverty trap' to describe the ways in which means tests penalised paid workers. In May 1997 Field was appointed Minister for Welfare Reform, with the brief to 'think the unthinkable' on social policy. In part, Field's attitude to behaviour was influenced by his Christian beliefs – these underlay his views on the 'fallen side of mankind'. Like Murray, Field stressed the importance of self-interest. He believed that welfare affected people's attitudes and behaviour, and in part he came to this point of view through observing how welfare operated on the ground. At the same time, he differed from Murray in that he was seeking to reconstruct welfare, not to abolish it.[40]

In an early book on the underclass (1989), Field sought to reclaim the term for the liberal Left. He argued that important economic and social trends threatened to overturn the concept of citizenship as proposed by T. H. Marshall. Marshall had earlier written of history in terms of the successive emergence of political citizenship, economic citizenship, and social citizenship. One trend was the emergence of record postwar levels of unemployment. A second was widening class differentials. Another was the exclusion of the very poor from rising living standards. Finally, there was a significant change in the attitudes of those in mainstream society towards those who had failed to 'make it'. These changes, argued Field, had combined to 'produce an underclass that sits uncomfortably below that group which is referred to as living on a low income'.[41] Field claimed that the underclass lived under a form of 'political, social and economic apartheid', and that the emergence of this group marked a watershed in British working-class politics. The very poorest were separated, not only from other groups on low incomes, but more importantly from the working class. The difference was that the working class still shared with other classes the hope of rising living standards and opportunities.

Field claimed that the underclass comprised three groups – the long-term unemployed (especially older workers and school-leavers if they had never had a job); single-parent families; and elderly pensioners. He acknowledged that this typology was crude, and dangerously close to the arguments of Dahrendorf. There was a danger that the characteristics of the underclass could be seen as its causes, and this was a short step away from 'blaming the victim'. It was too similar to a culture of poverty approach. Field acknowledged that even in his own city of Birkenhead there was evidence that there was nothing new in a concentration on the moral weaknesses of the underclass. In the 1930s, for example, the local newspaper had carried stories about those who had allegedly stopped wanting to work.[42] Field argued that the personal pathologies of the underclass and its culture were induced by poverty and were only part of the problem. The underclass of working age was not responsible for its own exclusion. Rather its members wished to regain membership of the wider society, through having a job, and preferably as soon as possible. Field's analysis of underclass culture was thus that it was an adaptive response to the environment its members found themselves in. His attempt to combine behavioural and structural factors was similar to that of William Julius Wilson.

Field argued that there were six forces involved in a 'cycle of deprivation' that effectively locked the underclass in place. Unemployment had increased, and downward social mobility meant that many of the working class were unemployed. There were more temporary, part-time, and poorly-paid jobs, and the tax and benefits system destroyed initiative. The 1980s had seen a striking increase in owner-occupation and share-ownership. Finally, pension reforms meant that there was a strong chance that the most disadvantaged would have to subsist on a low income. Field claimed that since the election of the Conservative government in 1979, a minority of the population had become cut off from other people on low income. This underclass was thus increasingly isolated, in terms of income, life chances, and political aspirations. He wrote that 'psychologically, the underclass is being increasingly isolated by the growth of a drawbridge mentality amongst those who feel they are "making it" in Thatcher's Britain'.[43]

Field's book on the underclass provided an early example of ideas that he was later to develop into a blueprint for welfare reform. He argued, for instance, that Titmuss's influence on social policy had meant that discussions of the role of behaviour had been neglected. It was this that lay behind the invention of the term 'stakeholder welfare', and the ideas that Field would express in *Making Welfare Work*.[44] Field's approach to attitudes and behaviour was in some ways similar to that of Murray, though he was also concerned with the impact of structural factors on poverty and deprivation. It was therefore interesting to see how Field responded to Murray's article in the *Sunday Times Magazine*. Field reiterated that he believed that Britain did now have a group of people so poor they could be considered an underclass. Pensioners, for example, had been hit hard by the decision of the Government to break the link between pensions and rises in earnings or prices. Field echoed Murray in arguing that it was necessary to integrate the 'disillusioned young unemployed worker' back into mainstream society.[45] He claimed that it was crucial to enforce an availability-for-work test so that people took work when it was available. At the same time, Field remained hostile to the notion of a culture of poverty.

Field was not a lone voice. At a popular level, many in the 1980s found the term 'underclass' helpful in focusing attention on growing poverty and deprivation. Within the academic community there were some who argued that the underclass was an identifiable feature of the class system. The sociologist W. G. Runciman, for instance, included the underclass among the seven classes that he claimed constituted British society. He wrote '[that] there is below the two working classes an underclass which constitutes a separate category of roles is as readily demonstrable as that there is an upper class above the middle class in contemporary British society'.[46] But this was not workers systematically disadvantaged in the labour market, but people unable to participate in the labour market at all, and living permanently on benefits. Many were members of ethnic minorities, or single mothers, and some were both. Runciman noted that the 'submerged tenth' of Edwardian society had included not just vagrants and petty criminals, but also casual labourers. Also in this group were the long-term unemployed who might supplement their benefits by undeclared work, begging, or petty theft. Aware of these historical continuities, he suggested that if the stereotypical member of the underclass in 1910 had been the 'loafer' – a white male casual labourer living in rented accommodation – in 1980 it was a single mother from an ethnic minority living in council housing and entirely dependent on state benefit.[47]

Others agreed with Dahrendorf that the underclass posed interesting theoretical problems for social citizenship. Maurice Roche suggested that its members were excluded from citizenship or disdainful of it, and represented a limit beyond which the order of the democratic and welfare state and civil society broke down. He noted that neoconservatives (like Murray) claimed that the welfare state was partly responsible for the growth of the underclass. Thus the dominant paradigm in the postwar welfare state had been responsible for the progressive breakdown of the very social citizenship it had sought to promote.[48] While this was a more abstract, theoretical argument, it appeared to concede that the underclass was an empirical reality.

The sociologist Alan Buckingham was a comparatively late entrant into the underclass debate. He set out to define the underclass and then test three competing theories. He traced what he termed behavioural, labour market, and critical approaches to the underclass, and attempted to evaluate them using the National Child Development Study. Buckingham argued from this data that an underclass did exist, suffering from a lack of qualifications, low cognitive ability, and chronic joblessness. Furthermore Buckingham claimed the underclass was distinct from the working class in terms of patterns of family formation, work commitment, and political allegiance. Buckingham noted that debate about the underclass had often been divided along ideological lines, and he conceded that further analysis was required. However he concluded from his analysis that 'the distinct attitudes of the underclass, when coupled with evidence of inter- and intra-generational stability of membership, provide early evidence that a new social class, the underclass, may now exist in Britain'.[49]

More common was the view that a growing underclass was potentially a very important development, but remained a matter of empirical investigation. These commentators continued to struggle with the issue of how the underclass might best be defined. At a seminar funded by the Joseph Rowntree Foundation and organised by the Policy Studies Institute, David J. Smith proposed that the underclass could not be defined as a group characterised by a culture of dependency, or as the political undeserving poor. The underclass also fell outside a Marxist class system. Instead he saw it as being comprised of 'family units having no stable relationship at all with the "mode of production" – with legitimate gainful employment'.[50] For Smith, the idea of an underclass only made sense if there was some stability in its membership. However he also resisted the idea that people in a 'secondary' labour market, where jobs offered poor security and low pay, or were part-time, were also in the underclass. It was difficult to define the 'secondary labour market', and many of these jobs were an additional source of income for the family unit. On structure and agency, Smith suggested that the underclass might be defined in structural terms, but it could be cultural factors that determined economic power, and consigned some people to the underclass. Others struggled with the same problems. Whether the underclass was defined as the 'secondary' labour market, including ethnic minorities and unskilled female workers; the long-term unemployed; families dependent on benefits; or simply as people on low incomes, there appeared to be little or no empirical evidence for its existence.

Sociologists interested in changes in Britain's employment structure sought to explore the idea that the most significant source of social change had been the growth of an underclass that cut across traditional class divisions. Duncan Gallie, for instance, attempted to explore whether there was evidence that an underclass, of the type previously described by Giddens, was emerging in Britain. The arguments of Giddens relied on a particular view of the way that the employment structure had evolved, and on a growing distinction between 'primary' and 'secondary' sector jobs. Nevertheless there was little evidence, Gallie argued, of a growth of 'secondary sector' jobs that were poorly paid, short-term, and where untrained labour was tightly supervised. There was little evidence that internal labour markets had become widespread in British industry, and not much sign of an expansion in temporary jobs. In the case of ethnic minorities, Gallie thought there was little evidence that their undoubted disadvantage in the labour market was being translated into the 'revolutionary' consciousness described by Giddens. As far as women were concerned, they suffered gender inequalities at work, and were concentrated in routine non-manual work and lower-skilled manual work. But as with the ethnic minorities, the high degree of internal differentiation within their employment meant they were unlikely to develop a sense of common economic interest.[51]

Even so, Gallie conceded it was possible that the concept of the underclass might be useful in highlighting the social position and attitudes of the unemployed. The emergence of mass unemployment in the 1980s seemed to indicate that a major divide was opening up between those in and out of work. There was no doubt, suggested Gallie, that unemployment led to deprivation. However the fact that the overall level of unemployment was relatively stable hid the fact that as far as individual people were concerned, there was much movement in and out of employment. In 1985, for instance, half of the people becoming unemployed found work again within three months. Even the long-term unemployed were very heterogeneous, in terms of the reasons why they became unemployed, their personal characteristics, and their age. Psychological depression and a lack of financial resources made collective action difficult, and there was evidence that their plight engendered sympathy rather than hostility from employed manual workers. Overall, Gallie argued that there was little evidence from the labour disadvantages experienced by ethnic minorities, women, or the unemployed that they were of a type that supported the emergence of an underclass. Rather, the idea of an underclass relied on lumping together very different types of labour-market disadvantage. It was unlikely that this would create a distinctive cultural identity and lead to political radicalism. Finally the idea of an underclass took little account of the way institutions tended to adapt to, and contain, new types of demand. In general, Gallie argued that predictions of the emergence of an underclass had proved 'largely unfounded'.[52]

Gallie further explored the particular case of the unemployed using data on six labour markets collected for the Economic and Social Research Council (ESRC)'s Social Change and Economic Life Initiative. Gallie provided a helpful definition of the underclass – it was a social stratum that suffered prolonged labour market marginality; it experienced greater deprivation than the manual working class; and it had its own subculture. In order to test if it existed, Gallie provided empirical evidence on the work histories and attitudes of employed and unemployed people. Three of the labour markets (Swindon, Aberdeen, and Northampton) had been economically buoyant in the 1980s, while three (Coventry, Rochdale, and Kircaldy) had experienced prolonged recession. However, Gallie found from past work histories that the long-term unemployed were no more likely than the employed to have changed jobs frequently, and they did not have a markedly lower commitment to work than those in employment. There was no doubt that the unemployed suffered serious disadvantage. But there was little evidence that this supported some sense of cultural distinctiveness. The unemployed neither engaged in direct action nor became politically passive, and in fact increased their support for the Labour Party.[53] Thus the evidence fitted neither the conservative nor the liberal versions of the underclass thesis.

Gallie's arguments were similar to those of Ross McKibbin on the 'social psychology' of unemployment in the 1930s, and it was striking that it was the same areas, South Wales and the North East, that experienced high unemployment. In 1989, Hartlepool was again in decline following the rundown of shipbuilding and restructuring of steel production. Lydia Morris and Sarah Irwin used Hartlepool to explore whether there really was any dividing line between an underclass and the rest of the population. They selected three groups of households – couples where the man had been unemployed continuously in the last 12 months; couples in which the man had been in the same job in the last 12 months; and couples where the man had started a job within the last 12 months, though he might be employed or unemployed. The idea was to compare the work histories and characteristics of these three groups, and to explore two definitions of the underclass. These were non-participation and systematic disadvantage in the labour market. The study did show that between the long-term unemployed and the securely employed there was a group of male workers experiencing broken employment interspersed with short-term unemployment. This suggested that the underclass might not consist only of the unemployed. Overall, however, Morris and Irwin found that the characteristics of the 'under-employed', although disadvantaged, were too heterogeneous for the group to be seen as a class. Evidence of mutual aid and informal exchange throughout the whole sample population tended to rule out the idea of a distinctive underclass culture.[54]

Gordon Marshall, Stephen Roberts and Carole Burgoyne set out to explore whether class analysis was undermined by its neglect of economically-inactive people. W. G. Runciman, for example, had argued that the underclass constituted one of the seven classes in British society. Marshall, Roberts, and Burgoyne noted several points about the underclass. First, the underclass was characterised as being excluded from society on account of its extreme deprivation (due to poverty or lack of employment), or was seen as at variance with mainstream behaviour and values. Second, in practice, most researchers associated it with either extreme poverty or long-term unemployment. Third, it was widely held that the underclass had a distinctive subculture of cynicism, resignation, and despair. Marshall, Roberts, and Burgoyne admitted that fatalism was a rather imprecise concept. However from interview data they did not find that the chronically economically-inactive were more prone to defeatism and mistrust than those in employment. Moreover their evidence suggested that in terms of attitudes the groups usually said to comprise the underclass were not distinct from the rest of the population. Marshall, Roberts, and Burgoyne therefore concluded of the underclass that 'the concept itself looks increasingly flawed, and certainly fails to provide a platform from which to launch a convincing critique of class analysis because of its "missing millions".[55]

Other researchers looked at the underclass from the perspective of housing, drawing on local case studies. Peter Lee argued that debates about new forms of poverty were incomplete, and needed to explain new spatial patterns of poverty and deprivation. He argued that local housing and economic conditions, along with welfare delivery, interacted to produce new regions of social exclusion. However while showing an appreciation of the historical dimension to the underclass discourse, Lee noted disagreement over definitions, and rejected the underclass as an explanatory device, since in his view it concentrated too heavily on the role of welfare dependency. Rather (and drawing on a case-study of the northern town of Morecambe) Lee argued that it was housing that created and sustained deprivation.[56]

In the 1980s, unemployment grew particularly rapidly in the Republic of Ireland, and here, too, researchers were attracted to the underclass concept as a possible explanation, or result of, social change. Between 1980 and 1987, unemployment in Ireland increased to 232,000, or nearly 18% of the workforce. Brian Nolan and Christopher T. Whelan adopted Duncan Gallie's three-part definition of the underclass. They were particularly interested in William Julius Wilson's argument that weak labour-force attachment and social isolation created a vicious circle and distinctive underclass subcultural characteristics. The Irish data certainly showed that labour market marginality was associated with a level of deprivation significantly greater than that experienced by the rest of the manual working class. However, this group was not concentrated in urban centres, though its members tended to live in rented urban public-sector housing. Nolan and Whelan concluded that since there was little evidence for subcultural characteristics, the underclass framework was redundant, and it was sufficient to refer to marginalization and deprivation. They argued that:

> widespread long-term unemployment, the concentration of the unemployed in public sector housing, and the existence of significant pockets of concentrated deprivation do not, of themselves, generate the cultural distinctiveness that characterizes an underclass.[57]

Other researchers looked at households that were classed as 'economically inactive'. At the Policy Studies Institute seminar, Nick Buck used data on labour market behaviour to explore how far it was possible to identify and measure an underclass. Like Smith, Buck defined the underclass as families that did not have a stable relationship with legitimate gainful employment. He analysed economic activity at the household or family level, focusing on households with no labour market activity, measuring how their numbers had changed in the 1980s, and what characteristics they possessed. Longitudinal data was not available. But data from the Labour Force Survey indicated that the estimated total population in 'inactive' couple households grew from 1.96m in 1979 (4.2% of the total population in working age households), to 4.58m in 1986 (9.9% of the total population). All of these groups had expanded rapidly at a time of rising national unemployment. But Buck argued the rationale for defining an underclass remained problematic. For most people, unemployment came as an interruption to a normal working life, and was not a permanent condition. In the words of Buck, these people were 'not so much stable members of an underclass as unstable members of the working class'.[58]

If one persistent defining characteristic of the underclass has been its relationship to stable working patterns, another is its attitudes towards work and the family, and its involvement in the mainstream economic and political processes of society. Anthony Heath used the 1987 British Election Survey and the 1989 British Social Attitudes Survey to see if the underclass had distinctive attitudes, and in particular if there was evidence of a 'culture of dependency'. He defined the underclass as those dependent on benefits, though excluding pensioners. Heath argued that this data confirmed that the underclass was poor, lacked educational qualifications, lived in rented accommodation, and was less likely to correspond to the nuclear family ideal. It indicated, though, that the underclass made up only a quarter of residents even in the poorest neighbourhoods, suggesting that it was unlikely it had a separate culture. Compared to the rest of the population, the underclass had similar attitudes towards children, but different attitudes towards marriage. With work, members of the underclass were more likely to give financial reasons for not working, but overall the evidence did not provide support for a 'culture of dependency'. As far as politics was concerned, the underclass was more cynical, but nevertheless turnout at elections was still quite high (68%). Heath concluded that the differences that did exist were not evidence of a distinct culture, and that the underclass was heterogeneous, both in terms of its members and their attitudes.[59]

Other studies, including some based on diaries and interviews, were similarly dismissive of the idea that the underclass might have a separate culture. One by Elaine Kempson, then at the Policy Studies Institute, attempted to look at the lives of people on low income. Her study combined 31 studies commissioned by the Joseph Rowntree Foundation as part of its social policy and housing research programmes. These had drawn on detailed accounts by 2,100 people in a wide range of circumstances, and on some 300 interviews. But Kempson concluded that while her study showed that some people managed their limited budget better than others, it demonstrated little evidence of fecklessness among the poor. She argued:

> One thing is clear from the analysis in this report – people who live on low incomes are not an underclass. They have aspirations just like others in society: they want a job; a decent home; and an income that is enough to pay the bills with a little to spare.[60]

Thus it appeared that when the concept of the underclass was tested against the empirical evidence, there was little support that it existed. First, there was little evidence of the expansion of secondary labour markets, or of a growth in the radical potential of ethnic minority groups or female workers. Second, although undoubtedly deprived, even the long-term unemployed were too hetereogeneous a group to constitute an underclass; they seemed as committed to work as the employed; and what political energies they had were directed through conventional channels into increased support for the Labour Party. Third, the Irish data showed that groups which occupied a marginal position in relation to the labour market were not concentrated in urban centres, and undermined the argument that weak labour force attachment and social isolation created a vicious circle. Fourth, unemployment statistics hid movement in and out of unemployment, and the 'under-employed' did not seem to be a separate class with a distinctive subculture. As in the USA, panel data of income dynamics indicated that within the low income population there was much movement in and out of poverty. Fifth, survey material and qualitative data suggested that the aspirations and attitudes of those on low incomes were the same as the rest of society. The argument of David J. Smith was that although the existence of the underclass could not be proven, it might turn out to be a good way of explaining the society that would be created if current conditions persisted.[61] As the Eugenics Society in the 1930s never tired of repeating, more research was needed.

In these respects, the underclass debate in Britain in the 1980s was similar in shape if not in scale to that in the United States. The apparent lack of empirical evidence led many to reject the term 'underclass' outright. John Macnicol, for example, was one of the first to examine the historical antecedents of the term, and point out the recurring nature of this phenomenon. Writing of the research undertaken as a result of Sir Keith Joseph's 1972 speech on the cycle of deprivation, he argued that in all the painstaking and expensive research 'surprisingly little cognisance was taken of the history of the concept'. Macnicol claimed that the concept of an inter-generational underclass displaying a high concentration of social problems had been reconstructed periodically over the previous 100 years. It was defined as 'remaining outwith the boundaries of citizenship, alienated from cultural norms and stubbornly impervious to the normal incentives of the market' [62] While there were important changes in emphasis between these reconstructions, there were important continuities. The concept had been sustained in different ways – by simple class prejudice, theories of heredity in the interwar years, and later by psychological models of personal inadequacy. In fact, claimed Macnicol, 'underclass stereotypes have always been part of the discourse on poverty in advanced industrial societies'.[63]

Macnicol claimed that there were problems in defining the underclass. A populist version of the concept had been internalised by ordinary working-class people as the obverse of respectable. The underclass concept had to be differentiated from wider assumptions about the inheritance of intellect and ability. And both Right and Left had used the concept, with the latter using it to describe the casualties of capitalism.[64] Macnicol noted that the underclass concept had five elements. In the first place, it was an artificial administrative definition, where those who were defined as members of the underclass depended on their contact with particular institutions of the state. Second, the idea was mixed up with the separate question of inter-generational transmission of intelligence. Third, particular social traits were identified as being antisocial, while others were ignored. Fourth, the underclass could further be seen as a resource allocation problem. Finally, the concept tended to be supported by those with a conservative outlook on the potential role of state welfare in reducing social inequalities. It became therefore part of a conservative view of the causes of social problems and the correct solutions.[65]

Charles Murray's 1989 article in the *Sunday Times Magazine* also generated much hostility and criticism. Alan Walker argued that Murray's thesis was part of a long tradition of dividing people into two groups, those whose poverty was due to structural factors and those whose situation was their own fault. He suggested, first, that Murray had failed to provide any scientific evidence that an underclass existed, and second, that his guide to policy was at best misleading and at worst a dangerous diversion from poverty and deprivation. Thus the Murray argument fitted very neatly into the earlier legacy of the culture of poverty and cycle of deprivation, with its 'characteristic mixture of popular stereotypes, prejudice about the causes of poverty and ill-founded quasi-scientific notions'.[66] Walker was Professor of Social Policy at the University of Sheffield. From evidence on unemployment and single mothers, Walker argued that there was no evidence of a different type of poverty, or of a subculture separated from the rest of society and with different values to it, or of a process of 'transmission and contamination'. For Walker, the problem was the degree of poverty, not the type of poverty. In general Murray's approach, like those before it, diverted attention from 'blaming the mechanisms through which resources are distributed'.[67]

Commentators were particularly critical of Murray's focus on single mothers. It was claimed that he had used statistics to present a picture of a growing army of one-parent families, mainly fatherless, who were dependent on state benefits.

But it was pointed out that statistics also showed that while the duration of single mothers on benefit increased (1981–87), they still spent shorter periods on benefit than divorced or widowed mothers. The main reason why single mothers did not spend long years on benefit was because they married. By the time a child was five years old, 60% of single mothers had married, and 70% by the time the child was 7 years old. It was claimed that it made little sense to point the finger at single mothers, and not at divorced or separated mothers. If these mothers remarried, they did not seem to be permanently rejecting either marriage or the role of men in families. Murray's solution of social reorganisation based on local community empowerment was also dismissed. Instead, the key was seen to be government helping mothers to combine their responsibilities in the home with paid employment.[68]

Some commentators focused on the gender politics of the popular underclass discourse. Kirk Mann and Sasha Roseneil, for example, argued that in 1993, in the wake of the James Bulger case, a high degree of consensus developed, uniting politicians and commentators in hostility to never-married mothers. In this process, never-married mothers were identified as the source and cause of juvenile crime. They located this discourse within the context of the restructuring of the welfare state, and as part of 'patriarchal reconstruction' which constituted a 'backlash' against long-term changes in gender relations and feminism. In 1993, they argued, moral panic, economic individualism, and anti-feminist backlash combined to make lone mothers the focus of public debate about the reproduction of the underclass. But Mann and Roseneil were also sceptical about the underclass concept itself. In their view, the concept had no theoretical coherence and only anecdotal evidence to support it. The fact that it had gained credibility from liberal and socialist commentators could not disguise the fact that it was a profoundly conservative and anti-feminist concept. Mann and Roseneil concluded that 'the threat we perceive comes not from the supposed constituents and reproducers of the underclass but from those who propagate the concept of a dangerous class'.[69]

Other commentators adopted an approach similar to that of Macnicol, in pointing to historical continuities in underclass concepts. Paul Bagguley and Kirk Mann, for example, noted that Murray drew on the key themes of a classic right-wing moral panic – illegitimacy, violent crime, and drop-out from the labour force. The underclass were seen as 'idle thieving bastards'. But in Britain, there was no evidence that an underclass had been comprised of the same groups since the 1880s. The criteria for defining it changed easily with changes in economic and social conditions, and the dominant ideas of the day had been consistently used by the middle class to redefine the poor. Bagguley and Mann were critical of the stance of William Julius Wilson, claiming that he further weakened the liberal position in that he appeared to support the culture of poverty notion, but provided no empirical evidence. In their view, the cycle of deprivation had been examined systematically in the 1970s and found wanting. In fact, the underclass was essentially 'a set of ideological beliefs held by certain groups among the upper and middle classes' which helped to sustain relations of domination of class, patriarchy, and race. The surprising feature for Bagguley and Mann was why both Left and Right found the concept so appealing when it had been destroyed by social scientific analysis. They suggested that 'perhaps the really dangerous class is not the underclass but those who have propagated the underclass concept'.[70] Bagguley and Mann concluded that because of its theoretical, methodological, and empirical flaws, the underclass concept was 'a demonstrably false set of beliefs'.[71]

Notwithstanding his arguments in the 1970s, John Westergaard, in a Presidential address to the British Sociological Association, claimed that the underclass concept was influential, not because it fitted the facts but because it was well attuned to the contemporary mood. British sociology, he claimed, showed resistance to the pressures of the 1980s. He claimed the concept existed in three versions – a 'moral turpitude' version, an 'outcast poverty' version, and a 'rhetorical' version. What they had in common was that they proposed the emergence of a significant minority who were outside mainstream society, and suggested that this divide was the most challenging line of social division for the future. While increased inequality was not in doubt, what was more unlikely was that the underclass represented a segregated minority, and the majority represented a classless commonality. In answer to the question of why the underclass concept was so popular, Westergaard suggested that it satisfied both Left and Right in acknowledging that poverty persisted alongside social class.[72] The movement was led more by the media than by social science. He suggested that changes in ideological fashion should be studied, both to see what they said about the mood of the times, and to establish whether they were empirically correct. In adopting this position, Westergaard echoed the work of Gans on the functions of the concept.

Discussions about the underclass debates in different countries were illuminating. Kirk Mann, for instance, attempted to examine how the underclass debate had developed in the United States, Britain, and Australia. He claimed that the observers who believed they were witnessing an underclass were unable to agree on what they had found; he argued that the idea was simply the most recent label for a 'class of failures'. Like Westergaard, Mann thought the observers might be more interesting than the observed. The debate was much more subdued in Britain than in the United States, but in Australia it was notable by its absence. Mann suggested this could be because Australia had better social scientists, or because the sense of 'otherness' embodied in the concept was complicated in Australia by the country's criminal past. More likely was that the Australian state had sought, through a high-wage economy and support for minimum wages, to incorporate groups, such as women, who would be excluded in Britain and the United States. The result was that there was little sense of danger generated by those who elsewhere might be consigned to the underclass – no acute racial divisions, and no riots. Mann concluded that while social divisions, poverty, and unemployment were key areas for research, policy recommendations that drew on the concept of the underclass were 'predicated on prejudice'.[73]

The underclass concept was juxtaposed with that of 'dependency culture'. Hartley Dean and Peter Taylor-Gooby suggested that whereas Thatcherism had sought to blame its victims by constructing the notion of 'dependency culture', its opponents had sought to blame government policy by constructing a socio-structural notion of the underclass. At the same time, the approach of Dean and Taylor-Gooby was to regard the two as 'discursive rather than objective phenomena'. They argued that:

> the underclass concept is most interesting, not for its explanatory value, but for the way in which it has so often drawn together and illuminated preoccupations with delinquency and dependency and for the way in which it permits often unspoken associations between the two.[74]

Dean and Taylor-Gooby were well aware of the assumptions that lay behind the impetus to define an underclass, and the historical dimension to the debate. They argued that the underclass theory reinforced a 'discursive network' of association between delinquency and dependency, crime and poverty, race and antisocial behaviour, and between immorality and single parenthood. Overall, the concept was nothing more than a 'symbolic manifestation of socially constituted definitions of failure'.[75] Yet although the term did not usefully define a real or tangible phenomenon, it nevertheless touched on real and important issues, to do with work, the family, and citizenship.

As we saw earlier, some commentators regarded the emergence of the underclass as a test of social citizenship. Yet for others, the concept of citizenship remained important, while that of the underclass was regarded as unhelpful. The Child Poverty Action Group, for example, argued that the term 'underclass' was effective in capturing the intensity of poverty, and the way that its different aspects compounded one another. Yet it argued that the term was imprecise and difficult to define empirically. There was little evidence to support the cultural interpretation, behavioural interpretations distracted attention from social and economic factors, and the phrase had negative connotations.[76] Its former Director, Ruth Lister, agreed that the use of such an imprecise and value-laden concept could weaken the claims of the poor to citizenship, even though it could also be effective as a means of putting poverty in the headlines. In her view, those who invoked the development of an underclass to make the case for the restoration of full citizenship rights for the poor were 'using a stigmatising label to make the case for non-stigmatising policies'.[77]

The republication of the two Murray pieces by the IEA in 1996, along with the earlier commentaries, provided an opportunity to take stock. A new introduction by Ruth Lister looked more widely at the concept of the underclass itself, the different ways it was understood, defined, and used, and their academic and political implications. Lister was well aware that the behavioural interpretation of the underclass had a long history. She suggested that arguments over the definition of the term had exposed the problems of using administrative criteria, such as 'dependency on the state'. Lister noted that empirical investigations of lone parenthood and unemployment had provided little support for the existence of an underclass. Moreover the language associated with the discourse was one of disease and contamination. Overall, Lister claimed that the focus on the behaviour and values of the underclass distracted attention from wider structural factors. Many had begun to prefer the term 'social exclusion', offering as it did a more dynamic focus on the processes and institutions that created and maintained disadvantage. Perhaps most importantly, for Lister, the concept of the underclass did not provide a means of reconciling more recent debates in social policy about the relative importance of agency and structure. For her, there was a fine line 'between acknowledging the agency of people in poverty and blaming them for that poverty'.[78]

Some of this work therefore began to move towards the concept of social exclusion based on social and legal status.[79] Researchers remained interested in questions of poverty, social isolation, and dispersion and concentration. However, in the British and increasingly influential European context, the language of the underclass was gradually being replaced by that of exclusion.[80] Whether the theory of social exclusion was marked more by continuity or change when compared with the concept of the underclass remained an open question. In using social exclusion, researchers were attempting to overcome the more pejorative aspects of the underclass debate; to look at a dynamic process, and to resolve questions of structure and agency. Nonetheless terms like 'cycle of deprivation' and 'underclass' continued to be used by politicians and policy makers, indicating that many remained unaware of this debate's historical legacy.

By the mid-1990s, the term 'underclass' had already begun to be replaced by the language of social exclusion. Even so, it is interesting to compare the debate about the underclass in Britain with its counterpart in America. There were some broad similarities in the different positions that commentators occupied in the debate. First, there was the stance, largely inspired by Charles Murray, that tended to define the underclass in behavioural terms, and examine trends in out-of-wedlock births, violent crime, and unemployment. As in *Losing Ground*, part of this argument was that changes in social policy had led individuals to alter their behaviour in ways that were damaging in the long term. Second, there was the position adopted by those like Frank Field, who were concerned about the impact of structural factors such as economic change and unemployment. They acknowledged that behaviour did have a role to play, and shared Murray's concerns about the 'decline' of the family. Then there were the agnostics, who regarded the underclass as a theoretical possibility, but in fieldwork on lone parenthood and unemployment found no empirical evidence. Fourth, there were those who rejected the term outright, arguing that though the concept was interesting in how it was defined and used, in the end it had no sociological value.

Murray was an important link in the debate on both sides of the Atlantic. However, these apparent similarities should not blind us to fundamental differences. First, the debate in the United States was much more 'racialised', with the place of black families playing a much more central role. Second, there was no real British counterpart to William Julius Wilson, and a much more deeply entrenched reluctance among social scientists in Britain to explore the role of behavioural and cultural factors in the perpetuation of poverty and deprivation. Third, the debate in Britain moved very quickly from a focus on the underclass *per se* to a much more general discussion about changes in the family, including the increase in out-of-wedlock births, the rise in divorce, the decline in marriage, and the rise in cohabitation. These characteristics reflected not so much trends in economic and social change in Britain and the United States – these were broadly similar – but differences in the earlier history of this discourse. Whereas the United States had engaged heavily in the debates about the culture of poverty, British commentators, particularly on the Left, had through the 1970s displayed almost total hostility to the notion of a cycle of deprivation. It was only in the 1990s, with the theory of social exclusion, that a means was found of bridging the age-old division between those who favoured structural and those who favoured cultural interpretations of the causes of poverty and deprivation. It is to social exclusion that we move in the final chapter.

9

Social Exclusion and Cycles of Disadvantage

As we have seen, the phrase 'underclass' was extremely influential in debates in both the United States and Britain in the 1980s. It continues to be used, particularly at a popular level and in the media. However, since the early 1990s, and among academics and policy-makers, the term has passed out of use, at least in Britain, and has been replaced by the term 'social exclusion', which is favoured by New Labour. In December 1997, in a speech given at Stockwell Park School, in the deprived London borough of Lambeth, Tony Blair outlined government plans to tackle the problem of social exclusion. The speech marked the launch of the Government's new Social Exclusion Unit, and the Prime Minister defined social exclusion in the following way:

> Social exclusion is about income but it is about more. It is about prospects and networks and life-chances. It's a very modern problem, and one that is more harmful to the individual, more damaging to self-esteem, more corrosive for society as a whole, more likely to be passed down from generation to generation, than material poverty.[1]

According to Blair, part of the answer lay in ensuring that those government departments concerned with the development of policy were co-ordinated more effectively. In a phrase that was to become a New Labour buzzword, 'joined up problems' demanded 'joined up solutions'. But Blair also argued that it was in people's own interests that social exclusion should be eliminated. The issue was 'as much about self-interest as compassion'.[2]

Blair's definition of social exclusion, with its emphasis on the structural causes of deprivation, its acknowledgement of the role of behavioural factors, and the stress on the way exclusion might be transmitted between generations immediately has echoes with the earlier underclass concepts with which this book has been concerned. This chapter asks whether social exclusion should be seen as a coda to this history. Is social exclusion simply the most recent in a series of similar labels that stretch back over the past 120 years, or is it something new and quite different? We look first at how the idea of social exclusion evolved in France, and how it has been subsequently embraced by other European countries. While the term 'underclass' was popular in Britain and the United States in the 1980s, in France debates around the issue of deprivation have always been framed by discourses of 'exclusion' and 'insertion'. We look at how the language of social exclusion was imported into Britain, and became part of the vocabulary of New Labour. Despite its appeal to academics and policy-makers, the concept of social exclusion has been challenged, as being centred on paid work, and difficult to test empirically. Finally, and in order to trace continuities and changes, we focus in particular on the way that New Labour has chosen to tackle child poverty. We argue that the nature of initiatives such as the Sure Start programme, and the language in which they are cast, indicate both important continuities and marked differences when compared with the cycle of deprivation research of the 1970s.

Since it was established in December 1997, the government's Social Exclusion Unit has issued a range of reports on subjects that have included truancy and school exclusion; 'rough sleepers'; teenage pregnancy; neighbourhood renewal; and child poverty. The thrust of this interpretation has been reflected in a plethora of government initiatives – the Sure Start programme for parents and children, Education and Health Action Zones, the New Deal for Communities, the Single Regeneration Budget, and many more. Much of the intellectual input into the work of the Social Exclusion Unit has been provided by the ESRC Research Centre for the Analysis of Social Exclusion (CASE), established at the London School of Economics in October 1997. In this respect, the issue of social exclusion provides a good example of the close ties that New Labour has developed with social science academics. Anne Power, for example, has argued that social exclusion is about 'the tendency to push vulnerable and difficult individuals into the least popular places, furthest away from our common aspirations'.[3] Inner-city areas and some large outlying council estates have become a 'receptacle for problems'. She points to the phenomenon of 'neighbourhood collapse', and the tendency of poorer neighbourhoods to form 'poverty clusters'. For Power, Professor of Social Policy, social exclusion is an urban issue.

But social exclusion is a term that has been imported into Britain, and the work of Hilary Silver has been important in exploring its origins. She points out that exclusion became the subject of discussion in France in the 1960s, and attributes the term 'social exclusion' to René Lenoir, then Secretary of State for Social Action in the Chirac Government. In 1974, for example, Lenoir estimated that 'the excluded' made up one-tenth of the French population. But it was only in the late 1970s that 'exclusion' was identified as the central problem of the 'new poverty'. Thus the term 'exclusion' referred to the rise in long-term and recurrent unemployment, and also to important changes in social relations – family break-ups, single-member households, social isolation, and the decline of traditional class solidarity based on unions, workplaces, and networks. Exclusion was seen as the 'rupture of the social and symbolic bonds that should attach individuals to society'.[4] Conversely, the process of tackling exclusion, and of achieving goals of integration, cohesion, and solidarity was called 'insertion'. In France, the guaranteed minimum income, the *Revenu Minimum d'Insertion* (RMI) provided one example of an 'insertion' policy, designed to address exclusion. There was certainly a consensus on this issue, with Presidential candidates of both the Right and Left in 1988 strongly supporting the RMI and wider policies against exclusion.[5]

That is not to say that the meaning of exclusion was not contested, by both the *Front National* and the far Left. Moreover, in the 1980s the meanings of exclusion and insertion were expanded to cover emerging new social groups and problems. One example of this was the way in which 'insertion' policies shifted from the handicapped to 'youth in difficulty'. Another was the extent to which the twin themes of exclusion and insertion were increasingly concerned with the integration of ethnic minority groups. Silver describes how young *beurs*, second generation North African migrants from the housing projects of the *banlieues*, the suburbs or outskirts of the cities, argued through their cultural associations that since they lived in France they should have full citizenship rights. An official policy was adopted to integrate migrants, that managed to keep the key elements of Republican solidarity discourse, but also tried to marry these with multicultural meanings of integration. Following disturbances on the suburban housing estates, the 'exclusion' discourse also encompassed the issue of the *banlieues*. Thus in terms of public policy in France, the many meanings of 'exclusion' were expanded in the 1980s. These included wider questions that were to do with the perceived challenge of integrating migrants; problems faced by young people; and the exclusion that resulted from economic change.[6]

From France, the discourse of exclusion spread rapidly across Western Europe, and was adopted by the European Commission. The White Paper that it published in 1994, entitled *Growth, Competitiveness, Employment*, called for a resolution to fight social exclusion. Graham Room has noted of the history of research on poverty sponsored by the European Union that by the time the third programme was launched (1990–94), social exclusion had become the fashionable terminology. What was interesting was the way that social exclusion was part of a continental, and particularly French, tradition of social analysis that was very different from what might be called the 'Anglo-Saxon' tradition of Rowntree and Townsend. Room argued that whereas the notion of poverty has tended to focus on distributional issues, and the lack of resources at the disposal of an individual or household, social exclusion has been concerned with relational issues, such as inadequate social participation, lack of social integration, and lack of power. In the latter, society is seen as a status hierarchy or number of different collectivities, bound together by sets of mutual rights and obligations that are rooted in some broader moral order.[7] Thus social exclusion is 'the process of becoming detached from the organisations and communities of which the society is composed and from the rights and obligations that they embody'.[8]

These differences meant that researchers struggled to decide how social exclusion might be distinguished from older concepts of poverty and deprivation, and whether it was in the end a useful idea. Jos Berghman, for example, has argued that the importance of social exclusion lies in the fact that it is a more comprehensive term, and refers to a dynamic process. Whereas poverty has to do with a lack of resources, social exclusion is more comprehensive, and is about 'much more than money'. Berghman tended to restrict the use of 'poverty' to the lack of a disposable income, while social exclusion referred to the breakdown of the main social systems that should guarantee citizenship rights. He concluded that poverty might best be seen as part of, or a specific form of, social exclusion. Another way of distinguishing the two might be to view social exclusion as a process, and poverty as the outcome.[9] Other researchers remained cautious, arguing that an emphasis on the 'multidimensional' nature of poverty could have the effect of obscuring the dynamic processes involved. They argued that researchers should continue to draw on the insights offered by traditional research into poverty, into the relationship between resources and deprivation, and the dynamics that lay behind patterns of disadvantage.[10] More recent work has indicated that the different ways in which social exclusion have been defined have continued to pose problems for researchers trying to operationalise the concept.[11]

As in the United States, data from longitudinal studies were recognised as playing a key role. It was argued that making time more explicit in the way that poverty and social exclusion were conceptualised, defined, and measured helped to clarify the differences between them. Robert Walker, for example, found from longitudinal data for the Netherlands and Germany that although most 'spells' of poverty were short, much poverty was accounted for by a small number of people who were in the midst of very long 'spells' of poverty. He suggested that there was 'not one kind of poverty but many', with different implications for social exclusion. Qualitative research, too, seemed to indicate that the different patterning of poverty over time, and the varying trajectories that people followed, meant poverty had different social meanings and there were different risks of social exclusion. What was most useful about the availability of better longitudinal data, suggested Walker, was that it would help to illuminate causes. Previous debates had adopted a view that was static, that individuals were poor because of their attitudes and behaviour, or because of structural factors such as low-paid jobs and processes in the labour market. But the triggers that precipitated poverty might embrace both personal and structural factors. This could help in understanding poverty and social exclusion, and the relationship between them. Walker speculated that it was probable that poverty was neither a sufficient nor a necessary factor in social exclusion, although certain kinds of poverty might contribute to a risk of exclusion. In these cases, social exclusion could be a 'destination on a journey through poverty'.[12]

Debates in France and other countries have led Hilary Silver to distinguish between three different paradigms of social exclusion, each based on a different conception of integration and citizenship. Like Thomas Kuhn, she uses the word 'paradigm' to refer to conceptual frameworks within which scientific theories are developed. She claims that, first, a 'solidarity' paradigm is evident in France, where exclusion is the 'breakdown of a social bond between the individual and society that is cultural and moral, rather than economically interested'. Secondly, a paradigm of 'specialisation' can be found, where exclusion is really a reflection of social discrimination. Thirdly, there is a 'monopoly' paradigm, that describes a process whereby powerful groups in society restrict the access of outsiders to resources through a process of 'social closure'. Silver claims that the 'monopoly' paradigm, in particular, draws on earlier discourses on the underclass and citizenship.[13] What these paradigms really mean in practice, and whether they can usefully be distinguished at all, remains uncertain. What is clear is that Silver is right in pointing out that, like 'underclass', the phrase 'social exclusion' has become a keyword, a term with its own history that can serve a variety of political purposes.[14]

A different way of approaching the same issue is to ask why 'poverty discourses' seem to vary according to the country in which they have evolved. As we saw in the previous chapter, Kirk Mann had begun to do this in asking why there was no underclass discourse in Australia. Hilary Silver argues that 'poverty discourses' tend to be nationally specific. For example, the 'exclusion' rhetoric is dominant in France partly because the connotations it evokes come out of the dominant French Republican ideology of *solidarisme*. The term 'underclass', on the other hand, has more to do with liberal and conservative ideologies of citizenship, rejected by French Republicans, which have played a key role in many aspects of British and American social policies. Whereas in Britain and the United States the 'underclass' discourse has been the most common, in France it is the 'exclusion' discourse that tends to dominate. Silver suggests that one reason for this may be because the 'new poverty' really is different in France compared to Britain and the United States, although politics may also have a role to play. A second possibility is that in the 1980s the Socialists were in power in France, while it was the Republicans and Conservatives that governed in the United States and Britain. Whatever the reason for these differences, Silver concludes that these variations in labelling the poor are best examined:

> in the context of conflicting paradigms of national identity, political ideology and social science ... Depending upon the paradigm in which they are embedded, poverty discourses attribute responsibility for the problem and shape the policy agenda.[15]

Silver suggests that even when they are imported from other countries, 'poverty discourses' change their meaning to fit dominant national paradigms. This is relevant and helpful in understanding how the concept of social exclusion has been imported into Britain, and how its meaning has been blended with other influences. In the 1990s, some commentators thought that social divisions seemed to be widening and hardening. In his influential book *The State We're In* (1995), the journalist Will Hutton had written of a new '30/30/40' society, where around 30% of the population were disadvantaged, including the unemployed and those excluded from the labour market; 30% were marginalised and insecure, since their jobs did not provide any tenure; and 40% were privileged, with secure employment. Hutton found a world of 'us' and 'them' where a privileged class was:

> favoured with education, jobs, housing and pensions. At the other end of the scale more and more people discover they are the new working poor, or live off the state in semi-poverty. Their paths out of this situation are closing down as the world in which they are trapped becomes meaner, harder and more corrupting.[16]

In between these two groups were growing numbers of people who were more insecure, worried about losing their jobs, and about maintaining a decent standard of living. Hutton concluded there was a 'general sense of fear and beleaguerment'.[17]

Groups such as the Child Poverty Action Group (CPAG) were equally aware of these widening inequalities, and, as we saw in the previous chapter, by the mid-1990s had begun to move away from the concept of the underclass towards that of social exclusion. This reflected the influence of the earlier European debates, and also the increasing emphasis placed on citizenship. In part, too, social exclusion offered a means of describing poverty that had fewer pejorative connotations. For instance, the CPAG published *Britain Divided: The Growth of Social Exclusion in the 1980s and 1990s* (1997). Individuals as well as pressure groups began to rethink the way that they had conventionally viewed poverty. Peter Townsend, for example, arguably the dominant figure in this field, now admitted that he had earlier been wrong in thinking that the term 'social exclusion' was a diversion from more important issues. He conceded that social exclusion was crucial, because of the way it focused attention on the denial of rights, and on the ways in which needs were created and controlled by external forces.[18] Nevertheless he remained reluctant to engage with questions of behaviour.

Intellectuals close to New Labour helped to popularise the concept of social exclusion. In his influential book on the 'Third Way', Anthony Giddens has argued that social exclusion can occur both at the bottom of society and at the top – in the former, when people are cut off from the opportunities that society has to offer, and in the latter, when the more affluent groups withdraw from public institutions. Moreover Giddens suggests that social exclusion at the bottom may be both economic and cultural. In declining communities, housing falls into disrepair, and a lack of job opportunities produces educational disincentives, leading to social instability and disorganisation. Giddens argues that, like social exclusion at the top, that at the bottom is self-reproducing, though it is not clear what he means by this. His solutions include any strategies that break the poverty 'cycle', particularly education and training, but especially involvement in the labour force. Conventional poverty programmes should be replaced with community-focused approaches that emphasise support networks, self help, and a culture of 'social capital'.[19] In all of this, Giddens can be seen to have been heavily influenced by the interpretation of William Julius Wilson of 'concentration effects' in American cities.

Giddens has been influenced both by longitudinal studies, and also by the revival of interest in questions of agency among social policy specialists, that has stressed the ability of individuals to influence their own circumstances. Giddens has noted, for example, that longitudinal research has shown how poverty is not a permanent condition, even though more people experience it than was previously thought. But equally, Giddens has argued that to be excluded is not the same as to be powerless to influence one's own circumstances, writing 'the social and economic factors that can lead to exclusion are always filtered through the way individuals react to the problems that confront them'.[20] Solutions should therefore have an 'enabling' approach, building on the action strategies of the poor, with a stress on initiative and responsibility. Evidence from Germany, on coping strategies, has concluded that 'poverty has many faces'. Giddens concedes that specific help is needed for the long-term poor. It is neither necessary, nor desirable, however that it should come only from government – more innovative policies will draw on a range of agencies.[21] Social exclusion directs attention to the social mechanisms that produce or sustain deprivation, and research might usefully focus on how people get out of poverty.

How did New Labour come to adopt social exclusion as the label for its attempts to tackle poverty? In some respects, the ideas embodied in the concept simply represented an updating of Peter Townsend's earlier formulation of poverty as relative deprivation. In his book *Poverty in the United Kingdom* (1979), Townsend had made a crucial contribution to the poverty debate in writing that:

> Individuals, families and groups in the population can be said to be in poverty when they lack the resources to obtain the types of diet, participate in the activities and have the living conditions and amenities which are customary, or are at least widely encouraged or approved, in the societies to which they belong. Their resources are so seriously below those commanded by the average individual or family that they are, in effect, excluded from ordinary living patterns, customs and activities.[22]

Although Townsend focused on poverty, he stressed how the lack of resources that characterised the poor meant they were unable to participate in activities that other people would regard as normal. The task for academics was to construct social surveys that captured this sense of relative deprivation. This approach was subsequently applied in Britain in the early 1980s, in the 'Breadline Britain' survey, which similarly defined poverty in terms of 'an enforced lack of *socially perceived* necessities'.[23]

Townsend's theory of 'relative deprivation' in some respects anticipated the idea of social exclusion. But arguably more important was the way that New Labour was much more prepared to consider the influence of behaviour on poverty and deprivation than the Labour Party had been previously. As we have seen in earlier chapters, it has been argued that in America the publication of the Moynihan Report (1965) led to a void in which Liberals were unwilling to discuss issues of race and poverty. In Britain too, the postwar period (what is often called the Titmuss era) had been marked by a refusal to consider that poverty could have anything other than structural causes. But this was increasingly questioned by some thinkers and policy makers on the Left. One of the most important was the Labour MP Frank Field, whom we have previously encountered as a writer on the underclass in the 1980s. In his important book *Making Welfare Work* (1995), Field argued that welfare had to be based on a realistic view of human nature, since self-interest, not altruism, was the main driving force of mankind. Influenced in part by his Christian beliefs, Field wrote that 'welfare influences behaviour by the simple device of bestowing rewards (benefits) and allotting punishments (loss of benefits) ... the nature of our character depends in part on the values which welfare fosters'.[24] Thus Field advocated a system of 'stakeholder welfare', where welfare aimed to maximise self-improvement, reflected the significance of self-interest, and rewarded good behaviour.

Field was subsequently criticised for using the terms 'behaviour' and 'character' interchangeably, and for evoking the judgementalism of the nineteenth-century Charity Organisation Society. It was suggested that this had links with the debates on the social residuum in the 1880s, and problem families in the 1950s.[25] What is clear is that Field, and New Labour more generally, had been heavily influenced by American writers such as Charles Murray and Lawrence Mead. Alan Deacon claims more generally that the Blair administration has looked to America for ideas for welfare reform, and that the language in which these policies are presented and justified has drawn heavily on that of American politicians and commentators. New Labour's debate on welfare marked its response to the challenge of Murray and Mead to pay more attention to issues of personal responsibility and moral obligation. Field was influenced by his Christian beliefs in coming to this conclusion, and other key members of the Blair government followed a type of Christian Socialism that made it possible to address inequalities while at the same time acknowledging the role of behaviour. It has been suggested, therefore, that the approach of the Blair government to welfare reform has been rooted in 'Anglicised communitarianism'. A welfare system was envisaged which was active rather than passive; which combined opportunity and responsibility; and which was based around paid work. Deacon concludes that the influence of American thinking has been crucial to the shift from 'the problem of inequality to the problem of dependency', and in increasing the attention New Labour has paid to issues of values and social morality.[26]

The important differences between Britain and America notwithstanding, with regard to welfare reform New Labour has been more influenced by the experience of the United States than by that of France. As David Marquand has noted, 'the Blair government looks across the Atlantic for inspiration, not across the channel'.[27] In particular, Blair and other intellectuals on the Left have been influenced by the American emphasis on communitarianism. Its leading advocate, Amitai Etzioni, had written for example that 'we are a social movement aiming at shoring up the moral, social, and political environment. Part change of heart, part renewal of social bonds, part reform of public life'.[28] Thus he had drawn attention to the roles of the family; schools; the 'social webs' that bind individuals together; and the overarching values that a national society embodies. Anthony Giddens, too, has argued that civic decline is real and visible, and is seen in 'the weakening sense of solidarity in some local communities and urban neighbourhoods, high levels of crime, and the break-up of marriages and families'.[29] Similarly, civic involvement is least developed in areas and neighbourhoods marginalised by the sweep of economic and social change. One of the lessons of the 1960s social engineering experiments, contends Giddens, has been that external forces can best be mobilised to support local initiative.

These different influences – of the new emphasis on behaviour, of debates about American welfare reform, and of communitarianism – can be seen in a speech given by Tony Blair in June 1997, at the Aylesbury estate in the London borough of Southwark. This preceded the speech in December 1997, at the Stockwell Park School in Lambeth, that marked the launch of the Social Exclusion Unit. The Prime Minister stated that the Government would deal with those living in poverty – what he called the 'forgotten people'. But he stressed it was not just a question of poverty, but one of fatalism, and about 'how to recreate the bonds of civic society and community in a way compatible with the far more individualistic nature of modern, economic, social and cultural life'.[30] Blair continued:

> there is a case not just in moral terms but in enlightened self interest to act, to tackle what we all know exists – an underclass of people cut off from society's mainstream, without any sense of shared purpose.[31]

What was needed was a modern civic society based on an ethic of mutual responsibility and duty. Although problems were caused by changes in the nature of work, and long-term unemployment, there was also the danger that people were becoming detached from society, and from citizenship in its widest sense. Welfare had to be reshaped to reward hard work. Solutions were long-term; would require greater co-ordination across government departments than previously; and would be based on policies that had been shown to work.[32]

Blair's use of the term 'underclass' was interesting, and it is partly a recognition of these diverse influences that has led other observers to contest the meaning of social exclusion in Britain. Ruth Levitas, for example, has argued that social exclusion has become integrated into a new 'hegemonic discourse', where it is contrasted with integration into the labour market, and actually obscures inequalities. She claims the discourse treats social divisions endemic to capitalism as resulting from an abnormal breakdown in the social cohesion which should be maintained by the division of labour. Although linked to Townsend's theory of relative deprivation, social exclusion 'actually obscures the questions of material inequality it was originally intended to illuminate'.[33] Levitas argues that the concept of social exclusion operates to devalue unpaid work, and to obscure the inequalities between paid workers, as well as to disguise the fundamental social division between the property-owning class and the rest of society. Like Hilary Silver, Levitas has argued that social exclusion is embedded in three different discourses – a redistributionist discourse that is primarily concerned with poverty; a moral 'underclass' discourse that focuses on the moral and behavioural delinquency of the excluded; and a social integrationist discourse whose focus is on paid work. And she agrees with Silver that one reason why social exclusion has been so powerful a concept has been because it can have different meanings and move between these discourses. She writes that like the word 'underclass', the phrase 'social exclusion' can, almost unnoticed, 'mobilise a redistributive argument behind a cultural or integrationist one – or represent cultural or integrationist arguments as redistributive'.[34] The claim of Levitas is that New Labour has moved away from a concern with poverty towards an inconsistent combination of the moral 'underclass' approach with an emphasis on social integration whose focus is on paid work.

It is not surprising that New Labour has attracted the interest of academics interested in the way that words are used. In *New Labour, New Language?*, Norman Fairclough offers a more intensive study of New Labour speeches and policy documents. He makes the point that whereas Labour uses the word 'poverty' in an international context, it tends to use social exclusion for domestic policy. As in other areas of policy, claims Fairclough, New Labour tends to favour lists of achievements, rather than explanations of the relationship between causes and outcomes, and the relationships between different problems and agencies.[35] For

New Labour, social exclusion is a condition people are in, not something that is done to them. Words such as 'exclusion' are used more than verbs such as 'exclude', and the focus is on outcome rather than process. Like Levitas, Fairclough believes there is evidence that the behavioural and moral delinquency suggested by the term 'underclass' has been carried over into the construction of social exclusion. New Labour did not settle immediately on social exclusion – for a time it used both social exclusion and the 'underclass'. Fairclough agrees with Levitas that the New Labour discourse of social exclusion is based in part on a 'social integrationist' discourse that emphasises the importance of paid work. Thus when opening the CASE at LSE in November 1997, Harriet Harman, then Minister of Social Security, argued that:

> work helps to fulfil our aspirations – it is the key to independence, self-respect and opportunities for advancement ... work brings a sense of order that is missing from the lives of many unemployed young men.[36]

And Fairclough supports Levitas in arguing that social exclusion combines this with a moral underclass discourse, where exclusion is due to deficiencies in the culture of the excluded. It is the perceived cultural deficiencies of socially excluded people that provide the justification for government interventions to change cultures. In February 1999, for example, Alistair Darling, then Minister of Social Security, announced an internal audit of Government action to tackle poverty. Darling wrote that 'we know too well the effect that years of unemployment or illness have on individuals. It demoralises. People come to expect nothing different. And, in turn, their children expect no better for themselves'.[37] In fact, suggests Fairclough, there is evidence that the socially excluded develop their own (effective but at times illegal) social capital and social networks to survive. These are a rational response to the situation that people find themselves in. Fairclough concludes that New Labour is committed to 'tackling' social exclusion because of a combination of compassion and self-interest. Alleviation of social exclusion has replaced the longer-term Labour goal of equality, which is based on the belief that capitalist societies create inequalities and conflicting interests. He claims that social exclusion focuses on those who are excluded from society, shifts attention away from inequalities and conflicts of interests, and assumes there is nothing wrong with contemporary society as long as it is made more inclusive through government policy.[38]

The analyses of Levitas and Fairclough have been concerned with discourses and language, but on an empirical level, researchers have found it difficult to find evidence of social exclusion on the ground. Tania Burchardt, Julian Le Grand, and David Piachaud suggested that 'an individual is socially excluded if (a) he or she is geographically resident in a society and (b) he or she does not participate in the normal activities of citizens in that society'.[39] They tried to operationalise a definition of social exclusion based around five types of activity: consumption, savings, production, political engagement, and social interaction. This was because they thought there were five dimensions for 'normal activities' – to have a reasonable standard of living; to possess a degree of security; to be engaged in an activity which is valued by others; to have some decision-making power; and to be able to draw support from immediate family, friends and a wider community. Using the British Household Panel Survey, and interviews conducted in the years 1991–95, they found that for individuals there were strong associations between exclusion on one dimension and exclusion on another, and between exclusion in one year and exclusion in subsequent years. However, very few people were excluded on all dimensions in any one year, and most were not excluded on any dimension. Burchardt, Le Grand, and Piachaud concluded that using these indicators there was no clear-cut category of socially excluded people. It seemed better to treat different dimensions of exclusion separately than to think of the socially excluded as being one homogeneous group.[40] Thus, as with the underclass debate in the 1980s, some attempts to find empirical evidence for social exclusion have been unsuccessful.

Summaries of research have explored the meaning of social exclusion, acknowledging that because it is a broad term, views on its causes can differ markedly. Some, as in the underclass debate, put individual behaviour and morals at the centre; others highlight the role of institutions and systems; and others emphasise discrimination and lack of rights. One of the important points is that is necessary to look not just at material resources but at other indicators of deprivation or of an inability to participate in society. This work has concluded, for example, from the evidence of income dynamics that 'there is little evidence in the UK for a permanently excluded "underclass", doomed from childhood'.[41] Hence it has been argued that social exclusion can change the way people think about poverty and deprivation, and that traditional concerns with poverty need not be left behind.

Whether this is actually true in practice can be explored in relation to government initiatives on child health. How far do these illustrate links between social exclusion, the policies endorsed by New Labour, and earlier underclass concepts? One of the key aims of New Labour is to tackle child poverty. In the Beveridge Lecture, given at Toynbee Hall, London, in March 1999, Tony Blair made a historic commitment to end child poverty within 20 years. Blair said he would 'set out our historic aim that ours is the first generation to end child poverty forever, and it will take a generation. It is a 20-year mission, but I believe it can be done'.[42] He presented a blueprint for a new modern popular welfare state that incorporated some of the thinking that Frank Field had put forward in *Making Welfare Work*. The welfare state would tackle child poverty, social exclusion, and the decay of communities. But people also had a responsibility to take the opportunities that were offered. The welfare state should be an enabler, not a provider. Most help should go to those in most need, but fraud and abuse should also be rooted out. Public-private partnerships and voluntary organisations would have an increasingly important role in delivering welfare. And welfare was not just about benefits, but about services and community support.[43]

Preliminary analysis has indicated that the aim of ending child poverty within 20 years is unlikely to be achieved with current policies.[44] More relevant to the discussion here is that New Labour has been concerned to strike a balance between responsibility and opportunity. Its policy on child poverty provides a good example of the 'third way' on welfare. Thus the ending of child poverty is often presented less as an objective in itself, and more as a means of reducing inequalities in opportunity. The emphasis that people should take up the opportunities that are offered has led New Labour to revisit earlier debates, including the cycle of deprivation research of the 1970s. In the Beveridge Lecture, Blair continued:

> we need to break the cycle of disadvantage so that children born into poverty are not condemned to social exclusion and deprivation. That is why it is so important that we invest in our children.[45]

Since then, the phrases 'cycle of deprivation' and 'cycle of disadvantage' have become a feature of the language of New Labour. As the *Opportunity for All* White Paper stated in 1999:

> The key to tackling disadvantage in the future is the eradication of child poverty. Children who grow up in disadvantaged families generally do less well at school, and are more likely to suffer unemployment, low pay and poor health in adulthood. This poverty of opportunity is then more likely to be experienced by the next generation of children … We need to break the cycle of deprivation, to stop it being transmitted through generations.[46]

The third annual report on poverty (2001) argued that 'for far too many children, disadvantage in early life leads to poor outcomes in adulthood that perpetuate the transmission of poverty across the generations'.[47]

The use of the phrases 'cycle of disadvantage' and 'cycle of deprivation', and the emphasis on the transmission of poverty between generations is one of the most striking aspects of New Labour policy in the field of child health. It immediately evokes echoes of the cycle of deprivation hypothesis advanced by Sir Keith Joseph in 1972, and explored in the transmitted deprivation research programme of the 1970s and 1980s. This hint is confirmed by the existence of a more explicit attempt to revisit the earlier research programme, and to link academics and policy-makers. In November 1997, a conference entitled 'New Cycles of Disadvantage' was organised by CASE on behalf of the ESRC. The aim was to broaden Treasury links with sociologists and social policy specialists. The Treasury was interested in cycles of disadvantage for three reasons. First, its core aim was to raise the sustainable growth rate and increase opportunities for everyone to share in the benefits of growth. Second, Treasury policy cut across different government departments, and cycles of disadvantage were seen to result from multiple problems that required multiple solutions. Third, substantial amounts of public expenditure were devoted to mitigating the effects of cycles of disadvantage.[48]

The aim was to revisit the idea of cycles of deprivation in light of new evidence, and the subsequent conference indicated some new elements when compared to the earlier SSRC/DHSS research programme. One was the emphasis placed on the evidence for genetic influences on individual differences in anti-social and other behaviour. Another was the availability of new longitudinal studies, which meant more importance was attached than previously to income mobility and poverty dynamics, with evidence indicating that the poor do not generally remain persistently poor. In the earlier programme, Sir Keith Joseph had been an important personal influence, and disputes between civil servants and social scientists one of the most interesting features. And there was much reference to the role of place in 'poorer neighbourhoods', to drugs and crime, and to single parenthood. Despite these differences, the November 1997 conference illustrated interesting continuities with the earlier cycle of deprivation debates. The conference was introduced by Professor Michael Rutter, then Professor of Child Psychiatry and Honorary Director of the Medical Research Council Child Psychiatry Unit, who had been closely involved with the original SSRC/DHSS research programme. Academics seemed no closer to deciding if a cycle of deprivation actually existed, or to detecting 'transmission' mechanisms and risk. Similar continuities with the 'cycle of deprivation' research are evident in some of the reports produced by CASE at the LSE. John Hobcraft has looked at what he calls the 'intergenerational and life-course transmission' of social exclusion, examining the influences of childhood poverty, family disruption, and contact with the police. The source of Hobcraft's data was the same longitudinal survey that Essen and Wedge had used twenty years earlier, the National Child Development Study.[49]

Howard Glennerster has made the point that whereas in the 1960s it was sociologists and anthropologists that influenced the culture of poverty debate, today it is economists, with their manipulation of large-scale panel datasets, that dominate the discussions of poverty and lifetime inequality.[50] As we have seen in both the American and European contexts, one of the most important sources of data on the dynamics of poverty has been the availability of longitudinal data sets. More attempts have been made, in recent research, to examine the dynamics of poverty – how families move in and out of poverty, and how long they stay there. In the early 1970s, preliminary analysis of the PSID data seemed to show that the bulk of those in poverty were poor for only a few years. The poor were a heterogeneous group, including a small minority who were persistently poor. This was important, because claims about dependency and a separate lifestyle among the poor rested on assumptions about the long-term nature of poverty. More recently, other researchers have used the PSID data to look at the length of 'spells' spent in poverty. Mary Jo Bane and David Ellwood, for example, used the PSID data for the years 1970–82 to look more closely at what they called 'spell durations and exit probabilities' – 45% of spells ended within a year, and 70% of the spells were over within three years. Although many people had very short spells of poverty, the few with very long spells accounted for the bulk of all poverty, and represented the majority of the poor at any given time. In general, they agreed that those living in poverty were a very heterogeneous group.[51]

The influential Bane and Ellwood article was published in 1986, and gradually British commentators began to use panel data to look more closely at income dynamics among the low-income population. The British Household Panel Survey seemed to indicate that there was much movement in and out of poverty. Steven Webb argued from a preliminary analysis of the data that:

> there is not a single homogeneous group who are 'the poor' and whose lot is permanently to remain poor. Rather, fluctuations in personal circumstances lead to considerable variations in living standards even from one year to the next.[52]

Yet others have used the same data to argue that most income changes from one year to the next are not very great. Sarah Jarvis and Stephen Jenkins compared income distribution to a tall apartment building with the numbers of residents on different floors corresponding to the concentration of people at different real income levels. Jarvis and Jenkins found that there was much mobility in household net income from one year to the next. But most income changes from one year to the next were not very large, and there were substantial 'permanent' income differentials. Jarvis and Jenkins remarked wryly that few of those living in the basement changed places with those in the penthouse.[53] Simon Burgess and Carol Propper have agreed that any snapshot picture hides the degree of mobility that does exist, and in general their analysis has confirmed that of Jarvis and Jenkins. People move out of poverty, but generally to an income level that is not much higher. Movements in and out of poverty are not random, and are associated with employment and family status. Burgess and Propper concluded that the key factors in determining household income were labour market factors such as labour supply, earnings generation, and household formation, and also what they referred to as 'dissolution processes' such as marriage, divorce, and fertility.[54]

This new research using panel datasets dominated a further workshop at the Treasury in November 1998, which considered the evidence on persistent poverty and lifetime inequality. It was claimed that looking at the dynamics of poverty and inequality of opportunity made it possible to pinpoint the processes and events that led people to be at greater risk of low income and poorer life chances. This data could provide evidence to underpin policy. What was evident in the discussion was the importance attached to childhood poverty, and to policies for early intervention to prevent 'downward cycles of deprivation and create upward cycles'.[55] Equally, this data had an important influence on Treasury proposals to modernise the tax and benefit system, published in March 1999. It was again suggested that by understanding the factors that influenced people's trajectories through life, it would become possible to develop strategies to reduce events that meant people were at greater risk of economic disadvantage. Government could work to promote factors that helped people climb a 'ladder of opportunity'.[56] In particular, the evidence was interpreted as showing that the life chances of people are determined by who their parents are, rather than by their own talents and efforts. The Treasury argued that:

> Childhood disadvantage frequently leads to low educational attainment, low educational attainment leads to low pay and low employment, which in turns leads to low income and denial of opportunity for the next generation. There are strong links between people's own life chances and those of their parents and possibly even grand-parents.[57]

Thus success in education was the most important 'transmission mechanism' for cycles of disadvantage. It was argued that children who grew up in disadvantaged families were more likely as adults to be teenage mothers; live in social housing; be dependent on benefit; and have a low income.[58]

The Treasury document indicated that evidence from the Cross-Departmental Review of Young Children in the Comprehensive Spending Review had convinced the government that resources should be devoted to a new programme to pioneer a co-ordinated approach to services for families with children under four. It was claimed that there were 'risk factors' that could affect educational performance, which was a good indicator of later success in the labour market and more widely. Multiple risk factors greatly increased the chance of later social exclusion. Equally, there were 'protective factors' that could counter risk, including strong early attachments to adults and parental interest. These could explain how children from apparently different backgrounds could differ in their achievements. The Treasury argued that effective interventions involved parents as well as children; were non-stigmatising (for example they avoiding labelling problem families); targeted a number of factors; lasted long enough to make a real difference; were based on the involvement of parents and local communities; and were sensitive to the needs of parents and children.[59]

The Treasury claimed that services for children cost around £10 billion a year, but were driven by vertically separated agencies, leading to fragmentation and a lack of co-ordination. The result has been that the government has used the Sure Start initiative to target these patterns of childhood disadvantage. The Sure Start initiative further illustrates the influence of the experience of the United States, since it is modelled on the earlier American Head Start programme. Sure Start has aimed to promote the physical, intellectual, and emotional development of children to make sure they are ready to thrive when they go to school. Sure Start areas are located in some of the most disadvantaged areas of the country. It works with parents and parents-to-be to provide better access to family support; advice on children's development; health services; and early learning. Its objectives include: to improve social and emotional development; improve health; improve children's ability to learn; and strengthen families and communities. By the end of 2001, there were more than 260 local programmes planned or in operation.

Given the background to this initiative, including the earlier ESRC and Treasury seminars, it is not surprising that the rhetoric of Sure Start has contained echoes of the 1972 cycle speech and transmitted deprivation research programme. In April 2000, a report in the *Guardian* argued that Sure Start provided a means of tackling the 'cycle of deprivation'.[60] Similarly, an editorial in the *British Medical Journal* in July 2001 argued that the result of social exclusion could be that children living in poverty 'may enter a cycle of poor educational achievement, unmanageable behaviour, drug misuse, unemployment, teenage pregnancy, homelessness, crime, and suicide'.[61] But differences in this vocabulary also reflect the uncertainty of New Labour about the relative importance to be attached to behavioural and structural causes of deprivation. In the introductory booklet to the fifth wave of Sure Start programmes, it is the phrase 'cycle of disadvantage' that is most apparent. The declared aim of Sure Start is:

> To work with parents-to-be, parents and children to promote the physical, intellectual and social development of babies and young children – particularly those who are disadvantaged – so that they can flourish at home and when they get to school, and thereby break the cycle of disadvantage for the current generation of young children.[62]

It is claimed that Sure Start is founded on evidence that sustained support for children can help them succeed at school and help reduce crime, unemployment, teenage pregnancy, and other economic and social problems.[63] The *Breaking the Cycle* Report (2004) by the Social Exclusion Unit, for example, refers to an 'intergenerational cycle of deprivation', along with the 'transmission' and 'inheritance' of disadvantage.[64]

Alan Deacon suggests from these and other sources that New Labour's understanding of the cycle of disadvantage has drawn on five conflicting interpretations of continuities in disadvantage. First, the cultural explanation of the culture of poverty; second, the rational explanation associated with Charles Murray; third, a permissive explanation linked to the work of Lawrence Mead; fourth, the adaptive explanation adopted by William Julius Wilson among others; and fifth, the structural explanation that denies the role of behavioural factors and is embodied in William Ryan's book *Blaming the Victim*. Deacon has compared New Labour's approach to child poverty with the earlier research into transmitted deprivation in the 1970s. He concludes that New Labour's interpretation of the cycle of disadvantage does recognise the significance of structural factors, and in general its rhetoric is closer to the adaptive explanation. However, its emphasis that people should take full advantage of the opportunities that are created also reflects elements of the rational, permissive, and cultural explanations. Thus in Deacon's words, New Labour seeks both to 'level the playing field' and to 'activate the players'.[65]

In some respects, this shift in the policy agenda has been paralleled by a move in the stance adopted by academic commentators. David Piachaud, for example, has acknowledged that the government has tackled child poverty in three main ways, by promoting paid employment through the New Deal and other measures; by redistributing money to children with the working families tax credit; and by tackling long-term causes of poverty, such as teenage births and exclusion from school. Yet Piachaud has also argued that the quality of children's lives, and their opportunities in later life, depend on much more than their material circumstances. Tackling poverty is not enough, and there needs to be a broader radical vision of public policy for childhood. For instance, the nutrition of children is poor because many housing estates have only corner shops with no fresh food and high prices; families are bombarded with the advertising of junk foods; and many parents know very little about nutrition, having learned little from their parents. Thus the influences on children's lives and opportunities are complex – improving education requires not only good schools and teachers, but parental involvement and encouragement. Government, Piachaud argues, should focus on achieving childhoods that are 'happy, healthy and fulfilled and that nurture young people who are civilised and educated'.[66]

Other commentators appear increasingly interested in debates around questions of behaviour and motivation. Julian Le Grand, for instance, has argued that assumptions governing human motivation – the desires or preferences that incite action – and agency – the capacity to undertake that action – are key to the design and implementation of public policy. Policy-makers fashion policies on the assumption that both those who implement the policies and those who benefit from them will behave in certain ways. Le Grand uses the metaphors of knights, knaves, pawns, and queens to characterise changing attitudes to questions of motivation and behaviour. He has argued, for example, that in the era of the classic welfare state (1945–79), public servants were seen as being motivated mainly by their professional ethic and were concerned with the interests of those they were serving. They worked in the public interest, and were seen as public spirited altruists (or knights). Taxpayers were similarly knightly in their willingness to pay taxes. Individuals in receipt of the benefits of the welfare state, on the other hand, were seen as essentially passive, or pawns, content with a universal but fairly basic standard of service. However after 1979, claims Le Grand, there were serious assaults on assumptions about motivation and behaviour. It was argued that the behaviour of public officials and professionals could be better understood if they were seen to be self-interested. The idea that knightly behaviour characterised those who pay for welfare was also challenged. Finally it was seen as undesirable that the users of services were treated as passive recipients – rather the consumer should be king. The logic was that the most obvious mechanism of service delivery was the market.[67]

Le Grand argues it is not implausible to describe the bundle of assumptions concerning human behaviour that characterised the democratic socialist welfare state as one 'designed to be financed and operated by knights for the benefit of pawns'.[68] Nevertheless he admits that his analysis may well be too simplistic a means of capturing the complexity of the realities of human motivation and agency. There are many kinds of knight and knave, and individuals are not simply pawns or queens. Moreover he makes a distinction between attitudes and the actual delivery of policy, conceding the postwar history of social security is characterised by the successive development of different forms of checks and balances to control the behaviour of people termed the work-shy, scroungers, and loafers. Le Grand notes that there was a constant tension between the assumption that welfare recipients were essentially passive – pawns – and the assumption that they had some capacity for agency – knaves – and responded to the incentives with which they were faced.

Changing approaches to poverty are perhaps best illustrated by the work of Ruth Lister, who in the 1990s was extremely hostile to underclass formulations. She now notes that experiences and understandings of poverty are shaped by both socioeconomic and cultural contexts, and argues that there should be less emphasis on the measurement of poverty, and more attention to its conceptual dimensions. Poverty has to be understood as social relations, since poverty has been constructed by the 'non-poor'. Thus Lister concedes that discourse (including underclass discourse) has been important, in constructing the poor as different or 'other'. Furthermore she devotes more attention to agency, acknowledging that agency was denied by postwar British social policy, and arguing that it is access to resources that mediates the link between agency and structure. Lister suggests that the interplay between agency and structure is at the heart of contemporary efforts to theorise the dynamics of poverty, with researchers conceding that movements in and out of poverty are the result of individual actions, as well as wider economic and social processes along with government policies. Thus agency has to be understood within the context of structural, cultural, and policy constraints. People are actors within their own lives, but within the bounds of constraints. Thus Lister seems more prepared than previously to accept that poverty is a relational and symbolical as well as material phenomenon. She argues that the ways in which people conceptualise poverty affect their understanding and attitudes towards poverty, and hence their determination to do something about it.[69]

Alan Deacon has commented that explorations of agency are now at the heart of debates about welfare reform. As the work of Le Grand and Lister illustrates, agency has been understood in different ways by different commentators. The main question has been how people are able to act independently, and how far their behaviour is constrained by social structures. But Deacon has also noted that the idea of agency raises issues of motivation and capacity. One of the reasons why agency was neglected by social scientists in the postwar period, he suggests, was because it was associated with a punitive individualism associated with the nineteenth-century Poor Law. This was seen to have re-emerged in the debate about problem families in the 1950s, the cycle of deprivation in the 1970s, and the underclass in the 1980s. A concern with agency was thus associated with a moral and judgemental approach to welfare. Thus Deacon suggests that while scholars seek to develop new ways of understanding agency and structure in relation to poverty, debates about welfare continue to be 'preoccupied by the spectre of dependency and the attribution of blame'.[70] This further underlines how a proper understanding of the historical dimensions of the underclass concept in the period 1880–2000, its changing form and function, is essential for contemporary debates.

As we have seen, the concept of social exclusion emerged in France, and was associated with a relational view of poverty that was very different to the traditional British concern with individual and household resources. From the mid-1990s, New Labour adopted the language of social exclusion. In part, this reflected a determination to focus on the structural causes of deprivation, and to use the new evidence on poverty dynamics that resulted from the availability of longitudinal data sets. Nevertheless part of the appeal of social exclusion to New Labour has been that it has made it possible to combine a commitment to tackle poverty with a cultural interpretation that reflects the importance it attaches to behaviour, and to people taking advantage of the opportunities that are offered to them. In this, as in the 'Americanisation' of debates on welfare, New Labour has arguably been much more influenced by experiences on the other side of the Atlantic than across the Channel. In Britain, social exclusion has remained a contested concept, with its opponents arguing that it reflects an undue emphasis on the importance of paid work, illustrates continuities with the earlier underclass debates, and is difficult to test empirically.

These points are brought out well in relation to the particular issue of child health. On the one hand, New Labour has made a commitment to ending child poverty, and shown a recognition of the role of structural factors. As Glennerster has noted, it is economists who now dominate the debate with large-scale data sets. But on the other hand, the emphasis on the cycle of disadvantage in the Sure Start initiative, and the stress given to the transmission of poverty between generations, shows how the Blair government has drawn on aspects of the earlier cycle of deprivation debate. It is for this reason, among others, that it has been suggested that Sir Keith Joseph is the intellectual godfather of New Labour. At the time of writing, there are signs that social exclusion itself is less prominent than previously in the hands of both policy makers and academics. What is clear is that the approach of social scientists to poverty at the start of the 21st century shows the legacy of earlier underclass concepts on on-going debates about agency, structure, and public policy.

Conclusion

This book has been concerned with the invention and re-invention of the concept of the underclass and related ideas in the period 1880–2000. In terms of earlier work, it has been the alleged emergence of the underclass in the 1980s that has been given most attention; and the earlier antecedents are much less recognised. One of the aims of this book has been to ensure that sociologists and policy-makers are more aware of the historical dimension to these debates. Having charted the rise and fall of successive labels, we are now in a position to draw out some general themes that have emerged. First, in relation to changes and continuities in how the underclass has been defined. Second, in terms of which individuals and groups have been doing the defining. Third, with regard to the question of whether there is sufficient similarity between these ideas to sustain the argument that there is a linear process at work. Fourth, in terms of how and why these concepts emerge, including processes of policy transfer, especially between the USA and Britain. Fifth, with regard to the impact of these concepts on practical policy-making.

What is in no doubt is that there have been a series of similar labels, both in terms of earlier antecedents and in the particular period 1880–2000. Ideas of the deserving and undeserving poor were evident in the early modern period, and are arguably timeless. But in the modern period there have been at least eight reconstructions. In the 1880s, social investigators such as Charles Booth became concerned about the emergence of a social residuum in London. In turn, this was replaced by anxieties about the unemployable in the writings of William Beveridge and the Webbs in the early 1900s. While this language was less evident in the social surveys published in the first decade of the twentieth century, the 1920s and early 1930s were characterised by the search for a social problem group. In the early postwar period, this metamorphosed into the problem family notion of the 1950s, which cast a powerful spell over volunteers involved in the Family Service Units, public health doctors, and some social workers.

The fifth reconstruction of the concept was in terms of Oscar Lewis's notion of the culture of poverty in the 1960s. Interestingly, it was not the culture of poverty but the British theory of the 'problem family' that was more influential on Sir Keith Joseph when he came up with the cycle of deprivation in his 1972 speech. But it was again the United States that was the real driving force behind the concept of the underclass in the 1980s. At the same time, the idea of an underclass also became attractive to observers of economic change and social polarisation in Britain. Finally, we have explored the ways in which the theory of social exclusion has attempted to shed its links with these earlier labels, but nevertheless continues to have echoes with the underclass discourse. Continuities are also evident in specific aspects of policy on child health, most obviously in the way that the phrase 'cycle of deprivation' continues to be used in relation to child poverty and the Sure Start initiative for pre-school children.

But while it is comparatively easy to trace this process, though requiring some fascinating historical detective work, it is more difficult to account for its longevity as a recurring phenomenon. It is important to try to distinguish underclass stereotypes from related, but more general, ideas about the deserving and undeserving poor; about unemployment and public attitudes towards scroungers; and about behaviour more generally. As John Macnicol has previously argued, underclass concepts have a number of different strands. One is the way that they have been used to signify and denote the alleged behavioural inadequacies of the poor, whether an inability to form attachments to other individuals and agencies, a failure to plan for the future, or a tendency to engage in crime and other forms of antisocial behaviour. Second, there is the use of the phrase to denote the ways in which wider structural processes, whether technological and economic change, unemployment, racial and social segregation in cities, or the move to a post-industrial economy, have contributed to a situation in which groups with poor access to education and skills risk being left behind. Third is the recurring belief in inter-generational continuities, whether of cultural aspirations and habits, or in terms of poverty and teenage pregnancy. Fourth is the belief that the underclass exists separately from the working class, as a subset or what has been called the lower class. Fifth is the combination of rhetorical symbolism and empirical complexity, where the term 'underclass' has served as a powerful metaphor for social change on the one hand, but where its supporters have also searched – without much success – for empirical proof of its existence.

This historical investigation also illustrates marked differences in these concepts and in the individuals or organisations that have used them. In many cases it has been individuals who have had a prominent role, such as Charles Booth in the 1880s, Oscar Lewis in the 1960s, and Sir Keith Joseph in the 1970s, though it has been more central to the thinking of some than to others. At other times, voluntary organisations and professional groups have been more prominent, such as the Eugenics Society in the 1930s, the Women's Group on Public Welfare in the 1940s, and the Family Service Units of the 1950s. For these individuals and organisations, underclass stereotypes have had important scapegoating and legitimising functions. It is only more recently that government has taken a more active role in sponsoring research, and interestingly the studies sponsored by the DHSS/SSRC Working Party on Transmitted Deprivation in fact found little evidence to support the original cycle of deprivation hypothesis. The involvement of the Social Exclusion Unit and Treasury in more recent debates about social exclusion suggests a move away from individuals and voluntary organisations to more centralised policy research processes, illustrating how arguments about behaviour have become more central to public policy.

What support, then, does this survey offer for the framework proposed by Gans? As we saw in the Introduction, Gans has argued that the 'label formation' process includes a number of interested parties – label makers (both alarmists and counters), label users, legitimaters, the labelled themselves, and finally the romanticisers who revive old labels. It certainly is the case, as has been suggested in the American context, that terms follow a trajectory of emergence, popularity, the acquiring of a pejorative character, and then a falling out of favour. The role of the 'alarmists' does appear critical, since discussions of this type are invariably provoked by alarm about the characteristics of the relevant groups and its members. Similarly the role of the 'legitimators' is also important, although as we have seen, they can include academics, professionals, journalists, and politicians. The role of the popular media shows some important continuities, wider changes in its technology and scale notwithstanding. In the 1880s it was contemporary periodicals and newspapers that were crucial to the propagation of the concept of the social residuum. Similarly a hundred years later, in the 1980s, it was again magazines and newspapers that were crucial to the rise of interest in the underclass, specifically through Ken Auletta's *New Yorker* articles, and the way that the *Sunday Times* sponsored the visits of Charles Murray to Britain. In between, the role of the media was much more muted and the influence of the ideas themselves was limited to a professional rather than a popular arena. The role of the 'romanticisers' seems less evident – once concepts have dropped out of favour and popular usage it is difficult for them to make a comeback.

Arguably the most important aspect of this story is the question of whether there is sufficient linearity between these related concepts to support the argument that there has been a successive reinvention of the underclass concept over the past 120 years. Clearly the economic, political, and social landscape within which these ideas have evolved has changed dramatically. The way that the concept has been defined in different periods has said as much about broader trends in the economy and labour market, the role of women and the emphasis placed on the family, migration and urbanisation, and ideas about behaviour and agency as about the underclass itself. At various times it has been joblessness, household squalor, mental health, long-term poverty, illegitimacy, and crime that have been drawn into underclass stereotypes. Ideas of class formation and biological determinism have played into this, as well as eugenics and a vague and indefinable fear of the 'other'. The social problem group of the 1930s represented a medicalisation of the concept of the residuum, while it was the idea of 'trans-mission', more usually associated with infectious disease, that was central to the cycle of deprivation research of the 1970s. Nevertheless, this study has also sought to bring out some of the striking continuities between these ideas – in terms of the alleged physical and mental characteristics of the poor; the stress placed on inter-generational continuities; and the focus on behavioural inadequacies.

It is arguable that there are chronological gaps in the history, periods when no underclass concept was available or taken up by social investigators. At these times, a more structural interpretation of poverty and unemployment seemed to be dominant. These include the periods from the outbreak of the First World War to the late 1920s; the shorter period of 1937–43; and perhaps the period from 1972 to the early 1980s, when social scientists resisted the imposition of the cycle of deprivation hypothesis. Some of the chronological stepping-stones were more about processes than the delineation of the parameters of a social group, most obviously in the case of the cycle of deprivation, and less obviously with the culture of poverty, and the processes by which one concept replaces another remain unclear. But what is perhaps more noticeable is that these periods are remarkably brief. Above all, the argument that the postwar period was dominated by an emphasis on structural factors, and by economic determinism on the part of social researchers, or by 'knightly' behaviour by professionals in the public sector, seems difficult to sustain in light of the evidence presented here. Rather it appears that at most times in the period 1880–2000, there was a variant of the underclass theory available to researchers, although of course the scale and influence of the ideas have varied greatly. This, in turn, problematises attempts to identify shifts (as has been suggested of the Rowntree survey) between behavioural and structural interpretations.

If we focus on those periods when the ideas appear to undergo a period of transition, contradictions appear to emerge. It has been proposed, for example, that the idea of the social residuum evaporated during the First World War, when the advent of full employment suggested that those previously deemed 'unem-ployable' had never really existed. But conversely, it was during the Second World War that the notion of the problem family emerged to replace the theory of the social problem group. We can date the timing of this with some precision – to the *Our Towns* report, published by the Women's Group on Public Welfare in March 1943. Similarly the problem family undermines the argument that underclass stereotypes are most likely to emerge in periods of economic dislocation, when attention tends to become focused on the behavioural inadequacies of a 'reserve army of labour'. In fact, the problem family notion, although never a major aspect of discussions of social policy, coexisted in 1950s Britain with full employment, economic optimism, and a strong belief in the nuclear family.

The history of the concept of the underclass offers an interesting perspective on debates about policy transfer between the USA and Britain. The current literature on policy transfer stresses the need to consider not just what is transferred, but the motivations of those involved. The history of the underclass concept shows the complexities inherent in policy transfer. It would seem at first glance that Britain has been more influenced by the USA than vice versa. In the early 1900s, eugenists in Britain were well-aware of the American studies of the Jukes and Kallikak families. The 1980s underclass debate is perhaps the clearest example, with the early debates occurring in the USA, and with one mechanism being quite clear – the invitation that the *Sunday Times Magazine* extended to Charles Murray in 1989. But in other cases, there has been considerable resistance to American ideas. In the late 1960s, for example, British social researchers were resistant to the notion of the culture of poverty, the creation of Educational Priority Areas and Community Development Projects notwithstanding, and it is clear that Sir Keith Joseph's hypothesis of the cycle of deprivation owed much more to his earlier interest in the idea of the problem family. The contemporary emphasis on social exclusion originally owed more to ideas from across the Channel than to ideas from across the Atlantic. It would seem, therefore, that while there are similarities in timing between the invention of underclass concepts in Britain and the USA, the form that they took was often very different, reflecting the different histories, ethnic mix, and political cultures of the two countries. Most evident was the much stronger connection with race that was forged with the underclass concept in the USA.

Although assessing 'influence' is notoriously difficult, it is also worth pausing to ask what practical impact these ideas had on actual policy-making. The different concepts were undoubtedly of considerable interest to social commentators, but did they actually influence real policy-making on the ground? In the case of the early concepts, there seems to have been little direct influence. Neither the theory of the social residuum, nor the idea of the unemployable, nor the notion of the social problem group appears to have influenced policy directly. Some of the ideas were relatively short-lived, and in any case attempts at legislation, whether to segregate mental defectives or to introduce voluntary sterilisation, were unsuccessful. Much later, in the case of the cycle of deprivation, the theory was viewed with hostility by social science researchers, and there was a marked disjunction between the ideas as expressed by Sir Keith Joseph and what the researchers actually found. In the 1980s it seems that the underclass concept again had little direct influence on policy – in Britain, for instance, the failure to find empirical support for the existence of an underclass weakened its claims to exert a direct influence on policy.

In other cases there has been a clearer link between the ideas and particular policy initiatives. In the case of the unemployable, there was a broad link with policies on the administration of unemployment relief in the interwar period, which it has been argued was dominated by the 'search for the scrounger'. Very similar debates were evident some fifty years later, in the 1980s, when the renewal of debates about the 'workshy' had a powerful influence on the 1989 Social Security Act. The idea of the problem family was central to the identity of the Family Service Units, and there was a direct link too with local authorities, first through local Health Departments and then in the 1960s through Children's Departments. It has been argued that the culture of poverty theory did influence the American 'War on Poverty', and British equivalents were apparent in the Educational Priority Areas and Community Development Projects. While the underclass notion was arguably less influential, the Charles Murray analysis, on the allegedly detrimental effects of benefits on behaviour, was of considerable interest to policy-makers. Finally the concept of social exclusion has had an important influence on New Labour policy, and indeed the idea of a cycle of deprivation has been reborn in relation to the Sure Start initiative. Thus as social scientists have become more concerned to unravel the relative influences of agency and structure in the causation of poverty and deprivation, governments have shown increasing interest in ways of influencing behaviour, whether in terms of public health policy or 'worklessness'.

What is apparent is that the concept of the underclass has been periodically invented and re-invented in Britain and the USA over the past 120 years. The persistence of the 'underclass' and related ideas suggests that this process of word substitution is likely to survive and perhaps flourish in the future. There are several reasons for the apparent resilience of the concept. First, the unresolved issue of the relative importance of behavioural and structural factors in the causation of poverty and deprivation. It is in part this that gives the concept much of its ambiguity and flexibility. Second, the relatively early stage (at least in Britain) of such potentially important data-sources as panel data on poverty dynamics and income mobility. Third, the continued likely pace of technological change, globalisation, and economic uncertainty which together are likely to continue to raise the spectre, both real and imagined, of groups perceived as 'left behind' or 'cut off' from the mainstream working class. Fourth, the value of the concept as a convenient symbol and metaphor for fears and anxieties whose empirical reality remains unproven. While there has already been some repackaging of terms such as 'hard to reach', the exact forms that these labels will take can only be guessed at. But together these forces should ensure that the future of the underclass concept will be as interesting as its past.

Notes

Notes to Introduction

1 http://www.cabinet-office.gov.uk/seu
2 Ibid.
3 Cabinet Office, Prime Minister's Strategy Unit, *Personal Responsibility and Changing Behaviour: The State of Knowledge and its Implications for Public Policy* (London, 2004).
4 John Hills, 'Does a Focus on "Social Exclusion" Change the Policy Response?', in John Hills, Julian Le Grand and David Piachaud (eds.), *Understanding Social Exclusion* (Oxford, 2002), p. 236.
5 Ruth Levitas, *The Inclusive Society? Social Exclusion and New Labour* (London, 1998), pp. 7–28.
6 Norman Fairclough, *New Labour, New Language?* (London, 2000), p. 52.
7 'Education Drive to Focus on the Poor', *Guardian*, 11 April 2000, p. 4.
8 Cited in John Macnicol, 'Social Politics in the 1960s: The Great Society and Social Democracy', *Open University A317: Focus Points 7 and 8 Essays* (Milton Keynes, 1985), p. 116.
9 David Gordon and Paul Spicker (eds.), *The International Glossary on Poverty* (London, 1999), pp. 34–35, 38, 54, 70, 84, 108, 138.
10 *Oxford English Dictionary* (Oxford, 1989), Vol. XVIII, p. 958.
11 Hugh Macdiarmid, *The Company I've Kept: Essays in Autobiography* (London, 1966), p. 124.
12 *Oxford English Dictionary*, p. 958.
13 Raymond Williams, *Keywords: A Vocabulary of Culture and Society* (New York, 1976, Fontana edn., 1983).
14 John Macnicol, 'In Pursuit of the Underclass', *Journal of Social Policy*, 16 (3) (1987), p. 299.
15 Karl Marx, *Capital: A Critique of Political Economy: The Process of Capitalist Production*, translated from the fourth German edition by Eden and Cedar Paul (London, 1867, 1965 edn.), pp. 698–709.
16 Norman Ginsburg, *Class, Capital and Social Policy* (London, 1979), p. 33. See also Chris Grover and John Stewart, *The Work Connection: The Role of Social Security in British Economic Regulation* (Basingstoke, 2002), pp. 19–21.
17 William Julius Wilson, 'Cycles of Deprivation and the Underclass Debate', *Social Service Review*, 59 (1985), p. 546.

18   Erol R. Ricketts and Isabel V. Sawhill, 'Defining and Measuring the Underclass', *Journal of Policy Analysis and Management*, 7 (1988), pp. 316–25.

19   Robert Aponte, 'Definitions of the Underclass: A Critical Analysis', in Herbert J. Gans (ed.), *Sociology in America* (Westbury Park, California, 1990), pp. 117–18.

20   David J. Smith, 'Defining the Underclass', in David J. Smith (ed.), *Understanding the Underclass* (London, 1992), p. 4.

21   David Willetts, 'Theories and Explanations of the Underclass', in Smith (ed.), *Understanding the Underclass*, p. 49.

22   Macnicol, 'In Pursuit of the Underclass', pp. 299–300.

23   Hartley Dean and Peter Taylor-Gooby, *Dependency Culture: The Explosion of a Myth* (Hemel Hempstead, 1992), pp. 27, 44.

24   Ibid., p. 302.

25   David Matza, 'The Disreputable Poor', in Reinhard Bendix and Seymour Martin Lipset (eds.), *Class, Status and Power: Social Stratification in Comparative Perspective* (London, 1953, second edn., 1966), pp. 289–302.

26   Ibid., p. 302.

27   David Matza, 'Poverty and Disrepute', in Robert K. Merton and Robert A. Nisbet (eds.), *Contemporary Social Problems* (New York, 1961, third edn., 1971), p. 605.

28   Chaim Waxman, *The Stigma of Poverty: A Critique of Poverty Theories and Policies* (New York, 1977, 1983 edn.), pp. 25–26, 71–72, 100, 128.

29   Charles A. Valentine, *Culture and Poverty: Critique and Counter-Proposals* (Chicago, 1968), pp. 45–47.

30   Michael Morris, 'From the Culture of Poverty to the Underclass: An Analysis of a Shift in Public Language', *American Sociologist*, 20, 2 (1989), pp. 123–33.

31   Michael B. Katz, *The Undeserving Poor: From the War on Poverty to the War on Welfare* (New York, 1989), pp. 196, 235.

32   Michael B. Katz, 'The Urban "Underclass" as a Metaphor of Social Transformation', in Michael B. Katz (ed.), *The "Underclass" Debate: Views from History* (Princeton, 1993), p. 22.

33   Michael B. Katz, *Improving Poor People: The Welfare State, the "Underclass", and Urban Schools as History* (Princeton, 1995), pp. 65–71, 97–98.

34   Herbert J. Gans, 'Deconstructing the Underclass: The Term's Dangers as a Planning Concept', *Journal of the American Planning Association*, 56, 3 (1990), pp. 271–77.

35   Ibid.

36   Herbert J. Gans, 'Positive Functions of the Undeserving Poor: Uses of the Underclass in America', *Politics and Society*, 22, 3 (1994), pp. 269, 271–79, 279–81.

37   Herbert J. Gans, *The War Against the Poor: The Underclass and Antipoverty Policy* (New York, 1995), pp. 18–32.

38   Bill Jordan, *Poor Parents: Social Policy and the 'Cycle of Deprivation'* (London, 1974).

39   Peter Golding and Sue Middleton, *Images of Welfare: Press and Public Attitudes to Poverty* (Oxford, 1982), pp. 6–56, 239–44.

40   Geoffrey Pearson, *Hooligan: A History of Respectable Fears* (London, 1983), p. 242.

41   Macnicol, 'In Pursuit of the Underclass', pp. 293–318, p. 296.

42   Ibid., pp. 315–16.

43 John Macnicol, 'From "Problem Family" to "Underclass", 1945–95', in Rodney Lowe and Helen Fawcett (eds.), *Welfare Policy in Britain: The Road From 1945* (London, 1999), pp. 69–93.

44 John Macnicol, 'Perspectives on the Idea of an "Underclass"', in John Edwards and Jean-Paul Révauger (eds.), *Discourse on Inequality in France and Britain* (Aldershot, 1998), pp. 161–74. See also John Macnicol, 'Is There an Underclass? The Lessons from America', in Michael White (ed.), *Unemployment, Public Policy and the Changing Labour Market* (London, 1994), pp. 29–39.

45 Dean and Taylor-Gooby, *Dependency Culture*, pp. 26–50.

46 Pete Alcock, *Understanding Poverty* (London, 1993), pp. 28–29, 190–98.

47 Tony Novak, 'Poverty and the "Underclass"', in Michael Lavalette and Alan Pratt (eds.), *Social Policy: A Conceptual and Theoretical Introduction* (London, 1997), pp. 214–27.

48 John Dixon, Kerry Carrier, and Rhys Dogan, 'On Investigating the "Underclass": Contending Philosophical Perspectives', *Social Policy & Society*, 4, 1 (2005), pp. 21–30.

49 Kirk Mann, *The Making of an English 'Underclass': The Social Divisions of Welfare and Labour* (Buckingham, 1992), pp. 1–2, 106–7, 160, 165.

50 Lydia Morris, *Dangerous Class: the Underclass and Social Citizenship* (London, 1994), pp. 80, 129–31, 157–59, 165, 174–75. See also Lydia Morris, 'Dangerous Classes: Neglected Aspects of the Underclass Debate', in Enzo Mingione (ed.), *Urban Poverty and the Underclass: A Reader* (Oxford, 1996), pp. 160–75.

51 See for example, David P. Dolowitz, 'Policy Transfer: A New Framework of Policy Analysis', in David P. Dolowitz, Rob Hulme, Mike Nellis, and Fiona O'Neill, *Policy Transfer and British Social Policy: Learning from the USA?* (Buckingham, 2000), pp. 9–37.

52 Peter Taylor-Gooby, 'The Empiricist Tradition in Social Administration', *Critical Social Policy*, 2 (1981), pp. 6–21.

53 Ramesh Mishra, 'The Academic Tradition in Social Policy: The Titmuss Years', in Martin Bulmer, Jane Lewis and David Piachaud (eds.), *The Goals of Social Policy* (London, 1989), pp. 64–83.

54 S. M. Miller, 'Introduction: The Legacy of Richard Titmuss', in Brian Abel-Smith and Kay Titmuss (eds.), *The Philosophy of Welfare* (London, 1987), p. 65.

55 Michael Titterton, 'Managing Threats to Welfare: The Search for a New Paradigm of Welfare', *Journal of Social Policy*, 21 (1992), pp. 1–23.

56 Eithne McLaughlin, 'Researching the Behavioural Effects of Welfare Systems', in Jane Millar and Jonathan Bradshaw (eds.), *Social Welfare Systems: Towards a Research Agenda* (Bath, 1996), pp. 57–82.

57 Fiona Williams and Jane Pillinger, 'New Thinking on Social Policy Research into Inequality, Social Exclusion and Poverty', in Miller and Bradshaw, *Social Welfare Systems*, p. 3.

58 Ibid.

59 Fiona Williams, Jennie Popay, and Ann Oakley, 'Changing Paradigms of Welfare', in Fiona Williams, Jennie Popay, and Ann Oakley (eds.), *Welfare Research: A Critical Review* (London, 1999), pp. 2–16.

60 Fiona Williams and Jennie Popay, 'Balancing Polarities: Developing a New Framework for Welfare Research', in Williams, Popay and Oakley, *Welfare Research*, pp. 156–83.

61   Julian Le Grand, 'Knights, Knaves or Pawns? Human Behaviour and Social Policy', *Journal of Social Policy*, 26, 2 (1997), p. 157. See also Julian Le Grand, *Motivation, Agency, and Public Policy: Of Knights & Knaves, Pawns & Queens* (Oxford, 2003).

62   Ibid.

63   Alan Deacon, 'Welfare and Character', in IEA Health and Welfare Unit, *Stakeholder Welfare* (London, 1996), pp. 60–74.

64   Frank Field, *Reflections on Welfare Reform* (London, 1998), p. 53.

65   See for example, Alan Deacon, 'Re-Reading Titmuss: Moralism, Work and Welfare', *University of Leeds Review*, 36 (1993), pp. 89–105; Alan Deacon, 'Richard Titmuss: 20 Years On', *Journal of Social Policy*, 22, 2 (1993), pp. 235–42; Alan Deacon, 'The Dilemmas of Welfare: Titmuss, Murray and Mead', in S. J. D. Green and R. C. Whiting (eds.), *The Boundaries of the State in Modern Britain* (Cambridge, 1996), pp. 191–212.

66   Alan Deacon and Kirk Mann, 'Agency, Modernity and Social Policy', *Journal of Social Policy*, 28, 3 (1999), p. 418.

67   Alan Deacon, 'Learning from the US? The Influence of American Ideas Upon 'New Labour' Thinking on Welfare Reform', *Policy & Politics*, 28 (2000), pp. 5–18.

68   Alan Deacon, *Perspectives on Welfare: Ideas, Ideologies and Policy Debates* (Buckingham, 2002).

69   Alan Deacon, '"Levelling the Playing Field, Activating the Players": New Labour and the "Cycle of Disadvantage"', *Policy & Politics*, 31 (2) (2003), pp. 123–37.

70   Ruth Lister, *Poverty* (Cambridge, 2004), pp. 100–12, 126–27, 145–49. See also Alan Deacon, 'Review Article: Different Interpretations of Agency within Welfare Debates', *Social Policy & Society*, 3, 4 (2004), pp. 447–55.

71   John Welshman, 'The Unknown Titmuss', *Journal of Social Policy*, 33, 2 (2004), pp. 225–47.

72   Williams and Pillinger, 'New Thinking on Social Policy Research into Inequality, Social Exclusion and Poverty', p. 6; Lister, *Poverty*, p. 103.

Notes to Chapter 1: Regulating the Residuum

1   See for example, B. B. Gilbert, *British Social Policy, 1914–1939* (London, 1970).

2   David Ward, *Poverty, Ethnicity, and the American City, 1840–1925: Changing Conceptions of the Slum and the Ghetto* (Cambridge, 1989), pp. 86–93.

3   Gareth Stedman Jones, *Outcast London: A Study in the Relationship Between Classes in Victorian Society* (Oxford, 1971, Peregrine edn., 1984), pp. 283–89.

4   Ibid., pp. 303–8.

5   Ibid., p. 11.

6   Ibid., pp. 303–21.

7   Ibid., p. 336.

8   Ibid. See also James H. Treble, *Urban Poverty in Britain 1830–1914* (London, 1979), pp. 110–113.

9   E. P. Hennock, 'Poverty and Social Theory in England: The Experience of the Eighteen-Eighties', *Social History*, 1 (1976), pp. 90–91.

10 José Harris, 'Between Civic Virtue and Social Darwinism: The Concept of the Residuum', in David Englander and Rosemary O'Day (eds.), *Retrieved Riches: Social Investigation in Britain 1840–1914* (Aldershot, 1995), pp. 76–78.

11 Ibid., p. 68.

12 Ibid., pp. 82–83.

13 Ibid., p. 80.

14 Marc Brodie, *The Politics of the Poor: The East End of London 1885–1914* (Oxford, 2004), pp. 13, 205.

15 Thomas More, *Utopia*, translated with an introduction by Paul Turner (1516, Penguin edn., 1965).

16 Thomas Robert Malthus, *An Essay on the Principle of Population and A Summary View of the Principle of Population* edited with an introduction by Anthony Flew (1798 and 1830, Penguin edn., 1970), p. 98.

17 Ibid., p. 73.

18 Jordan, *Poor Parents*, pp. 17–22. See also Golding and Middleton, *Images of Welfare: Press and Public Attitudes to Poverty*, pp. 15–17.

19 See for example E. P. Thompson and Eileen Yeo (eds.), *The Unknown Mayhew: Selections from the Morning Chronicle 1849–50* (Harmondsworth, 1971, Penguin edn. 1973).

20 Jennifer Davis, 'The London Garrotting Panic of 1862: A Moral Panic and the Creation of a Criminal Class in Mid-Victorian England', in V. A. C. Gatrell, Bruce Lenman, and Geoffrey Parker (eds.), *Crime and the Law* (London, 1980), pp. 190–213.

21 Louis Chevalier, *Laboring Classes and Dangerous Classes in Paris During the First Half of the 19th Century* (Princeton, 1973).

22 Daniel Pick, *Faces of Degeneration: A European Disorder, c.1848–c.1918* (Cambridge, 1989); Jennifer Davis, 'Jennings' Buildings and the Royal Borough: The Construction of the Underclass in Mid-Victorian England', in David Feldman and Gareth Stedman Jones (eds.), *Metropolis London: Histories and Representations Since 1800* (London, 1989), pp. 11–39.

23 Karl Marx and Frederick Engels, 'The Communist Manifesto', reprinted in Karl Marx and Frederick Engels, *Selected Works: In One Volume* (London, 1968), p. 44.

24 Cited in Harris, 'Between Civic Virtue and Social Darwinism', p. 74.

25 Frederick Engels, 'Preface to the Peasant War in Germany', reprinted in Karl Marx and Frederick Engels, *Selected Works: In One Volume* (London, 1968), p. 240.

26 Nikolai Bukharin, *Historical Materialism: A System of Sociology* (New York, 1925, 1965 edn., translation from the 3rd Russian edn.), pp. 282–84, 289–90.

27 Ibid.

28 Harris, 'Between Civic Virtue and Social Darwinism', p. 74.

29 Ibid., p. 75.

30 Alsager Hay Hill, *Our Unemployed: An Attempt to Point out Some of the Best Means of Providing Occupation for Distressed Labourers; With Suggestions on a National System of Labour Registration; and other Matters Affecting the Well-Being of the Poor* (London, 1868), pp. 8–10, 28.

31 Hennock, 'Poverty and Social Theory in England', p. 67.

32 Peter Keating (ed.), *Into Unknown England 1866–1913: Selections from the Social Explorers* (Manchester, 1976), pp. 11–32.

33   William Booth, *In Darkest England: And the Way Out* (London, 1890), pp. 12, 17–23.

34   Alfred Marshall, 'The Housing of the London Poor: 1: Where to House Them', *Contemporary Review*, 45 (1884), p. 226.

35   Ibid.

36   Ibid, p. 231.

37   Arnold White, 'The Nomad Poor of London', *Contemporary Review*, 47 (1885), pp. 714–26.

38   H. M. Hyndman, 'The English Workers as they Are', *Contemporary Review*, 52 (1887), pp. 122–36.

39   Samuel A. Barnett, 'A Scheme for the Unemployed', *Nineteenth Century*, 24 (1888), pp. 753–63.

40   Ibid.

41   PP 1884–85, XXX, *First Report of Her Majesty's Commissioners for Inquiring into the Housing of the Working Classes* (c. 4402), p. 15.

42   Ibid.

43   Ibid., p. 16. See also PP 1896, IX, *Report from the Select Committee on Distress from Want of Employment; Together with the Proceedings of the Committee, Minutes of Evidence, Appendix, and Index*, pp. ii, viii, xiv–xv.

44   Stedman Jones, *Outcast London*, p. 321.

45   See for example, John Brown, 'Charles Booth and Labour Colonies, 1889–1905', *Economic History Review*, 2nd series, XXI (2) (1968), pp. 349–60.

46   Harris, 'Between Civic Virtue and Social Darwinism', pp. 80–82.

47   Jane Lewis, 'Social Facts, Social Theory and Social Change: The Ideas of Booth in Relation to Those of Beatrice Webb, Octavia Hill and Helen Bosanquet', in Englander and O'Day (eds.), *Retrieved Riches*, pp. 51, 55, 59, 63.

48   Hennock, 'Poverty and Social Theory in England', pp. 67–91; Peter Hennock, 'Concepts of Poverty in the British Social Surveys from Charles Booth to Arthur Bowley', in Martin Bulmer, Kevin Bales, and Kathryn Kisk Sklar (eds), *The Social Survey in Historical Perspective 1880–1940* (Cambridge, 1991), pp. 189–97.

49   Ernest Aves, 'Obituary: Charles Booth', *Economic Journal*, 26 (1916), pp. 537–42. On Booth see for example, Wayne K. D. Davies, 'Charles Booth and the Measurement of Urban Social Character', *Area*, 10 (1978), pp. 290–96; Michael Cullen, 'Charles Booth's Poverty Survey: Some New Approaches', in T. C. Smout (ed.), *The Search for Wealth and Stability: Essays in Economic and Social History Presented to M. W. Flinn* (London, 1979), pp. 159–74; Paul Spicker, 'Charles Booth: The Examination of Poverty', *Social Policy & Administration*, 24 (1) (1990), pp. 21–38; Kevin Bales, 'Lives and Labours in the Emergence of Organised Social Research, 1886–1907', *Journal of Historical Sociology*, 9 (2) (1996), pp. 113–38; Kevin Bales, 'Popular Reactions to Sociological Research: The Case of Charles Booth', *Sociology*, 33 (1) (1999), pp. 153–68.

50   Charles Booth, 'The Inhabitants of Tower Hamlets (School Board Division), Their Condition and Occupations', *Journal of the Royal Statistical Society*, 50 (1887), p. 375.

51   Ibid., p. 329.

52   Ibid.

53   Ibid.

54   Ibid., p. 337.

55   Ibid.

56 Ibid., p. 335.

57 Ibid.

58 Ibid.

59 Ibid., p. 375.

60 Ibid.

61 Charles Booth, 'Condition and Occupations of the People of East London and Hackney, 1887', *Journal of the Royal Statistical Society*, 51 (1888), pp. 276–309.

62 Ibid., p. 299.

63 Ibid., p. 305.

64 Charles Booth, *Life and Labour of the People in London: First Series: Poverty. 1. East, Central and South London* (London, 1904), p. 150.

65 Charles Booth, *Life and Labour of the People in London: Second Series: Industry. 5. Comparisons, Survey and Conclusions* (London, 1904), p. 73.

66 Booth, *First Series: Poverty. 1*, p. 176.

67 Ibid., p. 38.

68 Ibid., p. 39.

69 Hennock, 'Poverty and Social Theory in England', p. 75.

70 Harris, 'Between Civic Virtue and Social Darwinism', pp. 78–81.

71 Stedman Jones, *Outcast London*, p. 321.

72 Booth, *In Darkest England*, pp. 19–23.

73 Alfred Marshall, *Principles of Economics: An Introductory Volume* (London 1890, ninth Variorum edn., 1961), p. 2.

74 PP 1896, XI, *Report from the Select Committee on Distress from Want of Employment; Together with the Proceedings of the Committee, Minutes of Evidence, Appendix, and Index*, p. ii.

75 Ibid., p. xiii.

76 Ross McKibbin, 'Class and Poverty in Edwardian England', in Ross McKibbin, *The Ideologies of Class* (Oxford, 1991), pp. 167–96.

77 A. McBriar, *An Edwardian Mixed Doubles: The Bosanquets Versus the Webbs* (Oxford, 1987), pp. 10–14, 369. See also Stefan Collini, 'Hobhouse, Bosanquet and the State: Philosophical Idealism and Political Argument in England 1880–1918', *Past and Present*, 72 (1976), pp. 86–111, pp. 87, 91–92.

78 H. Dendy, 'The Industrial Residuum', in Bernard Bosanquet (ed.), *Aspects of the Social Problem by Various Writers* (London, 1895, Kraus reprint edn., 1968), p. 82.

79 Ibid., p. 83. See also McBriar, *An Edwardian Mixed Doubles*, pp. 124–25.

80 Ibid., p. 102. See also Pauline M. H. Mazumdar, 'The Eugenists and the Residuum: The Problem of the Urban Poor', *Bulletin of the History of Medicine*, 54 (2) (1980), p. 206.

81 Helen Bosanquet, *The Strength of the People: A Study in Social Economics* (London, 1902, reprinted 1996), pp. 113–14.

82 Jane Lewis, 'The Place of Social Investigation, Social Theory and Social Work in the Approach to Late Victorian and Edwardian Social Problems: The Case of Beatrice Webb and Helen Bosanquet', in Bulmer, Bales, and Kisk Sklar (eds), *The Social Survey in Historical Perspective*, pp. 158–62; Lewis, 'Social Facts, Social Theory and Social Change', pp. 49–66.

83 Harris, 'Between Civic Virtue and Social Darwinism', p. 72.

Notes to Chapter 2: A Trojan Horse

1 Sidney and Beatrice Webb, *Industrial Democracy* (London, 1897, 1902 edn.), p. 785.

2 Ibid. On the unemployable see also John Burnett, *Idle Hands: The Experience of Unemployment, 1790–1990* (London, 1994), pp. 156, 160, 220, 305.

3 Webbs, *Industrial Democracy*, p. 787.

4 Ibid., p. 789.

5 National Committee to Promote the Break-Up of the Poor Law, *The Minority Report of the Poor Law Commission: Part II: The Unemployed* (London, 1909), p. 236.

6 Ibid., pp. 210–11.

7 Lewis, 'The Place of Social Investigation', pp. 148–69; Lewis, 'Social Facts, Social Theory and Social Change', pp. 49–66.

8 Sidney and Beatrice Webb, *English Poor Law History: Part II: The Last Hundred Years: Volume II* (London, 1929), p. 710.

9 Ibid., p. 668; José Harris, *Unemployment and Politics: A Study in English Social Policy 1886–1914* (Oxford, 1972), p. 349, note 1.

10 Geoffrey Drage, *The Unemployed* (London, 1894), p. 142.

11 Ibid., p. 154.

12 Percy Alden, *The Unemployed: A National Question* (London, 1905), p. 17.

13 Ibid., pp. 17–31.

14 Ibid., p. 17.

15 Ibid., p. 18.

16 Ibid., p. 28.

17 Ibid., p. 144.

18 PP 1906, CIII, (Cd. 2852, 2891, 2892), *Report of the Departmental Committee on Vagrancy*, p. 1.

19 Ibid., pp. 120–21.

20 Ibid., p. 27.

21 Ibid., pp. 74–85.

22 Edmond Kelly, *The Unemployables* (London, 1907), p. 10.

23 José Harris, *William Beveridge: A Biography* (Oxford, 1977), pp. 103–6.

24 Ibid., pp. 120–21.

25 W. H. Beveridge, and H. R. Maynard, 'The Unemployed: Lessons of the Mansion House Fund', *Contemporary Review*, 86 (1904), pp. 629–38.

26 William Beveridge, *Unemployment: A Problem of Industry* (London, 1909), pp. 134, 137.

27 Ibid., p. 137.

28 Ibid., pp. 135–36, 138, 148–49.

29 Harris, *William Beveridge*, pp. 141–43.

30 Jonathan Bradshaw, 'Preface', in B. Seebohm Rowntree, *Poverty: A Study of Town Life* (London, 1901, 2000 facsimile edn., Bristol), p. xx.

31 Asa Briggs, 'Seebohm Rowntree's *Poverty: A Study of Town Life* in Historical Perspective', in Jonathan Bradshaw and Roy Sainsbury (eds.), *Getting the Measure of Poverty: The Early Legacy of Seebohm Rowntree* (Aldershot, 2000), pp. 5–22.

32   Alan Gillie, 'Rowntree, Poverty Lines and School Boards', in Jonathan Bradshaw and Roy Sainsbury (eds.), *Getting the Measure of Poverty: The Early Legacy of Seebohm Rowntree* (Aldershot, 2000), pp. 85–108.

33   Benjamin Seebohm Rowntree, *Poverty: A Study of Town Life* (London, 1901, second edn., 1902), pp. vii–x.

34   Ibid.

35   Ibid., p. 5.

36   Ibid., pp. 295, 304.

37   Hennock, 'Concepts of Poverty', p. 191.

38   Rowntree, *Poverty: A Study of Town Life*, p. 45.

39   Ibid., p. 46.

40   Ibid., pp. 207, 216–21.

41   Ibid., p. 47.

42   Ibid., pp. 140–42.

43   Ibid.

44   Ibid., pp. 144–45.

45   *The Times*, 16 September 1902, p. 4, col. f; cited in Bernard Harris, 'Seebohm Rowntree and the Measurement of Poverty, 1899–1951', in Jonathan Bradshaw and Roy Sainsbury (eds.), *Getting the Measure of Poverty: The Early Legacy of Seebohm Rowntree* (Aldershot, 2000), p. 69. I am grateful to Bernard Harris for this reference.

46   *The Times*, 4 October 1902, p. 11, col. f.

47   Cited in Gillie, 'Rowntree, Poverty Lines and School Boards', p. 97.

48   J. H. Veit-Wilson, 'Paradigms of Poverty: A Rehabilitation of B. S. Rowntree', *Journal of Social Policy*, 15 (1986), pp. 97–98.

49   Harris, 'Seebohm Rowntree and the Measurement of Poverty', pp. 60–84.

50   Bradshaw, 'Preface', pp. xxix, xxxi, xxxviii–xl.

51   Hennock, 'Concepts of Poverty', p. 206.

52   A. L. Bowley and A. R. Burnett-Hurst, *Livelihood and Poverty: A Study in the Economic Conditions of Working-Class Households in Northampton, Warrington, Stanley and Reading* (London, 1915), p. 33, table VII, p. 38.

53   Ibid., pp. 41–42, table IX.

54   Ibid., p. 47.

55   Hennock, 'Concepts of Poverty', p. 209.

56   A. L. Bowley and Margaret H. Hogg, *Has Poverty Diminished? A Sequel to "Livelihood and Poverty"* (London, 1925), pp. 1–26.

57   R. H. Tawney, *Poverty as an Industrial Problem* (London, 1913), p. 4.

58   Ibid., p. 11.

59   Ibid., p. 12.

60   Ibid., p. 15.

61   B. Seebohm Rowntree and Bruno Lasker, *Unemployment: A Social Study* (London, 1911), pp. v–xvii.

62   Ibid., p. 173.

63   Ibid., pp. 178–79.

64   Ibid., p. 182.

65   Ibid., pp. 185–86.

66   Ibid., p. 193.

67   Ibid., p. 199.

68   Victor Branford, *Interpretations and Forecasts: A Study of Survivals and Tendencies in Contemporary Society* (London, 1914), pp. 71–72. This is quoted in McKibbin, 'Class and Poverty in Edwardian England', p. 169.

69   McKibbin, 'Class and Poverty in Edwardian England', p. 168.

70   See for example, Noel Whiteside, 'Unemployment and Health: An Historical Perspective', *Journal of Social Policy*, 17, 2 (1988), pp. 177–94; Richard Smith, *Unemployment and Health: A Disaster and a Challenge* (Oxford, 1987).

71   Alan Deacon, *In Search of the Scrounger: The Administration of Unemployment Insurance in Britain 1920–1931* (London, 1976).

72   Marie Jahoda, Paul F. Lazarsfeld, and Hans Zeisel, *Marienthal: The Sociography of an Unemployed Community* (1933, English edn., London, 1972), pp. 4–14.

73   Ibid., p. 87.

74   Philip Eisenberg and Paul F. Lazarsfeld, 'The Psychological Effects of Unemployment', *Psychological Bulletin*, 35 (1938), pp. 358–90.

75   James L. Halliday, 'Psychoneurosis as a Cause of Incapacity Among Insured Persons: A Preliminary Enquiry', *British Medical Journal* (Supplement) (1935), i, pp. 85–88, 99–102.

76   Ibid., p. 100.

77   E. Wight Bakke, *The Unemployed Man: A Social Study* (London, 1933), pp. xiii–xviii, 45–49, 70–71.

78   Ibid., pp. 182, 193, 251.

79   Jahoda, Lazarsfeld, and Zeisel, *Marienthal*, p. xi.

80   R. I. McKibbin, 'The "Social Psychology" of Unemployment in Interwar Britain', in P. J. Waller (ed.), *Politics and Social Change in Modern Britain: Essays Presented to A. F. Thomson* (Brighton, 1987), pp. 161–91. This has been reprinted as Ross McKibbin, 'The "Social Psychology" of Unemployment in Interwar Britain', in McKibbin, *Ideologies of Class*, pp. 228–58.

81   David Caradog Jones, *The Social Survey of Merseyside* (Liverpool, 1934), vol 2, pp. 380–81.

82   Ibid., vol 2, p. 381.

83   Ibid., vol 3, p. 445.

84   Ibid., vol 3, p. 449.

85   Macnicol, 'In Pursuit of the Underclass'.

86   Pilgrim Trust, *Men Without Work: A Report Made to the Pilgrim Trust* (Cambridge, 1938), p. 173.

87   Marie Jahoda, 'The Impact of Unemployment in the 1930s and the 1970s', *Bulletin of the British Psychological Society*, 32 (1979), pp. 309–14; Marie Jahoda, *Employment and Unemployment: A Social-Psychological Analysis* (Cambridge, 1982), p. 21.

88   Adrian Sinfield, *What Unemployment Means* (Oxford, 1981), p. 37. Although see also Helen Ritchie, Jo Casebourne and Jo Rick, *Understanding Workless People and Communities: A Literature Review* (London, 2005).

Notes to Chapter 3: In Search of the Social Problem Group

1 David Barker, 'How to Curb the Fertility of the Unfit: The Feeble-Minded in Edwardian Britain', *Oxford Review of Education*, 9 (3) (1983), p. 197.

2 Donald MacKenzie, 'Eugenics in Britain', *Social Studies of Science*, 6 (1976), pp. 499–532; L. J. Ray, 'Eugenics, Mental Deficiency and Fabian Socialism Between the Wars', *Oxford Review of Education*, 9 (3) (1983), pp. 213–22; Ian Brown, 'Who were the Eugenists? A Study of the Formation of an Early Twentieth-Century Pressure Group', *History of Education*, 17 (4) (1988), pp. 295–307; G. R. Searle, 'Eugenics and Class', in Charles Webster (ed.), *Biology, Medicine and Society 1840–1940* (Cambridge, 1981), pp. 217–42; Dorothy Porter, '"Enemies of the Race": Biologism, Environmentalism, and Public Health in Edwardian England', *Victorian Studies* (1991), pp. 159–78.

3 Michael Freeden, 'Eugenics and Progressive Thought: A Study in Ideological Affinity', *Historical Journal*, 22 (3) (1979), pp. 645–71; Greta Jones, 'Eugenics and Social Policy Between the Wars', *Historical Journal*, 25 (3) (1982), pp. 717–28.

4 See for example Patricia Potts, 'Medicine, Morals and Mental Deficiency: The Contribution of Doctors to the Development of Special Education in England', *Oxford Review of Education*, 9 (3) (1983), pp. 181–96; Patricia L. Garside, '"Unhealthy Areas": Town Planning, Eugenics and the Slums, 1890–1945', *Planning Perspectives*, 3 (1988), pp. 24–46; R. A. Soloway, *Democracy and Degeneration: Eugenics and the Declining Birthrate in Twentieth Century Britain* (Chapel Hill, 1990); John Welshman, 'Eugenics and Public Health in Britain, 1900–40: Scenes from Provincial Life', *Urban History*, 24 (1) (1997), pp. 56–75; Mathew Thomson, *The Problem of Mental Deficiency: Eugenics, Democracy, and Social Policy in Britain c.1870–1959* (Oxford, 1998).

5 John Macnicol, 'Eugenics and the Campaign for Voluntary Sterilisation in Britain Between the Wars', *Social History of Medicine*, 2 (1989), pp. 149–54.

6 Mazumdar, 'The Eugenists and the Residuum', pp. 204–15.

7 Jones, 'Eugenics and Social Policy Between the Wars', pp. 723–26; Greta Jones, *Social Hygiene in Twentieth Century Britain* (London, 1986), pp. 88–111.

8 Soloway, *Democracy and Degeneration*, pp. 170–71, 190–91.

9 Desmond King, *In the Name of Liberalism: Illiberal Social Policy in the United States and Britain* (Oxford, 1999), pp. 79–81.

10 Macnicol, 'In Pursuit of the Underclass', pp. 300–313. The debt that this chapter owes to the work of Macnicol will be obvious.

11 Tim Cresswell, *The Tramp in America* (London, 2001), p. 114.

12 Ibid., p. 129.

13 PP 1929–30, XVII, *Report of the Departmental Committee on the Relief of the Casual Poor* (Cmd. 3640), pp. 8–11, 17.

14 Ibid., pp. 13–14.

15 Ibid., p. 16.

16 Ibid., pp. 23, 49.

17 Ibid., pp. 13–14.

18 H. Llewellyn-Smith (ed.), *The New Survey of London Life and Labour* (London, 1932), vol. 3., p. 261.

19 Ibid., pp. 259–60.

20 Ibid., p. 24.

21 Ibid., p. 255.

22 Ibid., pp. 280–81.

23 Nels Anderson, *The Hobo: The Sociology of the Homeless Man* (Chicago, 1921, Phoenix edn., 1961), p. 136.

24 Frank Gray, *The Tramp: His Meaning and Being* (London, 1931), pp. 19–20.

25 Ibid., p. 23.

26 Ibid., pp. 58, 79–80.

27 Macnicol, 'In Pursuit of the Underclass', p. 301. See also G. R. Searle, 'Eugenics and Politics in Britain in the 1930s', *Annals of Science*, 36 (1979), pp. 159–69.

28 C. E. Rosenberg, 'The Bitter Fruit: Heredity, Disease, and Social Thought in Nineteenth-Century America', *Perspectives in American History*, 8 (1974), pp. 189–235.

29 Robert L. Dugdale, *The Jukes: A Study in Crime, Pauperism, Disease, and Heredity* (New York 1877, Arno Press edn. 1970), pp. 13, 68–70; Cresswell, *The Tramp in America*, p. 114.

30 Dugdale, *The Jukes*, pp. iv–v.

31 Ibid., p. 3.

32 Ibid., pp. 3–4.

33 Henry Herbert Goddard, *The Kallikak Family: A Study in the Heredity of Feeblemindedness* (New York, 1912, Arno Press edn. 1973), pp. 116–17.

34 Ibid., pp. 18–30.

35 Ibid., p. 69.

36 Ibid., pp. 104–14. See also Ray, 'Eugenics, Mental Deficiency and Fabian Socialism', pp. 219–20.

37 Mark H. Haller, *Eugenics: Hereditarian Attitudes in American Thought* (New Brunswick, NJ, 1963, paperback edn., 1984), p. 106.

38 Contemporary Medical Archives Centre, Wellcome Institute, London (hereafter CMAC) SA/EUG, F2, F3, F4.

39 Cited in Mazumdar, 'The Eugenists and the Residuum', p. 212.

40 E. J. Lidbetter, 'Pedigrees of Pauper Stocks', in *Eugenics, Genetics and the Family: The Second International Congress of Genetics* (London, 1921), i, pp. 391–97.

41 CMAC SA/EUG, C209: 'Mr E. J. Lidbetter'.

42 Ibid., Secretary of the Eugenics Society to W. P. Crawford Greene, 25/1/28.

43 Ibid., C. P. Blacker to E. J. Lidbetter, 27/6/31.

44 E. J. Lidbetter, 'The Social Problem Group', *Eugenics Review*, 24, 1 (1932), pp. 7–9.

45 Ibid., pp. 10–12.

46 E. J. Lidbetter, *Heredity and the Social Problem Group, Volume 1* (London, 1933), p. 18.

47 CMAC, SA/EUG, C209: J. C. Pringle to C. P. Blacker, 16/10/33.

48 CMAC, SA/EUG, C57: A. M. Carr-Saunders to C. P. Blacker, 17/11/33.

49 Ibid., C. P. Blacker to A. M. Carr-Saunders, 20/11/33.

50 Macnicol, 'In Pursuit of the Underclass', pp. 308–10.

51 Board of Education and Board of Control, *Report of the Mental Deficiency Committee* (London, 1929), Parts 1 and 2, p. iii.

52 Ibid., Part 3, paras. 96–102.

53 Ibid., Part 3, pp. 81–82, para. 93.

54 Ibid., Part 2, pp. 83, para. 91, Part 3, pp. 79–80, para. 91.

55 Bernard Mallet, 'The Social Problem Group', *Eugenics Review*, 23, 3 (1931), pp. 203–6. See also CMAC, SA/EUG, D197: 'The Social Problem Group'.

56 CMAC, SMOH/B2/I: minutes of meeting 9/3/33, p. 42; CMAC SA/EUG C32 II: C. J. Bond, 'Are our Children To-Day As Good as Their Grandfathers?', radio broadcast, Birmingham, 20/9/33, p. 2.

57 CMAC, SA/EUG, D197: letter from C. P. Blacker, 21/5/32.

58 CMAC, SA/EUG, C209: C. P. Blacker to E. J. Lidbetter, 2/11/32.

59 Ibid., pp. 21, 41–42, 54, 57; King, *In the Name of Liberalism*, p. 79.

60 Macnicol, 'Eugenics and the Campaign for Voluntary Sterilisation', pp. 154–59; King, *In the Name of Liberalism*, p. 72.

61 PP 1933–34, XV (Cmd. 4485), *Report of the Departmental Committee on Sterilisation*.

62 Ibid., p. 21.

63 Jones, *Social Hygiene in Twentieth Century Britain*, p. 99; Macnicol, 'Eugenics and the Campaign for Voluntary Sterilisation', pp. 159–69; King, *In the Name of Liberalism*, pp. 91–94.

64 Macnicol, 'In Pursuit of the Underclass', p. 310.

65 Caradog Jones papers, University of Liverpool, D48/i, iv: David Caradog Jones, *Power: A Gift to Ordinary People: The Autobiography of David Caradog Jones* (1973).

66 David Caradog Jones, 'An Account of an Inquiry into the Extent of Economic Moral Failure Among Certain Types of Regular Workers', *Journal of the Royal Statistical Society*, 76, 5 (1913), pp. 520–33.

67 Macnicol, 'In Pursuit of the Underclass', pp. 310–11.

68 David Caradog Jones (ed.), *The Social Survey of Merseyside* (Liverpool, 1934), vol 3., p. 394.

69 Ibid., p. 546.

70 Ibid., pp. 546–47.

71 Caradog Jones papers, D48/4/5: cuttings from the *Liverpool Post*, 22/6/34; *Daily Dispatch*, 21/6/34 and 22/6/34.

72 Ibid., cutting from the *Political Quarterly*, January – March 1935.

73 Ibid., cutting from the *New Statesman and Nation*, 7/7/34.

74 CMAC, SA/EUG, C193: D. Caradog Jones to C. B. S. Hodson, 24/9/29.

75 Caradog Jones papers, University of Liverpool, D48/4/4.

76 Ibid., David Caradog Jones, 'Mental Deficiency on Merseyside: Its Connection with the Social Problem Group', *Eugenics Review*, pp. 97–105.

77 Cited in Macnicol, 'In Pursuit of the Underclass', p. 311.

78 Caradog Jones (ed.), *Social Survey of Merseyside*, vol 3., pp. 403, 405.

79 Searle, 'Eugenics and Politics in Britain in the 1930s', pp. 150–69; Kevles, *In the Name of Eugenics*, pp. 164–75; Macnicol, 'In Pursuit of the Underclass', p. 313; Garside, '"Unhealthy Areas"', pp. 40–42.

80 CMAC, SA/EUG, C209: E. J. Lidbetter to C. P. Blacker, 13/1/36.

81 C. P. Blacker (ed.) *A Social Problem Group?* (Oxford, 1937), p. 2.

82 Ibid., p. 6.

83 R. B. Cattell, *The Fight for our National Intelligence* (London, 1937), p. 108.

84 Blacker (ed.), *A Social Problem Group?*, p. v.

85 R. M. Titmuss, *Poverty and Population: A Factual Study of Contemporary Social Waste* (London, 1938), p. 288.

86 CMAC SA/EUG C209: C. P. Blacker to E. J. Lidbetter, 19/4/44.

87 Ibid., C. P. Blacker to E. J. Lidbetter, 8/6/44.

88 CMAC SA/EUG, C58: A. M. Carr-Saunders to C. P. Blacker, 16/6/44.

89 Ibid., C. P. Blacker to A. M. Carr-Saunders, 20/6/44.

90 Caradog Jones papers, D48/2 (I), KK: D. Caradog Jones, *The Social Problem Group: Poverty and Subnormality of Intelligence*, reprinted from the *Canadian Bar Review* (March, 1945), pp. 44–50.

91 Ibid., pp. 2–4.

92 D. Caradog Jones, *Social Surveys* (London, 1949), pp. 125, 130.

93 E. T. Ashton, 'Problem Families and their Household Budgets', *Eugenics Review*, 48, 2 (1956), pp. 98–100.

Notes to Chapter 4: The Invention of the Problem Family

1 R. C. Wofinden, 'Problem Families', *Public Health*, 57 (1944), p. 137.

2 John Welshman, 'In Search of the "Problem Family": Public Health and Social Work in England and Wales, 1940–1970', *Social History of Medicine*, 9 (3) (1996), pp. 447–65.

3 Pat Starkey, 'The Medical Officer of Health, the Social Worker, and the Problem Family, 1943 to 1968: The Case of Family Service Units', *Social History of Medicine*, 11, 3 (1998), pp. 421–41.

4 Pat Starkey, 'The Feckless Mother: Women, Poverty and Social Workers in Wartime and Post-War England', *Women's History Review*, 9, 3 (2000), pp. 539–57.

5 Alan Cohen, *The Revolution in Post-War Family Casework: The Story of Pacifist Service Units and Family Units 1940–1959* (Lancaster, 1998); Pat Starkey, *Families and Social Workers: The Work of Family Service Units 1940–1985* (Liverpool, 2000).

6 Macnicol, 'From "Problem Family" to "Underclass", 1945–95', pp. 69–93. See also Macnicol, 'In Pursuit of the Underclass'.

7 *Social Insurance and Allied Services: Report by Sir William Beveridge* (London, 1942).

8 Women's Group on Public Welfare, *Our Towns: A Close Up* (Oxford, 1943), p. xiii. On the Our Towns report see, for example, John Welshman, 'Evacuation, Hygiene, and Social Policy: The *Our Towns* Report of 1943', *Historical Journal*, 42 (3) (1999), pp. 781–807.

9 *Eugenics Review*, 35 (1943), p. 13.

10 C. G. Tomlinson, *Families in Trouble: An Enquiry into Problem Families in Luton* (Luton, 1946), p. 11.

11 Ibid., pp. 3–13, 29–37.

12 CMAC, SA/EUG C193: D. Caradog Jones, 'Notes on Tomlinson's Report', 5/7/46.

13 C. P. Blacker, 'Social Problem Families in the Limelight', *Eugenics Review*, 38 (1946), pp. 117–27.

14 CMAC SA/EUG L58: minutes of the Problem Families Committee, 18/7/47.

15 Ibid., minutes of the Problem Families Committee, 10/10/47; CMAC SA/EUG D169: Eugenics Society Problem Families Committee, 'Problem Families: Proposed Pilot Inquiries', 11/47, p. 1.

16 CMAC SA/EUG L59: Problem Families Committee, circulated papers 1947–49.

17 CMAC SA/EUG D169: Eugenics Society Problem Families Committee, 'Problem Families: Proposed Pilot Inquiries', 11/47, p. 6; CMAC SA/EUG L58: minutes of the Problem Families Committee, 30/1/48, p. 3.

18 CMAC SA/EUG L58: minutes of the Problem Families Committee, 30/1/48.

19 CMAC SA/EUG D169: C. P. Blacker, 'Problem Families Committee', 15/2/48, pp. 3–4.

20 National Archives, Kew, London, MH 134/181: Problem Families Committee, 'Problem Families: Six Pilot Enquiries', 3/48, p. 4.

21 CMAC SA/EUG L58: minutes of the Problem Families Committee, 1/4/49, p. 3.

22 R. C. Wofinden, *Problem Families in Bristol* (London, 1950), p. 47.

23 *Medical Officer* (1951), p. 137.

24 CMAC SA/EUG D171: E. O. Lewis to C. P. Blacker, 1/2/52.

25 Richard Titmuss papers, British Library of Political and Economic Science (BLPES), London, 4/545: R. Titmuss to C. P. Blacker, 3/1/52.

26 Ibid., p. 5.

27 C. P. Blacker, *Problem Families: Five Enquiries* (London, 1952), pp. 12–20.

28 Ibid., pp. 29–34, 79–83.

29 See for example, Greta Jones, *Social Hygiene in Twentieth Century Britain* (London, 1986); R. Soloway, *Democracy and Degeneration: Eugenics and the Declining Birthrate in Twentieth Century Britain* (Chapel Hill, 1990); P. M. H. Mazumdar, *Eugenics, Human Genetics and Human Failings: The Eugenics Society, Its Sources, and its Critics in Britain* (London, 1992).

30 Macnicol, 'From "Problem Family" to "Underclass", 1945–95', pp. 77–81.

31 D. Morgan, 'The Acceptance by Problem Families in Southampton of a Domiciliary Birth Control Service', in J. E. Meade and A. S. Parkes (eds.), *Biological Aspects of Social Problems* (Edinburgh and London, 1965), pp. 201–2.

32 C. P. Blacker and L. N. Jackson, 'Voluntary Sterilisation for Family Welfare: A Proposal by the Simon Population Trust', *Lancet*, (1966), i, pp. 971–74.

33 Eric McKie, *Venture in Faith: The Story of the Establishment of the Liverpool Family Service Unit and the Development of the Work with 'Problem Families'* (Liverpool, 1963), p. 12.

34 Ibid., pp. 18–35.

35 Tom Stephens, 'Sixty-Two Problem Families', *Social Welfare*, 5 (1944), pp. 328–29.

36 Starkey, 'The Medical Officer of Health, the Social Worker, and the Problem Family', p. 423.

37 Tom Stephens, *Problem Families: An Experiment in Social Rehabilitation* (London, 1945), pp. vii, 2–6.

38 Ibid., p. 6.

39 Ibid., pp. 46–72.

40 *British Medical Journal* (1946), i, p. 166.

41 *Lancet* (1946), i, p. 928.

42   David Jones, 'Family Service Units for Problem families', *Eugenics Review*, 41 (1950), pp. 171–79.

43   McKie, *Venture in Faith*, pp. 69–91.

44   D. L. Woodhouse, 'Casework with Problem families', *Case Conference*, 5 (1958), p. 38.

45   David Jones, 'Some Notes on Measuring the Results of Family Casework with "Problem Families"', *Social Work*, 21 (1964), pp. 3–11.

46   B. M. Spinley, *The Deprived and the Privileged: Personality Development in English Society* (London, 1953), p. 75.

47   Ministry of Health, Department of Health for Scotland, *Report of the Working Party on Social Workers in the Local Authority Health and Welfare Services* (London, 1959), pp. 45, 122–23.

48   Rodney Lowe and Paul Nicholson (eds.), 'The Formation of the Child Poverty Action Group', *Contemporary Record*, 9 (1995), pp. 612–37.

49   *British Medical Journal* (1954), ii, p. 639.

50   Wofinden, 'Problem Families', p. 137.

51   R. C. Wofinden, 'Problem Families', *Eugenics Review*, 38 (1946), pp. 127–32.

52   C. O. Stallybrass, 'Problem Families', *Medical Officer*, 75 (1946), p. 89.

53   Ibid., p. 91.

54   C. O. Stallybrass, 'Problem Families', *Social Work*, 4, 2 (1947), p. 30.

55   Ibid., p. 35.

56   S. W. Savage, 'Rehabilitation of Problem Families', *Medical Officer*, 75 (1946), p. 86.

57   J. L. Burn, *Recent Advances in Public Health* (London, 1947), p. 203.

58   C. Fraser Brockington, 'Problem Families', *Medical Officer*, 77 (1946), pp. 75–77.

59   See, for example, Percy Ford, C. J. Thomas, and E. T. Ashton, *Problem Families: The Fourth Report of the Southampton Survey* (Oxford, 1955).

60   A. C. Stevenson, *Recent Advances in Social Medicine* (London, 1950), p. 138.

61   C. Fraser Brockington, *The Health of the Community: Principles of Public Health for Practitioners and Students* (London, 1954), pp. 216–20.

62   Margaret MacEwan, *Health Visiting: A Textbook for Health Visitor Students* (London, 1951, 1957 edn.), pp. 58–59.

63   N. R. Tillett, 'The Derelict Family', *New Statesman and Nation* (28 April, 1945), p. 270.

64   Joint Circular from the Home Office, Ministry of Health and Ministry of Education, *Children Neglected or Ill-Treated in Their Own Homes*, 31 July 1950.

65   Cited in MacEwan, *Health Visiting*, pp. 58–59.

66   Ministry of Health, *On the State of the Public Health, 1951* (London, 1953), p. 134.

67   Ministry of Health, *Annual Report of the Ministry of Health, 1953* (London, 1954), p. 129.

68   Ministry of Education, *The Health of the School Child, 1950 and 1951* (London, 1952), p. 44.

69   Ministry of Health, Department of Health for Scotland, Ministry of Education, *An Inquiry into Health Visiting: Report of a Working Party on the Field of Work, Training and Recruitment of Health Visitors* (London, 1956), pp. 100–1.

70   B. Andrews and J. S. Cookson, 'Problem Families: A Practical Approach', *Medical Officer*, 88 (1952), pp. 118–19.

71   R. C. Wofinden, 'Unsatisfactory Families: Two Approaches to the Problem', *Medical Officer*, 94 (1955), pp. 384–87.

72   George Godber, 'Health Services, Past, Present and Future', *Lancet* (1958), ii, pp. 2–6.

73   *Medical Officer* (1957), p. 246.

74   Starkey, 'The Medical Officer of Health, the Social Worker, and the Problem Family', pp. 421, 439.

75   W. H. Parry, C. H. Wright, and J. E. Lunn, 'Sheffield Problem Families: A Follow-Up Survey', *Medical Officer*, 118 (1967), pp. 130–32.

76   C. H. Wright and J. E. Lunn, 'Sheffield Problem Families: A Follow Up Study of Their Sons and Daughters', *Community Medicine*, 126, 22 (1971), p. 307.

77   See for example, J. Peel, 'A Fertility Control Experiment Among Problem Families', *Medical Officer*, 116 (1966), pp. 357–58; A. Midwinter, P. M. Rich, and W. B. Fletcher, 'A Contraceptive Clinic for Problem and Potential Problem Families: a Preliminary Report on the First Year', *Medical Officer*, 118 (1967), pp. 29–31.

78   DHSS, *On the State of the Public Health, 1968* (London, 1969), p. 95.

79   W. L. Tonge, D. S. James, and S. M. Hillam, *Families Without Hope: A Controlled Study of 33 Problem Families* (Ashford, 1975).

80   Noel Timms, 'Taking Social Work Seriously: The Contribution of the Functional School', *British Journal of Social Work*, 27 (1997), pp. 723–37.

81   Women's Group on Public Welfare, *Our Towns*; University Press of Liverpool, *Our Wartime Guests – Opportunity or Menace?* (London, 1940), p. 39.

82   See for example, P. Seed, *The Expansion of Social Work in Britain* (London, 1973); Penelope Hall, *Reforming the Welfare: The Politics of Change in the Personal Social Services* (London, 1976); Eileen Younghusband, *Social Work in Britain, 1950–1975: A Follow-Up Study*, 2 vols. (London, 1978); Joan Cooper, *The Creation of the British Personal Social Services, 1962–1974* (London, 1983).

83   *Medical Officer* (1952), p. 277.

84   *Social Work* (1953), pp. 797–801.

85   E. E. Irvine, 'Research into Problem Families: Theoretical Questions Arising from Dr Blacker's Investigations', *British Journal of Psychiatric Social Work*, 5 (1954), pp. 24–33.

86   David Donnison, *The Neglected Child and the Social Services* (Manchester, 1954), p. 116.

87   Noel Timms, 'Problem Family Supporters', *Case Conference*, 1 (1954), pp. 28–31.

88   W. Baldamus and N. Timms, 'The Problem Family: A Sociological Approach', *British Journal of Sociology*, 6 (1955), pp. 318–27.

89   R. K. Merton, *Social Theory and Social Structure* (New York, 1949, 1957 edn.), pp. 187–89.

90   Noel Timms, 'Social Standards and the Problem Family', *Case Conference*, 2 (1956), pp. 2–3.

91   A. F. Philp and N. Timms, *The Problem of the Problem Family: A Critical Review of the Literature Concerning the 'Problem Family' and its Treatment* (London, 1957), p. v.

92   Ibid., p. 7.

93   Ibid., pp. 9, 25–28, 63–68.

94   David Donnison, 'The Problem of "the Problem Family"', *Case Conference*, 3, 10 (1957), pp. 308–9.

95　G. Rose, 'Co-Ordinating Committees', *Case Conference*, 4 (1957), pp. 41–47, 75–78, 111–14.

96　J. Warham, and S. McKay, 'Working with the Problem Family', *Social Work*, 16 (1959), p. 127.

97　Ministry of Health *et al*, *Report of the Working Party on Social Workers*, pp. 80–81, 217.

98　Barbara Wootton, *Social Science and Social Pathology* (London, 1959), pp. 51–62, 337.

99　See for instance, Harriett Wilson, 'Problem Families and the Concept of Immaturity', *Case Conference*, 6 (1959), pp. 115–18; E. E. Irvine, 'Some Notes on Problem Families and Immaturity', *Case Conference*, 6, 9 (1960), pp. 225–28.

100　V. Wimperis, *The Unmarried Mother and her Child* (London, 1960), pp. 62, 285.

101　Noel Timms, *Casework in the Child Care Service* (London, 1962), p. 135.

102　Harriett Wilson, *Delinquency and Child Neglect* (London, 1962), pp. 34–39, 109–11, 148–59, 162–63.

103　Paul Halmos (ed.) *The Canford Families: A Study in Social Casework and Group Work* (Keele, 1962), pp. 229–35; Olive Stevenson, 'Co-Ordination Reviewed', *Case Conference*, 9, 8 (1963), pp. 208–12.

104　M. P. Hall, *The Social Services of Modern England* (London, 1952, 1965 edn.), p. 169.

105　Home Office, *Report of the Committee on Children and Young Persons* (Cmnd. 1191) (London, 1960); Home Office, *Report of the Committee on Local Authority and Allied Personal Social Services* (Cmnd. 3703) (London, 1968).

106　Home Office, *Report of the Committee on Children and Young Persons*, pp. 8–20.

107　Home Office, *Report of the Committee on Local Authority and Allied Personal Social Services*, pp. 25–28, 119.

Notes to Chapter 5: Chasing the Culture of Poverty

1　Edward James, *America Against Poverty* (London, 1970), pp. 86–107. For an overview of the history of area-based initiatives see Pete Alcock, '"Maximum Feasible Understanding" – Lessons from Previous Wars on Poverty', *Social Policy & Society*, 4, 3, (2005), pp. 321–29.

2　James L. Sundquist, 'Origins of the War on Poverty', in James L. Sundquist (ed.), *On Fighting Poverty: Perspectives from Experience* (London, 1969), p. 30; James L. Sundquist, 'The End of the Experiment?', in Sundquist, *On Fighting Poverty*, pp. 242–51.

3　John G. Wofford, 'The Politics of Local Responsibility: Administration of the Community Action Program – 1964–1966', in Sundquist, *On Fighting Poverty*, pp. 71–73.

4　Quoted in A. H. Halsey, 'Government Against Poverty in School and Community', in Dorothy Wedderburn (ed.), *Poverty, Inequality and Class Structure* (Cambridge, 1974), p. 139, footnote 11.

5　Alice O'Connor, *Poverty Knowledge: Social Science, Social Policy, and the Poor in Twentieth-Century U.S. History* (Princeton, 2001), p. 99.

6　Susan Rigdon, *The Culture Façade: Art, Science and Politics in the Work of Oscar Lewis* (Urbana and Chicago, 1988), pp. 49–50.

7　Oscar Lewis, *Five Families: Mexican Case Studies in the Culture of Poverty* (New York, 1959, 1962 edn.), p. 1. See also Gans, *The War Against the Poor*, pp. 24–25, 156, footnote 64.

8　Rigdon, *The Culture Façade*, pp. 54–63.

9　Ibid., pp. 64–68.

10　Oscar Lewis, *La Vida: A Puerto Rican Family in the Culture of Poverty – San Juan & New York* (New York, 1966, London, 1967 edn.), p. xxxix.

11　Ibid., p. xli.

12　Ibid.

13　Ibid., p. xliv.

14　Ibid., p. xlviii. See also Oscar Lewis, 'The Children of Sanchez, Pedro Martinez, *and* La Vida', *Current Anthropology*, 8 (5) (1967), pp. 480–500.

15　Rigdon, *The Culture Façade*, p. 87.

16　Katz, *The Undeserving Poor*, pp. 16–19.

17　Michael Harrington, *The Other America: Poverty in the United States* (Harmondsworth, 1962), pp. 23–24.

18　O'Connor, *Poverty Knowledge*, p. 123.

19　Edward C. Banfield, *The Unheavenly City Revisited: A Revision of the Unheavenly City* (Boston, 1974), pp. 12, 53–54.

20　Ibid., pp. 61–63, 235.

21　Rigdon, *The Culture Façade*, p. 177.

22　Ibid., p. 180.

23　James Leiby, *A History of Social Welfare and Social Work in the United States* (New York, 1978), p. 317.

24　Robert E. Park, 'The City: Suggestions for the Investigation of Human Behavior in the Urban Environment', in Robert E. Park, Ernest W. Burgess and Roderick D. McKenzie, *The City* (Chicago, 1925), pp. 4, 24–25.

25　Ibid., pp. 45–46.

26　E. Franklin Frazier, *The Negro Family in the United States* (Chicago, 1939, revised and abridged edn., 1948, 1966 edn.), p. 363.

27　Ibid., pp. 363–68.

28　Ibid.

29　William Foote Whyte, *Street Corner Society: The Social Structure of an Italian Slum* (Chicago, 1943, second edn., 1955), pp. 273–74, 358.

30　Allison Davis, 'The Motivation of the Underprivileged Worker', in William Foote Whyte (ed.), *Industry and Society* (New York, 1946, 1971 reprint), pp. 84–106.

31　Allison Davis, *Social-Class Influences Upon Learning* (Cambridge, Mass., 1948), pp. 11–13, 18, 24–37.

32　Walter B. Miller, 'Lower Class Culture as a Generating Milieu of Gang Delinquency', *Journal of Social Issues*, 14 (3) (1958), pp. 5–19.

33　Ibid.

34　Hyman Rodman, 'On Understanding Lower-Class Behaviour', *Social and Economic Studies*, 8 (1959), pp. 444–46, 447–49.

35　Hyman Rodman, 'The Lower-Class Value Stretch', *Social Forces*, 42 (1963), p. 209.

36　Ibid., p. 215. See also Hyman Rodman, *Lower-Class Families: The Culture of Poverty in Negro Trinidad* (London, 1971), pp. 192–93, 195, 197–98.

37　Herbert J. Gans, *The Urban Villagers: Group and Class in the Life of Italian-Americans* (New York, 1962), p. 249.

38   Elliot Liebow, *Tally's Corner: A Study of Negro Streetcorner Men* (Boston, 1967), pp. 4–5, 11, 208–13, 214–22.

39   Ibid., pp. 222–31.

40   Valentine, *Culture and Poverty*, pp. 23–24.

41   Ibid., pp. 43–45.

42   Nathan Glazer, 'Foreword', in Frazier, *Negro Family in the United States*, p. vii.

43   Daniel P. Moynihan, *The Negro Family: The Case for National Action* (Washington, 1965), pp. 3–14. See also Lee Rainwater and William L. Yancey, *The Moynihan Report and the Politics of Controversy* (London, 1967), pp. 3–30.

44   Ibid., pp. 30–45.

45   See for example, William Ryan, 'Savage Discovery: The Moynihan Report', in Rainwater and Yancey, *The Moynihan Report*, pp. 457–62; Herbert J. Gans, 'The Negro Family: Reflections on the Moynihan Report', in Rainwater and Yancey, *The Moynihan Report*, pp. 445–57; Valentine, *Culture and Poverty*, pp. 31–35.

46   Jack L. Roach and Orville R. Gursslin, 'An Evaluation of the Concept "Culture of Poverty"', *Social Forces*, 45, 3 (1967), pp. 383–92.

47   Valentine, *Culture and Poverty*, pp. 5–13.

48   Ibid., pp. 57–67.

49   Ibid., pp. 141–47.

50   See also Charles Valentine, 'Culture and Poverty: Critique and Counter-Proposals', *Current Anthropology*, 10 (2–3) (1969), pp. 181–201; Charles Valentine, 'The "Culture of Poverty": Its Scientific Significance and its Implications for Action', in Eleanor Burke Leacock (ed.), *The Culture of Poverty: A Critique* (New York, 1971), pp. 193–225.

51   Eleanor Burke Leacock, 'Introduction', in Leacock, *Culture of Poverty*, pp. 10–11.

52   Ibid., p. 34.

53   William Ryan, *Blaming the Victim* (New York, 1971), pp. 113–19, 122–35.

54   Valentine, *Culture and Poverty*, pp. 94–97.

55   Ulf Hannerz, *Soulside: Inquiries into Ghetto Culture and Community* (New York, 1969), pp. 181–82, 200.

56   Lee Rainwater, *Behind Ghetto Walls: Black Families in a Federal Slum* (Chicago, 1970), pp. 396–97.

57   Ibid., pp. 1, 5–6, 365–66.

58   Herbert J. Gans, 'Poverty and Culture: Some Basic Questions about Methods of Studying Life-Styles of the Poor', in Peter Townsend (ed.), *The Concept of Poverty: Working Papers on Methods of Investigation and Life-Styles of the Poor in Different Countries* (London, 1970), p. 155.

59   Rodman, *Lower-Class Families: The Culture of Poverty in Negro Trinidad*.

60   David Harrison, 'The Culture of Poverty in Coconut Village: A Critique', *Sociological Review*, 24 (1976), pp. 832–36.

61   Ibid., pp. 843–46, 851, 854–56. See also Hyman Rodman, 'Culture of Poverty: The Rise and Fall of a Concept', *Sociological Review*, 25 (1977), p. 867.

62   Macnicol, 'Social Politics in the 1960s', pp. 106–17.

63   Elizabeth Bott, *Family and Social Network: Roles, Norms, and External Relationships in Ordinary Urban Families* (London, 1957, second edn., 1971), pp. 306–7.

64 Keith G. Banting, *Poverty, Politics and Policy: Britain in the 1960s* (London, 1979), pp. 109–38.

65 Department of Education and Science, *Children and Their Primary Schools: A Report of the Central Advisory Council for Education (England)* (London, 1967), vol 1.

66 Ibid., vol 1., pp. 57–59, paras. 151–54.

67 Ibid., vol 1., p. 436, para. 1186.

68 British Library of Political and Economic Science, London: Titmuss Papers 2/209, cutting from the *Economist*, 4/2/67, p. 405.

69 A. H. Halsey (ed.), *Educational Priority: Volume 1: EPA Problems and Policies* (London, 1972), pp. 13, 16–19.

70 Martin Loney, *Community Against Government: The British Community Development Project 1968–78 – A Study of Government Incompetence* (London, 1983), pp. 18–25.

71 Ibid., pp. 55–56.

72 Ibid., pp. 56–59.

73 Ibid., pp. 60–68.

74 Macnicol, 'Social Politics in the 1960s', p. 115.

75 Social Science Research Council, *Research on Poverty: An SSRC Review of Current Research* (London, 1968), pp. 8–10.

76 Ibid.

77 Ken Coates and Richard Silburn, *Poverty: The Forgotten Englishmen* (Harmondsworth, 1970, 1973 edn.), p. 153.

78 Ibid., pp. 166–67.

79 Ibid., p. 168.

80 Peter Townsend, 'Measures and Explanations of Poverty in High Income and Low Income Countries: The Problems of Operationalizing the Concepts of Development, Class and Poverty', in Peter Townsend (ed.), *The Concept of Poverty*, pp. 41, 44–45.

81 Ibid.

82 Peter Townsend, *Poverty in the United Kingdom: A Survey of Household Resources and Standards of Living* (Harmondsworth, 1979), pp. 65–70.

83 Dorothy Wedderburn, 'A Cross-National Study of Standards of Living of the Aged in Three Countries', in Townsend, *Concept of Poverty*, p. 203.

84 Jordan, *Poor Parents*, pp. 123–42.

85 Howard Glennerster, *US Poverty Studies and Poverty Measurement: The Past Twenty-Five Years*, CASEpaper 42 (London, 2000), p. 8.

86 William Julius Wilson, 'The Underclass: Issues, Perspectives, and Public Policy', in William Julius Wilson (ed.), *The Ghetto Underclass: Social Science Perspectives* (London, 1993), pp. 4–5.

Notes to Chapter 6: Sir Keith Joseph and the Cycle of Deprivation

1 On Joseph see for example the biography by Andrew Denham and Mark Garnett, *Keith Joseph* (Chesham, 2001); Andrew Denham and Mark Garnett, 'From the "Cycle of Enrichment" to the "Cycle of Deprivation": Sir Keith Joseph, "Problem Families"

and the Transmission of Disadvantage', *Benefits*, 35, 10, 3 (2002), pp. 193–98. For the relevant archival sources see John Welshman, 'Ideology, Social Science, and Public Policy: The Debate over Transmitted Deprivation', *Twentieth Century British History*, 16, 3 (2005), pp. 306–41.

2 Andrew Denham and Mark Garnett, 'From "Guru" to "Godfather": Keith Joseph, New Labour and the British Conservative Tradition', *Political Quarterly*, 72 (2001), pp. 97–106.

3 *The Times*, 12 December 1994, p. 21.

4 Nicholas Timmins, *The Five Giants: A Biography of the Welfare State* (London, 1995; second edn, 2003), pp. 289–90.

5 Keith Joseph, 'The Cycle of Family Deprivation', reprinted in Keith Joseph, *Caring for People* (London, 1972), p. 32. The abridged version is in Eric Butterworth and Robert Holman (eds.), *Social Welfare in Modern Britain* (London, 1975), pp. 387–93.

6 Keith Joseph, 'The Cycle of Family Deprivation', p. 32.

7 Ibid., p. 33.

8 Ibid.

9 Ibid., p. 34.

10 Ibid., p. 37.

11 Ibid., p. 39.

12 Ibid., p. 46.

13 *The Times*, 30 June 1972, p. 17.

14 Denham and Garnett, *Keith Joseph*, pp. 264–68.

15 *The Times*, 21 October 1974, p. 3.

16 Margaret Wynn and Arthur Wynn, 'Can Family Planning do More to Reduce Child Poverty?', *Poverty*, 29 (1974), pp. 17–20. An earlier biographer of Joseph claims that the 1972 speech went through eleven drafts. See Morrison Halcrow, *Keith Joseph: A Single Mind* (London, 1989), pp. 51–52, 83–84.

17 Denham and Garnett, *Keith Joseph*, pp. 268–69; on Arthur Wynn, see the obituary in the *Guardian*, 29 September 2001.

18 Denham and Garnett, *Keith Joseph*, p. 269.

19 *The Times*, 21 October 1974, p. 1.

20 Ibid.

21 Richard Berthoud, 'Transmitted Deprivation: The Kite That Failed', *Policy Studies*, 3, 3 (1983), p. 151. I am grateful to Alan Deacon for this reference.

22 Denham and Garnett, *Keith Joseph*, p. 221.

23 Keith Joseph, *Social Security: The New Priorities* (London, 1966), p. 7.

24 Ibid., p. 16.

25 Ibid., p. 17.

26 Ibid., pp. 19, 27.

27 Ibid., p. 33.

28 Keith Joseph, *Changing Housing* (London, 1967), p. 4.

29 Keith Joseph, *Freedom under the Law* (London, 1975), p. 9.

30 Charles Webster, *The Health Services Since the War, ii, Government and Health Care: The British National Health Service, 1958–1979* (London, 1996), p. 426.

31   While the two theories are related, it is confusing to link them. See for example Robert Holman, *Poverty: Explanations of Social Deprivation* (London, 1978).

32   Denham and Garnett, *Keith Joseph*, p. 224.

33   SSRC/DHSS, *Transmitted Deprivation: First Report of the DHSS/SSRC Joint Working Party on Transmitted Deprivation* (London, 1974); Berthoud, 'Transmitted Deprivation', p. 155.

34   SSRC/DHSS, *Transmitted Deprivation*, foreword.

35   Ibid., para. 5.

36   Ibid., paras. 5–12.

37   Ibid., para. 19.3.

38   DHSS, *The Family in Society: Preparation for Parenthood. An Account of Consultations with Professional, Voluntary and Other Organisations, October 1972 to February 1973* (London, 1974), pp. 5–8.

39   DHSS, *The Family in Society: Dimensions of Parenthood. A Report of a Seminar held at All Souls College, Oxford 10 – 13 April 1973* (London, 1974), p. 8.

40   Peter Townsend, 'The Cycle of Deprivation: The History of a Confused Thesis', in British Association of Social Workers, *The Cycle of Deprivation: Papers Presented to a National Study Conference, Manchester University, March, 1974* (Birmingham, 1974), p. 8.

41   Ibid.

42   Jordan, *Poor Parents*, pp. 8, 173–75.

43   Robert Holman, 'Poverty: Consensus and Alternatives', *British Journal of Social Work*, 3 (1973), pp. 431–46.

44   Holman, *Poverty*, pp. 112–36.

45   SSRC/DHSS, *Transmitted Deprivation*, foreword.

46   Berthoud, 'Transmitted Deprivation', pp. 157, 162.

47   Ibid., p. 155.

48   Michael Rutter and Nicola Madge, *Cycles of Disadvantage: A Review of Research* (London, 1976), pp. 5–6.

49   Ibid., p. 30.

50   Ibid., pp. 246–48.

51   Ibid., pp. 255–56.

52   Ibid., pp. 303–4.

53   Ibid., p. 327.

54   See W. L. Tonge, J. E. Lunn, M. Greathead, S. McLaren and C. Bosanko, 'Generations of "Problem Families" in Sheffield', in Nicola Madge (ed.), *Families at Risk* (London, 1983), p. 57.

55   Israel Kolvin, F. J. W. Miller, D. Mc.I. Scott, S. R. M. Gatzanis and M. Fleeting, *Continuities of Deprivation? The Newcastle 1000 Family Study* (Aldershot, 1990), pp. 4–6.

56   Townsend, *Poverty in the United Kingdom*, pp. 70–71.

57   Mildred Blaxter, *The Health of Children: A Review of Research on the Place of Health in Cycles of Disadvantage* (London, 1981), pp. 1–8; Mildred Blaxter, *Mothers and Daughters: A Three-Generational Study of Health Attitudes and Behaviour* (London, 1982), pp. 1–5, 184–95.

58   Juliet Essen and Peter Wedge, *Continuities in Childhood Disadvantage* (London, 1982; repr. 1986), pp. 1–3, 11–12, 162.

59 Alan Murie, *Housing Inequality and Deprivation* (London, 1983), pp. 227–36; Pauline Ashley, *The Money Problems of the Poor: A Literature Review* (London, 1983), pp. 165–73; Jo Mortimore and Tessa Blackstone, *Disadvantage and Education* (London, 1982), pp. 1–4, 172–82.

60 A. B. Atkinson, A. K. Maynard and C. G. Trinder, *Parents and Children: Incomes in Two Generations* (London, 1983), pp. 176–84.

61 Roger Fuller and Olive Stevenson, *Policies, Programmes and Disadvantage: A Review of the Literature* (London, 1983), pp. vii–viii, 4–7.

62 Frank Coffield, Philip Robinson, and Jacquie Sarsby, *A Cycle of Deprivation? A Case Study of Four Families* (London, 1980), p. 159.

63 Ibid., p. 161.

64 Ibid., pp. 201–2.

65 Ibid., pp. 163–64.

66 Ibid., pp. 169–70.

67 Frank Coffield, *Cycles of Deprivation* (Durham, 1982), pp. 10–12.

68 Berthoud, 'Transmitted Deprivation', p. 160.

69 Ibid., p. 164.

70 Muriel Brown and Nicola Madge, *Despite the Welfare State* (London, 1982), pp. 2–3.

71 Ibid., pp. 26–27.

72 Ibid., p. 178.

73 Ibid., pp. 262, 266.

74 Ibid., pp. 268–69.

75 Berthoud, 'Transmitted Deprivation', p. 166.

76 Denham and Garnett, *Keith Joseph*, pp. 369–73, 421.

77 *The Times*, 12 December 1994, p. 19.

78 *Guardian*, 11 April 2000; Denham and Garnett, *Keith Joseph*, p. 429.

Notes to Chapter 7: Uncovering the Underclass – America

1 Ken Auletta, 'A Reporter at Large: The Underclass – I', *New Yorker*, 16 November 1981, p. 63.

2 See for example Jacqueline Jones, *The Dispossessed: America's Underclasses from the Civil War to the Present* (New York, 1992).

3 Jonathan Simon, *Poor Discipline: Parole and the Social Control of the Underclass, 1890–1990* (Chicago, 1993), pp. 258–59.

4 Ibid., pp. 5, 139–41.

5 Katz, *The "Underclass" Debate*.

6 Gunnar Myrdal, *Challenge to Affluence* (London, 1963), p. 40.

7 Ibid., p. 19.

8 Ibid., p. 53.

9 John C. Leggett, *Class, Race, and Labor: Working Class Consciousness in Detroit* (New York, 1968), pp. 14–15.

10 Ibid., pp. 116–18.

11 See for example, Morris, 'From the Culture of Poverty to the Underclass', pp. 126–32.

12   John Macnicol, 'Nightmare on Easy Street', *Times Higher Education Supplement*, 29 June 1990, p. 15.

13   Herbert J. Gans, 'From "Underclass" to "Undercaste": Some Observations About the Future of the Postindustrial Economy and its Major Victims', *International Journal of Urban and Regional Research*, 17 (1993), pp. 327–28.

14   'The American Underclass: Destitute and Desperate in the Land of Plenty', *Time*, 110, 29 August 1977, pp. 34–41. See also Aponte, 'Definitions of the Underclass', pp. 120–21.

15   Auletta, 'A Reporter at Large: The Underclass – I', p. 92.

16   Ibid., pp. 92–105.

17   Ibid., p. 105.

18   Ken Auletta, 'A Reporter at Large: The Underclass – III', *New Yorker*, 30 November 1981, p. 117.

19   Ibid., pp. 135, 168. See also Ken Auletta, *The Underclass* (New York, 1982).

20   Nicholas Lemann, 'The Origins of the Underclass: Part 1', *Atlantic Monthly*, June 1986, p. 35.

21   Ibid., p. 53.

22   Nicholas Lemann, 'The Origins of the Underclass: Part 2', *Atlantic Monthly*, July 1986, p. 4.

23   Ibid., p. 68.

24   Charles Murray, *Losing Ground: American Social Policy, 1950–1980* (New York, 1984), pp. 8–9.

25   Ibid., p. 58.

26   Ibid., pp. 64–65.

27   Ibid., pp. 73–74, 80–81.

28   Ibid., pp. 126–27.

29   Ibid., pp. 154–55.

30   Ibid., p. 155.

31   Ibid., pp. 156–62.

32   Ibid., pp. 167–68, 181–91.

33   Ibid., p. 219.

34   Ibid., p. 236.

35   Deacon, *Perspectives on Welfare: Ideas, Ideologies and Policy Debates*, pp. 40–41.

36   Clement Cottingham, 'Introduction', in Clement Cottingham (ed.), *Race, Poverty and the Urban Underclass* (Lexington, 1982), p. 3.

37   Ibid., pp. 1, 3.

38   Kenneth B. Clark and Richard P. Nathan, 'The Urban Underclass', in National Research Council, *Critical Issues for National Urban Policy: A Reconnaissance and Agenda for Further Study* (Washington, 1982), p. 33.

39   Ibid., pp. 44–45.

40   Ibid., p. 50.

41   Richard P. Nathan, 'Will the Underclass Always be With Us?', *Society* (March–April, 1987), pp. 57–62.

42   Ibid., p. 62.

43   George Cabot Lodge and William R. Glass, 'The Desperate Plight of the Underclass', *Harvard Business Review*, 60 (1982), pp. 60–71.

44 Myron Magnet, 'America's Underclass: What To Do?', *Fortune*, 11 May 1987, p. 80.

45 Gaither Loewenstein, 'The New Underclass: A Contemporary Sociological Dilemma', *Sociological Quarterly*, 26 (1985), p. 37.

46 Ibid., pp. 37–38.

47 Ricketts and Sawhill, 'Defining and Measuring the Underclass', p. 320.

48 Ibid., pp. 316–25. See also Ronald B. Mincy, 'The Underclass: Concept, Controversy and Evidence', in Sheldon Danziger *et al* (eds.), *Confronting Poverty: Prescriptions for Change* (New York, 1994), p. 145.

49 Christopher Jencks, 'Is the American Underclass Growing?', in Christopher Jencks and Paul E. Peterson (eds.), *The Urban Underclass* (Washington, D.C., 1991), pp. 28–100.

50 William Julius Wilson, 'The Underclass: Issues, Perspectives, and Public Policy', in William Julius Wilson (ed.), *The Ghetto Underclass: Social Science Perspectives* (New York, 1993), p. 2.

51 'Social Distress and the Urban Underclass', in Donald A. Hicks (ed.), *Urban America in the Eighties: Perspectives and Prospects* (New Brunswick, 1982), pp. 53–63.

52 John Kasarda, 'Caught in the Web of Change', *Society* (1983), pp. 41–47. See also John D. Kasarda, 'Introduction', in Hicks, *Urban America in the Eighties*, pp. v–x; John D. Kasarda, 'Structural Factors Affecting the Location and Timing of Urban Underclass Growth', *Urban Geography*, 11 (1990), pp. 234–64.

53 Douglas G. Glasgow, *The Black Underclass: Poverty, Unemployment, and Entrapment of Ghetto Youth* (San Francisco, 1980), p. vii.

54 Ibid., p. ix.

55 Ibid., p. 3.

56 Ibid., pp. 5–7, 8–11, 173.

57 Alphonso Pinkney, *The Myth of Black Progress* (Cambridge, 1984), pp. 115–34.

58 William Julius Wilson, *The Declining Significance of Race: Blacks and Changing American Institutions* (Chicago, 1978), pp. 22–23, 144, 152–54.

59 William Julius Wilson, *The Truly Disadvantaged: The Inner City, The Underclass, and Public Policy* (Chicago, 1987), pp. 3–10, 12.

60 Ibid., pp. 13–18.

61 Ibid., pp. 163, 165–87. See also William Julius Wilson, 'Studying Inner-City Social Dislocations: The Challenge of Public Agenda Research: 1990 Presidential Address', *American Sociological Review*, 56 (1991), pp. 4–6.

62 Wilson, *The Truly Disadvantaged*; Wilson, 'The Underclass: Issues, Perspectives, and Public Policy', pp. 12–13.

63 Ibid., pp. 18–19, 158–59.

64 Wilson, 'The Underclass: Issues, Perspectives, and Public Policy', pp. 4–5.

65 Wilson, 'Studying Inner-City Social Dislocations', p. 10.

66 Wilson, 'The Underclass: Issues, Perspectives, and Public Policy', p. 11.

67 Ibid., p. 163.

68 Wilson, *The Truly Disadvantaged*, p. 7.

69 Wilson, 'Studying Inner-City Social Dislocations', p. 6.

70 Ibid., p. 23.

71 Douglas S. Massey and Nancy A. Denton, 'Trends in the Residential Segregation of Blacks,

Hispanics, and Asians: 1970–1980', *American Sociological Review*, 52 (1987), pp. 802–25; Douglas S. Massey and Nancy A. Denton, 'The Ecology of Inequality: Minorities and the Concentration of Poverty, 1970–1980', *American Journal of Sociology*, 95 (1990), pp. 1153–88; Douglas S. Massey and Nancy A. Denton, *American Apartheid: Segregation and the Making of the Underclass* (Cambridge, Mass., 1993).

72 Paul A. Jargowsky and Mary Jo Bane, 'Ghetto Poverty in the United States, 1970–1980', in Jencks and Peterson, *The Urban Underclass*, pp. 235–73.

73 Greg J. Duncan, *Years of Poverty, Years of Plenty: The Changing Economic Fortunes of American Workers and Families* (Ann Arbor, Michigan, 1984), pp. 3–6.

74 James N. Morgan *et al.*, *Five Thousand American Families – Patterns of Economic Progress*, vol. 1 (Ann Arbor, Michigan, 1974), p. 339. See also Greg Duncan and Daniel Hill, 'Attitudes, Behaviour, and Economic Outcomes: A Structural Equations Approach', in *Five Thousand American Families*, vol. 3, pp. 61–100.

75 Duncan, *Years of Poverty, Years of Plenty*, pp. 5–6, 14–28, 65.

76 Ibid., p. 34.

77 Ibid., pp. 60–61.

78 Ibid., pp. 82–83, 91.

79 Ibid., p. 71.

80 Douglas Muzzio, 'The Smell in the Urban Basement', *Urban Affairs Quarterly*, 19 (1983), pp. 133–43.

81 William Kornblum, 'Lumping the Poor: What *is* the "Underclass"?', *Dissent* (Summer, 1984), pp. 295–302.

82 Emmett D. Carson, 'The Black Underclass Concept: Self-Help vs. Government Intervention', *American Economic Review*, 26 (1986), p. 348.

83 Ibid., pp. 347–50.

84 Aponte, 'Definitions of the Underclass: A Critical Analysis', pp. 117–37.

85 Sheldon Danziger and Peter Gottschalk, 'Earnings Inequality, the Spatial Concentration of Poverty, and the Underclass', *American Economic Review*, 77 (1987), pp. 211–15.

86 Sheldon Danziger and Peter Gottschalk, *America Unequal* (Cambridge, Mass., 1995), pp. 12–13, 188, note 13.

87 Walter W. Stafford and Joyce Ladner, 'Political Dimensions of the Underclass Concept', in Gans (ed.), *Sociology in America*, p. 139.

88 Ibid., pp. 138–53.

89 Adolph Reed, 'The Underclass as Myth and Symbol: The Poverty of Discourse About Poverty', *Radical America*, 24 (1990), Part 1, pp. 21–40.

90 Michael W. Sherraden, 'Working Over the "Underclass"', *Social Work*, 29, 4 (1984), pp. 391–92.

91 Morris, 'From the Culture of Poverty to the Underclass', pp. 126–32.

92 Herbert J. Gans, 'Deconstructing the Underclass: The Term's Dangers as a Planning Concept', *Journal of the American Planning Association*, 56 (1990), pp. 271–77.

93 Gans, 'From "Underclass" to "Undercaste"', p. 334.

94 Herbert J. Gans, 'Positive Functions of the Undeserving Poor: Uses of the Underclass in America', *Politics and Society*, 22 (1994), pp. 269, 271–79, 279–81.

95 Katz, *Improving Poor People*, pp. 65–71, 97–98.

96 Katz, *The Undeserving Poor*, pp. 196, 235.

97 Katz, 'The Urban "Underclass" as a Metaphor of Social Transformation', p. 22.

98 John Macnicol, 'Is There an Underclass?: The Lessons from America', in Michael White (ed.), *Unemployment, Public Policy and the Changing Labour Market* (London, 1994), p. 29.

99 Macnicol, 'Nightmare on Easy Street', p. 15.

100 Macnicol, 'Is There an Underclass?', pp. 29–39.

Notes to Chapter 8: Uncovering the Underclass – Britain

1 Robert Moore, 'Citizenship and the Underclass', in Harry Coenen and Peter Leisink (eds.), *Work and Citizenship in the New Europe* (Aldershot, 1993), p. 51.

2 Andrew Adonis and Stephen Pollard, *A Class Act: The Myth of Britain's Classless Society* (London, 1997), p. 16.

3 Robert Macdonald, *Youth, the 'Underclass' and Social Exclusion* (London, 1997), pp. 5–6.

4 *Oxford English Dictionary* (Oxford, 1985), vol. xviii, p. 958. See also H. MacDiarmid, *Company I've Kept* (1966), vol iv., p. 124.

5 Richard Titmuss, 'Goals of Today's Welfare State', in P. Anderson and R. Blackburn (eds.), *Towards Socialism* (Ithaca, 1965), p. 363.

6 Anthony Giddens, *The Class Structure of the Advanced Societies* (London, 1973), pp. 112, 184.

7 Ibid., p. 289.

8 Ibid., pp. 216–20.

9 Moore, 'Citizenship and the Underclass', p. 52.

10 John Westergaard and Henrietta Resler, *Class in a Capitalist Society: A Study of Contemporary Britain* (London, 1975), p. 356.

11 John Rex and Sally Tomlinson, *Colonial Immigrants in a British City: A Class Analysis* (London, 1979), pp. 16, note 9, 33.

12 Ibid., p. 104.

13 John Rex, *The Ghetto and the Underclass: Essays on Race and Social Policy* (Aldershot, 1988), pp. 28–29, 33, 112–13.

14 Robert Miles, *Racism and Migrant Labour* (London, 1982), p. 153; Michael Keith and Malcolm Cross, 'Racism and the Postmodern City', in Malcolm Cross and Michael Keith (eds), *Racism, the City and the State* (London, 1993), pp. 11–15.

15 Townsend, *Poverty in the United Kingdom*, p. 920.

16 Ralf Dahrendorf, 'The Erosion of Citizenship and its Consequences for us all', *New Statesman*, 12 June 1987, p. 12.

17 Ibid., p. 13.

18 Ibid.

19 Ibid., p. 14.

20 Ibid., p. 15.

21 Charles Murray, 'Underclass', in Charles Murray, *The Emerging British Underclass* (London, 1990), p. 3.

22 Ibid., pp. 1–3.

23 Ibid., p. 5.

24 Ibid., p. 13.

25 Ibid.

26 Ibid., p. 17.

27 Ibid., pp. 17–23.

28 Ibid., p. 25.

29 Ibid., p. 35.

30 Charles Murray, 'Rejoinder', in Murray, *Emerging British Underclass*, p. 68.

31 David G. Green, 'Foreword', in Murray, *Emerging British Underclass*, p. vi.

32 Charles Murray, *Underclass: The Crisis Deepens* (London, 1994), pp. 2–3.

33 Ibid., pp. 6–9.

34 Ibid., p. 11.

35 Ibid., p. 15.

36 Ibid., p. 32.

37 Melanie Phillips, 'Where are the New Victorians?', in Murray, *Underclass: The Crisis Deepens*, p. 62.

38 Ibid., p. 60. On this theme, see also Norman Dennis and George Erdos, *Families Without Fatherhood* (London, 1992, second edn., 1993).

39 David Willetts, 'Theories and Explanations of the Underclass', in Smith, *Understanding the Underclass*, pp. 48–54.

40 See for example, Deacon, *Perspectives on Welfare*.

41 Frank Field, *Losing Out? The Emergence of Britain's Underclass* (Oxford, 1989), p. 2.

42 Ibid., pp. 4–7.

43 Ibid., pp. 8, 101, 195–96.

44 Deacon, *Perspectives on Welfare*, pp. 44–45.

45 Frank Field, 'Britain's Underclass: Countering the Growth', in Murray, *Emerging British Underclass*, pp. 37–41, p. 40.

46 W. G. Runciman, 'How Many Classes Are There in Contemporary British Society?', *Sociology*, 24 (1990), p. 388.

47 Ibid., pp. 388–90.

48 Maurice Roche, *Rethinking Citizenship: Welfare, Ideology and Change in Modern Society* (Cambridge, 1992), p. 57.

49 Alan Buckingham, 'Is There an Underclass in Britain?', *British Journal of Sociology*, 50, 1 (1999), pp. 49–75.

50 Smith, 'Defining the Underclass', p. 4.

51 Duncan Gallie, 'Employment, Unemployment, and Social Stratification', in Duncan Gallie (ed.), *Employment in Britain* (Oxford, 1988), pp. 465–71.

52 Ibid., pp. 467–74, 488.

53 Duncan Gallie, 'Are the Unemployed an Underclass? Some Evidence from the Social Change and Economic Life Initiative', *Sociology*, 28 (3) (1994), pp. 737–57.

54 Lydia Morris and Sarah Irwin, 'Employment Histories and the Concept of the Underclass', *Sociology*, 26 (3) (1992), pp. 401–20; L. D. Morris, 'Is There a British Underclass?', *International Journal of Urban and Regional Research*, 17 (3) (1993), pp. 404–12. See also

Lydia Morris, *Social Divisions: Economic Decline and Social Structural Change* (London, 1995), pp. 57–74.

55   Gordon Marshall, Stephen Roberts and Carole Burgoyne, 'Social Class and Underclass in Britain and the USA', *British Journal of Sociology*, 47, 1 (1996), pp. 22–44. See also Lydia Morris and John Scott, 'The Attenuation of Class Analysis: Some Comments on G. Marshall, S. Roberts and C. Burgoyne, "Social Class and the Underclass in Britain and the USA"', *British Journal of Sociology*, 47, 1 (1996), pp. 45–55.

56   Peter Lee, 'Housing and Spatial Deprivation: Relocating the Underclass and the new Urban Poor', *Urban Studies*, 31, 7 (1994), pp. 1191–2009.

57   Brian Nolan and Christopher T. Whelan, *Resources, Deprivation, and Poverty* (Oxford, 1996), pp. 152–78.

58   Nick Buck, 'Labour Market Inactivity and Polarisation: A Household Perspective on the Idea of an Underclass', in Smith, *Understanding the Underclass*, p. 19.

59   Anthony Heath, 'The Attitudes of the Underclass', in Smith, *Understanding the Underclass*, pp. 32–47.

60   Elaine Kempson, *Life on a Low Income* (London, 1996), pp. 28, 163.

61   David J. Smith, 'The Future of the Underclass', in Smith, *Understanding the Underclass*, p. 95.

62   Macnicol, 'In Pursuit of the Underclass', pp. 293–96.

63   Ibid.

64   Ibid., pp. 296, 299–300.

65   Ibid., p. 315.

66   Alan Walker, 'Blaming the Victims', in Murray, *Emerging British Underclass*, pp. 49–58.

67   Ibid.

68   Joan C. Brown, 'The Focus on Single Mothers', in Murray, *Emerging British Underclass*, pp. 43–48.

69   Kirk Mann and Sasha Roseneil, '"Some Mothers do 'Ave 'Em": Backlash and the Gender Politics of the Underclass Debate', *Journal of Gender Studies*, 3 (3) (1994), pp. 317–31.

70   Paul Bagguley and Kirk Mann, 'Idle Thieving Bastards? Scholarly Representations of the "Underclass"', *Work, Employment & Society*, 6, 1 (1992), pp. 114–19.

71   Ibid., pp. 119–25.

72   John Westergaard, 'About and Beyond the "Underclass": Some Notes on Influences of Social Climate on British Sociology Today', *Sociology*, 26 (1992), pp. 575–81.

73   Kirk Mann, 'Watching the Defectives: Observers of the Underclass in the USA, Britain and Australia', *Critical Social Policy*, 14 (2) (1994), pp. 80–96.

74   Dean and Taylor-Gooby, *Dependency Culture*, p. 28. See also Hartley Dean, 'In Search of the Underclass', in Phillip Brown and Richard Scase (eds.), *Poor Work: Disadvantage and the Division of Labour* (Buckingham, 1991), pp. 23–39.

75   Ibid., p. 49.

76   Carey Oppenheim and Lisa Harker, *Poverty: The Facts* (London, 1996), pp. 17–19.

77   Ruth Lister, *The Exclusive Society: Citizenship and the Poor* (London, 1990), pp. 24–26.

78   Ruth Lister, 'In Search of the "Underclass"', in Ruth Lister (ed.), *Charles Murray and the Underclass: The Developing Debate* (London, 1996), pp. 1–18.

79   Moore, 'Citizenship and the Underclass', p. 62.

80 Sebastian Herkommer and Max Koch, 'The "Underclass": A Misleading Concept and a Scientific Myth? Poverty and Social Exclusion as Challenges to Theories of Class and Social Structure', in Paul Littlewood, Ignace Glorieux, Sebastian Herkommer, and Ingrid Jonsson (eds.), *Social Exclusion in Europe: Problems and Paradigms* (Aldershot, 1999), pp. 89–111.

Notes to Chapter 9: Social Exclusion and Cycles of Disadvantage

1 http://www.cabinet-office.gov.uk/seu
2 Ibid.
3 Anne Power, *Poor Areas and Social Exclusion*, CASEpaper 35 (London, 2000).
4 Hilary Silver, 'Social Exclusion and Social Solidarity: Three Paradigms', *International Labour Review*, 133 (1994), pp. 531–78, pp. 534–35.
5 Ibid., pp. 534–35.
6 Ibid.
7 Graham Room, 'Poverty and Social Exclusion: The New European Agenda for Policy and Research', in Graham Room (ed.), *Beyond the Threshold: The Measurement and Analysis of Social Exclusion* (Bristol, 1995), pp. 1–9.
8 Graham Room, 'Conclusions', in Room, *Beyond the Threshold*, p. 243.
9 Jos Berghman, 'Social Exclusion in Europe: Policy Context and Analytical Framework', in Room, *Beyond the Threshold*, pp. 10–28.
10 Brendan J. Whelan and Christopher T. Whelan, 'In What Sense is Poverty Multidimensional?', in Room, *Beyond the Threshold*, p. 29.
11 Paul Littlewood and Sebastian Herkommer, 'Identifying Social Exclusion: Some Problems of Meaning', in Littlewood, Glorieux, Herkommer, and Jonsson (eds.), *Social Exclusion in Europe: Problems and Paradigms*, pp. 1–21.
12 Robert Walker, 'The Dynamics of Poverty and Social Exclusion', in Room, *Beyond the Threshold*, pp. 102–28.
13 Silver, 'Social Exclusion and Social Solidarity', pp. 539–43, 549–72.
14 Raymond Williams, *Keywords: A Vocabulary of Culture and Society* (New York, 1976, Fontana edn., 1983).
15 Hilary Silver, 'Culture, Politics and National Discourses of the new Urban Poverty', in Enzo Mingione (ed.), *Urban Poverty and the Underclass: A Reader* (Oxford, 1996), p. 113.
16 Will Hutton, *The State We're In* (London, 1995), pp. 2–3.
17 Ibid., pp. 9–10.
18 Peter Townsend, 'Redistribution: The Strategic Alternative to Privatisation', in Alan Walker and Carol Walker (eds.), *Britain Divided: The Growth of Social Exclusion in the 1980s and 1990s* (London, 1997), p. 269.
19 Anthony Giddens, *The Third Way: The Renewal of Social Democracy* (Cambridge, 1998), pp. 103–4, 109–10, 117.
20 Anthony Giddens, *The Third Way and its Critics* (Cambridge, 2000), pp. 105–6.
21 Ibid., pp. 109–11, 114.
22 Townsend, *Poverty in the United Kingdom*, p. 31.
23 Joanna Mack and Stewart Lansley, *Poor Britain* (London, 1985), p. 45.

24 Frank Field, 'Making Welfare Work: The Underlying Principles', in Frank Field, *Stakeholder Welfare* (London, 1996), p. 9. See also Frank Field, 'A Rejoinder', in Field, *Stakeholder Welfare*, pp. 107–14.

25 Alan Deacon, 'Welfare and Character', in Field, *Stakeholder Welfare*, pp. 60–74.

26 Alan Deacon, 'Learning from the US? The Influence of American Ideas Upon "New Labour" Thinking on Welfare Reform', *Policy and Politics*, 28, 1 (2000), pp. 5–18.

27 David Marquand, 'Moralists and Hedonists', in David Marquand and Anthony Seldon (eds.), *The Ideas that Shaped Post-War Britain* (London, 1996), p. 20.

28 Amitai Etzioni, *The Spirit of Community: Rights, Responsibilities and the Communitarian Agenda* (1993, Fontana edn., 1995), pp. 247–48.

29 Giddens, *The Third Way*, pp. 78–82.

30 http://www.cabinet-office.gov.uk/seu

31 Ibid.

32 Ibid.

33 Ruth Levitas, 'The Concept of Social Exclusion and the new Durkheimian Hegemony', *Critical Social Policy*, 46 (1996), pp. 5–20.

34 Ruth Levitas, *The Inclusive Society? Social Exclusion and New Labour* (London, 1998), p. 27.

35 Fairclough, *New Labour, New Language?*, pp. 51–53. See also Robert Furbey, 'Urban "Regeneration": Reflections on a Metaphor', *Critical Social Policy*, 19 (1999), pp. 419–43.

36 Fairclough, *New Labour, New Language?*, p. 57.

37 Ibid., p. 61.

38 Ibid., pp. 62–65.

39 Tania Burchardt, Julian Le Grand, and David Piachaud, 'Social Exclusion in Britain 1991–1995', *Social Policy & Administration*, 33 (1999), p. 229.

40 Ibid., p. 241.

41 Hills, 'Does a Focus on "Social Exclusion" Change the Policy Response?', in Hills, Le Grand, and Piachaud (eds.), *Understanding Social Exclusion*, p. 236.

42 Tony Blair, 'Beveridge Revisited: A Welfare State for the 21st Century', in Robert Walker (ed.), *Ending Child Poverty: Popular Welfare for the 21st Century* (Bristol, 1999), p. 16.

43 Ibid.

44 Jonathan Bradshaw, 'Child Poverty Under Labour', in Geoff Fimister (ed.), *An End in Sight?: Tackling Child Poverty in the UK* (London, 2001), pp. 9–27.

45 Blair, 'Beveridge Revisited: A Welfare State for the 21st Century', p. 16.

46 Department of Social Security, *Opportunity for All: Tackling Poverty and Social Exclusion* (Cm 4445) (London, 1999), p. 5.

47 Department of Social Security, *Opportunity for All: Making Progress* (Cm. 5260) (London, 2001), p. 40.

48 Anthony Lee and John Hills (eds.), *New Cycles of Disadvantage? Report of a Conference Organised by CASE on Behalf of ESRC for HM Treasury* CASEreport 1 (London, 1998), p. 26. Available at http://www.sticerd.lse.ac.uk/case.htm

49 John Hobcraft, *Intergenerational and Life-Course Transmission of Social Exclusion: Influences of Childhood Poverty, Family Disruption, and Contact with the Police*, CASEpaper 15 (London, 1998). Available at http://www.sticerd.lse.ac.uk/case.htm

50 Howard Glennerster, *US Poverty Studies and Poverty Measurement: The Past Twenty-Five Years* (London, 2000).

51 Mary Jo Bane and David T. Ellwood, 'Slipping into and out of Poverty: The Dynamics of Spells', *Journal of Human Resources*, 21 (1986), pp. 1–23.

52 Steven Webb, *Poverty Dynamics in Great Britain: Preliminary Analysis from the British Household Panel Survey* (London, 1995), pp. 17–18.

53 Sarah Jarvis and Stephen P. Jenkins, 'How Much Income Mobility is There in Britain?', *Economic Journal*, 108 (1998), pp. 428–43.

54 Simon Burgess and Carol Propper, 'Poverty in Britain', in Paul Gregg and Jonathan Wadsworth (eds.), *The State of Working Britain* (Manchester, 1999), pp. 269–72, 274. For an overview of the implications of dynamic analysis see Pete Alcock, 'The Influence of Dynamic Perspectives on Poverty Analysis and Anti-Poverty Policy in the UK', *Journal of Social Policy*, 33, 3 (2004), pp. 395–416.

55 HM Treasury, *Persistent Poverty and Lifetime Inequality: The Evidence*, CASEreport 5, HM Treasury Occasional Paper No. 10 (London, 1999), p. 120.

56 HM Treasury, *Tackling Poverty and Extending Opportunity: The Modernisation of Britain's Tax and Benefit System: Number Four* (London, 1999), p. 5, para. 1.05.

57 Ibid., p. 7, para. 1.13.

58 Ibid., pp. 26, 33, para. 3.17.

59 Ibid., p. 30, box 3.1.

60 *Guardian*, 11 April 2000, p. 4.

61 'Social Exclusion: Old Problem, New Name', *British Medical Journal*, 323 (2001), p. 174.

62 *Sure Start: Making a Difference for Children and Families*, p. 4. Available at http://www.surestart.gov.uk

63 Ibid., p. 8.

64 Office of the Deputy Prime Minister, *Breaking the Cycle: Taking Stock of Progress and Priorities for the Future: A Report by the Social Exclusion Unit* (London, 2004), pp. 10, 28, 73, 93, 138. However on the evidence see Elizabeth Such and Robert Walker, 'Falling Behind? Research on Transmitted Deprivation', *Benefits*, 35, 10, 3 (2002), pp. 185–92.

65 Alan Deacon, '"Levelling the Playing Field, Activating the Players": New Labour and "the Cycle of Disadvantage"', *Policy and Politics*, 31 (2) (2003), pp. 123–37.

66 David Piachaud, 'Child Poverty, Opportunities and Quality of Life', *Political Quarterly*, 72 (2001), pp. 446–53.

67 Le Grand, 'Knights, Knaves or Pawns? Human Behaviour and Social Policy', pp. 149–69; Le Grand, *Motivation, Agency and Public Policy*, pp. 2–11.

68 Le Grand, *Motivation, Agency and Public Policy*, p. 7.

69 Lister, *Poverty*, pp. 3, 7, 99–123, 124–57, 188–89.

70 Deacon, 'Review Article: Different Interpretations of Agency within Welfare Debates', pp. 447–55. See also Alcock, 'Maximum Feasible Understanding', p. 328.

Select Bibliography

PRIMARY SOURCES

Alden, Percy, *The Unemployed: A National Question* (London, 1905).

Anderson, Nels, *The Hobo: The Sociology of the Homeless Man* (Chicago, 1923, Phoenix edn., 1961).

Auletta, Ken, *The Underclass* (New York, 1982).

Bakke, E. Wight, *The Unemployed Man: A Social Study* (London, 1933).

Barnett, Samuel, 'A Scheme for the Unemployed', *Nineteenth Century*, 24 (1888), pp. 753–63.

Beveridge, W. H., *Unemployment: A Problem of Industry* (London, 1909).

Beveridge, W. H., and Maynard, H. R., 'The Unemployed: Lessons of the Mansion House Fund', *Contemporary Review*, 86 (1904), pp. 629–38.

Blacker, C. P., *A Social Problem Group?* (London, 1937).

Booth, Charles, 'The Inhabitants of Tower Hamlets (School Board Division), Their Condition and Occupations', *Journal of the Royal Statistical Society*, 50 (1887), pp. 326–401.

Booth, Charles, 'Condition and Occupations of the People of East London and Hackney, 1887', *Journal of the Royal Statistical Society*, 51 (1888), pp. 276–339.

Booth, Charles (ed.), *Life and Labour of the People in London*, 17 vols. (London, 1889–1903).

Booth, William, *In Darkest England and the Way Out* (London, 1890).

Bosanquet, Helen, *The Strength of the People: A Study in Social Economics* (London, 1902, reprinted 1996).

Bowley, A. L. and Burnett-Hurst, A. R., *Livelihood and Poverty: A Study in the Economic Conditions of Working-Class Households in Northampton, Warrington, Stanley and Reading* (London, 1915).

Brown, Muriel and Madge, Nicola, *Despite the Welfare State: A Report on the SSRC/DHSS Programme of Research into Transmitted Deprivation* (London, 1982).

Coates, Ken and Silburn, Richard, *Poverty: The Forgotten Englishmen* (Harmondsworth, 1970, 1973 edn.).

Coffield, Frank, Robinson, Philip, and Sarsby, Jacquie, *A Cycle of Deprivation? A Case Study of Four Families* (London, 1980).

Davis, Allison, 'The Motivation of the Underprivileged Worker', in William Foote Whyte (ed.), *Industry and Society* (New York, 1946, reprinted 1971), pp. 84–106.

Dendy, Helen, 'The Industrial Residuum', in Bernard Bosanquet (ed.), *Aspects of the Social Problem: By Various Writers* (London, 1895, reprinted 1968).

Drage, Geoffrey, *The Unemployed* (London, 1894).

Dugdale, Robert L., *The Jukes: A Study in Crime, Pauperism, Disease, and Heredity* (New York, 1877, reprinted 1970).

Frazier, Franklin E., *The Negro Family in the United States* (Chicago, 1939, new edn., 1966).

Gans, Herbert J., *The Urban Villagers: Group and Class in the Life of Italian-Americans* (New York, 1962).

Gans, Herbert J., 'Culture and Class in the Study of Poverty: An Approach to Anti-Poverty Research', in Herbert Gans, *People and Plans: Essays on Urban Problems and Solutions* (New York, 1968), pp. 321–46.

Gans, Herbert J., 'Poverty and Culture: Some Basic Questions About Methods of Studying Life-Styles of the Poor', in Peter Townsend (ed.), *The Concept of Poverty* (London, 1970), pp. 146–64.

Goddard, Henry Herbert, *The Kallikak Family: A Study in the Heredity of Feeblemindedness* (New York, 1912, new edn., 1973).

Halsey, A. H. (ed.), *Educational Priority: Volume 1: EPA Problems and Policies* (London, 1972).

Halsey, A. H., 'Government Against Poverty in School and Community', in Dorothy Wedderburn (ed.), *Poverty, Inequality and Class Structure* (Cambridge, 1974), pp. 123–39.

Hannerz, Ulf, *Soulside: Inquiries into Ghetto Culture and Community* (New York, 1969).

Harrington, Michael, *The Other America: Poverty in the United States* (Harmondsworth, 1962).

Herrnstein, Richard J., and Murray, Charles, *The Bell Curve: Intelligence and Class Structure in American Life* (New York, 1994).

Hill, Alsager Hay, *Our Unemployed* (London, 1868).

Holman, Robert, *Poverty: Explanations of Social Deprivation* (London, 1978).

Hyndman, H.M., 'The English Workers as They Are', *Contemporary Review*, 52 (1887), pp. 122–36.

Jahoda, Marie, Lazarsfeld, Paul F., and Zeisel, Hans, *Marienthal: The Sociography of an Unemployed Community* (1933, English edn., London, 1972).

Jordan, Bill, *Poor Parents: Social Policy and the 'Cycle of Deprivation'* (London, 1974).

Joseph, Keith, 'The Cycle of Family Deprivation', in Keith Joseph, *Caring for People* (London, 1972), pp. 29–46.

Kelly, Edmond, *The Unemployables* (London, 1907).

Leacock, Eleanor Burke (ed.), *The Culture of Poverty: A Critique* (New York, 1971).

Lemann, Nicholas, 'The Origins of the Underclass: Parts 1 and 2', *Atlantic Monthly* (June 1986), pp. 31–55 (July 1986), pp. 54–68.

Lewis, Oscar, *Five Families: Mexican Case Studies in the Culture of Poverty* (New York, 1959).

Lewis, Oscar, *The Children of Sanchez: Autobiography of a Mexican Family* (New York, 1961).

Lewis, Oscar, *La Vida: A Puerto Rican Family in the Culture of Poverty – San Juan & New York* (London, 1967).

Lewis, Oscar, *A Study of Slum Culture – Backgrounds for La Vida* (New York, 1968).

Lidbetter, E. J., 'The Social Problem Group', *Eugenics Review*, 24 (1932), pp. 7–12.

Lidbetter, E.J., *Heredity and the Social Problem Group: Volume 1* (London, 1933).

Liebow, Elliot, *Tally's Corner: A Study of Negro Streetcorner Men* (Boston, 1967).

Mallet, Bernard, 'The Social Problem Group', *Eugenics Review*, 23 (1931), pp. 203–6.

Marshall, Alfred, 'The Housing of the London Poor: 1: Where to House Them', *Contemporary Review*, 45 (1884), pp. 224–31.

Marshall, Alfred, *Principles of Economics: An Introductory Volume* (London, 1890, new edn., 1961).

Miller, Walter, 'Lower Class Culture as a Generating Milieu of Gang Delinquency', *Journal of Social Issues*, 14 (3) (1958), pp. 5–19.

Moynihan, Daniel P., *The Negro Family: The Case for National Action* (Washington, 1965).

Murray, Charles, *Losing Ground: American Social Policy, 1950–1980* (New York, 1984).

Murray, Charles, *The Emerging British Underclass* (London, 1990).

Murray, Charles, *Underclass: The Crisis Deepens* (London, 1994).

Myrdal, Gunnar, *Challenge to Affluence* (London, 1963).

Pilgrim Trust, *Men Without Work: A Report Made to the Pilgrim Trust* (Cambridge, 1938).

Rainwater, Lee, *Behind Ghetto Walls: Black Families in a Federal Slum* (Chicago, 1970).

Rainwater, Lee and Yancey, William L., *The Moynihan Report and the Politics of Controversy* (Cambridge, Mass., 1967).

Rodman, Hyman, 'On Understanding Lower-Class Behaviour', *Social and Economic Studies*, 8 (4) (1959), pp. 441–50.

Rodman, Hyman, 'The Lower-Class Value Stretch', *Social Forces*, 42, 2 (1963), pp. 205–15.

Rodman, Hyman, *Lower-Class Families: The Culture of Poverty in Negro Trinidad* (London, 1971).

Rowntree, Benjamin Seebohm, *Poverty: A Study of Town Life* (London, 1901).

Rowntree, Benjamin Seebohm and Lasker, Bruno, *Unemployment: A Social Study* (London, 1911).

Rutter, Michael and Madge, Nicola, *Cycles of Disadvantage: A Review of Research* (London, 1976).

Shostak, Arthur B. and Gomberg, William (eds.), *Blue-Collar World: Studies of the American Worker* (Englewood Cliffs, NJ, 1964).

Social Science Research Council, *Research on Poverty: An SSRC Review of Current Research* (London, 1968).

Sundquist, James L., 'Origins of the War on Poverty', in James L. Sundquist (ed.), *On Fighting Poverty* (New York, 1969), pp. 6–33.

Tawney, R. H., *Poverty as an Industrial Problem* (London, 1913).

Townsend, Peter, 'The Meaning of Poverty', *British Journal of Sociology*, 13 (3) (1962), pp. 210–27.

Townsend, Peter (ed.), *The Concept of Poverty: Working Papers on Methods of Investigation and Life-Styles of the Poor in Different Countries* (London, 1970).

Townsend, Peter, 'The Cycle of Deprivation – The History of a Confused Thesis', in British Association of Social Workers, *The Cycle of Deprivation: Papers Presented to a National Study Conference, Manchester University, March, 1974* (Birmingham, 1974), pp. 8–22.

Valentine, Charles A., *Culture and Poverty: Critique and Counter-Proposals* (Chicago, 1968).

Webb, Sidney and Beatrice, *Industrial Democracy* (London, 1897, new edn., 1902).

Wedderburn, Dorothy (ed.), *Poverty, Inequality and Class Structure* (Cambridge, 1974).

White, Arnold, 'The Nomad Poor of London', *Contemporary Review*, 47 (1885), pp. 714–26.

Whyte, William Foote, *Street Corner Society: The Social Structure of an Italian Slum* (Chicago, 1943, second edn., 1955).

Wofinden, R.C., 'Problem Families', *Public Health*, 57 (1944), pp. 136–39.

Women's Group on Public Welfare, *Our Towns: A Close Up* (London, 1943).

Wootton, Barbara, *Social Science and Social Pathology* (London, 1959).

SECONDARY SOURCES

Alcock, Pete, *Understanding Poverty* (London, 1993).

Alcock, Pete, 'The Influence of Dynamic Perspectives on Poverty Analysis and Anti-Poverty Policy in the UK', *Journal of Social Policy*, 33, 3 (2004), pp. 395–416.

Aponte, Robert, 'Definitions of the Underclass: A Critical Analysis', in Herbert J. Gans (ed.), *Sociology in America* (Westbury Park, Calif., 1990), pp. 117–37.

Bagguley, Paul and Mann, Kirk, 'Idle Thieving Bastards? Scholarly Representations of the "Underclass"', *Work, Employment & Society*, 6 (1) (1992), pp. 113–26.

Bane, Mary Jo and Ellwood, David T., 'Slipping into and out of Poverty: The Dynamics of Spells', *Journal of Human Resources*, 21 (1986), pp. 1–23.

Banting, Keith G., *Poverty, Politics and Policy: Britain in the 1960s* (London, 1979).

Berthoud, Richard, 'Transmitted Deprivation: The Kite that Failed', *Policy Studies*, 3 (3) (1983), pp. 151–69.

Blair, Tony, 'Beveridge Revisited: A Welfare State for the 21st Century', in Robert Walker (ed.), *Ending Child Poverty: Popular Welfare for the 21st Century?* (Bristol, 1999), pp. 7–18.

Bradshaw, Jonathan, 'Preface', in B. Seebohm Rowntree, *Poverty: A Study of Town Life* (1901, new edn., Bristol, 2000), pp. xix–lxxxii.

Bradshaw, Jonathan and Sainsbury, Roy (eds.), *Getting the Measure of Poverty: The Early Legacy of Seebohm Rowntree* (Aldershot, 2000).

Brodie, Marc, *The Politics of the Poor: The East End of London 1885–1914* (Oxford, 2004).

Brown, John, 'Charles Booth and Labour Colonies', *Economic History Review*, 21 (2) (1968), pp. 349–61.

Bryson, Alex and Jacobs, John, *Policing the Workshy: Benefit Controls, The Labour Market and the Unemployed* (Aldershot, 1992).

Buckingham, Alan, 'Is There an Underclass in Britain?', *British Journal of Sociology*, 50 (1) (1999), pp. 49–75.

Bulmer, Martin, Bales, Kevin, and Kish Sklar, Kathryn (eds.), *The Social Survey in Historical Perspective 1880–1940* (Cambridge, 1991).

Burchardt, Tania, Le Grand, Julian, and Piachaud, David, 'Social Exclusion in Britain 1991–1995', *Social Policy & Administration*, 33 (3) (1999), pp. 227–44.

Burgess, Simon and Propper, Carol, 'Poverty in Britain', in Paul Gregg and Jonathan Wadsworth (eds.), *The State of Working Britain* (Manchester, 1999), pp. 259–75.

Byrne, David, *Social Exclusion* (Buckingham, 1999).

Cabinet Office, Prime Minister's Strategy Unit, *Personal Responsibility and Changing Behaviour: The State of Knowledge and its Implications for Public Policy* (London, 2004).

Centre for the Analysis of Social Exclusion, HM Treasury, *Persistent Poverty and Lifetime Inequality: The Evidence* (London, 1999).

Chevalier, Louis, *Laboring Classes and Dangerous Classes in Paris During the First Half of the 19th Century* (London, 1973).

Clark, Kenneth B. and Nathan, Richard P., 'The Urban Underclass', in National Research Council, *Critical Issues for National Urban Policy: A Reconnaissance and Agenda for Further Study* (Washington, 1982), pp. 33–53.

Cottingham, Clement (ed.), *Race, Poverty, and the Urban Underclass* (Lexington, 1982).

Cresswell, Tim, *The Tramp in America* (London, 2001).

Dahrendorf, Ralf, 'The Erosion of Citizenship and its Consequences for us All', *New Statesman*, 113 (1987), pp. 12–15.

Danziger, Sheldon and Gottschalk, Peter, 'Earnings Inequality, the Spatial Concentration of Poverty, and the Underclass', *American Economic Review*, 77 (2) (1987), pp. 211–15.

Danziger, Sheldon and Gottschalk, Peter, *America Unequal* (Cambridge, Mass., 1995).

Davis, Jennifer, 'Jennings' Buildings and the Royal Borough: The Construction of the Underclass in Mid-Victorian England', in David Feldman and Gareth Stedman Jones (eds.), *Metropolis London: Histories and Representations Since 1800* (London, 1989), pp. 11–39.

Deacon, Alan, 'The Dilemmas of Welfare: Titmuss, Murray and Mead', in S. J. D. Green and R. C. Whiting (eds.), *The Boundaries of the State in Modern Britain* (Cambridge, 1996), pp. 191–212.

Deacon, Alan, 'Learning from the US? The Influence of American Ideas Upon "New Labour" Thinking on Welfare Reform', *Policy and Politics*, 28 (2000), pp. 5–18.

Deacon, Alan, *Perspectives on Welfare: Ideas, Ideologies and Policy Debates* (Buckingham, 2002).

Deacon, Alan, 'Echoes of Sir Keith? New Labour and the Cycle of Disadvantage', *Benefits*, 10, 3 (2002), pp. 179–84.

Deacon, Alan, '"Levelling the Playing Field, Activating the Players": New Labour and the "Cycle of Disadvantage"', *Policy and Politics*, 31 (2) (2003), pp. 123–37.

Deacon, Alan, 'Review Article: Different Interpretations of Agency within Welfare Debates', *Social Policy & Society*, 3, 4 (2004), pp. 447–55.

Deacon, Alan, and Mann, Kirk, 'Agency, Modernity and Social Policy', *Journal of Social Policy*, 28, 3 (1999), pp. 413–35.

Dean, Hartley, 'In Search of the Underclass', in Phillip Brown and Richard Scase (eds.), *Poor Work: Disadvantage and the Division of Labour* (Buckingham, 1991), pp. 23–39.

Dean, Hartley, 'Poverty Discourse and the Disempowerment of the Poor', *Critical Social Policy*, 35, 12, 2 (1992), pp. 79–88.

Dean, Hartley and Taylor-Gooby, Peter, *Dependency Culture: The Explosion of a Myth* (Hemel Hempstead, 1992).

Denham, Andrew and Garnett, Mark, *Keith Joseph* (Chesham, 2001).

Denham, Andrew and Garnett, Mark, 'From the "Cycle of Enrichment" to the "Cycle of Deprivation": Sir Keith Joseph, "Problem Families" and the Transmission of Disadvantage', *Benefits*, 10, 3 (2002), pp. 193–98.

Dixon, John, Carrier, Kerry, and Dogan, Rhys, 'On Investigating the "Underclass": Contending Philosophical Perspectives', *Social Policy & Society*, 4, 1 (2005), pp. 21–30.

Dolowitz, David P., 'Policy Transfer: A New Framework of Policy Analysis', in David P. Dolowitz with Rob Hulme, Mike Nellis, and Fiona O'Neill, *Policy Transfer and British Social Policy: Learning from the USA?* (Buckingham, 2000), pp. 9–37.

Duncan, Greg J., *Years of Poverty Years of Plenty: The Changing Economic Fortunes of American Workers and Families* (Ann Arbor, Michigan, 1984).

Englander, David, and O'Day, Rosemary (eds.), *Retrieved Riches: Social Investigation in Britain 1840–1914* (Aldershot, 1995).

Fairclough, Norman, *New Labour, New Language?* (London, 2000).

Field, Frank, *Losing Out: The Emergence of Britain's Underclass* (Oxford, 1989).

Field, Frank, *Making Welfare Work: Reconstructing Welfare for the Millennium* (London, 1995).

Field, Frank, *Stakeholder Welfare* (London, 1996).

Field, Frank, *Reflections on Welfare Reform* (London, 1998).

Gallie, Duncan, 'Employment, Unemployment and Social Stratification', in Duncan Gallie, (ed.), *Employment in Britain* (Oxford, 1988), pp. 465–92.

Gallie, Duncan, 'Are the Unemployed an Underclass? Some Evidence from the Social Change and Economic Life Initiative', *Sociology*, 28 (3) (1994), pp. 737–57.

Gans, Herbert J., 'Deconstructing the Underclass: The Term's Dangers as a Planning Concept', *Journal of the American Planning Association*, 56 (3) (1990), pp. 271–77.

Gans, Herbert J., 'From "Underclass" to "Undercaste": Some Observations about the Future of the Postindustrial Economy and its Major Victims', *International Journal of Urban and Regional Research*, 17 (3) (1993), pp. 327–35.

Gans, Herbert J., 'Positive Functions of the Undeserving Poor: Uses of the Underclass in America', *Politics and Society*, 22 (3) (1994), pp. 269–83.

Gans, Herbert J., *The War Against the Poor: The Underclass and Antipoverty Policy* (New York, 1995).

Giddens, Anthony, *The Class Structure of the Advanced Societies* (London, 1973).

Giddens, Anthony, *The Third Way: The Renewal of Social Democracy* (Cambridge, 1998).

Giddens, Anthony, *The Third Way and its Critics* (Cambridge, 2000).

Glasgow, Douglas G., *The Black Underclass: Poverty, Unemployment, and Entrapment of Ghetto Youth* (San Francisco, 1980).

Gordon, David and Spicker, Paul (eds.), *The International Glossary on Poverty* (London, 1999).

Le Grand, Julian, 'Knights, Knaves or Pawns? Human Behaviour and Social Policy', *Journal of Social Policy*, 26 (2) (1997), pp. 149–69.

Le Grand, Julian, *Motivation, Agency and Public Policy: Of Knights & Knaves, Pawns & Queens* (Oxford, 2003).

Harris, Bernard, 'Seebohm Rowntree and the Measurement of Poverty, 1899–1951', in Bradshaw and Sainsbury (eds.), *Getting the Measure of Poverty*, pp. 60–84.

Harris, José, *Unemployment and Politics: A Study in English Social Policy 1886–1914* (Oxford, 1972).

Harris, José, *William Beveridge: A Biography* (Oxford, 1977).

Harris, José, 'Between Civic Virtue and Social Darwinism: The Concept of the Residuum', in Englander and O'Day (eds.), *Retrieved Riches*, pp. 67–88.

Hennock, E. P., 'Poverty and Social Theory in England: The Experience of the Eighteen-Eighties', *Social History*, 1 (1976), pp. 67–91.

Hennock, E. P., 'Concepts of Poverty in the British Social Surveys From Charles Booth to Arthur Bowley', in Bulmer, Bales, and Kish Sklar (eds.), *Social Survey*, pp. 189–216.

Hills, John, Le Grand, Julian, and Piachaud, David (eds.), *Understanding Social Exclusion* (Oxford, 2002).

Jacobs, John, 'The Scroungers who Never Were: The Effects of the 1989 Social Security Act', in Robert Page and John Baldock (eds.), *Social Policy Review 6* (Canterbury, 1994), pp. 126–45.

James, Edward, *America Against Poverty* (London, 1970).

Jarvis, Sarah and Jenkins, Stephen P., 'How Much Income Mobility is There in Britain?', *Economic Journal*, 108 (1998), pp. 428–43.

Jencks, Christopher and Peterson, Paul E. (eds.), *The Urban Underclass* (Washington, 1991).

Jones, Gareth Stedman, *Outcast London: A Study in the Relationship Between Classes in Victorian Society* (Oxford, 1971, new edn., 1984).

Jones, Greta, *Social Hygiene in Twentieth Century Britain* (London, 1986).

Katz, Michael, *The Undeserving Poor: From the War on Poverty to the War on Welfare* (New York, 1989).

Katz, Michael B. (ed.), *The "Underclass" Debate: Views from History* (Princeton, 1993).

Katz, Michael B, *Improving Poor People: The Welfare State, The 'Underclass', and Urban Schools as History* (Princeton, 1995).

Kempson, Elaine, *Life on a Low Income* (York, 1996).

Lee, Anthony and Hills, John, *New Cycles of Disadvantage? Report of a Conference Organised by CASE on Behalf of ESRC for HM Treasury* (London, 1998).

Leggett, John C., *Class, Race, and Labor: Working Class Consciousness in Detroit* (New York, 1968).

Levitas, Ruth, *The Inclusive Society? Social Exclusion and New Labour* (London, 1998).

Lewis, Jane, 'The Place of Social Investigation, Social Theory and Social Work in the Approach to late Victorian and Edwardian Social Problems: The Case of Beatrice Webb and Helen Bosanquet', in Bulmer, Bales and Kish Sklar (eds), *Social Survey*, pp. 148–69.

Lewis, Jane, 'Social Facts, Social Theory and Social Change: The ideas of Booth in Relation to those of Beatrice Webb, Octavia Hill and Helen Bosanquet', in Englander and O'Day (eds.), *Retrieved Riches*, pp. 49–66.

Lister, Ruth (ed.), *Charles Murray and the Underclass: The Developing Debate* (London, 1996).

Lister, Ruth, *Poverty* (Cambridge, 2004).

Littlewood, Paul *et al*, *Social Exclusion in Europe: Problems and Paradigms* (Aldershot, 1999).

Loney, Martin, *Community Against Development: The British Community Development Project 1968–78 – A Study of Government Incompetence* (London, 1983).

Macdonald, Robert (ed.), *Youth, the 'Underclass' and Social Exclusion* (London, 1997).

Macnicol, John, 'In Pursuit of the Underclass', *Journal of Social Policy*, 16 (3) (1987), pp. 293–318.

Macnicol, John, 'Is there an Underclass? The Lessons from America', in Michael White (ed.), *Unemployment, Public Policy and the Changing Labour Market* (London, 1994), pp. 29–39.

Macnicol, John, 'Perspectives on the Idea of an Underclass', in John Edwards and Jean-Paul Révauger (eds.), *Discourse and Inequality in France and Britain* (Aldershot, 1998), pp. 161–74.

Macnicol, John, 'From "Problem Family" to "Underclass", 1945–95', in Rodney Lowe and Helen Fawcett (eds.), *Welfare Policy in Britain: The Road from 1945* (London, 1999), pp. 69–93.

Mann, Kirk, *The Making of an English 'Underclass'? The Social Divisions of Welfare and Labour* (Buckingham, 1992).

Mann, Kirk, 'Watching the Defectives: Observers of the Underclass in the USA, Britain and Australia', *Critical Social Policy*, 14 (2) (1994), pp. 79–99.

Mann, Kirk and Roseneil, Sasha, '"Some Mothers Do 'Ave 'Em": Backlash and the Gender Politics of the Underclass Debate', *Journal of Gender Studies*, 3, 3 (1994), pp. 317–31.

Marshall, Gordon, Roberts, Stephen and Burgoyne, Carole, 'Social Class and Underclass in Britain and the USA', *British Journal of Sociology*, 47, 1 (1996), pp. 22–44.

Massey, Douglas S. and Denton, Nancy A., *American Apartheid: Segregation and the Making of the Underclass* (Cambridge, Mass., 1993).

Matza, David, 'The Disreputable Poor', in Reinhard Bendix and Seymour Martin Lipset (eds.), *Class, Status and Power: Social Stratification in Comparative Perspective* (London, 1953, new edn., 1966), pp. 289–302.

Matza, David, 'Poverty and Disrepute', in Robert K. Merton and Robert A. Nisbet (eds.), *Contemporary Social Problems* (New York, 1961, third edn., 1971), pp. 601–56.

McKibbin, Ross, 'Class and Poverty in Edwardian England', in Ross McKibbin, *The Ideologies of Class: Social Relations in Britain 1880–1950* (Oxford, 1990), pp. 167–96.

McKibbin, Ross, 'The "Social Psychology" of Unemployment in Inter-War Britain', in McKibbin, *Ideologies of Class*, pp. 228–58.

McLanahan, Sara and Garfinkel, Irwin, 'Single Mothers, the Underclass, and Social Policy', *Annals of the American Academy of Political and Social Science*, 501 (1989), pp. 92–104.

Mingione, Enzo (ed.), *Urban Poverty and the Underclass: A Reader* (Oxford, 1996).

Morris, L. D., 'Is there a British Underclass?', *International Journal of Urban and Regional Research*, 17 (3) (1993), pp. 404–12.

Morris, Lydia, *Dangerous Class: The Underclass and Social Citizenship* (London, 1994).

Morris, Lydia and Irwin, Sarah, 'Employment Histories and the Concept of the Underclass', *Sociology*, 26 (3) (1992), pp. 401–20.

Morris, Michael, 'From the Culture of Poverty to the Underclass: An Analysis of a Shift in Public Language', *American Sociologist*, 20 (2) (1989), pp. 123–33.

Nolan, Brian and Whelan, Christopher T., *Resources, Deprivation, and Poverty* (Oxford, 1996).

Novak, Tony, 'Poverty and the "Underclass"', in Michael Lavalette and Alan Pratt (eds.), *Social Policy: A Conceptual and Theoretical Introduction* (London, 1997), pp. 214–27.

O'Connor, Alice, *Poverty Knowledge: Social Science, Social Policy and the Poor in Twentieth Century US History* (Princeton, 2001).

Office of the Deputy Prime Minister, *Breaking the Cycle: Taking Stock of Progress and Priorities for the Future: A Report by the Social Exclusion Unit* (London, 2004).

Oppenheim, Carey and Harker, Lisa, *Poverty: The Facts* (London, 1996).

Pick, Daniel, *Faces of Degeneration: A European Disorder, c.1848–c.1918* (Cambridge, 1989).

Pinkney, Alphonso, *The Myth of Black Progress* (Cambridge, 1984).

Presidents' Commission for a National Agenda for the Eighties, 'Chapter Five: Social Distress and the Urban Underclass', in Donald A. Hicks (ed.), *Urban America in the Eighties: Perspectives and Prospects* (New Brunswick, 1982), pp. 53–63.

Rex, John, *The Ghetto and the Underclass: Essays on Race and Social Policy* (Aldershot, 1988).

Ricketts, Erol R. and Sawhill, Isabel V., 'Defining and Measuring the Underclass', *Journal of Policy Analysis and Management*, 7 (1988), pp. 316–25.

Rigdon, Susan M., *The Culture Façade: Art, Science and Politics in the Work of Oscar Lewis* (Urbana and Chicago, 1988).

Ritchie, Helen, Casebourne, Jo, and Rick, Jo, *Understanding Workless People and Communities: A Literature Review* (London, 2005).

Robinson, Fred, and Gregson, Nicky, 'The "Underclass": A Class Apart?', *Critical Social Policy*, 34 (1992), pp. 38–51.

Room, Graham (ed.), *Beyond the Threshold: The Measurement and Analysis of Social Exclusion* (Bristol, 1995).

Schmitter Heisler, Barbara, 'A Comparative Perspective on the Underclass: Questions of Urban Poverty, Race, and Citizenship', *Theory and Society*, 20 (4) (1991), pp. 455–83.

Silver, Hilary, 'Social Exclusion and Social Solidarity: Three Paradigms', *International Labour Review*, 133 (1994), pp. 531–78.

Smith, David J. (ed.), *Understanding the Underclass* (London, 1992).

Starkey, Pat, 'The Medical Officer of Health, the Social Worker, and the Problem Family, 1943 to 1968: The Case of Family Service Units', *Social History of Medicine*, 11 (3) (1998), pp. 421–41.

Starkey, Pat, 'The Feckless Mother: Women, Poverty and Social Workers in Wartime and Post-War England', *Women's History Review*, 9 (3) (2000), pp. 539–57.

Starkey, Pat, *Families & Social Workers: The Work of Family Service Units 1940–1985* (Liverpool, 2000).

Such, Elizabeth, and Walker, Robert, 'Falling Behind? Research on Transmitted Deprivation', *Benefits*, 10, 3 (2002), pp. 185–92.

Timmins, Nicholas, *The Five Giants: A Biography of the Welfare State* (London, 1995, second edn., 2003).

Townsend, Peter, *Poverty in the United Kingdom: A Survey of Household Resources and Standards of Living* (Harmondsworth, 1979).

Treble, James H., *Urban Poverty in Britain 1830–1914* (London, 1979).

Walker, Alan, and Walker, Carol (eds.), *Britain Divided: The Growth of Social Exclusion in the 1980s and 1990s* (London, 1997).

Ward, David, *Poverty, Ethnicity, and the American City, 1840–1925: Changing Conceptions of the Slum and the Ghetto* (Cambridge, 1989).

Webb, Steven, *Poverty Dynamics in Great Britain: Preliminary Analysis from the British Household Panel Survey* (London, 1995).

Welshman, John, 'In Search of the "Problem Family": Public Health and Social Work in England and Wales, 1940–70', *Social History of Medicine*, 9 (3) (1996), pp. 447–65.

Welshman, John, 'The Social History of Social Work: The Issue of the "Problem Family", 1940–70', *British Journal of Social Work*, 29 (1999), pp. 457–75.

Welshman, John, 'Evacuation, Hygiene, and Social Policy: The *Our Towns* Report of 1943', *Historical Journal*, 42 (3) (1999), pp. 781–807.

Welshman, John, 'The Cycle of Deprivation and the Concept of the Underclass', *Benefits*, 10 (3) (2002), pp. 199–205.

Welshman, John, 'The Unknown Titmuss', *Journal of Social Policy*, 33, 2 (2004), pp. 225–47.

Welshman, John, 'Ideology, Social Science, and Public Policy: The Debate over Transmitted Deprivation', *Twentieth Century British History*, 16, 3 (2005), pp. 306–41.

Welshman, John, 'The Concept of the Unemployable', *Economic History Review* (forthcoming).

Westergaard, John, 'About and Beyond the "Underclass": Some Notes on Influences of Social Climate on British Sociology Today', *Sociology*, 26 (1992), pp. 575–87.

Williams, Fiona, Popay, Jennie, and Oakley, Ann (eds.), *Welfare Research: A Critical Review* (London, 1999).

Veit Wilson, J. H., 'Paradigms of Poverty: A Rehabilitation of B. S. Rowntree', *Journal of Social Policy*, 15 (1986), pp. 69–99.

Wilson, William Julius, 'Cycles of Deprivation and the Underclass Debate', *Social Service Review*, 59 (1985), pp. 541–59.

Wilson, William Julius, *The Truly Disadvantaged: The Inner City, The Underclass, and Public Policy* (Chicago, 1987).

Wilson, William Julius, 'The Underclass: Issues, Perspectives, and Public Policy', *Annals of the American Academy of Political and Social Science*, 501 (1989), pp. 182–92.

Wilson, William Julius, *The Ghetto Underclass: Social Science Perspectives* (London, 1993).

Index

Abel-Smith, Brian 102
Aberdeen 171
Aberdeen, University of 121
Abnormal families 78
Abortion 113
Absolute poverty 33
Abyss 9
Adonis, Andrew 157
Age discrimination 10
Agency xi, xxiii–xxvii, 96, 170, 180, 189,
    200–3, 207, 210
Aid for Families with Dependent Children
    (AFDC) xv, 96, 136–37, 167
Alcock, Pete xxi
Alden, Percy 24
All Souls College, Oxford 114, 116
Altruism xxv, 190, 201
American Civil War 128
American Dream 87
American Planning Association 153
Anarchism 7
Anderson, Nels 49
Anthropology 88–92, 93, 96–97, 106, 115,
    121, 196
Anti-social behaviour 196
Aponte, Robert xiii, 151
Area-based initiatives 100, 121
A Social Problem Group? (1937) 62–63
Atkinson, Tony 114, 121
Atlantic Monthly, The magazine
    132–33
Attitude scales 40
Auletta, Ken 127, 131–32, 134, 138–39,
    141–42, 149, 161, 207
Australia 178–79, 187

Bagguley, Paul 177–78
Balliol College, Oxford 26
Balzac, Honoré de 6
Bane, Mary Jo 147, 197
Banfield, Edward C. 91, 131–32
Banlieues 185
Barker family 121–22
Barnett, Samuel A. 2–3, 10–11, 16, 20
Beggars 7, 14, 51, 131, 169
Behavioural dependency xxvi
Behind Ghetto Walls (1970) 98
Belgium 25, 32
Bell, Lady Florence 17
Bentham, Jeremy 5
Berghman, Jos 186
Berthoud, Richard 114, 117–18, 123–24
Betting 32–33, 42
Beurs 185
Beveridge Lecture (1999) 194–95
Beveridge, William xxviii, 12, 21, 26, 28,
    42–43, 45, 48, 205
Biological casualties 71
Biological determinism 83, 207
Birkenhead 164, 168
Birmingham 7, 75, 110, 159–60
Birth control 45, 47, 73, 80
Bitter Cry of Outcast London, The (1883–84) 9
Blacker, Carlos P. 54–55, 57–59, 62–63, 70–73,
    119
Blair, Tony ix–x, xxvii, 183, 190–92
Blaming the victim xviii, xxv, 102, 116, 154,
    168, 180
Blaming the Victim (1971) 98, 200
Blaxter, Mildred 121
Board of Control 56, 58

Board of Education 56

Booth, Charles xxviii, 1–3, 11–14, 16–17, 19–24, 29–30, 33, 36, 38, 45, 49, 63, 69, 119, 205–6

Booth, William 2, 9, 16

Bosanquet, Bernard 18–19

Bosanquet, Helen xxviii, 2, 13, 17, 19, 20, 23, 32

Boston 94

Boston College 151

Bott, Elizabeth 100

Bovis construction company 107

Bowley, Arthur xxviii, 21, 29, 34–36, 43–45, 63

Boyd Orr, John 62

Boyle, Edward 100

Bradford 75

Bradshaw, Jonathan 29, 34

Branford, Victor 38, 43

Breadline Britain survey 190

Breaking the Cycle (2004) 199

Bright, John 7–8

Bristol 68, 71–72, 75, 77, 79–80

Bristol, University of 114

Britain Divided (1997) 188

British Election Survey (1987) 174

British Federation of Social Workers 81

British Household Panel Survey (BHPS) 194, 197

British Medical Association 59

British Medical Journal 199

British Social Attitudes Survey (1989) 174

British Sociological Association 178

Brock, Laurence 58

Brockington, C. Fraser 78

Brodie, Marc 4

Brookings Institution 140

Brown, John 12

Brown, Muriel 123–26

Buck, Nick 173–74

Buckingham, Alan 169–70

Buckinghamshire 165

Bukharin, Nikolai 7

Bulger, James 177

Burchardt, Tania 193–94

Burgess, Simon 197

Burgoyne, Carole 172–73

Burn, J. L. 78

Burnett-Hurst, A. R. 34–35

Burns, John 26

Burt, Cyril 54, 56

Cabot Lodge, George 139

California, University of (Berkeley) xiv

Cambridge Institute of Criminology 109

Caradog Jones, David 41, 47, 57, 59–65, 70–71

Care Committees 37

Carr-Saunders, A. M. 54–55, 63

Carson, Emmett D. 150–51

Carter, Jimmy 141

Casual earnings 13

Casual employment 15, 28, 36

Casual labour 14, 24, 28, 37, 42–43, 50, 169

Casual poor 17, 48

Casual wards 25–26, 48, 50

Catholic Church 59

Cattell, Raymond 62

Census data 138, 140, 147, 162, 164–65

Central Association for Mental Welfare 56, 58

Central Statistical Office 114

Centre for the Analysis of Social Exclusion (CASE) (London) 184, 193, 195–96

Centre for Policy Studies (London) 108

Challenge to Affluence (1963) 129

Chance, William 26

Character 11–13, 16, 18–20, 22, 24, 26–28, 37, 42–43, 53, 71, 73–74, 190

Charities 10, 31, 51, 61, 77

Charity Organisation Review 18, 32

Charity Organisation Society (COS) xii, xxvi, 2, 8, 17, 21, 34, 46, 55, 190

Charterhouse School 26

Chicago 131–33, 142

Chicago School 49, 92–93, 138

Chicago, University of 144, 146, 151

Chief Medical Officer 79–80

Child poverty xxvii, xxix, 107, 184, 194–200, 203, 206

Child Poverty Action Group (CPAG) 76, 110, 167, 179, 188

Children and their Primary Schools (1967) 100

Children and Young Persons Act (1963) 68, 80, 84

Children's Departments 68, 80, 84, 210

Children of Bondage 93

Children of Sanchez, The (1961) 89

Chirac, Jacques 184

Christian Socialism 190

Church, A. G. 58

City University of New York 140, 150

Civilising process 166

Clark, Kenneth B. 138

Class 'A' (Booth) 13–15, 33

Class 'A' (Rowntree) 31–33

Class 'B' (Booth) 13–15, 21

Cleveland 147

Clinical psychology 89

Coates, Ken 102–5

Coffield, Frank 121–24

Cohen, Alan 68

Cold War 88

Columbia University (New York) 26, 39, 153

Committee for Legalising Eugenic Sterilisation 58

Common lodging houses 49–50

Communist Manifesto (1848) 6

Communitarianism 191

Community action 87, 101–2, 108

Community Action Areas 87, 101

Community Action Programme 87

Community Development Projects (CDPs) 101–2, 105, 113, 209–10

Comprehensive Spending Review 198

Concentration effects xvii, 145, 153, 189

Conservative Party 107, 110–11, 164, 168, 187

Conservative Political Centre 112

Contemporary Review, The 9–10, 27

Cooper, Yvette 126

Co-ordinating Committees 82–84

Coping xxiii, xxv, 189

Corner men 14

Cornerville 93

Cottingham, Clement 138

Coventry 101, 171

Cresswell, Tim 47, 50

Criminal class 6, 14, 19, 26

Criminal justice system 128, 164

Criminals 13, 22, 24, 28, 52, 57, 60–61, 63, 69, 92, 124, 128, 130–33, 139, 150, 162–67, 169, 178, 180

Cuba 90

Cultural sociology 17

Culture of poverty 69, 73, 85, 87–106, 111, 114–17, 119, 121–22, 126–27, 130–32, 140–41, 144–46, 150–54, 157, 160–61, 164, 168–69, 176, 178, 181, 196, 205–10

Cycle of deprivation 65, 69, 73, 84–85, 88, 90, 96, 102, 106–27, 157–58, 161, 168, 175–76, 178, 180–81, 184, 195–96, 198–99, 202–3, 205–10

Cycles of disadvantage 107, 118–20, 125, 164, 184–203

Dack family 53

Dahrendorf, Ralf 161, 168–69

Daily Dispatch, The newspaper 60

Daily News, The newspaper 54

Dangerous class xxviii, 2, 6, 19, 64, 177–78

Danziger, Sheldon 151

Dark Ghetto (1960) 138

Darling, Alistair 193

Darwin, Charles 3

Das Capital xii

Davis, Allison 93

Davis, Jennifer 6

Deacon, Alan xxvi, 190–91, 199–200, 202

Dean, Hartley xiii, xxi, 179

Deep South 93

Degeneration 3, 10, 12, 16, 19, 43, 50–52, 55, 63, 110

Delinquency 83, 92–94, 113, 179

Democrat Party 130

Dendy, Mary 17

Denmark 25

Denton, Nancy A. 146–47
Department of Education and Science 114
Department of Health and Social Security
  (DHSS) 107–8, 111, 114–20, 125, 196,
  207
Department of Housing 114
Department of Social and Administrative
  Studies (Oxford) 101
Departmental Committee on the Relief of the
  Casual Poor (1929–30) 48
Departmental Committee on Vagrancy
  (1904–06) 25–26, 48
Departmental Committee on Voluntary
  Sterilisation (1932) 58–60, 63–64
Derelict families 76–77
Deserving and undeserving poor x–xi, xiv,
  xvii–xviii, xxviii, 2–4, 8, 17–20, 34, 91, 154,
  162, 170, 205–6
Detroit 129, 158
Deviance xiv, 82, 130, 150–52
Dimensions of Parenthood (1974) 116
Discouraged workers 135
Discourses xxviii, 130, 173, 176–77, 179–81,
  183, 185, 187–88, 192, 201, 206
Dispossessed 128
Disreputable poor xiv–xvi
District nurses 70
Divorce Reform Act (1969) 165
Dock strike (1889) 3, 9, 16
Donnison, David 81–82, 102
Drage, Geoffrey 24
Dregs xv, 49, 57
Drink 15, 32–33, 61
Dugdale, Robert 51
Duncan, Greg 148–49
Durham, University of 123

Eastabrook, Arthur H. 52
East Coast 93
Easterhouse estate (Glasgow) 164
Eastern Europe 9, 90
Economically inactive households 163–64,
  172–74

Economic and Social Research Council
  (ESRC) xxiii–xxvii, 171, 184, 195, 199
Economic Club 18
Economic moral failure 59
Economic Opportunity Act (1964) 87, 101
Economist, The 100
Edgbaston speech 110–11
Education Action Zones x, 184
Educational Priority Areas (EPAs) 88, 100–1,
  105, 209–10
Education vouchers 125
Efficiency and Empire (1901) 10
Eisenberg, Philip 39
Ellwood, David 197
Employment 15
Engels, Frederick xii, 6–7
Entry-level jobs 143
Essen, Juliet 121, 196
Essex, University of 104, 114
Ethnography 88, 93, 97–98, 106
Etzioni, Amitai 191
Eugenics xvii, 1, 26–27, 31–32, 34, 45–65, 68,
  77–80, 110–11, 126, 207
Eugenics Review 53–54, 70
Eugenics Society xx, xxviii, 44–45, 53–65, 68,
  70–75, 77–79, 81, 83, 85, 158, 175, 206
Eugenic Sterilisation Law (Germany) (1933)
  59
European Commission 185
European Union 185
Euthanasia 59
Evacuation xxviii, 65, 69, 77, 80
Exeter, University of 105, 116

Fabian Society xxiii, xxvi, 21, 46
Fairclough, Norman x–xi, 192–93
Family allowances 69, 111, 146
Family departments 82
Family failure 76
Family pedigrees 53, 55, 63
Family planning 80, 87, 109–11, 113–14
Family Service Units xx, 64, 68–69, 74–76,
  79–85, 205–6, 210
Family Welfare Association 81

Farm colonies 17, 24–25
Fathers 162, 166
Feckless mothers 68
Fecklessness 72
Feebleminded 46, 48, 50–53, 56–57, 60, 67
Field, Frank xxvi, 111, 167–69, 181, 190, 194
Fielding family 121–22
First World War xxii, 3, 21, 23–24, 34, 36, 43, 45, 53, 56, 59, 65, 85, 208
Fitness 46
Five Families (1959) 89
Football hooliganism 161
Forgotten people ix, 191
Fowler, Norman 110
Fox, Evelyn 56
Fractional selection xv
France x, 159, 183–85, 187, 202
Frazier, Franklin 92–93, 95–98, 106
Freedman, Maurice 114
Front National 185
Fuller, Roger 121

Gallie, Duncan 170–73
Galton, Sir Francis 45
Gambling 32, 40
Gangs 94
Gans, Herbert xvii, xxii, 94, 97–100, 153–54, 178, 207
Garrotting panic (1862) 6
Genetics 83, 196
Genuinely seeking work 38, 50
Germany 25, 32, 159, 186, 189
Ghetto poor 146–47
Ghettos 133, 138–39, 144–48, 157
Giddens, Anthony 158–59, 170–71, 188–89, 191
Giddings, Franklin H. 51
Glass, William R. 139
Ginsburg, Norman xii
Glasgow, Douglas 141–43
Glasgow, University of 117
Glazer, Nathan 96
Glennerster, Howard 106, 196, 203

Goddard, Henry Herbert 51
Golding, Peter xviii
Gottschalk, Peter 151
Gray, Frank 49
Greater San Juan (Puerto Rico) 89
Great Society 137
Green, David G. 164
Growth, Competitiveness, Employment (1994) 185
Guardian, The newspaper x, 199
Gulbenkian Foundation 102
Gursslin, Orville 96

Habitual criminals 27, 51
Habitual Criminals Act (1869) 6
Habitual slum dwellers 57
Habitual vagrants 25–27, 48–50
Hall, Penelope 83
Halsey, A. H. xi, 101–2
Hannerz, Ulf 97–99, 129, 141, 145, 155
Happy Hickory family 53
Hard to reach xiv, 210
Harman, Harriet 193
Harrington, Michael 91
Harris, Elisha 51
Harris, José 3, 7, 12–13, 16, 19, 26–28
Harrison, David 99
Harrow School 107
Hartlepool 165, 172
Harvard Business School 139
Harvard University 137
Has Poverty Diminished? (1925) 36
Hay Hill, Alsager 8
Head lice 79
Head Start 199
Health Action Zones x, 184
Health visitors 70, 73, 78–82, 84
Heath, Anthony 174
Heath, Edward 110–11
Heinemann series on transmitted deprivation 120–25
Helpable and unhelpable 18
Hennock, Peter 3, 8, 13, 16, 31
Heredity 51–55, 58, 60–61, 64–65, 82, 176

Heredity and the Social Problem Group (1933) 63

Herefordshire 78–79

Heroin 127

Hertfordshire 78

Hill folk 5

Hill, Octavia 13, 21

Hills, John x

Hispanics 131, 138–39, 142, 144, 152

Historical materialism 7

Hobcraft, John 196

Hobo, The (1921) 49

Hogben, Lancelot 54, 62

Holland 25

Holman, Bob 117

Holy Trinity Church (Liverpool) 73

Home helps 79–80, 112

Home-made casualties 112

Home Office 79, 101–2, 105

Homelessness 73, 199

Homeless Persons Act (1977) 163

Home-Start 125

Hooliganism xviii

Horder, Lord 63, 71

Hostels 73–74, 77, 110

Howard University 92, 142

Hugo, Victor 6

Hull 57

Hungate (York) 30

Hustlers 132

Hutton, Will 188

Huxley, Julian 54

Hyndman, H. M. 2, 10, 16, 20

Idlers 11

Illegitimacy xx, 51–52, 92, 94, 96, 111, 128, 130, 133–40, 155, 162–67, 176–77, 180–81, 207

Illegitimacy ratios 135, 162, 164

Illinois, University of 88

Immaturity 76, 83

Imperial College, London 104

Improvidence 72

Incentive structures 137

Income dynamics x, 175, 194, 210

Income Support 166

In Darkest England and the Way Out (1890) 9, 16

India 90

Industrial communities 12

Industrial Democracy (1897) 22–23

Industrial schools 14, 37

Infant mortality 31, 63

Ingleby report (Report of the Committee on Children and Young Persons) (1960) 84

Insertion 183–85

Instability or infirmity of character 71–72

Institute for Economic Affairs (IEA) (London) 162, 164, 180

Institute of Psychiatry (London) 114, 118

Institute of Social Anthropology (Oxford) 114

Interdepartmental Committee on Physical Deterioration (1904) 2

Intergenerational continuities xvi, 31, 51, 53–65, 80, 87, 89–90, 106–7, 109, 112–13, 115, 118–21, 123, 125, 129, 138, 143, 149, 152, 158, 166, 170, 175–76, 183, 195–96, 198, 203, 206, 208

Intractable ineducability 71–73

Invulnerables 124

Ireland, Republic of 173–75

Irregular employment 15

Irregular labour 14

Irresponsibility 72, 93

Irvine, Elizabeth 81

Irwin, Sarah 172

Italian migrants 93–95

Jahoda, Marie 39, 42

Jargowsky, Paul A. 147

Jarvis, Sarah 197

Jencks, Christopher 140

Jenkins, Stephen 197

Jewish migrants 9

Johnson, Lyndon B. 87

Jones, Greta 46

Jones, Jacqueline 128

Jordan, Bill xvii, 5, 105, 116
Joseph, Sir Keith xviii, xxviii, 73, 106–14, 116,
   118–20, 122–23, 125–26, 157, 175, 195–96,
   203, 205, 206, 209
Joseph Rowntree Foundation xxiv, 170, 174
Journal of the Royal Statistical Society 13–15,
   59
Judgementalism xxvi
Jukes family 51–53, 152, 209
Juvenile labour 36

Kallikak family 51, 53, 152, 209
Kasarda, John 141–42
Katz, Michael xvi–xvii, xxiv, 90, 129, 154
Keating, Peter 9
Keele, University of 121
Kelly, Edmond 26
Kempson, Elaine 174–75
Kennedy, John 87, 91
Kent 80
Keynesianism 62, 65
Keywords (1976) xii
King, Desmond 46, 59
King's School, Chester 59
Kinship 89
Kircaldy 171
Knaves xxv, 200–1
Knights xxv, 200–1, 208
Kolvin, Israel 120
Kornblum, William 150
Kuhn, Thomas 187

Labelling xiv–xviii, 81, 91, 122, 128, 130, 154,
   183, 187, 205, 207
Labour colonies 1, 3, 9, 12, 15–16, 20, 22,
   24–28, 38, 43, 50, 52
Labour Commission 24
Labour exchanges 12, 28, 42, 48, 50
Labour force attachment 144, 173, 175
Labour force participation rates 135, 138, 163
Labour Force Survey 174
Labour market segmentation theory 140
Labour Party 46, 50, 59, 64, 70, 164, 172, 175,
   190

Labour tests 27
Ladner, Walter W. 151–52
Lamar University 140
Lamont, Norman 110
Lamport and Holt Steamship Company
   12
Lane Committee 113
Latent poverty 134–38
La Vida (1966) 89, 104
Lazarsfeld, Paul 39–40
Leacock, Eleanor Burke 97–98
Lee, Peter 173
Leeds 107–8, 111
Leggett, John 129–30, 141, 158–59
Le Grand, Julian xxv, 193–94, 200–2
Leiby, James 92
Leicester 75, 80
Leisure class xv, 13
Lemann, Nicholas 127, 132–34, 139, 141
Lenoir, René 184
Less eligibility 5
Levitas, Ruth x, 192–93
Lewis, E. O. 48, 56–57, 60, 72
Lewis, Jane 13, 19, 21, 23
Lewis, Oscar xvi–xvii, xxviii, 17, 69, 88–92,
   96–99, 102, 104–6, 114, 116, 119, 122,
   130–32, 134, 141, 144–45, 157, 205–6
Lidbetter, E. J. 47, 53–55, 116, 119
Liebow, Elliot 95, 97–98, 106, 129, 143
Life and Labour of the People of London
   (1889–1903) 12–13, 15–16
Life skills 127, 131
Lister, Ruth xxvii, 179–80, 201–2
Livelihood and Poverty (1915) 34–36
Liverpool 12, 47, 57, 59, 73–77, 101, 165
Liverpool Post, The 60
Llewellyn-Smith, Hubert 49
Loafers xxvi, 11, 13–15, 17, 40, 169, 201
Loane, Margaret 17
Local authorities 71, 75–77, 79, 81–83, 108,
   210
Local Education Committees 56
Local Improvement Committees 8
Loewenstein, Gaither 140

London:
  Aylesbury housing estate ix, 191
  Bethnal Green 14, 53
  Deptford 49
  East End 4, 29, 53–65
  Hackney School Board Division 14
  Islington 49
  Jennings' Buildings 6
  Kensington 6, 49, 71–72
  Lambeth 183, 191
  Mansfield House Settlement 24
  Mile End 13
  Newham 101
  Paddington 49
  Poplar 13, 49
  Shoreditch 14, 17
  Southwark 49, 101, 191
  Stepney 13, 49
  St George's in the East 13
  St Pancras 49
  Stockwell Park School ix, 183, 191
  Tower Hamlets 13–14
  Toynbee Hall 2, 10, 194
  Westminster 108
  Whitechapel 13
  Woolwich 49
London matchgirls strike (1888) 9
London School of Economics 34, 36, 54,
  81–82, 123, 158, 184, 193, 196
Lone mothers xx, 5, 51–52, 92, 94, 96, 111,
  128, 130, 133–40, 155, 162–67, 176–77,
  180–81, 207
Loney, Martin 101–2
Longitudinal data sets 109, 115, 121, 147–49,
  174, 186, 189, 196, 202
Lord Mayor's Fund 27
Losing Ground (1984) 134–38, 141, 144, 155,
  162–64, 167, 180
Lower-class culture 87–89, 91–96, 105, 129,
  133, 206
Lower-class value stretch 94, 97–98
Low Pay Unit 167
Lujan, Carolina 89
Lumpenproletariat xii, xv, xxviii, 2, 6, 7, 19, 130

Luton 70–72

Macdiarmid, Hugh xii
Maclean, John xii, 158
Macmillan, Harold 108
Macnicol, John xii–xiii, xviii–xxii, 45–47,
  55, 59–60, 68, 99, 132, 154–55, 175–77,
  206
Madge, Nicola 114, 118–20, 122–26
Magdalen College, Oxford 107
Magnet, Myron 139
Mainstream working class 129–30, 160
Making Welfare Work (1995) 168, 190, 194
Maladjustment 109, 117–18
Mallet, Bernard 57
Malthus, Thomas 2, 5
Manchester 74–75, 78, 81, 165
Manhattan Institute 137
Mann, Kirk xxi–xxii, xxvi, 177–79, 187
Manpower Demonstration Research
  Programme 127
Mansion House Unemployed Committee 24,
  27
Marginal working class 129–30
Marienthal (Austria) 38–39, 42
Marie Stopes Foundation 73
Marquand, David 191
Marshall, Alfred 3, 9, 16, 20
Marshall, Gordon 172–73
Marshall, T. H. 167
Martin family 121–22
Marxism xii-xiii, xxvi, 2, 6–7, 19, 130, 138,
  150, 160, 170
Massey, Douglas S. 146–47
Matza, David xiv, xvii
Mayhew, Henry 6, 162
Mazumdar, Pauline 46
McBriar, Angus 18
McKibbin, Ross 17, 40–41, 172
McLaughlin, Eithne xxiv
Mead, Lawrence xxvi, 190, 199
Medical Officers of Health (MOsH) xx, 45,
  57, 67–73, 76–80, 82, 84
Medical Research Council 114

Medical Research Council Child Psychiatry Unit 196
Memphis 147
Mental deficiency 1, 4, 17, 24, 45–46, 48–52, 56–61, 63–65, 69, 77, 209
Mental health 58, 73, 91, 132
Mental poverty 64
Merseyside Social Survey (1934) 41, 59–61, 65
Merton, Robert 82
Mexico 90–91
Mexico City 89
Michigan, University of 147–49, 151
Middlesbrough 165
Middleton, Sue xviii
Middle-Way 62, 65
Migration 132–33, 141–42, 144–48, 159, 207
Miller, Mike xxiii
Miller, Walter B. 94–95, 97, 100
Milwaukee 147
Minimum standard 35
Ministry of Education 79
Ministry of Health 58, 72, 75, 77, 79
Ministry of Labour 41
Mishra, Ramesh xxiii
Monetarism 108
Moore, Robert 157, 159
Moral Education League 46
Morally deficient 22, 61
Morecambe 173
More, Thomas 2, 5
Morning Post, The newspaper 27
Morris, Lydia xxii, 172
Morris, Michael xvi, 151, 153
Mott, Frederick 54
Moynihan, Daniel Patrick 96
Moynihan Report (1965) xxvi–xxvii, 88, 96–97, 106, 144, 190
Murray, Charles xxii, xxvi, 134–39, 141, 155, 157, 162–69, 176–77, 180–81, 190, 199, 207–8, 210
Muzzio, Douglas 149–50
Myrdal, Gunnar xii, xvii, 129–31, 141, 153, 158
Myth of Black Progress, The (1984) 143

Nam family 53
Nathan, Richard P. 138
National Association for the Care and Control of the Feebleminded 46
National Association for the Promotion of Social Science 8
National Casework Committee 74
National Child Development Study (NCDS) 109, 115, 121, 169–70, 196
National Children's Bureau 121
National Conference on the Prevention of Destitution (1911) 53
National efficiency 10, 45
National Health Service Act (1946) 77
National Research Council Committee on National Urban Poverty (USA) 138
National Unemployed Workers Movement 38
Nazi social policy 59, 65, 70
Negro families 88, 91–93, 96
Negro Family, The (1965) 96
Negro Family in the United States, The (1939) 92, 96
Neighbourhood collapse 184
Neighbourhood renewal ix, 184
Neo-classical economics 18
Neo-Marxism 129, 158
Netherlands 186
Never-married mothers 177
Newark, University of 39
Newcastle-upon-Tyne 57, 59, 101, 120
Newcastle-upon-Tyne, University of 120
New Deal for Communities x, 184, 200
New Haven, University of 153
New Labour x–xi, xxvii, xxix, 107–8, 126, 183–203, 210
New Labour, New Language? (2000) 192
New Liberals 2
Newman, George 56
New Poor Law 4
New Statesman, The periodical 61, 161
New Survey of London Life and Labour (1930–35) 48–49, 60
New York 89, 127, 131, 142

New Yorker, The magazine 127, 131, 133, 142, 161, 207
New York Prison Association 51
New York University 146
Nineteenth Century, The 10
Nolan, Brian 173
Nomad poor 10, 20
Northampton 34, 171
North Carolina at Chapel Hill, University of 142
North Lawndale (Chicago) 133
Northwestern University 152
Norwich 79
Nottingham 103–5
Novak, Tony xxi
Nursery classes 69, 87, 100, 108
Nutrition 62, 67, 200

Oakley, Ann xxiv–xxv
O'Connor, Alice 88, 91
Office of Economic Opportunity 87
Office of Policy Planning and Research 96
Ohio 53
Old age pensions 1, 24, 49
One Nation conservatism xxvii
Opportunity for All (1999) 195
Other America, The (1962) 90
Our Towns (1943) 65, 69–70, 75, 77, 80, 208
Our Unemployed (1868) 8
Outcast London (1971) 2, 24
Outdoor relief 51, 56
Outline of a Work Entitled Pauper Management Improvement (1798) 5
Overcrowding 10, 32, 100, 113, 120
Oxford English Dictionary xii, 158
Oxford University Institute of Statistics 34

Pacifist Service Units 73–77, 81, 84
Panel Study of Income Dynamics (PSID) 147–50, 155, 196–97
Paradigms xxiii–xxv, xxvii, 187
Parenting 109, 114, 124
Park, Robert 92
Parker, Roy 114

Parole 128
Participant observation 121
Paterson, Ada 121
Pauperism 3, 11, 51, 53–54, 65, 69
Pauperism and the Endowment of Old Age (1892) 12
Paupers xv, 6, 15–16, 46, 52–54, 57, 60, 62, 64
Pauper schools 14
Pawns xxv, 200–1
Peace Corps 87, 137
Pearson, Geoffrey xviii
Peasants 7
Peasant War in Germany (1870) 7
Pembroke College, Cambridge 59
Pennsylvania 137
Persistently poor 149
Persistent poverty 151, 153–54, 197
Personal social services 81, 84, 114
Phantom army 3
Philadelphia 147
Philanthropy 21
Phillips, Melanie 166
Philp, Fred 82
Physical disabilities 58
Physical efficiency 29, 33
Physionomy 6
Piachaud, David 193–94, 200
Pilgrim Trust survey (1938) 41
Pillinger, Jane xxiv, xxviii
Piney family 53
Pinkney, Alphonso 143
Plowden Report (1967) 100–1
Police 6, 95, 196
Policy Studies Institute 170, 173–74
Policy transfer xxii, 99, 205, 209
Political Quarterly, The 60
Pollard, Stephen 157
Polytechnic Institute of Brooklyn 97
Poor Law 3–5, 8, 17, 23, 28, 53, 202
Poor Law Act (1598) 4
Poor Law Amendment Act (1834) 5–6
Poor Law Guardians 11, 56, 61
Poor relief 5, 10, 17

Popay, Jennie xxiv–xxv
Poverty 110
Poverty: A Study of Town Life (1901) 29–34
Poverty clusters 184
Poverty cycle 9, 92, 189
Poverty dynamics xxvii, 32, 109, 132, 196, 198, 201–2, 210
Poverty in the United Kingdom (1979) 104, 160–61, 189
Poverty line 33–35, 49, 63, 134, 139, 149
Poverty spells 186, 197
Poverty: The Forgotten Englishmen (1970) 103
Poverty trap 167
Powell, Allan 57
Powell, Enoch 111
Power, Anne 184
Preparation for Parenthood (1974) 116
Pre-School Playgroups Association 108
President's Commission for a National Agenda for the Eighties 142
Primary amentia 56
Primary poverty 29–30, 32–35
Princeton, University of 138–39, 150
Principles of Economics (1890) 16
Pringle, J. C. 55
Prison 51, 110, 128, 163
Problem families 64–65, 67–85, 87, 102–4, 107, 111–13, 119–20, 122–23, 125, 127, 157–58, 190, 198, 202, 205–10
Problem Families Committee 71–73, 77, 84
Problem of the 'Problem Family', The (1957) 82
Proletariat 6–7, 129
Promising families 73
Propper, Carol 197
Prostitution 51–52, 57, 62
Pruitt-Igoe project (St Louis) 98–99
Psychiatric social work 81, 83
Psychiatry 46, 50, 80, 83, 91, 100, 120, 196
Psychological Institute, University of Vienna 39
Psychological traits 89–90, 176
Psychology 82, 83, 88, 90–91, 120–22, 153, 176

Public health xxviii, 22, 58, 70, 77–78, 80–81, 84–85, 87, 205, 210
Puerto Rico 89, 91

Quasi-markets xxv
Queens 200–1
Questions of circumstance 15
Questions of habit 15

Race xxvi, 69, 88, 92, 96, 128–30, 134, 141, 144, 146–47, 155, 160–61, 178–79, 181, 209
Radzinowicz, Leon 63
Rainwater, Lee 97–99, 129, 141, 155
Ratan Tata Foundation 36
Rational choice 12, 16
Reading 34–35, 57
Reading, University College 34
Recuperation centres 80
Red Cross 73
Reed, Adolph 152
Reform Bills (1866–67) 3
Reform eugenics 62
Rehabilitation families 74
Relative deprivation 33, 189, 192
Relative poverty 33
Report on Social Insurance and Allied Services (1942) 26, 65, 69
Republican Party 130, 187
Reserve army of labour xii–xiii, xx, 208
Residuum 1–20, 64, 75, 85, 127, 158, 190, 205–10
Residuum mentality 12
Resler, Henrietta 159
Respectable fears xviii
Respectable poor 166
Retreatism 82
Revenu Minimum d'Insertion (RMI) 185
Rex, John 159–60
Ricketts, Erol R. xiii, 140, 151
Rigdon, Susan 88, 90–92
Roach, Jack 96
Roberts, Stephen 172–73
Robert Taylor Homes housing project (Chicago) 132

Rochdale 171

Roche, Maurice 169

Rockefeller Foundation 54, 60

Rodman, Hyman 94, 97–99

Room, Graham 185

Rosenberg, Charles 50

Roseneil, Sasha 177

Rotherham 67, 71–72

Rough sleepers ix, 184

Rowntree, Benjamin Seebohm xxviii, 1, 9, 21, 29–37, 43, 45, 63, 185, 208

Royal Commission on the Aged Poor (1893) 9

Royal Commission on the Care and Control of the Feebleminded (1904–08) 2

Royal Commission on the Housing of the Working Classes (1885) 2, 9, 11

Royal Commission on Labour (1891–94) 9

Royal Commission on the Poor Law (1905–09) 2, 12, 21–23, 43

Royal Commission on Population 63

Royal Statistical Society 13–15, 59

Runciman, W. G. 169, 172

Russia 32

Rutter, Michael 114, 118–21, 124, 196

Ryan, William 97–98, 200

Salford 78, 81

Salvation Army 2, 9

Sampling 29, 34–35, 54, 115

Sam Sixty family 53

Sanitary inspectors 70

Savage, S. W. 78

Sawhill, Isabel xiii, 140, 151

School Board visitors 14–15

School Health Service 79

School Medical Service 69

Scientific racism xvii

Scotland 120

Scroungers xxvi, 21, 38, 43, 201, 206, 209

Secondary labour markets 140, 170, 175

Secondary poverty 29–30, 32–34

Second International Eugenics Congress (1920) 53

Second Reform Act (1867) 7–8, 20

Second World War xxii, xxviii, 26, 34, 58, 63, 69–70, 73–74, 77, 92–93, 109, 155, 208

Seebohm Report (1968) 67, 84, 101

Segregation 1, 12, 20, 25, 52–53, 57–58, 64, 77, 85

Select Committees on Distress from Want of Employment (1894–96) 2, 17, 20

Self-help 18

Sharecroppers 133

Sheffield 75, 78, 80, 109, 113, 120, 122

Sheffield, University of 176

Sherraden, Michael 152–53

Sherwell, Arthur 30

Shirkers 37

Shriver, Sargent 87

Silburn, Richard 102, 103–5

Silver, Hilary 184–85, 187, 192

Simon, Jonathan 128

Simon Population Trust 73

Sinfield, Adrian 42

Single Regeneration Budget x, 184

Skidders xv

Slavery 92, 133

Slum culture 91

Smith, David J. xiii, 170, 173, 175

Smith, Howard 127

Social action 19

Social administration xxiii, 82, 105, 117, 158

Social capital 189, 193

Social casework xv, xxvi, 74, 76, 81, 83, 102

Social casualties 71

Social citizenship xxii

Social control 128

Social Darwinism 4, 12, 20, 29, 43, 150

Social Democratic Foundation 2

Social disorganisation 133

Social exclusion ix–x, xxiv, 126, 159, 173, 180–81, 184–203, 205–10

Social Exclusion Unit ix, 183–84, 191, 199, 207

Social failure 53

Social inefficiency 57, 65

Social investigation xvi, 9, 12–13, 16–17,

21–22, 29, 33, 43, 53, 67, 97, 205–10

Social medicine 78

Social Pathology and Social Science (1959) 83

Social pest 52

Social policy xxiii, xxvi, 82, 87, 99–100, 107–8, 111–12, 114–15, 117, 134, 136, 163, 196

Social problem group 45–65, 67, 69–70, 72, 76, 81, 83–85, 127, 158, 205–10

Social Problem Group Investigation Committee 57, 62

Social psychology of unemployment 21, 38–42, 172

Social reconstruction 65, 70

Social residuum 1–20, 64, 75, 85, 127, 158, 190, 205–10

Social Security Act (1989) 210

Social Security Act amendments (USA) (1962 and 1967) 87

Social Security: The New Priorities (1966) 112

Social sediment 75

Social science 83, 85, 88, 96, 102, 104–5, 117–18, 127, 152, 178, 181, 184, 187

Social Science Research Council (UK) (SSRC) 102, 105, 107–8, 111, 114–20, 125, 196, 207

Social Science Research Council Committee for Research on the Urban Underclass (USA) 140

Social Services Departments 84

Social surveys 29–38, 70, 82–83, 190

Social work xv, 19, 21, 30, 46, 50, 58, 67, 69, 74, 76, 78, 80–85, 95, 101–2, 105, 109–10, 112, 116, 122, 142, 152, 205

Society for the Relief of Distress in East London 8

Society of Friends 73

Sociological Society 38

Sociology 82–83, 91–93, 98, 104–6, 118, 121, 143, 153, 159, 169–75, 178, 196, 205

Solidarity 184–85, 187, 191

Soloway, R. A. 46

Soulside (1969) 99

Southampton 57, 73, 78

Special schools 61

Spence, James 120

Stafford, Joyce 151–52

Stakeholder welfare xxvi, 190

Stallybrass, C. O. 77–78

Stanley, H. M. 9

Stanley (County Durham) 34

St Anne Street (Liverpool) 73

Starkey, Pat 67–68

State intervention 19, 33

State We're In, The (1995) 188

Stedman Jones, Gareth 2–3, 12, 21, 24, 155

Stephens, Tom 74–76

Sterilisation 1, 10, 20, 46–47, 50–52, 57–59, 62, 64–65, 73, 77, 85, 209

Stevenson, Olive 121

Stigma xiv–xv, xvii, xxiii, 17, 115, 137, 144, 154, 180, 198

Stockholm, University of 129

Street arabs 14

Strength of the People, The (1902) 19

Sub-average types 62

Subcultures 89–99, 105, 115, 117, 119, 130, 141, 171–76

Submerged social stratum 10, 20

Submerged tenth 16, 69

Subnormal types 41, 60–61

Suburbs 130–31, 133, 141–42, 144–48, 163, 185

Suffrage 7–8

Sunday Times, The newspaper 162, 164, 168, 176, 207–8

Supplementary Benefit 110

Sure Start ix, 107, 126, 184, 199, 203, 206, 210

Surrey 165

Survey Research Center (University of Michigan) 147

Survival of the fittest 15

Swindon 171

Switzerland 159

Syphilis 47

Tally's Corner (1967) 95, 97, 143

Tawney, R. H. 36–37, 43

Taylor-Gooby, Peter xiii, xxi, xxiii, 179

Teenage pregnancy ix, 184, 198–200, 206

Temperamental instability 70

Temperance Problem and Social Reform, The (1899) 30

Tepoztlan (Mexico) 88

Thailand 137

Thatcher, Margaret xxvi–xxvii, 108, 126, 163, 168, 179

Third Way x, 159, 188, 195

Thomas Coram Research Unit 118

Thrift 15, 26, 89

Time magazine 131, 133, 141

Times, The newspaper 33, 54, 108, 110–11, 126

Timmins, Nicholas 108

Timms, Noel 80–83

Titmuss, Richard xxi, xxiii, xxv–xxviii, 63, 71–73, 82, 84, 105, 158, 168, 190

Titterton, Michael xxiii–xxv

Tomlinson, C. G. 71

Tomlinson, Sally 159–60

Tonge, W. L. 120

Townsend, Peter xxi, xxiii, 33–34, 104–5, 116, 120, 160–61, 185, 188–90, 192

Tramp, The (1931) 49

Tramping 50

Transmission xv, 16, 58, 60–61, 98, 106–7, 113, 116, 118, 123–25, 143, 145, 149, 151, 158, 166, 176, 183, 195–96, 198–99, 203, 208

Transmitted deprivation 111–26, 195, 199, 200

Treasury 196–99, 207

Tredgold, Alfred F. 56, 61

Trinidad 94, 99

Trinity College, Cambridge 34

Trojan Horse 21

Truancy ix, 184

Tuberculosis 58, 61, 77

Undercaste 153–54

Underclass i–xxix, 127–55, 157–81, 183–203, 205–10

Underklass xii

Unemployable 19–44, 60, 63–64, 128–29, 158, 160, 205–10

Unemployables, The (1907) 26

Unemployed 14–15, 28, 57, 61

Unemployment 13, 21–22, 24, 26–28, 32–33, 36–38, 43, 50, 57, 62–63, 89, 95, 115, 121, 127–30, 132–39, 141, 143–48, 153, 155, 161–67, 171–72, 175, 179–81, 184–85, 192, 206

Unemployment: A Problem of Industry (1909) 27, 29, 48

Unemployment insurance 28, 38, 40–42, 209

Unfit 15, 20, 31, 54, 60

Unfitness 10, 31, 46

Unheavenly City Revisited, The (1974) 91

United States x–xi, 87–106, 127–55

United States Agency for International Development 137

Unmarried mothers 83, 110

Unreachables 131

Unsatisfactory households 76

Urban Institute (New York) 140

Urban Programme 101, 108, 110

Urban and Regional Research Centre (Princeton) 138

Urban Villagers, The (1962) 94, 97

USSR 109

Utopia (1516) 5

Vagrancy 4, 7, 10, 25, 27, 47–51, 169

Valentine, Charles xvi, 95–98, 106

Veblen, Thorstein xv

Veit-Wilson, John 33

Venereal disease 77

Vineland (New Jersey) 51

Voluntary organisations 73–76, 79–80, 116, 207

Vulnerability xxiii, 112, 160

Walker, Alan 176

Walker, Robert 186

War on Poverty xxviii, 87, 90, 100–1, 104–5, 130, 134–38, 210

Ward, David 1

Warner, Amos 92

Warrington 34

Wartime xxii, xxviii, 3, 21, 23–24, 26, 29, 34, 36, 43, 45, 53, 56, 58–59, 63, 65, 69–70, 73–74, 77, 85, 92–93, 109, 155, 208
Warwickshire 71–72
Washington 95, 98
Washington University 152
Watts (Los Angeles) 142
Waxman, Chaim xv
Web of deprivation 122–23
Webb, Beatrice xxviii, 19, 21–24, 28–29, 42–43, 45, 155, 205
Webb, Sidney xxviii, 21–22, 24, 28–29, 42–43, 45, 155, 205
Webb, Stephen 197
Wedderburn, Dorothy 104
Wedge, Peter 121, 196
Welfare dependency 96, 130, 132, 134–39, 147–49, 152, 155, 169, 173
Welfare State 26, 73
Welfare to work xxvii
Westergaard, John 159, 178
West Lancashire Association for Mental Welfare 60–61
West Riding of Yorkshire 71–72, 78
Whelan, Christopher T. 173
White, Arnold 10, 16, 20
Whitehouse, Mary 110
Whyte, William Foote 93
Wight Bakke, E. 40
Wildcat Skills Training Center (New York) 127, 131
Willetts, David xiii, 166–67
Williams, Fiona xxiv–xxv, xxviii
Williams, Raymond xii

Willmott, Peter 117
Wilson Government 101
Wilson, William Julius xiii, xvi–xvii, 97, 99, 106, 134, 139, 141, 143–47, 151–53, 155, 157, 160, 168, 173, 177–78, 181, 189, 199
Winston Street (Washington) 98
Wofinden, R. C. 67, 72, 77
Wokingham 165
Women's Group on Public Welfare 65, 69, 206, 208
Women's Voluntary Service 73
Wood, Arthur 56
Wood Committee on Mental Deficiency (1924–29) 46, 54, 56–58, 60, 64–65, 72, 112, 116, 119
Wootton, Barbara 83
Worcestershire 78
Workfare 139–40, 146
Workhouse 5, 32, 48
Working Families Tax Credit 200
Working Party on Transmitted Deprivation 114–26, 207
Worklessness 210
Work shy xxvi, 37, 41, 43, 201, 209
Wynn, Arthur and Margaret 110–11

Yale, University of 40
York 9, 29–35, 37, 45, 75
Young, Hilton 59
Young, Michael 102
Younghusband Report (1959) 76, 83

Zeisel, Hans 39